Developing Voice Through the
LANGUAGE ARTS

Developing Voice Through the
LANGUAGE ARTS

Kathryn Henn-Reinke
University of Wisconsin, Oshkosh

Geralyn A. Chesner
Alverno College

SAGE Publications
Thousand Oaks ▪ London ▪ New Delhi

For information:

Sage Publications, Inc.
2455 Teller Road
Thousand Oaks, California 91320
E-mail: order@sagepub.com

Sage Publications Ltd.
1 Oliver's Yard
55 City Road
London EC1Y 1SP
United Kingdom

Sage Publications India Pvt. Ltd.
B-42, Panchsheel Enclave
Post Box 4109
New Delhi 110 017 India

Printed in the United States of America

Library of Congress Cataloging-in-Publication Data

Henn-Reinke, Kathryn.
Developing voice through the language arts / Kathryn Henn-Reinke, Geralyn A. Chesner.
    p. cm.
Includes bibliographical references and index.
ISBN 1-4129-1811-1 (cloth) 9781412918114
   1. Language arts (Elementary) 2. Language arts (Secondary) 3. Reflective teaching.
I. Chesner, Geralyn A. II. Title.
LB1576.H3337 2007
372.6—dc22   2006014041

This book is printed on acid-free paper.

06 07 08 09 10 11 9 8 7 6 5 4 3 2 1

Acquisitions Editor:	Diane McDaniel
Associate Editor:	Elise Smith
Editorial Assistant:	Erica Carroll
Production Editor:	Diane S. Foster
Copy Editor:	Barbara Coster
Typesetter:	C&M Digitals (P) Ltd.
Proofreader:	Gillian Dickens
Indexer:	Molly Hall
Cover Designer:	Michelle Kenny

Acknowledgments:

List of Standards from Standards for the English Language Arts, copyright © 1996, International Reading Association and the National Council of Teachers of English. Reprinted with permission.

D'Nealian Manuscript Alphabet from D'Nealian Handwriting, copyright © 2007 by Pearson Education, Inc. Reprinted by permission.

D'Nealian ® Handwriting is a registered trademark of Donald Neal Thurber.

Brief Contents

Detailed Contents

5. Language, Word Study, and the Tools of Writing 145

Preface

*T*he language arts are the intellectual tools we use to learn about the world. Reading, writing, listening, speaking, viewing, and visually representing are considered the primary language arts and are often also referred to as literacy skills. The language arts are seldom used in isolation, and when they are integrated in learning experiences, we have a greater opportunity to make sense of the world around us. Children who are interested in how animals are taken care of at the zoo might watch videos on the subject, visit the zoo, listen to a presentation by the zookeeper, read books about zoos, draw pictures, write in a zoo journal, and share what they learned with their class. These children learned not just from reading about zoos but from all of the experiences as well. As they learned new concepts, they assimilated the new information with what they already knew and refined their understanding of how animals are cared for at the zoo. This example highlights the important role that each of the language arts plays in learning and the extended value of integrating the language arts.

The purpose of this text is to provide K–8 (early childhood to early adolescence) teachers with a solid framework for teaching, learning, and assessing in the language arts that reflects current research on how children develop as literate persons and the use of national standards to guide the development of literacy.

Literacy **standards** established by the International Reading Association and the National Council of Teachers of English are designed to meet the needs of all students with a wide array of learning abilities, styles, and situations. The standards represent a comprehensive overview of learning across the grade levels and language areas, and as such provide a useful tool in planning, implementing, and assessing literacy.

The following table details where the standards for the English language arts are represented within the text most evidently. They are integrated into the text where some chapters clearly delineate their inclusion, and others include the standards but are not explicitly stated. For example, Standard 11 states that students participate as knowledgeable, reflective, creative, and critical members of a variety of literacy communities. We believe that as students self-assess their development in the language arts, they can be reflecting critically on their understanding and competence. Therefore, although not directly stated, Chapter 11 and many others include representations of this standard. Included in the ancillary materials are activities that encourage the reader to further explore how the language arts standards guide the teaching, learning, and assessment of language arts in kindergarten through Grade 8 classrooms.

The philosophical basis for the text comes from a sociocultural constructivist viewpoint, with a focus on the development of *voice through the language arts*. As children learn about the world through the language arts, they voice their

	Ch 1	Ch 2	Ch 3	Ch 4	Ch 5	Ch 6	Ch 7	Ch 8	Ch 9	Ch 10	Ch 11	Ch 12
Standard 1		X	X	X	X	X	X	X	X	X	X	X
Standard 2		X	X			X	X	X	X	X	X	X
Standard 3		X	X	X	X	X	X	X	X	X	X	X
Standard 4			X	X	X	X		X	X	X	X	X
Standard 5				X	X		X	X	X	X	X	X
Standard 6		X	X	X	X	X	X	X	X	X	X	X
Standard 7		X	X					X	X	X	X	X
Standard 8		X	X	X	X	X	X	X	X		X	X
Standard 9	X	X	X			X	X			X	X	X
Standard 10		X	X	X	X	X	X	X	X	X	X	X
Standard 11	X	X	X	X		X	X			X	X	X
Standard 12		X	X	X	X	X	X	X	X	X	X	X

understandings and opinions. The broader their knowledge of the world around them, the more capable they are likely to become in making connections and drawing conclusions, thus developing their own literate voices.

Curriculum is viewed as a seamless *cycle of teaching, learning, and assessment* in this text. Teachers plan for instruction based on the perceived needs and interests of their students. Using national, state, and/or district standards appropriate for the group of learners, they select learning experiences that match the academic, developmental, and social needs of the students and that promise to develop critical thinking skills. Students engage in the learning experiences and are guided by the teacher to (a) connect learning to what they already know and understand and to (b) determine how new concepts extend their understanding of the world. Throughout the learning experiences, teachers monitor student progress, and students self-assess their own progress and understanding. Teachers adjust their teaching based on feedback from these observations and self-assessments.

This text encourages teachers to take a *reflective approach* to preparing to teach language arts, viewing not only their students as language users and learners but to begin with themselves as literate models for their students. This notion is based on the belief that teachers who continually develop as literate persons bring a rich appreciation of literacy and communication to the classroom and are more likely to inspire students to appreciate and grow in the language arts. Indeed, teachers ought to read and investigate a wide range and variety of genres of literature if their students are to build enthusiasm for reading and other literate activities.

A *balanced literacy approach* is the framework for this text. This approach organizes reading and writing into four categories: reading/writing aloud, shared reading/writing, guided reading/writing, and independent reading/writing. Listening, speaking, viewing, and visually representing are also integral components of the balanced literacy approach. This approach is explored at each of the developmental levels, that is, early childhood, middle childhood, and early adolescence, represented in this text. Although there may be overlap in many of the components at each of these levels, unique characteristics of the approach are highlighted at each level.

An emphasis on diversity, children's literature, critical thinking, and technology in relation to the language arts in the K–8 classroom is a thread running through this text. We believe that the way one approaches teaching language arts is rooted in an understanding of the philosophy that underlies how children learn and develop as literate persons.

Diversity exists in many forms within a classroom—racial, linguistic, learning needs, gender, and so on. Children who are able to learn about people who are different from themselves are often able to determine how people are similar and different and are more likely to develop greater understanding of differences. Diversity can be explored through the language arts in a variety of ways as children come to understand more about themselves and others around them.

Due to the influx in today's schools of students whose first language is a language other than English, another emphasis is based on meeting the diverse needs of **English language learners.** These students have special needs in relation to their literacy development, and the materials used in the language arts classroom should reflect the variety of cultures in the United States especially, but also the world. As well, students with exceptional needs require teachers of language arts and literacy who understand their particular learning needs. Surely this will continue to be an important consideration in all K–8 classrooms.

A great deal of emphasis is devoted to selecting and using quality *children's/ young adult literature* in learning experiences with students. Differences between reading and listening comprehension are emphasized, and suggestions are made for ways to motivate students to become enthused about books and to appreciate listening to literature. Examples of both narrative and expository text are featured throughout the text. A bibliography of literature that is discussed throughout the chapter is included at the end of each chapter to allow readers the opportunity to build a collection of children's literature resources they may use in their own teaching.

At every age/ability level, the focus of all teaching, learning, and assessment should be centered on the development of **critical thinking skills.** Students may learn specific skills and strategies in each learning experience, but it is the cumulative development of higher-level thinking skills that makes students more well rounded and independent learners. More independent learners bring a set of well-developed thinking strategies to each learning experience.

Children of today are growing up in an ever-changing technology-rich world. It is important to guide them in the use of *technology* as part of the language arts. Specific suggestions are made for use of technology in the classroom, and numerous resources and Web sites are referenced that may be used by teachers and/or their students.

The No Child Left Behind Act (2001) has reinforced the importance of standardized testing, and this language arts text assists preservice and inservice teachers in understanding how assessment is a critical element that drives the curriculum.

Features of the Text

Several special features are included in *Developing Voice Through the Language Arts* to provide preservice and inservice teachers with opportunities to collaboratively analyze concepts and constructs, make inferences, and evaluate understanding.

Reflection is emphasized in the following features:

- Before We Begin
- Stop to Think
- Reflection Journal
- End-of-Chapter Reflection

Application to actual teaching is explored through the following components:

- Context Setting
- A View From Home
- Planning for Teaching
- A View From the Classroom
- Connections With the Field

Links between language arts theory and practice are found in the Theory Into Practice feature, as well as in detail in Part III as classroom settings are highlighted.

REFLECTION

Before We Begin

These reflection points enable the reader to explore beliefs, assumptions, and practices on key aspects of the chapter prior to reading as a means for setting context.

Stop to Think

Questions and statements are posed to encourage readers to reflect on what they have read and how new understandings will be applied in actual classroom practice.

Reflection Journal

Each chapter contains recommendations for reflection in a journal that students will keep throughout the course, and ideally, beyond the course. This reflection feature includes topic suggestions and prompts that relate to major concepts featured in the chapter.

End-of-Chapter Reflection

Reflective prompts at the end of each chapter enable readers to determine how well the concepts were understood. They are also a means to set goals for additional preparation for teaching.

APPLICATION

Context Setting: After reading this chapter, you will be able to . . .

Each chapter begins with a listing of the most important outcomes to be gained. The outcomes are linked to classroom practice.

A View From Home

Brief vignettes provide readers with the opportunity to reflect on how literacy in children is developed and supported by family practices. Readers are encouraged to consider links between home and school communication activities that may further strengthen literacy development.

Planning for Teaching

Another feature includes suggestions for applying what was learned in the chapter. Preservice and inservice teachers will reflect on areas of teaching, learning, and assessment they will need to take into consideration as they begin their teaching careers.

A View From the Classroom

Narrative and concrete examples of teaching and learning experiences are found in this revealing feature as well as questions encouraging readers to readily apply what is being learned.

Connections With the Field

One of the goals of this text is to bridge the gap between teacher preparation and actual classroom teaching. As many colleges of education incorporate a field component into their methods courses, this text will take this into account and incorporate practical suggestions related to the content with which readers may experiment while in a field setting.

THEORY TO PRACTICE

Theory Into Practice

A wide range of activities are provided in this feature to enable students to make connections between theoretical constructs and aspects that relate to actual classroom practice.

Organization of the Text

This text is divided into three sections.

Part I: Understanding Language Arts

Part I includes a discussion of what literacy is and provides a framework for teaching the language arts.

Part II: Frameworks and Approaches to Teaching, Learning, and Assessing in the Language Arts

Part II outlines the teaching, learning, and assessment considerations for each of the language arts.

Part III: Language Arts Teaching, Learning, and Assessing From Early Childhood to Early Adolescence

Part III features detailed classroom vignettes that highlight application of an integrated language arts curriculum at the early childhood, middle childhood, and early adolescence levels. The chapters may be read sequentially with the text or used to supplement previous chapters.

The three parts of this book may be accessed in various ways. Part III can be read before reading Parts I and II to provide an overview of what language arts looks like at the various age/grade levels. Reading Part III after reading Part I and/or Part II is another option. Using this method could help the reader understand what language arts might look like in a classroom in relation to the content and concepts previously read. One other method would be to use Part III as a guidebook in classroom learning experiences with children, both in preservice work and while teaching.

Instructor's Resources CD

This CD offers the instructor a variety of resources to supplement the book material, including lecture outlines, PowerPoint® lecture slides, sample syllabi, video clips with student exercises, Web resources, reflection portfolio guidelines, and more. We've also provided additional activities and resources to help instructors integrate the in-text pedagogical resources (A View From the Classroom, Theory Into Practice, etc.) into their classroom discussions. Also included is a Test Bank, which consists of 35–40 multiple-choice questions with answers and page references, as well as 15–20 short answer and 5–10 essay questions for each chapter. An electronic Test Bank is also available so that instructors can create, deliver, and customize tests and study guides using Brownstone's Diploma test bank software.

Web-Based Student Study Site

http://www.sagepub.com/dvtlastudy

This Web-based student study site provides a variety of additional resources to enhance students' understanding of the book content and take their learning one step further. The site includes a comprehensive Study Guide, which consists of learning objectives, key terms, activities, reflection portfolio guidelines, flash cards, practice tests, and more. Also included are special features, such as the Links to Standards from U.S. States and associated activities, Children's Literature Selections, Reflection Exercises, Learning from Journal Articles, and PRAXIS.

Student Resources CD

This CD is bound into each copy of the *Developing Voice Through the Language Arts* textbook and offers students some additional resources to enhance their understanding of the book content. In particular, this CD includes a variety of video clips to accompany each chapter that demonstrate key teaching and learning techniques. The video clips are accompanied by a variety of exercises and questions to promote further comprehension of the material discussed in each chapter.

Reference

No Child Left Behind Act. (2001). Conference Report to Accompany H.R. 1, Report No. 107-334, House of Representatives, 107th Congress, 1st Session.

Acknowledgments

We are particularly grateful to Kathi Glick and Joelle Quimby and their students for allowing us to spend several months observing and interviewing them for Chapters 10 and 12 of this text. The many teachers whose classrooms we visit on an ongoing basis have given us wonderful insights into good teaching in the language arts. Several of those classrooms are highlighted throughout this text, including Paula Henn, María Gonzalez de Nuñez, Sharon Shermerhorn, María Godina, Lorena Gueny, Lori Menning, Luz Lebrón, and Lillian Lawrence. Our thank-you also goes to John W. Stewig, who provided initial guidance in writing a language arts textbook.

The numerous reviewers of this text have given us invaluable suggestions for revising and editing our early drafts. The peer reviewers include Debra Farrer, California University of Pennsylvania; Rose Casement, University of Michigan-Flint; Candice Marie Moench, Wayne State University; Patricia Baldwin, College of Saint Rose; and Robin Love, San Jose State University. Peg Dettlaff has also been a valued editor through all stages of this project.

We would like to extend special thanks to Dr. Jacqueline Hansen, Assistant Professor in the Department of Early Childhood and Elementary Education at Murray State University, and the students in her language arts course who class tested and provided feedback on Chapters 4, 5, and 8.

We would like to thank the staff at Sage who encouraged us throughout the process of creating this text. The guidance of Diane McDaniel was especially critical. In addition, Erica Carroll, Elise Smith, Diane Foster, Barbara Coster, and Marta Peimer were helpful in assisting us through the technical aspects of bringing the text to publication.

part 1

Understanding Language Arts

Language arts is a content area in the elementary and middle school that is a framework for many forms of communication. Part I of this text details the need for teachers to be reflective as communicators themselves in order to be effective teachers of students who learn the language arts. Chapter 1 will assist you in thinking about your language arts background and experiences in becoming a literate person, and it provides you with some suggestions for linking to the literacy of your students. Chapter 2 provides background for understanding the six components of language arts, as well as philosophical frameworks undergirding teaching, learning, and assessing the language arts in elementary and middle school.

Becoming a Reflective Teacher

Context Setting:

After reading this chapter, you will be able to

- Begin examining your own literacy and the relationship between this and teaching children to become literate
- Create a literacy learning environment that encourages children to view language arts as an exciting and integral part of their lives

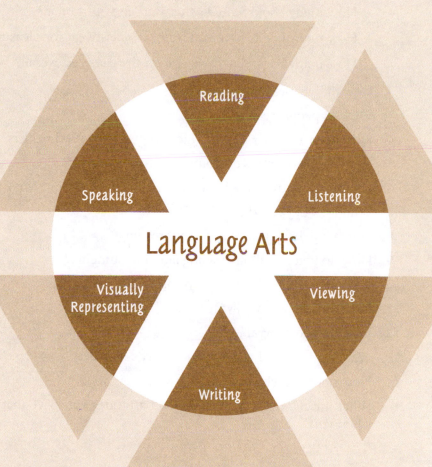

Before We Begin

- Think of the most valuable learning experiences that you have had with reading and writing throughout your formal schooling. How did it make you feel about yourself as a learner, and what did you learn about your own literacy development?

Literacy Survey

Complete the following survey as a means for thinking about your own literacy development:

1. If you had to guess,

   How many books would you say you owned?

   How many books would you say are in your house?

   How many books have you read in the last year for pleasure?

   How many books have you read in the last year overall?

2. How did you learn to read?

3. Why do people read?

4. How does a teacher decide which students are good readers?

5. What kinds of books do you like to read and why?

6. Have you ever reread a book? If yes, which one(s) and why?

7. Who are your favorite authors?

8. In general, how do you feel about reading?

9. How do you feel about reading aloud to students?

10. Are you a writer? Why or why not?

11. How did you learn to write?

12. Why do people write?

13. What do you think a good writer needs in order to write well?

14. How does a teacher decide what writing is good?

15. What are the reading strategies and attitudes you have that you use when you

    Read fiction?

    Read nonfiction?

    Read poetry?

    Read children's books?

    Read _____ (fill in the blank with another genre of your choice)

Exploring Your Assumptions About Teaching, Learning, and Assessing

We all can think back to our experiences in elementary school when we were children. There are those that stay with us for both positive and negative reasons. I (Geri) recall the weekly spelling bees, where two teams of students would line up on opposite sides of the classroom with each student taking a turn at spelling the word the teacher recited and put into a sentence. If the word was spelled correctly, the student would go to the back of the line, continuing to be a part of the team. If the word was incorrectly spelled, the student had to dejectedly sit down in the middle of the classroom between the two teams, excluded from the bee. Luckily, I was a good speller, for I did not have to sit down until after most of the other students had already misspelled words. I remember the stigma attached to those who misspelled a word early on.

There were many things I learned through this activity, most of them not evident until further reflection many years later. I was taught that academic competition was a good thing and that being one of the best in the class at spelling was desirable. I knew that I was not learning how to spell or be a better speller through this activity, as I already knew how to spell the words. I knew, as did all of the other students, that spelling bees were another way of "testing" our spelling ability, even though the format for this test allowed us to move about with our classmates and seemingly have some fun. Although it was never verbalized, I learned through these spelling bees that students who misspelled words early on were poor spellers and were looked upon as unworthy of staying in the game. Once sitting, their focus was no longer on spelling, as they tuned out and felt undeserving of being a part of the team. I learned that it was important to be able to stand and spell words correctly, out of context of any meaningful situation, and that this was a skill that was deemed desirable by my teachers.

In thinking about this experience today, I cannot help but question the underlying purpose for subjecting us to those weekly spelling bees. Everything we do is grounded on a set of beliefs and **assumptions** that we hold. Clearly, using spelling bees was a practice that was acceptable in my school and most likely something my teacher experienced as a student herself. Was she also a good speller as a child who did not fully understand the shame of those who were not good spellers—those who continually were relegated to their desks where those still standing could stare and judge? Would teachers who deeply reflect on what they teach, how they teach, and especially why they teach as they do subject their students to this kind of activity, which really is not an ideal learning experience for their students?

Teacher and researcher Stephen Brookfield (1992) believed that teachers need to uncover their own assumptions and reflect repeatedly on the validity of their assumptions if they are to engage in important teaching and provide meaningful learning for their students. He defines assumptions as those "taken for granted beliefs we have about reality" and "the rules of thumb that guide our actions" (p. 13). Frequently, our assumptions go unquestioned. Good teaching is grounded in reflecting on one's assumptions, practice, and planning (Newman, 1991). Not only must teachers think about their underlying common assumptions, but they also need to reflect on the theoretical assumptions that inform their teaching.

Teachers need to develop capabilities of assessing and adjusting their assumptions and beliefs related to how children learn and the most effective ways to teach. Our purpose for this text is to assist you in using reflection for envisioning and improving your teaching and to help direct student learning in language arts. We want you to become aware of your own thinking, both pedagogically and personally, in relation to literacy and student literacy development. We want you to value reflection as a way to become not just a better teacher of literacy but also a better teacher in general. Zeichner and Liston (1996) proclaimed that reflection involves "self-analysis" done frequently, precisely what we are suggesting throughout this textbook by supplying a variety of prompts to encourage you to dig deeper into what you believe and why you believe what you do.

Learning From Reflection 1.1

Try your hand at this now: number from 1 to 10 and on each line write a sentence that begins "I believe." Complete each sentence in relation to what you believe about children and their development, their learning, and teaching children in general. There are no correct answers, and writing quickly without deep thinking about this task will get at your "taken for granted" beliefs that Brookfield discusses.

The purpose of reflecting on your personal literacy assumptions and experiences, as well as your learning of literacy-related research and teaching methods, is to examine your beliefs about teaching and learning and using and developing language. Although researchers and theorists with more experience in the field of literacy can provide some guidance as teachers, we are responsible for our own choices. Therefore, thinking about what you believe, and the assumptions that underlie your teaching, will make you a better teacher.

There are numerous ways to reflect on your teaching, including discussions with expert teachers, using think-aloud exercises where you verbalize your thinking out loud as a way to dig deeply at issues and assumptions, and writing and journaling (Daniels, 2002; Surbeck, Han, & Moyer, 1991; Wenzlaff, 1994). **Reflection** of any kind includes asking questions of oneself such as "What do I think?" "What should I do?" and "Why?" Inservice and preservice teachers *can* monitor their own teaching behaviors and assumptions. However, training and practice in becoming reflective teachers will better inform your process of thinking about your teaching (Brookfield, 1992; Wenzlaff, 1994). Throughout this text you will have numerous opportunities to try your hand at some of the methods for reflecting on your own teaching as a way to assist you on your way to becoming a **reflective teacher.** There are many methods for reflecting on your beliefs and practices, including journaling, a major form of reflection that we are asking you to engage in while reading this text. According to Hillocks (1995), the process of writing is a form of discovery by nature, and writing in a reflection journal in conjunction with reading this text will assist you in discovering your ideas and beliefs about language learning.

Beginning teachers often focus heavily on the how-tos rather than the whys. In my (Geri) own reflective journal that I kept during my first few years of teaching, I mirrored this with the comment "I know what to teach and usually how; it's the why I am not so set with." It is easy to evaluate what works and what does not in your classroom, based on student performance and engagement, but it is much more challenging to look deeper to explore why something does or does not work.

A View From the Classroom

Josette Stoneman, a seventh-grade teacher in her second year, felt she needed to engage more in thinking about her teaching of language arts to her students. She had three classes of seventh graders, and only one of them seemed to be really interested in language arts and motivated in her classroom. Her neighboring social studies teacher, Coraline Winch, suggested keeping a journal as a way for Josette to process her thoughts regarding how things went each day with her teaching and her students' engagement. She told her that it had helped her to get to the heart of what she was doing and not doing with her social studies instruction and content and helped her to feel better about what her students were learning. It was also helpful to Coraline in letting out frustration regarding what was not working but also in setting goals for trying new things to assist her students and improve her teaching. She also even offered to share some entries in her own journal to help Josette get started.

Reflection Journal 1.1

Now it is your turn to begin uncovering the whys as you go back to your list of 10 "I believe" sentences. After reading each statement, ask yourself, "Why do I believe this?" Recall some concrete experiences you have had that have helped to shape those experiences.

Why Reflect on Your Own Literacy?

We believe that in order to be **effective teachers of literacy**, reflection on your assumptions and experiences with literacy in your own life is necessary. It is difficult to teach something that is not of interest to you, as when I (Geri) had to teach about simple machines in science to my third-grade students. Sadly, science was not an interest of mine; however, it was mandated curricula, and therefore I needed to teach this content. Looking back, I know I could have taught this content more interestingly and made this learning more applicable had I been more interested myself. Reflection is a powerful thing. By reflecting back today and applying what I know from experience, simple machines *can* be interesting. I could have used methods of experimentation and made connections to machines in my students' daily lives to engage them more deeply in learning how machines work and their importance. I was not an effective teacher of science then, but if I were teaching science to third graders now, I would definitely take what I have learned and apply it to make the content and concepts important to my students. It would be a goal of mine to make this aspect of the curriculum more engaging.

As you read this, you may have answered no to the questions in the literacy survey at the beginning of the chapter asking "Are you a reader?" and "Are you a writer?" Through learning about literacy and how children develop as literate persons and through reflecting on your own assumptions and experiences with language arts and literacy, we hope that you will see the importance of being a reader and a writer to model these important lifelong skills to your students. Not only do teachers need to help children develop as literate persons, but they also need to model for their students that they are frequent users of literacy themselves. If at this time you cannot say you are excited about literacy in your own life and in the prospect of teaching these skills to your students, you need to set some goals for yourself.

Linking Your Literacy to That of Your Students

Perhaps a good way to move from a consideration of your own literacy to a focus on how to be a teacher of literacy would be to consider the links between the two levels, that is, teacher and student. It would be helpful to monitor your own continuing growth as a literate person while monitoring children's growth as well.

> What ideas do you currently have to guide your students in building positive attitudes toward reading, writing, listening, speaking, viewing, and visually representing?

Stop to Think

Exploring your attitude toward literacy would certainly be a good starting point. Although this may not have been something you thought much about before, now that your consciousness has been raised you will want to pay closer attention to how much you read and write, what types of reading and writing you do, and where you go to find reading and writing activities that you enjoy. You will also want to explore your listening, speaking, and viewing habits and determine areas on which you wish to focus. Interspersed throughout this chapter are questions that may guide you in thinking about yourself as a teacher of literacy.

Reflection Journal 1.2

Reflect on the range of reading and writing activities you typically engage in. Choose a period of time, for example, a day, week, or month, and keep a list of all the reading and writing, listening, speaking, and viewing that you do.

What do you notice about your reading and writing habits from this journal exercise? Do you gravitate to reading the same kind of book? Note your purposes for reading and writing. If you only read science fiction, for example, think about what else you might enjoy. If you only write papers for your classes, what could you write for fun?

> What will you do to guide students to read, write, talk, listen, view, and visually represent often and for a variety of purposes?

Stop to Think

Think about those with whom you share your reading and writing. You probably have certain people that you cannot wait to tell about a good book you just read.

Perhaps other people always seem to know about good books to read. It is not likely that you write out a list of questions or prepare a worksheet for them to complete. Instead, you probably have lively discussions about character motivation or the plot in novels. You give your opinions and puzzle together through confusing parts of informational text. You ask each other about what you think the author meant.

You may be wondering why we are having you reflect on your own literacy when you are so anxious to learn how to teach children to read and write. Nevertheless, think of this: if you are not enthusiastic about your own literacy, will you be able to motivate students to read and write widely? If you love to read and write, won't that excitement also be conveyed to your students? The good news is that it is never too late to expand one's literate activities. We build a much more dynamic classroom when we explore literate issues together with our students. Students generally follow the teacher's lead and are more inclined to reflect on their **literacy development** if they see their teacher engaged in the same kinds of reflection.

Stop to Think

How will you excite children about searching for new sources of reading and writing material? What opportunities will you provide to children to talk with their classmates about what they have read, written, or viewed?

There are many sources of inspiration to expand our appetites for interesting materials to read and write about. Where do you get your ideas? Do you peruse the new arrivals table at the library or bookstore, read print or electronic reviews, get ideas from friends and classmates, browse at the bookstore, or join book clubs? Is there a particular type of writing you would like to attempt or continue? Perhaps you would like to read what others have written in that genre.

It has been quite a long time since you learned to read and perhaps just as long since you thought about how well you read and **comprehend** text. Now would be a good time to start thinking about the strategies you use to get meaning from print. What do you do when you do not understand something you are reading for class? What do you do when you encounter new vocabulary? It would be interesting to begin examining whether you reread, use **prior knowledge,** rely on **context clues,** or skip the confusing parts of text. Do you stop regularly to monitor what you just read?

Reflection Journal 1.3

Choose some reading material that causes you to think deeply as you read. As you read, jot down in your journal what you did to make meaning of what you read, listing the strategies you used to comprehend the text. After discussing this exercise with classmates, consider whether there are additional strategies you could have used that would also have been helpful.

It is evident that as a capable reader, you use a variety of strategies to make meaning of what you read and write cohesively. These same strategies are ones that you will want your students to learn to use when they are also engaged in literate activity.

You probably have a picture in your mind of what you would like your class to be like: students engaged in stimulating learning experiences throughout the day, all of them loving to read and write, children who can articulately reveal their critical thinking skills as they share what they have learned. While it is possible to get to this point, it requires a process of helping students understand that embracing their literacy and its development can be enjoyable and profitable.

If you were to interview the most exemplary literacy teacher that you know and ask how he or she plans for a new school year, it is most certain that the teacher would talk about the kinds of things he or she does to create a literate classroom community. This means fostering an environment where children come to enjoy reading, writing, listening, speaking, and viewing because they have participated in authentic and engaging learning experiences. They use the language arts to learn rather than only learn the language arts. The former conjures up a picture of exciting study of interesting topics with stops along the way to learn needed skills and strategies. The latter sounds like a list of skills to be learned by completing boring workbook pages.

Creating a Literacy Learning Environment

An important beginning step is to develop a classroom environment that invites children to expand their literacy skills and supports their efforts to do so. Early educational theorists such as Froebel and Montessori espoused the need for creating a physical environment that is conducive to literacy learning (Morrow, 2004). Skolnick and Fraser (1994, p. 49) ask children to create a "Life Box" of treasures so class members get to know one another at the beginning of the year. An adaptation of this idea would have children construct "literacy boxes" that highlight significant literacy examples from their lives. As the teacher, you can share your box not only as a model of possible items to include but also as someone who values literacy in everyday life. Encourage students to include items that represent themselves as readers, writers, listeners, speakers, and viewers. Examples of things that I (Geri) would include would be a cereal box—to depict my love of reading anything you put in front of me any time of the day—and a special bookmark made for me by my niece that I use when reading books for pleasure and my journal. My literacy box (Kathy) would include books in Spanish by my favorite author, Isabel Allende, and drafts of some children's books I have been working on.

Theory Into Practice →

Sharing literature with students that includes characters who are literate in a variety of ways can help them see how literacy plays a role in their own lives. The following is a list of some recommended literature to share that highlights literacy in different ways.

Bunting, E. (1989). *The Wednesday Surprise*. Illustrated by Donald Carrick. Scott Foresman. Anna and her grandmother excitedly wait to share their secret with their family after many Wednesdays working together. The reader is led to believe that the grandmother is teaching her granddaughter to read, but in fact, it is the grandmother who becomes the reader.

DePaola, T. (1999). *26 Fairmount Avenue*. Scholastic. Parts of this text are good examples of being literate in a variety of ways. One chapter describes using visuals to portray one's ideas as Tomie is allowed to draw on the walls of their home being built before the plaster was put up. Another chapter details his excitement about going to see Disney's *Sleeping Beauty* in the theater after having the original version read to him many times over the years. Tomie describes his anger and his yelling at the screen when the movie doesn't accurately portray the "real" Sleeping Beauty.

Fox, M. (1985). *Wilfred Gordon Macdonald Partridge*. Illustrated by Julie Vivas. Kane/Miller. Young Wilfred learns how important memories are when elderly neighbors share their childhood memories with him through storytelling.

Hamley, D. (1988). *Hare's Choice*. Delacorte Press. Two children find a dead hare along the road and bring it to school to have a funeral and bury it. They determine that they need to write a story about its life, and the class collaborates on a story that they in turn read to younger students.

Heide, F. P. (1995). *Day of Ahmed's Secret*. Illustrated by Ted Lewin. Harper Trophy. Ahmed, after a long day doing chores for his family in Cairo, shares his joy with his family when he learns to write his own name.

Hest, A. (1995). *The Private Notebook of Katie Roberts, Age 11*. Illustrated by Sonya Lamut. Candlewick Press. Journal of a young girl in 1947 as she struggles with having to move from the city with her mother to her new home in the country. Sketches, along with the text, are a good model for the various ways to use a journal.

Little, J. (1986). *Hey World, Here I Am!* Illustrated by Sue Truesdell. Harper & Row. A small book of poems written by the character, Kate Bloomfield. We learn a lot about her daily life and her trials, tribulations, interests, and passions. An excellent model for writing poetry as a form of self-expression.

Richardson, A. (1974). *In Grandma's Attic* (Grandma's Attic Series). Illustrated by Dora Leder. D. C. Cook. Stories told by a grandmother to her granddaughter as the granddaughter finds items in the attic that intrigue her. Good model of being literate in an oral manner.

Rocklin, J. (1997). *For Your Eyes Only (FYEO)*. Illustrated by Mark Todd. Scholastic. The required writing assignment of keeping journals is reflected in two students' personal thoughts and characteristics, one including mostly writing, the other a variety of drawings. Good as a model for portraying one's ideas in a variety of formats.

It is important to consider the varying degree of literacy your students have attained and to encourage students to share their literacy experiences and development using all modes of language arts communication. Some students will not have many examples of being writers or readers in their lives and homes, but they will have extensive experiences with verbal literacy and storytelling. Modeling and discussing a variety of literate activities and examples will assist students to see the wide scope of literacy in their lives.

A View From Home

During journal writing one day, Carlos wrote about helping his grandmother tie a special quilt she was making for his mother. During a one-on-one conference with him later that day, his teacher engaged him in a discussion about his experience. He told her that his grandmother makes quilts for family members made up of cloth from clothing and other special cloth that represent special occasions and stories in their lives. He was helping his grandmother complete a quilt for his mother that included cloth from her college graduation gown, wedding dress, one of Carlos's baby outfits, and other special events that have marked her life. Each piece of the quilt has a story that accompanies it, and Carlos listens to his mother explain each piece and share her life with him in this unique way. Carlos has a small quilt his grandmother made for him, and it includes cloth pieces from events from his 8-year life.

In the above A View From Home vignette, Carlos's life quilt is another example of a part of his literate life, an oral component. Children should be taught to think about the many aspects of their literacy lives, not just reading and writing, and be encouraged to bring these types of things in to share with others.

Taking time for children to share the contents of their literacy boxes in large or small groups will be time well spent. Students will motivate one another as they get ideas from one another about literacy-related activities that look like a great deal of fun to pursue. It is also a meaningful opportunity for them to use their oral communication skills for authentic purposes.

The literacy boxes and literacy stories that your students share will provide you with insights into their attitudes toward language arts activities and their level of confidence in themselves as literate persons. The experience will shed more light on their interests as well. Note why they selected certain items for inclusion, that is, what does this tell you about what motivates these students? Note how their cultures and communities are reflected in their choices.

Before the children even arrive at school, a teacher can set the stage for developing a **literacy learning environment.** Sending a letter home to each child at the end of the summer describing language arts activities that they will engage in is one way to meet your students and set the context for focusing on literacy. Using a letter asking students to bring their favorite book on the first day too will tell them that you value their interests and reading habits. A classroom library and writing center is a signal of the importance of literacy development. Some new teachers will be lucky enough to inherit a classroom loaded with quality **trade books;** however, others will need to begin building a selection of books on their own. You can do this by checking out books from your school or local library, purchasing books at a used bookstore, keeping on the lookout for library book sales, as well as joining a teachers' book club as a means for obtaining books. Once the children arrive and you get to know them, you will ascertain their interests, and then the search will be on to find reading materials that reflect those interests. An easy and often effective way to hook some reluctant readers onto reading is to put something irresistible in their hands, such as a new and enticing book about dinosaurs for the first-grade child who lives and breathes these creatures.

A writing **center** stocked with a variety of writing and drawing utensils, computers, and many different kinds of paper and envelopes will lure many students into trying their hands at writing and will encourage the creation of student-made books. Devoting a section of the classroom library to student-authored books will be further incentive for students to create their own books for the classroom. Listening and speaking centers can be established where children listen to books on tape, create audiotapes of well-loved books, or read poetry aloud.

Having a beautifully appointed classroom library and well-organized centers that never get used or that are not designed for children to access easily render them quite useless. Time must be built into the schedule to use these resources on an ongoing basis. It is better to risk losing a book or two or having a few markers dry out, as making materials available for student access will more likely keep the students engaged in **literate activities.** Materials must be accessible for children to use when they need them.

Sometimes students do a much better job than teachers do of convincing their classmates to read particular books. All they need to say is "You've got to read this book. It's awesome!" and everyone will be clamoring to get his or her hands on it. It is clear, then, that children need opportunities to share what they read and write with others. Students may be given time to talk about books during language arts time, or they may write book critiques to be kept in a box for students to review when they are searching for a new book to read.

Encouraging and celebrating writing is also of critical importance. Among other places, students get ideas for writing from one another. Having an audience for one's writing provides greater motivation for students to do their best. Students who select interesting topics and/or write well-developed pieces serve as models for their classmates. Devoting time to celebrate students' accomplishments in writing can create a community of authors who continually strive to explore and improve their craft.

One way to get students thinking about their literacy development is by having them keep a log of what they read and write by recording the type of each book they read and piece they write. They and the teacher can see at a glance how many and the types of books they have read or the stories they have written. Taking time for children to review their logs enables them to set goals for what they wish to achieve before the next review. Comparing work over time is an effective method to help students recognize the progress they are making. When students compare writing done in September with what they are writing in November, they can readily see how much they have improved. Similarly, they will generally be reading books that are more challenging in November. For some students who lack motivation, noting a paucity of accomplishments will serve as an inspiration to work harder.

Surveys, like the one that begins this chapter, are a good way to begin the school year and explore student interest and attitudes toward language arts. You may also include questions that provide an indication of the **skills** and **strategies** students use in their reading and writing. Surveys can also be a good first step in introducing students to **self-assessment** of their work as they begin setting goals for areas they wish to improve.

Students will not automatically know how to self-assess their work or set goals. Without practice, a student setting a goal may say, "My goal is to be a better speaker." This goal is so broad that it is not helpful because it does not give the student specific ideas about what to do to improve. We need to teach children how to self-assess their development and help them determine what will move them forward. When students know how to do this, it makes them more independent in their learning. When students are motivated in this way, a community of learners begins to emerge where students are eager to learn and the teacher is there to spark their interest and guide their learning.

Not only is it important to reflect on and continue to develop your own literacy attitudes and habits, but also in modeling this, your students will continue to understand and embrace their own literate lives and development. The most important point that we would like you to take away from this chapter is that preparation to teach involves so much more than a nicely decorated classroom and language arts learning experiences that children will enjoy. We are in the business of helping children develop lifelong learning habits, and we cannot expect them to have positive attitudes about literacy if we do not model that enthusiasm ourselves daily. Children take cues from us, and they will never be fooled by a charlatan. In every classroom where children love to read and write, you will find a teacher who also loves to read and write.

End-of-Chapter Reflection

- Return to the literacy survey you completed at the beginning of this chapter as a way to begin setting goals for yourself. What literacy areas or topics are you most interested in learning more about? Where do you see a need to develop your understanding and teaching skills?
- Looking back at the most valuable learning experiences that you outlined at the beginning of the chapter, what do you believe were the assumptions and philosophies of your teachers related to their use of effective teaching methods and students as learners?

Planning for Teaching

1. Put together a literacy box of your own and include items that highlight you as a literate person. Include items such as favorite childhood books, books you are reading now, pieces of writing that you are proud of, a favorite writing utensil, or notes from an effective speech you gave. Share your literacy box with your classmates/colleagues to celebrate your literacy.

2. Sketch out a classroom map that includes areas that encourage children to read and write. Make sure to include such things as a classroom library, comfortable reading area, and centers for literate activity such as a writing and a listening and speaking center. What kinds of things would be in each area?

Connections With the Field

Visit a library in your community. Speak with a children's librarian regarding the resources he or she could provide for you and your students and the kinds of activities the library provides to promote literate activities. Spend some time browsing through the children's area of the library to familiarize yourself with the kinds of materials available for children. Ask the librarian what books are currently popular with children today. Check out a few of these books to begin building your knowledge of children's interests in literature.

Student Study Site

The Companion Website for Developing Voice Through the Language Arts

http://www.sagepub.com/dvtlastudy

Visit the Web-based student study site to enhance your understanding of the chapter content and to discover additional resources that will take your learning one step further. You can enhance your understanding of the chapters by using the comprehensive Study Guide, which includes learning objectives, key terms, activities, practice tests, and more. You'll also find special features, such as the Links to Standards from U.S. States and associated activities, Children's Literature Selections, Reflection Exercises, Learning from Journal Articles, and PRAXIS test preparation materials.

References

Brookfield, S. (1992). Uncovering assumptions: The key to reflective practice. *Adult Learning, 3,* 13–18.

Daniels, D. (2002). Becoming a reflective practitioner. *Middle School Journal, 33,* 52–59.

Hillocks, G. (1995). *Teaching writing as reflective practice.* New York: Teachers College Press.

Holdaway, D. (1980). *Independence in reading.* Portsmouth, NH: Heinemann.

Morrow, L. M. (2004). *Literacy development in the early years* (5th ed.). New York: Pearson.

Newman, J. (1991). *Interwoven conversations: Learning and teaching through critical reflection.* Toronto, Ontario, Canada: Ontario Institute for Studies in Education.

Skolnick, D., & Fraser, J. (1994). *On their way: Celebrating second graders as they read and write.* Portsmouth, NH: Heinemann.

Surbeck, E., Han, E. P., & Moyer, J. E. (1991). Assessing reflective responses in journals. *Educational Leadership, 48,* 25–27.

Wenzlaff, T. (1994). Training the student to be a reflective practitioner. *Education, 115,* 278–288.

Zeichner, K., & Liston, D. (1996). *Reflective teaching: An introduction.* Mahwah, NJ: Lawrence Erlbaum.

What Are the Language Arts?

Context Setting:

After reading this chapter, you will be able to

- Discuss how literacy instruction has changed over the years
- Detail the six language arts and the importance of their integration
- Describe language development of young learners
- Discuss language learning theories
- Compare acquisition of a first and second language

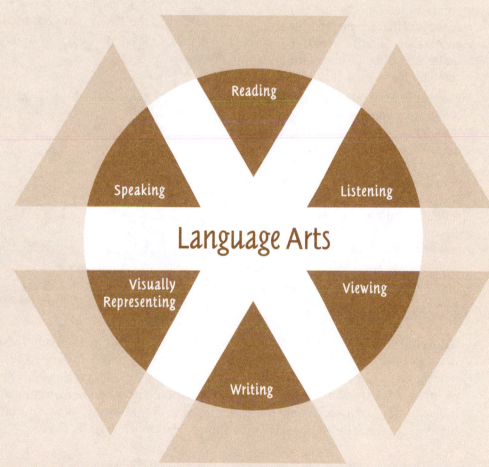

Before We Begin

- Think over your beliefs about how children learn and the types of learning experiences that support maximum learning for children. Make a list of the components that you would include in your philosophy of literacy development. Be prepared to share your ideas in small or large group discussion.

How Literacy Develops:
Literacy Acquisition Birth Through Grade 6

🏠 A View From Home

Curled up together in an overstuffed chair, Jasmine, wearing fuzzy-footed pajamas, and her mother are reading *Goodnight Moon*. As her mother reads the words, Jasmine points to the objects that the text conveys. "That's right," her mother encourages, "that's the mitten." Jasmine smiles up at her, pleased with herself at correctly identifying the object.

Raheem and his father prepare to go to the grocery store as his mother looks through the cupboards, listing off the items the family needs: "kidney beans, canned corn, flour." Raheem's father writes down the items as she says them and Raheem looks on. Later Raheem is scribbling on a pad of paper with a crayon and saying, "We need cheerios, pudding, and pizza."

Two-year-old Maria looks out the window from her car seat at passing objects.

Excitedly, after viewing the golden arches at McDonald's restaurant, she calls out, "French fries!"

Dominic, an 11-month-old baby, upon viewing the bottle being made for him, reaches out and calls "baba." His mother confirms his language and desire and says, "Yes, bottle. This is your bottle I'm warming up for you."

What is **literacy?** The definition has changed over the years from the narrow definition as the ability to read and write. As knowledge has expanded related to what it takes to be literate for life, the definition has broadened as well. The focus of literacy for this text and for your understanding as a teacher of language arts includes the ability to competently read, write, speak, listen, view, and comprehend language. The emphasis is on communication in all of its forms.

Stop to Think

If a child reads perfectly but does not understand anything that was read, is the child reading? If a child stumbles through reading but understands everything that was read, is the child reading? How would you define reading? How would you define literacy based on your own experiences?

Of course, as teachers we want our students to become literate persons, possessing refined skill in the ability to communicate effectively. Although you learned to read and write many years ago, it may not be clear as to exactly how you started on the path to becoming a literate person. This chapter will help you understand some of the underlying frameworks related to developing skill and ability in reading and writing, as well as becoming good listeners, speakers, and viewers.

Language Development

Begin with yourself as a starting point. Did you have older persons who read to you while you were snuggled up close? Did you have models of experienced readers, speakers, and writers use the language? Were you brought up in a household where language, both oral and written, was used purposefully on a continual basis? Even if you do not remember, it is likely that you learned to speak, listen, and even write through the models you were exposed to as a young child. Becoming literate is largely a social process (Wells, 1990). It has been shown that the more a child is exposed to language in its multiple forms through the support of experienced literate models, the more adept he or she is in learning and using language (Vygotsky, 1978).

It may seem miraculous that a child begins to learn the complex skills of communication without deliberate instruction. Although we may not realize it, children are receiving instruction in how to communicate through movement and listening they engage in from the moment they are born. It is believed that learning to communicate even begins before birth while a child is still in the womb. Although this complex understanding is too broad for the scope of this book, it is important to know that learning to communicate is an intricate process that begins early in a child's life. Development of oral language and its connection to success with learning to read has been researched and shown to have a positive correlation (Garcia, 2000; Ruddell, 1963). Therefore, encouraging oral development while children are young helps to develop the framework for future language development in all of its forms.

From early on, children begin to babble, producing a variety of sounds and experimenting with their voices in a number of ways. By about their first year, children begin to use some recognizable words that are associated with items and people in their worlds. At around 18 months of age, children begin to put two or more words together, such as "all done" and "night night." Young children enjoy rhyme, rhythm, and repetition in language and sound. Playing word games assists the children in hearing language and having models of language to foster further language development.

At around 3 years of age, the number of words children can say expands greatly. Young children often are quite animated, experimenting with sounds and verbal attempts at using language as they play and interact. This type of talk is often done while speaking to themselves and is an important step as they engage in using and practicing language and developing their language memories. Children at this stage of development are using their language capacities to make sense of their experience and world. This continues through the beginning stages of learning to read and write as well and is also the time in which young children begin asking many questions, often to the frustration of their parents (Vygotsky, 1978).

By the 5th year, children's spoken language is becoming more conventional as they start noticing words in their environment, certain advertisements, or characters on television or in the movies. By the time children begin school, most possess a burgeoning language base that will assist them as they engage in formal, structured learning experiences (Halliday, 1975).

Considerations of Cultural Differences in Language Development

Children bring their cultural backgrounds to school with them and they also bring a variety in rules and patterns of communication based on their experiences and cultural ways. It is important to honor the cultural literacy aspects of our students but also to model and teach the cultural literacy patterns that school expects (Delpit, 1988).

Second Language Acquisition

Some children acquire two or more languages from birth. They are referred to as **simultaneous bilinguals** (Ovando, Collier, & Combs, 2003). Their language development is often slightly delayed from the average **monolingual** child. They need additional time to sort out the complexities of the languages, since they are working with a vocabulary, a grammar, a syntax, and cultural expectations for communication from each language. They also need to determine which language to use with certain persons and in which situations. For example, when at Grandma's house, the language spoken is Farsi, and when at home, English is spoken. Although there may be a slight delay initially, most children quickly become **bilingual** or even **trilingual** when they have rich and consistent contact with the languages. For example, in some instances, the caretaker of the child may speak one language and the parents another. In other households, in an effort to maintain the languages of the parents/guardians, the father may speak one language to the child and the mother another.

Sequential bilinguals is the term used to refer to children who learn one language at birth and an additional language(s) after the first language is firmly established. This often occurs when children speak one language at home and learn another when they enter school. Second language acquisition for these students follows a pattern that is similar to that of their first language. Knowledge of the characteristics of these stages can be helpful for planning language arts instruction for English language learners (ELLs).

What Are the Language Arts?

The language arts typically consisted of four traditional processes: listening, speaking, reading, and writing. More recently, to address the expanding view of literacy and to encompass the highly visual nature of today's society, viewing and visually representing were added (*Standards for the English Language Arts,* 1996). Following is a brief introduction, as each of these processes is discussed at length with

Table 2.1 Stages of English Language Acquisition

At each stage, the student does the following:

1. Preproduction

(Students often experience a silent period during this stage)

- Relies on visual cues for meaning
- Uses gestures to indicate meaning
- Responds nonverbally to simple expressions or commands
- Relies on visual cues for meaning
- Uses gestures to indicate meaning
- Follows simple narrative expressed through spoken and visual material
- Initiates talk using single words or short phrases
- Begins to develop an understanding of word order and grammatical function

2. Early Production

- Initiates talk
- Begins to contribute to talk in whole-class situations
- Begins to initiate talk in small groups
- Begins to express ideas and feelings
- Talks about familiar topics in context
- Follows a sequence of instructions in familiar context
- Retells and discusses a simple story
- Engages in classroom and social talk with growing confidence

3. Intermediate

- Talks in a variety of situations with increasing fluency and confidence
- Demonstrates a growing control of semantic and syntactic features
- Engages in talk involving higher-level thinking skills
- Acquires a wide general vocabulary
- Follows most instructions
- Begins to adjust use of language to specific situations
- Begins to understand inferential language, for example, puns, irony, similes, metaphors

4. Advanced Intermediate

- Understands and uses English confidently in most contexts
- Recognizes a range of registers and uses these appropriately
- Becomes familiar with idiomatic use of English and culturally specific references
- Explores complex ideas in English
- Uses English fluently in most contexts

5. Advanced

- Uses English fluently and appropriately with an understanding of culturally specific references

SOURCE: Krashen & Terrell (1987).

examples in future chapters. Although each of the language arts is isolated below, typically no component stands alone without the use or integration of at least one of the others. They are interdependent, and the skills and processes used for each interconnect and are complementary to one another. Helping children become literate involves teaching them to use all six of the language arts. This text will assist you in teaching and integrating the language arts in a meaningful manner into your classroom and the lives of your students.

Listening

Listening is an interactive component of communication that is linked to all other communication skills, predominantly speaking. It involves the brain taking in and understanding language in the form of words and sentences and requires sustained attention. In simple terms, listening can be considered as hearing with a purpose.

Children utilize listening for much of their school experience and use these skills particularly during language arts instruction when listening to others during conversations about books, when someone is reading to them, either in person or on tape, and when listening to a partner share what he or she has written in a reading response log. Listening instruction is often neglected or marginalized because listening is done all the time, both in and out of school, and teachers mistakenly assume children should already have the skills needed to be effective listeners. However, instruction in listening is essential in the elementary classroom because of its prominence in the curriculum and in daily life, but also because it is not necessarily a skill that is just picked up naturally. It needs to be taught and practiced in a variety of contexts for a variety of listening purposes. Listening itself cannot be measured. We must gauge, therefore, how much children comprehend by what they do with what they have heard.

Speaking

Speaking, like listening, is a major learning activity and experience in classrooms, and it is often assumed that once children have learned to speak, they can do so with ease for a variety of purposes. As with listening, mastery through use is not the only or necessarily the most effective way to learn to talk with clarity and for a range of communication purposes. Talking occurs in the language arts when students respond to literature, their peers, and their teachers, as well as engage in reading aloud, **reader's theater,** and storytelling. Including instruction in effective speaking in the curriculum will allow children to share their ideas and learning in a verbal mode adeptly.

Reading

The process of **reading** is integral to a language arts curriculum, from learning to **decode** text to comprehending meaning. Children engage in reading throughout their school day and should learn a variety of strategies and skills to assist them in successfully reading a range of formats and genres for many purposes. Reading in the language arts can include such things as reading with a partner, reading aloud to allow the teacher to assess for fluency and strategy use, reading for pleasure, reading for research purposes, and performing reader's theater.

Writing

Writing is a process of putting ideas onto the page or electronic device. Children must learn what it entails to become proficient writers themselves. Understanding that writing is an important skill that is used for a variety of purposes in one's life stresses the value of writing. Writing and reading go hand in hand, and it is believed that having skill in one process assists with the other (Tierney & Shanahan, 2002). By reading many books of a favorite author, students might try using the author's writing style in their own writing pieces. By reading a certain **genre** of literature such as mysteries, children learn the essential components of a mystery and can then incorporate them into their own writing. Writing complements reading, as in the example of an 11-year-old child who reads an alphabet book he wrote and illustrated to a 5-year-old buddy.

Viewing

Children today live in a society that is inundated with visual images that they take in through television, the Internet, advertisements, print media, illustrations, and video and computer games. It is important that they learn how to decode and interpret visual images so that communication is clear and messages being sent through visuals can be critically evaluated. Children use **viewing** as they make meaning using the illustrations while reading a picture book or understanding a period of history while viewing and reading a timeline in a biography of Sacajewea or using Reader Rabbit (The Learning Company, 2006) software on the computer.

Visually Representing

Viewing is one part of the visual communication process, and another is creating or using visuals to communicate. Children represent their ideas visually when they draw pictures to accompany a story, design a poster in response to a text they have read, and create a newsletter from a research report using computer software. Possessing skills in representing ideas visually assists children in developing skill in a major communication process of today's world.

The Foundation of Language: The Four Cueing Systems

Engaging in communication is based on an understanding and application of four language or **cueing systems:** the **semantic system, syntactic system, pragmatic system,** and **graphophonemic system.** While being immersed in a culture of language, young children begin to understand and internalize the language systems even before they begin to talk themselves.

In order to understand these systems, consider the following sentence.

Kishia rolled the ball down the _____.

Consider the possibilities for completing this sentence. In order to fill in the blank, you need to have an understanding of **semantics**, the meaning system of language. Knowing that words put together in a sentence make meaning, you would use the semantic system to begin completing the sentence in a meaningful manner. You need to know what a ball is and its characteristics, such as the notion that it needs a semiflat surface in order to roll effectively.

You know that Kishia is a person, most likely a girl, and that sentences with a person in them are typically "doing" something. In this sentence, the girl named Kishia is rolling a ball down "something" and that "something" has to be a noun. Understanding the structure of language such as parts of speech, sentence structure, and rules of grammar represents using the **syntax** or structural system of language. Any of the following nouns would logically fit the sentence above. There are many possibilities. Can you think of others?

hallway	room	sidewalk	stairs	alley	hill

Now we will add an adjective to the sentence so that we can narrow down the noun that could possibly end the sentence.

Kishia rolled the ball down the *tree-lined* _____.

Now that *tree-lined* was added, you can make sense of the sentence using the syntax cueing system again, knowing that the adjective *tree-lined* describes the noun that fits into the blank. Now you go back to using semantics, knowing that for this sentence to be feasible, it has to make sense. The noun at the end of the sentence also has to be located out of doors because that is where trees typically are found. At this point, we can evaluate the options that were listed and decide that *hallway* and *room* are no longer possible for the sentence to make sense. The others, *sidewalk, stairs, alley,* and *hill,* are still viable options. Knowing that the word must be described by *tree-lined,* there are many more possibilities. Consider them altogether:

sidewalk	stairs	alley	hill	
road	street	avenue	parkway	boulevard

Another cueing system that allows an understanding and the utilization of language is **pragmatics,** the language system that deals with the social and cultural aspects of language use. If you are supplied with more knowledge or context surrounding this sentence, such as the sentences prior to this one in a text, you will learn that Kishia lives in a small rural community where there are many trees and farms. Knowing that typically there would not be alleys in a rural environment, or sidewalks, stairs, boulevards, avenues, or parkways, leaves the following noun options from the list:

hill   road   street

Any of these nouns would fit semantically, syntactically, and pragmatically and make sense in the sentence. The last cueing system that will assist you in further narrowing down the appropriate noun to complete this sentence is the **graphophonemic system,** the sound system of language. Although there are 26 letters in the English language, there are 44 sounds or phonemes, adding up to a large combination of letters and sounds to form many words with various pronunciations. We can add another clue that will demonstrate how using the phonological system is necessary to fully comprehend this sentence.

Kishia rolled the ball down the tree-lined s_____.

Now the only options from our list include *sidewalk* and *street* due to the first letter being an *s.* But this is not all that you need to read and fully comprehend the sentence. Young children begin to recognize words using the initial and final consonants in words, so when the last letter is added to the word in the sentence, the final word can be more accurately confirmed.

Kishia rolled the ball down the tree-lined s_____t.

It is evident that the word that fits in this sentence is *street.* This example demonstrates the complexity of learning to read and comprehend the written word. It is no wonder that it can be a challenge for some students.

Reading is abstract in that sounds in the language are represented by marks on a page. Some children find it difficult to make these abstract links. It may take them longer to sort this all out. Others learn to read the words, but they can't comprehend what they've read. Deliberate instruction in using the cueing systems will help most students continually improve their reading and communication ability. By understanding these foundations of English language learning, you can emphasize the components in your language arts curriculum and assist students in becoming more effective users of language.

Approaches to Teaching Language Arts

Communication is a complex process. Helping children to develop the ability to communicate effectively in a variety of modes and for a variety of purposes should include immersion in the language systems at birth and more systematic instruction when formal schooling begins. Historically, there have been a number of major approaches to language arts instruction, including the **traditional basal approach,** the **language experience approach,** the **whole language approach,** and the method of instruction on which this text is based, a **balanced or comprehensive approach.**

Traditional Basal Approach

The traditional basal approach to teaching reading and language arts has evolved over many decades. Language arts instruction using a traditional approach typically includes a **basal reading textbook** (one for language arts and one for reading) for instructional purposes and workbooks for practice in skill in such things as spelling, English grammar, and handwriting. Basals are typically textbooks developed for each grade level, and for reading they include a collection of written pieces that are organized by reading level or difficulty and skills that students progress through as they continue to develop reading ability. The first basal series included a textbook and a workbook for each student that included controlled vocabulary, parts of longer texts, systematic reading skill development, and a combination of genres of literature. Teachers' manuals accompanied each level of student text and provided explicit direction in instruction with the basals. Today, basal reader series are more sophisticated and inclusive, and in addition to the textbook, they include trade books (or children's books that can be bought in stores); cassettes and texts for listening and reading along; CD-ROMs that include quizzes, games, and skill practice; teacher resource materials such as charts and tests; and Internet links to related content and skill practice. An advantage of using a traditional basal approach to teaching reading includes having the materials already assembled and organized for teaching. As well, teachers' manuals provide support and direction for using the materials with students.

Basals for language arts are leveled as well, typically one text for each grade level, and include skills and exercises on such things as writing, grammar, usage, and spelling patterns. Often the skills and exercises are taught in isolation and not within a meaningful context, which can make learning more challenging than it needs to be.

Disadvantages of using basal series for language arts teaching and learning include the fact that basal reader series are written and constructed to meet the needs of students at each grade level and are supposed to have wide appeal. However, even though this is changing somewhat, because of basals' generic nature, not all children can find themselves, their experiences, and their cultures represented. In addition, authentic reading selections are often adapted and language simplified, thus causing the language to be stilted and challenging because it is unlike spoken language. As well, authentic texts that include illustrations are often cut due to space constraints, thus losing the original flavor and design of the book. Because a book publisher cannot know your students and their particular needs, teachers need to choose the components that best meet their students' development, adapting the basals rather than using them prescriptively. In the last decade or so, basal series have seen some changes in response to these criticisms; however, many literacy advocates suggest using them as a tool, not as the only source of teaching reading and literacy.

Language Experience Approach

Beginning in the 1950s through the 1970s, the language experience approach to teaching and learning language arts became popular. This teaching philosophy is based on the premise that learning to become literate capitalizes on the oral language of children and their experience. Children dictate stories and descriptions of personal experiences, and these become part of the materials used to teach and reinforce reading. Literacy is making meaning of language in its many forms, and this principle undergirds the language experience approach. Imagine the difficulty of reading about a topic in which you have no interest or background. If people with limited knowledge or interest in football were given a text to read about this sport, their ability to read the text would be hindered. They would find it extremely challenging to stay with the task and comprehend fully what was being read. The other major principle of the language experience approach is that children need many models of the written and spoken word and opportunities to experience it, and therefore access to books and authentic literature is essential. Using the language experience approach as one's language arts curriculum requires a teacher to develop learning experiences based on children's development and literacy needs. This in turn requires a teacher to be highly familiar not only with literature and materials but also students' individual development.

Whole Language Approach

Beginning to gain popularity in the 1980s, the whole language approach is based on the philosophy that language is best learned through authentic models of whole texts first, focusing on understanding and making meaning before breaking it down into its parts. This teaching philosophy emphasizes immersing children in authentic whole texts through read-alouds and shared reading and having a solid understanding that text should make sense and carry meaning before analyzing the individual words, sounds, and letters. This approach came into question in the 1990s, when many educators misunderstood whole language to be only a method or style of teaching without a solid underlying philosophical framework based on understanding how children learn to become literate.

Balanced or Comprehensive Approach

A balanced or comprehensive approach to teaching language arts integrates philosophies based in the traditional, language experience, and whole language approaches as it seeks to include a balance of teaching that is appropriate for student literacy development. It contains the belief that not all children become literate in the same way and that there must be a variety of methods and approaches available so that all can become successful. The principles of a balanced literacy approach include the following:

- Children learn to become literate when instructed with and engaged in literate tasks that are meaningful to their lives.

- Language arts instruction should be integrated, incorporating all facets of literacy—reading, writing, listening, talking, viewing, visually representing—as well as emphasized in content area learning experiences.

- Children engage in a variety of reading and writing activities (shared, guided, independent, read/write-alouds) to provide well-rounded opportunities to expand their literacy abilities.

- As children become literate, the teacher's role moves from being more directive to being more of a facilitator or guide (**scaffolding**) providing supports for learning.

Reflection Journal 2.1

Reflect on the reading program and activities you were involved in as a child learning to read. Recall the kinds of things you did during reading class. What made them good learning experiences and enjoyable to you? Were there any negative learning experiences? Do you believe all students felt the same way as you did? Describe why you feel this way. Which approach to literacy development was most likely being used (traditional, language experience, whole language, or balanced or comprehensive)?

Outside Influences on the Teaching of Language Arts

The **No Child Left Behind Act (NCLB)** (2001), enacted by the George W. Bush administration, has had a significant impact on language arts curricula in all 50 states. NCLB focuses on four principles: "stronger accountability for results, expanded flexibility and local control, expanded options for parents, and an emphasis on teaching methods that have been proven to work" (U.S. Department of Education, 2002). One of the guidelines that states accepting funding from NCLB[i] are required to meet is that all students become proficient readers by the year 2012.

Many challenges to the efficacy of the NCLB have been made by advocates for schools with high concentrations of poverty and/or ELLs, contending that the law does not adequately allow for the specialized needs of students in these populations (Goodman, Shannon, Goodman, & Rapaport, 2004). Some of the major provisions of the NCLB that impact language arts curricula and instruction are outlined below:

- Assessments will be created in each state that measure what children know and learn in reading and math in Grades 3–8. Student progress and achievement will be measured according to tests that will be given to every child every year.

- An increase in federal funding for reading must include scientifically proven methods of reading instruction through the President's Reading First plan.

- All LEP (limited English proficiency) students will be tested for reading and language arts in English after they have attended school in the United States for 3 consecutive years.

Given that it takes ELLs a minimum of 5 years (Cummins, 1980; Thomas & Collier, 1995) to become proficient in English, it is a difficult burden for ELLs to complete standardized tests after only 3 years of schooling in the United States. Scores from all students in the school are compiled to determine whether or not the school or district has made sufficient progress. The law further states that students must be in the United States for 3 consecutive years to allow for the fact that in the case of many migrant students, families may return to their country of origin for several weeks or months during the school year. Schools, teachers, students, and curricula, including language arts, are being affected by influences such as the No Child Left Behind Act. It is important that teachers stay attuned to what is happening at the state and national level.

Language Arts and Literacy Theory: The Beliefs Undergirding This Text

Reflection Journal 2.2

Think about what you would include in a philosophy statement related to becoming literate. What do you believe are the necessary components for becoming educated? Record the statement in your journal and revisit it from time to time to see if your beliefs change as you gain more experience. Some questions to consider:

- What do you believe is the real purpose of education in the United States?

- What characteristics should well-educated citizens in this country possess?

- Do all citizens and residents of this country have a right to be well educated?

- What do you think others believe about how education in this country should be structured and delivered?

- When designing an educational program, how important are the social and cultural contexts in which we live as compared to curriculum and content we want students to learn?

- Who should decide what is important for students to learn or how they should be taught?

If education is ultimately about guiding children to make greater sense of their worlds, we need to reflect on and understand the complexity of the educational process.

The remainder of this chapter focuses on philosophical considerations in relation to sociocultural contexts of learning and theories of cognition.

Socioculturalism

When parents have a choice, they put their children in the learning environment where they feel they will receive the best education possible that reflects their beliefs about the goals of education. For some parents this will mean selecting a school where specific religious values permeate all aspects of the academic, social or emotional, and even physical characteristics of the learning environment. Some parents select schools with a diverse population because they want their children to understand and appreciate cultural, religious, and economic diversity. Others want to ensure that their children's lives are not altered by interactions with children and families who are not like them. And many parents would select public or private schools that have good reputations for academic success, strong community involvement, and/or specialized curricula.

Thinking about the types of schools that exist and their missions helps to appreciate that education does not serve a single purpose in the United States, though there are many common beliefs. If we then consider the variety of educators, parents, and students within a single school or district, we find ourselves in the midst of the sociocultural context of education. "'Socio-cultural context' is a way of describing the social plane and cultural practices in which the learner and learning are situated" (Hammerberg, 2004, p. 650). The ways in which learning tasks occur both inside and outside of school will have an impact on how children learn in school. Family and community values and/or circumstances may be diverse or fairly homogeneous within a school community. In either case, however, what happens in school will be more effective when it links with students' lives outside of school and includes significant parental input (Delpit, 1996; Ladson-Billings, 2001). This is important to consider when teaching language arts to students who bring a wide array of cultures and experiences with them to school.

Historical Influences on Teaching and Learning

Many historical events as well as significant educational psychologists have influenced our present conceptualization of education. The influence of behavioral psychology in the United States plus the emergence of the industrial revolution early in the 20th century impacted the development of a curriculum that emphasized dispensing learning in small manageable elements to be learned incrementally. This is often referred to as the Transmission Model of Teaching and Learning, and it led educators to establish a firm curriculum for each grade level. In this model, classrooms are teacher centered, in that teachers dispense learning from the front of the classroom and children quietly and passively absorb what is taught. Tests are completed to demonstrate how well students could "recall" what they had been taught. Students are not required to complete projects, demonstrate their understanding, or reflect on their learning.

Learning to read was viewed as mastery of a hierarchy of phonics and word analysis skills. Each skill built on the previous skills, the assumption being that once all the skill levels were mastered, students would emerge as competent readers. Students first learned the letters of the alphabet, then letter sounds, and then blended the sounds to form words. Less emphasis was placed on reading for meaning. Penmanship was a major focus for writing with younger children. Other writing activities focused more on copying writing from the chalkboard and writing answers to comprehension questions. Little emphasis was placed on creative or process writing.

Active Constructive Process/Constructivism

In the mid-20th century, a number of psychologists emerged who had a profound impact on the way we view student learning. Each of them determined that the development of cognition and learning was heavily dependent on the child's ability to interact with the environment and use language to explore understanding. One of the most influential of this group, Jean Piaget (1955), concluded that children pass through a series of stages of cognition as they develop, though the exact age and amount of time children spend at each level may vary. In addition, there is only one order of the stages, and it is not possible to skip any of the stages. This concept of learning focuses exclusively on the development of the individual child and the kinds of learning experiences that will best enhance cognition at a particular stage of development. The four stages of development according to Piaget are outlined briefly in Table 2.2.

Table 2.2 Piaget's Stages of Development

Stage 1: Sensorimotor	Ages birth to 2 years	Mastery of concepts of objects; preverbal
Stage 2: Preoperational	Ages 2–7 years	Mastery of symbols; vocabulary and true language
Stage 3: Concrete operational	Ages 7–11 years	Mastery of classes, relations, and numbers; logical reasoning; and socialized speech
Stage 4: Formal operational	Ages 11 and older	Abstract reasoning and world of symbols

Theory of Cognition and Psychological Constructivism

Piaget's (1973, 1977) observations of children led him to the design of his *cognitive theory* of learning and forever changed the way we think about education. Contrary to the "transmission model" of learning, where it was believed that children were empty vessels and new learning could be poured in, Piaget determined that children actively construct their own understandings of the world. His theory of cognition includes four major components: *schema, equilibrium, assimilation,* and *accommodation.*

What we know about the world is arranged into weblike organizations within our brains. These organizations of experiences and understandings are called schemata. For example, if you hear the word *family,* a variety of images, memories, and thoughts come to mind. However, what comes to mind for you will not be the same for someone else, even for other members of your family, because you have had different experiences and have interpreted those experiences in unique ways.

You often hear the phrase "You could just see the wheels turning" when describing young children's efforts to learn something new. Often they will make several attempts before they figure it out. As human beings we strive for a state of equilibrium, where everything runs smoothly and everything makes sense to us. However, learning does not occur when we reach this state of equilibrium; it occurs in the "figuring it out" stage where we need to be pushed slightly beyond our comfort zone and stretched into considering new options. If the newly attained knowledge agrees with what we already know and/or believe, Piaget would say that we have "assimilated" the new knowledge. If the information causes us to alter what we know or believe, he would say that we have "accommodated" our current knowledge or beliefs to adjust to the new knowledge or beliefs.

These components of Piagetian theory lead us to understand that learning is an active process. Every new learning experience causes us to act on it and extend our knowledge base. New learning puts us in a state of disequilibrium, and since we always struggle to maintain a state of equilibrium within our bodies and our minds, we must actively explore whether or not to assimilate, accommodate, or even reject the new knowledge, depending on the understanding of the world that we are constructing. If children must actively explore how new learning fits with what they already understand, it was therefore logical for Piaget to recommend that children be exposed to hands-on and discovery types of learning, where they would be actively engaged in exploring new concepts.

Piaget's cognitive theory was reflected in language arts teaching, as it became important to make certain that students had sufficient background knowledge about reading topics, could draw conclusions, and could make connections to other stories, authors, and characters. Students write to explore character motivations and to make connections to their own lives. In these scenarios, children are not merely learning to read but, more important, reading to learn. The level of expectation mirrors the cognitive level of development of the children. The teacher helps students develop learning experiences and then guides them in their learning.

Psychological Constructivism

Understanding Piaget's theory of constructivism helps us examine how children learn and the stages of cognition they must pass through and the impact of the broader social context of learning.

> Think about the social context of a class that you particularly enjoyed and where you learned a great deal. What were the elements that made the social aspect of the class engaging? How did this context enhance your learning?

Theory Into Practice

Social Constructivism

Socioconstructivists took Piaget's theory one step further by examining the social role of the learning environment. These psychologists determined that students master new concepts by interacting with others (Bruner, 1986). Learning was not viewed as a purely individualistic phenomenon, as Piaget had suggested. Once students had developed prerequisite background understanding, they would benefit from interactions with teachers and peers. This would deepen their understanding of concepts and enable them to participate in more sophisticated interactions (Dillenbourg, Baker, Blaye, & O'Malley, 1994). Hands-on and discovery learning were important aspects of the social constructivist view of learning, but students' interactions with peers and adults in these learning experiences became crucial variables in examining their progress.

The collaborative aspect of social constructivism is clearly reflected in language arts programs that enable children to learn from each other in meaningful ways. Students join groups to read novels of their choosing, discuss how they interpret what they've read, and select ways to apply what they've learned. The teacher serves as a guide not only to extend student understanding of literacy but also to evaluate and continually improve their efficiency in working collaboratively.

Sociocultural Constructivism

Lev Vygotsky (1978) also examined the environment and its influence on learning, asserting that student learning is shaped and developed in large part by the environment in which students find themselves. Individual development occurs as a result of group interactions that result in group understandings, which are eventually internalized by the individual.

One of the centerpieces of the Vygotsky theory is the **zone of proximal development,** the distance between what the child is capable of doing alone and the problem-solving level accomplished with guidance. This connects to Vygotsky's belief that learning occurs first on a social level among individuals and is gradually internalized by each individual.

Stop to Think

Think of a course you took that was challenging or that required a new way of thinking or acting and was effective in the use of collaborative learning. Vygotsky's theory would suggest that learning in that course occurred similar to the following scenario: as a result of your interactions with the professor and your classmates and as your group began to understand the course concepts, you came little by little to understand how to do things or how to respond. This gave you more confidence, and you began to respond more fully because you now understood the concepts more fully. New ideas or suggestions would arise and be explored by the group. As a result of study and participation in class conversations, you could decide what the new information meant to you personally.

Assistance from the teacher, classmates, and/or collaborative group work assists learners in developing more in-depth understandings of the concepts. These supports are often referred to as scaffolding, similar to the scaffolding that is erected surrounding tall buildings as they are being built to help support the process (Bruner, 1986). Once the building has been constructed, the scaffolding is removed and the building is able to stand on its own. Piaget referenced assimilating or accommodating new knowledge within the learner. Vygotsky examined the social process of moving from inter- to intraunderstanding. Throughout this text, we explore ways to develop language arts learning experiences that reflect a sociocultural perspective, as this theory more fully reflects effective balanced teaching and learning.

What implication does scaffolding have for teaching language arts to children?   *Stop to Think*

Table 2.3 Constructivist Theories

	Psychological Constructivism	Social Constructivism	Sociocultural Constructivism
Major Theorist	Piaget	Bruner	Vygotsky
Goal of Education	Individual cognition Development	Individual cognition via social interaction	Education for social transformation
Learning Context	Individual context	Social context	Social context
Teaching/Learning Approach	Child-centered approach Knowledge construction Assimilation and accommodation Hands-on, discovery learning Tasks that challenge, encourage questioning	Application of Piagetian principles Focus on student interactions	Zone of proximal development Scaffolded instruction Piagetian principles Cultural contexts

Language Theorists and Language Theory

Based on the notion that effective learning occurs in a social context, some theorists have constructed models or conditions of learning that teachers may find useful in developing a philosophical approach to teaching, learning, and assessment. Two of the major theorists, Don Holdaway and Brian Cambourne, are represented below.

Holdaway's Model of Student Learning

Holdaway (1979) developed a simple but elegant model reflecting the role of both assisted and individual effort in learning grounded in a socioconstructivist perspective. The four elements of the cycle of learning include demonstration, participation, practice, and performance and are outlined below.

1. Teacher demonstration: Through modeling and directed instruction, the teacher introduces new aspects or concepts of learning. During this phase, students may be observers as the teacher provides deliberate instruction. Students who already understand the concepts may also serve as teachers.

2. Participation: Together the teacher and the students (or groups of students) engage in learning experiences designed to deepen the students' understanding of the concepts. This is a guided participation stage, and students are encouraged to take risks, knowing that the teacher or "expert" is available for assistance.

3. Practice: When the students demonstrate a basic competence with the new material, they work independently to further solidify understanding and practice the concepts.

4. Performance: The students share what has been accomplished or learned. They receive constructive feedback on their efforts from teachers and peers.

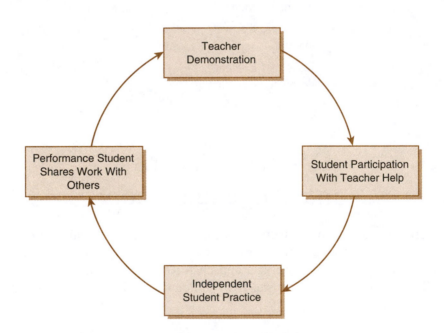

Figure 2.1 Holdaway's Model of Effective Student Learning

Cambourne's Conditions of Language Learning

Another theorist whose philosophy includes a sociocultural constructivist perspective is Australian educator Brian Cambourne (1988). He synthesized extensive observations of children to conclude that certain optimal interactions within the

Table 2.4 Cambourne's Conditions of Language Learning

Cambourne's Conditions	Language Arts Classroom Examples	Relationship to Sociocultural Constructivism
IMMERSION: Children need to be immersed in their learning through a variety of methods and activities.	Teachers plan activities that immerse children in literacy throughout the school day. The print-rich classroom is stocked with literacy materials for easy access.	Social role of learning is inherent. Learning from adults and peers is an active and consistent activity.
DEMONSTRATION: Adults model concepts/processes to be learned by students.	Teachers observe that the children need to know how to determine character traits in stories they read. Teachers model by reading a story and identifying the clues they use to determine character traits.	A first step in learning entails interactions with an individual who is more knowledgeable in the subject/concept.
USE: Children need adequate individual and group opportunities to use and practice their emerging skills, knowledge, and attitudes.	Children read a new story in pairs. They determine words, phrases, and pictures that reveal the traits of the characters in the story.	Learning is a shared, interactive process. Group processing results in a shared understanding of concepts that may not yet result in individual understanding.
EXPECTATION: Expectations for learning and self-management should be established. Teachers play an active role in holding high expectations for student learning and guiding them in meeting expectations.	Children review their work over a period of time and set goals in collaboration with their teachers for future development. They conference with their teachers regularly to monitor progress. They know they are expected to read and apply new strategies to their reading.	Over time, learners begin to internalize their own understanding of concepts.
APPROXIMATION: Children must try out new learning. They take risks to continually move closer to expectations. It is expected that they will make errors as they engage in practice.	Children analyze samples of quality descriptive writing and develop a set of criteria for good descriptive writing. They write descriptive pieces and compare them to the criteria, taking risks with a new genre of writing.	At both the group and individual level, children continually refine their understanding of concepts based on the approximations they make.
RESPONSE: Students need to receive constructive feedback from teachers and peers to help them adapt, modify, and extend learning.	Teachers conference with students to review their self-assessments of descriptive writing. Teachers review with children which criteria were met and help them set goals for next steps in descriptive writing. Students read their writing to a peer to receive response and feedback based on the developed criteria.	Individuals interact with peers and adults to receive feedback that helps them internalize individual understanding.

(Continued)

Table 2.4 (Continued)

Cambourne's Conditions	Language Arts Classroom Examples	Relationship To Sociocultural Constructivism
RESPONSIBILITY: Children are guided in accepting increasing responsibility for their own learning.	After students learn to evaluate the writing of others using a rubric, they are expected to self-assess their own work and edit and revise it to meet criteria.	As understanding moves from the group to the individual, students are more capable of taking on responsibility for their own learning.
ENGAGEMENT: Children need to be actively engaged in learning. To do this they need opportunities to study, explore, discuss, and reflect on what they are learning in a variety of groupings (individual, paired, small group, large group).	Students are immersed in meaningful and interesting areas of study. They have a variety of materials and learning experiences available to them. Venues are available for students to discuss and reflect on what they have learned. These conditions encourage student engagement.	At both the individual and group level, students determine meaning, internalize that meaning, and apply it to new levels of learning.

learning environment enhance students' understanding of the learning process and their role within it. The resulting "Conditions of Learning" encompass eight dynamic and interactive processes by which children learn: (1) immersion, (2) demonstration, (3) use, (4) expectation, (5) approximation, (6) response, (7) responsibility, and (8) engagement. These conditions form a framework for teaching, learning, and assessing in the language arts and are a guiding structure in this text.

Each of the conditions is outlined more fully in Table 2.4, including examples of how the conditions might be implemented in the classroom and their relation to a sociocultural constructivist viewpoint.

When all of Cambourne's conditions of learning are operational within a classroom, the stage is set for optimal learning and especially for language learning to take place. One of the major goals of Cambourne's conditions is that students will be guided little by little to take more responsibility for their own learning. An excellent model for assisting students to grow into becoming more responsible for their learning and support their development is the **gradual release of responsibility model** developed by Pearson and Gallagher (1983). This is similar to the scaffolding of learning prescribed by Bruner (1986), as discussed earlier in this chapter. As you can imagine, however, students do not automatically know how to judge their own work, set goals, or take responsibility for how well they do. Students who have been accustomed to submitting their work and then waiting for the teacher to inform them about how well they did on assignments may find it difficult to self-assess their own work accurately. The same may be true with "approximation." If students have been engaged in learning experiences that yielded only right and wrong answers or where grades were considered definitive measures of student progress, effectively examining their work in relation to a set of criteria can take some time.

Adapting Curriculum to Reflect and Appreciate Classroom Diversity

Constructivist theory is particularly effective when addressing the needs of a diverse classroom, since a constructivist classroom encourages students to interact and learn from one another's experiences. Even though a class may appear relatively homogeneous at the beginning of the year, an observant teacher will quickly realize that there is great variety in any group of children. The more that we get to know our students and their families, the more we will come to understand and appreciate these differences. Classroom diversity can be considered from a broad perspective, including race, gender, ethnicity, language background, religious affiliation, and special educational needs. These are the areas that readily come to mind when we think of diversity in the classroom; however, there are many other areas to consider. Gender differences may be apparent or subtle in a classroom. We hear a great deal about ensuring that girls do not come to think of themselves as less capable than boys or are not relegated to less academically rigorous classes than their male counterparts. Boys, on the other hand, are often compelled to make choices that society views as more "masculine," even though they may not match the interests or wishes of all male students. Some students learn quickly, others need more time to explore and think about new concepts, and still others have special educational needs that require adapted or modified curricula.

Linking students' home lives to their school lives is a positive way to connect the whole child to the learning experience. There are innumerable ways to make these kinds of links through the language arts. Viewing, speaking, and listening can be easily integrated by having children create posters or bulletin boards about themselves, their interests, and their families to be displayed in the classroom. Some teachers feature one child and his or her family each week. Providing opportunities for students to talk about themselves and their lives outside of school, especially as they relate to areas of study in the classroom, helps students appreciate each other and provides insights into the children's lives. Some children may not wish to talk about their lives outside of school for one reason or another, and these wishes should be respected. Other students may be too shy to share with the whole class but may be verbal in small groups. Children who are learning English and children with certain learning challenges may need extra time to think about and rehearse what they will say before they share with others.

A View From the Classroom

Lori teaches middle school migrant students in a Spanish, language arts class. She had them read *Cajas de Cartón* (*The Circuit*) (Jim.Jénez, 1997), which is based on a true story about the lives of a migrant family as they zigzag across the United States harvesting crops. Students created a T-chart to make reflections as they read the book. On the left side of the *T,* students recorded significant events from the story; this was also a method for practicing summarizing main ideas. On the other side of the *T,* similar events from their own lives or similar experiences they had heard about are recorded. At first the students had difficulty with this activity because they were not accustomed to making connections between school and home, but as Lori continued to model the strategy by sharing connections from her own life, their responses became richer. Many of these students were struggling to read in Spanish due to their mobile lifestyles, but because their interest level was high, they put tremendous effort into reading, discussing, and writing about the novel.

Language arts provides limitless venues for student diversity to be understood and celebrated. Selecting literature that reflects the experiences of the students in the classroom, and does so in an accurate and respectful manner, captures the attention of the students and makes them feel more connected to the school experiences. Oral and written reflections on the readings that require students to make connections between what they have read and their own experiences helps them become more reflective readers and writers.

Learning about students' backgrounds and interests may lead you to make selections for formal reading and writing experiences and help you select books for your classroom library. You will want to have a good variety of books available for independent reading. If students speak languages in addition to English or have unique background experiences, you may wish to (a) select books that are written in these languages or that reflect these experiences so that students can see themselves reflected in the literature they read as well as (b) share literature of varied cultures with all students.

Free-write journals also provide opportunities for students to record their experiences and reactions. Enabling students to share their journal entries on a voluntary basis helps them get to know each other and appreciate similarities and differences among class members. When students are particularly interested in a topic or reading materials that focus on conflict students might encounter, the journals are often great stepping-stones for class discussions.

Affording choices in how students complete learning experiences or projects allows them to represent their cultures and/or experiences if they so choose. For example, in the vignette about Lori's students, a final project might encourage them to reflect on what families do to mange a mobile lifestyle. Students might focus on the Jiménez family in the novel, compare their own experiences to the Jiménez family, or interview community members to get their perspectives.

Creating Home-School Literacy Connections

The importance of home-school connections cannot be overemphasized. When parents/guardians and teachers work together to provide the best education possible for children, the results are bound to be more positive than when parents/guardians are not included in this process. When all who care about a child hold the same expectations for student learning, work habits, and social interactions at school, a child has a clear picture of what is expected of him or her. When parents are informed about what children are learning in school and how they are being taught, it provides them with opportunities to extend that learning at home, and thus students see that academic learning occurs beyond the classroom. Perhaps even more important is that families and schools are likely to learn more about each other and adapt more effectively to one another's needs.

Often parents send their children to school and assume that everything will be the same as when they attended school. Providing information through an Open House, letters home, or parent or guardian workshops to highlight the philosophy and methodology of the school and your language arts curriculum will inform parents about how and why their children are being instructed in a particular manner. These meetings may also be used as a first step in guiding parents to work effectively with their children at home when completing homework and extending learning. Efforts should be made to emphasize that children will be more open to engaging in literacy activities with their parents/ guardians if the experiences are carried out in an enjoyable manner and if the children are able to complete the activities they are being asked to complete.

Teachers and administrators would do well to structure opportunities for parents to inform them about expectations they have for their children at home.

Knowing that children have extensive religious or cultural obligations beyond the classroom may have a bearing on the amount of work children are asked to do outside of school. Determining whether or not it is appropriate to integrate these activities into the curriculum would be a good discussion to have with parents. In cases where parents are learning English, it would be necessary to have translators present to facilitate communication among school personnel and family members. Calls home by fluent speakers of the home language may be more effective than letters home or may precede letters sent home in the first language of the family.

Parents/guardians can have a significant impact on the literacy development of their children. Encourage them to talk frequently with their children and engage them in various activities. Aside from forging positive relationships with their children, parents/guardians can teach their children a great deal about the world, and of course the more children know of the world, the more understanding they will bring to what they read and how they communicate. This relates to the notion of schema theory that was discussed earlier in this chapter. Even if children are hearing or reading about something new, it is more likely that they will be able to relate to and have a clearer understanding of new concepts if they have a broad range of experiences.

Parents/guardians should know of the importance of listening to their children and encouraging them to expand their thinking. Children solidify their understanding of concepts when they discuss them with others and hear other viewpoints. As they listen and discuss, their vocabularies increase as well. Parents/guardians will want to make these discussions positive and informal. They may share a wide range of visual and manipulative materials with children to strengthen their understanding. They may engage their children in activities along with them to also foster understanding. Some cultures teach their

A View From the Classroom

In studying the various eras in the evolution of the earth, children in Michigan learn that 350 million years ago, the Great Lakes region was one large tropical sea with a great deal of living coral. Children who live in this area may visit the western shores of Lake Michigan to search for Petoskey stones, which are fossilized coral remnants of the earlier era (Wargin, 2004). Local experts are invited in to share knowledge of the stones and the history they represent. Native American storytellers share legends of the stones and land formations. Children bring home trade books and read about the legends (Lewis, 2004; Wargin, 2004). Parents/guardians share their knowledge and perhaps even learn together as they work with children in completing related projects.

children in this fashion and do less verbalization, instead allowing their children to learn by working alongside older family members or experimenting on their own. Parents/guardians who are learning English should be assured that use of the home language is highly acceptable, especially since they may be able to express themselves much more fully in their native language.

Literacy researchers have done research on the correlation between the number of books in the home and the level of reading success in school. Across all economic levels, it is found that homes with more books produce children who are better readers. This is important information to share with families. Parents/guardians may wish to include more books among gifts they make to their children or may make more extensive use of their local libraries. Teachers may make arrangements with neighborhood libraries to feature library card applications, special story hours, or homework assistance. Reading Is Fundamental, Inc. (RIF) provides schools with free books to send home with children. This is another good source of books in the home.

Encouraging parents/guardians to establish regular routines for literacy activities may help busy families extend literacy interactions at home. Finding regular times and places for these activities is helpful. Reading at bedtime is a long-established tradition in many households but may be new in others. Some households include extended family members or older siblings who may be willing to help. Some parents may not be literate in English (or in their home language), but they can still support their children's education by ensuring that they do homework and read or write every evening.

Some children struggle in school, and sending homework they cannot complete on their own will frustrate the parents/guardians and further erode the self-efficacy of the child. In these instances, take care to send homework they can do with little or no support, as the child will feel more relaxed and the parents will be more likely to applaud the progress the child is making.

A View From the Classroom

Luz Lebrón, a fourth-grade teacher, has developed a successful method for teaching parents/guardians about working with their children at home. Luz teaches in a two-way bilingual school where half the students are English-dominant and half of the children are Spanish-dominant. Both groups of children become fluent in both languages by the time they complete the fifth grade. Luz recognizes that many of her families are not certain about how to help the children at home. She invites them to training sessions during the school day and in the evening. She demonstrates how to practice reading, use reading strategies, write for pleasure, practice spelling, and so on. She emphasizes keeping the homework sessions short,

(Continued)

(Continued)

focused, and positive and highlights the importance of establishing a homework routine with a regular time and quiet space.

After parents/guardians practice with each other, Luz brings in the children, and they try out the new techniques. It is touching to see how eagerly the adults and children approach their learning time together. Luz is a successful teacher, and in her classroom children experience high levels of success. She recognizes the

important role parents/guardians play in their children's education, and she provides them with the tools they need to be successful.

🚙 A View From the Classroom

Lorena is a Spanish bilingual first-grade teacher who has a clear understanding of the importance of communication between home and school. Family members are lined up outside her door before and after school every day. Her parent-teacher conference schedule is always full. How does she get so much more family involvement than other teachers in the building? The Chilean-born Lorena is Latina herself, so she has an understanding of the culture of her children, though cultural differences still exist between her background and that of her mostly Mexican and Puerto Rican–born students.

Lorena makes special efforts to get to know the families by personally inviting them into the classroom and getting to know them when they drop off and pick up their children. She always makes time for them, even though she must spend extra time after school to get ready for the next day. She recognizes that raising the children is a family affair, and often older siblings, grandparents, aunts, or

uncles may play a role in caring for the children. Lorena extends invitations to the entire family to come to school and knows that often everyone from the smallest baby to the oldest *abuelita* (grandma) may show up. She gets to know them all and respects the role they play with the children. In getting to know the families on a personal level, Lorena is earning their trust and respect. As the family members become more comfortable with her, they begin to share their family circumstances. Though life for these immigrant families is very difficult, many households are quite stable. One of her students cries easily, and she learns that his mother has not yet been able to come to the United States from Mexico with her two youngest children. Another girl is belligerent and is rude to her classmates, and Lorena learns that her parents are in the midst of a divorce. With this kind of information, Lorena has a better understanding of why her children react as they do, and she can make more informed judgments about how to work with them.

Little by little Lorena begins to make the academic expectations of her classroom known to the parents/guardians. Children bring home books in a plastic ziplock bag every night. They are to read them to someone in the family, and that person must sign a verification card. Lorena recognizes that many of her parents are not fully literate, even in Spanish, because they have not had much access to educational opportunities. Therefore she relies on anyone in the household who can help and makes certain the children know the material quite well before it goes home. She knows the strengths and weaknesses of each student, and she keeps the families informed about the progress of each one. She makes individualized recommendations for each child and sends home practice work in math or writing, for example, to strengthen areas where children need more practice.

Creating an Optimal Environment for Language Arts Learning

Think about courses where you learned the most. What are the elements that made it an optimal learning environment? Could you replicate these elements in a PK–8 (prekindergarten to eighth grade) classroom? Would these conditions be conducive for learning for all students, or would you have to consider alternatives for some students? What might these be?

Stop to Think

Children learn best in situations that represent Cambourne's conditions for learning, for example, the necessary resources are available, a stimulating curriculum exists, and students are expected to take responsibility for their progress. Beyond these conditions, it is of vital importance that a safe and secure environment be established where students feel free to take risks in exploring new concepts. This assumes that the teacher will guide students in mastering not only academic content but in developing social interaction skills as well. Students learn to work collaboratively in groups, use one another as resources in their learning, and grow as a community of learners.

In language arts this means that students are asked to respond to what they have read in genuine conversations, rather than merely answering questions for which there is a right or wrong answer. Their writing is designed to help them explore topics and express their opinions about them. They have many opportunities to create artistic, musical, or dramatic activities to demonstrate what they have learned. The classroom is stocked with a rich variety of literacy materials that stimulate students to explore areas of interest. Students move purposefully about the room as they complete their learning activities.

Differentiating Instruction for Meeting the Needs of All Students

As mentioned previously, not all children learn at the same rate and in the same way. Teachers must find ways to meet the needs of each child in their classrooms. Although this sounds rather daunting, there are some principles that teachers can put into practice to make teaching and learning more effective for all students:

1. Evaluate students' strengths and needs periodically to determine specific areas on which to focus

2. Establish groups of students that are flexible in nature to focus on identified areas of need

3. Determine the standards that students are required to meet and scaffold instruction to address them in a meaningful way for students; provide multiple opportunities for modeling and allowing students to practice the new concepts

4. Focus on the higher levels of **Bloom's taxonomy** (see Table 2.5) to challenge all students

5. Establish substantive and meaningful expectations for all students

6. Design open-ended learning experiences that enable students to complete the activities at their level of expertise

7. Assess the individual progress of students and note gains made over time; continually refine the curriculum to meet the changing needs of students

8. Support the efforts of each individual student in building confidence and self-esteem

Gifted Students

Students who are advanced in comparison to the rest of the class have a right to a curriculum that challenges them and moves them forward in their learning. Occasionally, students who are bored in school develop behavior issues because they are required to complete work that offers them little or no intellectual stimulation. An evaluation of their class work, as well as a review of test results,

Table 2.5 Bloom's Taxonomy

Benjamin Bloom (Bloom & Krathwohl, 1956) developed a taxonomy or a hierarchy of learning that identifies and ranks learning experiences from the simplest to the most complex. Obviously, the simplest learning experiences require the least amount of thinking and the most complex require maximum use of brainpower. Each of the levels in Bloom's taxonomy is briefly outlined below:

Recall: Students are asked to recall or reiterate what they learned without altering the information in any way. Matching or fill-in-the-blank assignments are examples of recall. Students merely "recall the correct answer."

Comprehension: Students go one step further when they comprehend what they have heard or read. They are required to demonstrate that they understood but are not required to do anything with their comprehension.

Application: Students apply understanding when they use information to complete a task.

Analysis: Students carefully review what they have read, listened to, or written to make judgments about what they have learned.

Synthesis: Students build on what they have learned and what they already understand to develop new conclusions or ideas.

Evaluation: Students evaluate what they have read, written, or listened to. They do not take information at face value but carefully review it against what they have researched and compare it to their prior knowledge.

will provide the teacher with an indication of the level of challenge needed. Using samples of classroom work alone may not be sufficient, as students who do not find the learning experiences beneficial may not complete their work or may do so with minimal effort. These students can be involved in learning experiences that require higher level and more in-depth thinking and reasoning. Working with gifted and talented programs and teachers will also help the classroom teacher design appropriate learning experiences for advanced students. Efforts should be made to make sure these students are included in the social fabric of the classroom and not left to spend most of their day working independently.

Students With Special Needs

It is much more common for students with special needs to be included in grade-level classrooms, since it has been recognized that they perform better in heterogeneous settings rather than being isolated in special education classrooms

(Hallahan & Kauffman, 2000; Smith, Polloway, Patton, & Dowdy, 1998). Classroom teachers who have not received extensive training in meeting the needs of special education students may be at a loss in determining how to develop appropriate curricula. Fortunately, many school districts have developed schedules that enable special education teachers to work in the grade-level classroom for certain portions of the day with the classroom teachers as they work collaboratively to determine the most effective instructional strategies for students. In other cases it is the responsibility of classroom teachers to seek out district-level resources to inform them about meeting individual needs. Each student with identified special education needs has an individual education plan (IEP), which outlines specific goals the child is expected to work toward. Paying special attention to the requirements of the IEP also assists teachers in planning. Many of the principles listed at the beginning of this section are also effective in working with students with special needs.

English Language Learners (ELLs)

Students who are in the process of learning English as a second (or subsequent) language need special consideration in relation to literacy development. All ELLs should be evaluated with a district- or state-approved measure of English language proficiency. The results of this measure places students on a continuum of English language acquisition of about six categories ranging from emergent to nearly proficient.

Ideally, students should begin reading in their dominant language, as they will bring more understanding to the endeavor. Frequently, teachers and administrators who do not have a background in best practices for ELLs will decide that ELLs will learn English more quickly if they are completely immersed in English and have little or no contact with their home language. On the surface this may seem like a logical assumption to make; however, just the opposite is true.

Our Beliefs About Language Arts Teaching, Learning, and Assessment

The way we teach reflects what we believe about how children learn best. As authors of this text, we have outlined our common beliefs (see the companion CD included with the book) regarding effective teaching, learning, and assessment in relation to the language arts. These beliefs form our philosophy about effective literacy instruction. No two teachers believe exactly the same things, and each person's philosophy is somewhat different. We have also included a brief description of how these beliefs might be reflected in classroom practice as a means for seeing how philosophy and practice go hand in hand.

Go to the CD now and read the authors' beliefs. Complete the worksheet that accompanies this component as a means for reflecting on your own beliefs.

Theory Into Practice

Your Beliefs Influence How You Teach

Your beliefs unquestionably influence how you teach. For example, judging from our belief statements above, we assume that children are capable of developing critical thinking skills and that they can handle a fair amount of responsibility at a relatively young age. We believe that they learn a great deal from one another and that children should be given opportunities to develop as fully as possible. Therefore, if we set up a classroom, you might expect to see students gathered in small groups to discuss personal reactions to stories they had read, determine cause and effect, or identify inferences that could be made from certain reading passages.

As you move through your teacher preparation program, you may find that your original views of education change or that your basic beliefs remain intact and you only refine them as you learn. This process of developing your teaching philosophy is an example of Piaget's concept of (a) accommodation, as you incorporate new ideas and beliefs, and (b) assimilation, as you solidify them into your foundational philosophy. The main point, however, is that you develop your own philosophy of teaching, learning, and assessment so that when you begin teaching, you will be more likely to teach from your convictions about how children learn best, rather than routinely following a teacher's guide.

Reflection Journal 2.3

Complete the following checklist by checking all the choices that apply.

When given the following choices about how to complete a project, what option(s) would you select and why?

__ work alone	__ write a report	__ create a visual display
__ work with others	__ give an oral	__ create a video presentation
__ create a computer	__ write and sing a song	__ perform a dramatic reenactment slide show

Share your choices with your classmates. Note the variety of responses within your group. Discuss why you chose the options you did. What does this make you think about making choices available to your students?

A View From Home

Chuck tells a story about his daughter's teacher and how he turned her school life around. April had struggled in school up to this point (about fifth grade), but this particular teacher helped her develop into a top-notch student. He taught her how to become a critical thinker, but mostly he made her believe in her own ability to be a good student by giving her the confidence to draw on strategies she'd learned to support learning when things got difficult in her courses. April went on to become salutatorian of her high school class, completed her master's degree in psychology, and has begun the process of applying to doctoral programs.

It is energizing to realize that a single teacher can have such an impact on the remainder of a person's life. We all should strive to be that teacher. A great part of this particular teacher's success came from the enthusiasm he had about learning and his ability to excite his students about learning. You can't pass on that type of enthusiasm if you don't already possess it within yourself. If you love to read and write, your students will pick up on that passion. If you do not really like to read and write but you do think you would be a wonderful teacher, it's not too late. Think about what you really enjoy and begin by reading books or magazines on that topic(s) and allow your interests to lead you.

End-of-Chapter Reflection

- Return to the philosophy statement that you wrote for Journal Entry 2.2. What implications does your philosophy have on how you will
  a. Structure learning in your classroom?
  b. Weigh the relative importance you place on both cognitive and affective aspects of learning?
  c. Organize your classroom for instruction?

- What are your beliefs about children and reading? And writing? Listening? Speaking? Visually representing? Viewing? Quickly write a few sentences detailing your beliefs about each of these components of language arts.

Planning for Teaching

1. Look at the language arts standards for your state. Ascertain the philosophical beliefs that are reflected through the standards statements.

2. Based on theories of student learning and effective teaching, what do you feel are some important things to implement during the first 2 weeks of the school year?

3. Critique a number of children's books that portray females, minorities, or children with special needs as main or significant characters. Examine the roles these characters play. Note whether these characters are cast as lively and vibrant personalities engaged in important decision-making roles, or are they helpless and dependent on those around them.

Connections With the Field

1. Visit a classroom that is relatively diverse. Ask the teacher how he or she represents the students' backgrounds in the classroom.

2. Work with school officials to interact with parents during PTO meetings or other parent gatherings. Engage parents in discussions that will lead to a better understanding of the families who attend the school. You may wish to use some of the questions below or develop your own. Be certain to have school officials review the questions first, to make certain they are appropriate for the audience. It may also be necessary to engage the services of an interpreter when parents are in the process of learning English:
   a. What would you like us to know about your community or children?
   b. What would help families be more involved in school activities?
   c. What things does the school do that are helpful to you and your children?
   e. What things would you like to see changed?
   f. What are your goals for your children (in general and in relation to language arts)?

3. Observe a successful language arts teacher in the field. List the elements of his or her teaching and assessing of language arts that you feel contribute to this teacher's successful teaching and the success of the learners.

Student Study Site

The Companion Website for Developing Voice Through the Language Arts

http://www.sagepub.com/dvtlastudy

Visit the Web-based student study site to enhance your understanding of the chapter content and to discover additional resources that will take your learning one step further. You can enhance your understanding of the chapters by using the comprehensive Study Guide, which includes learning objectives, key terms, activities, practice tests, and more. You'll also find special features, such as the Links to Standards from U.S. States and associated activities, Children's Literature Selections, Reflection Exercises, Learning from Journal Articles, and PRAXIS test preparation materials.

References of Children's/Young Adult Literature

Brown, M. W. (1991). *Goodnight moon*. New York: Harper Collins.

Jiménez, F. (1997). *Cajas de cartón*. Albuquerque: University of New Mexico Press.

Lewis, A. M. (2004). *Tears of Mother Bear*. Mackinac Island, MI: Mackinac Island Press.

Wargin, K. (2004). *The legend of the Petoskey stone*. Chelsea, MI: Sleeping Bear Press.

References of Professional Resources

Bloom, B. S., & Krathwohl, D. R. (1956). *Taxonomy of educational objectives: The classification of educational goals*. New York: Longman.

Bruner, J. (1986). *Actual minds, possible worlds*. Cambridge, MA: Harvard University Press.

Cambourne, B. (1988). *The whole story: Natural learning and the acquisition of literacy in the classroom*. New York: Ashton Scholastic.

Cummins, J. (1980). The construct of language proficiency in bilingual education. In J. E. Alatis (Ed.), *Georgetown University roundtable on language and linguistics* (pp. 76–93). Washington, DC: Georgetown University Press.

Delpit, L. (1988). The silent dialogue: Power and pedagogy in educating other people's children. *Harvard Educational Review, 58,* 280–298.

Delpit, L. (1996). *Other people's children: Cultural conflict in the classroom*. New York: New Press.

Dillenbourg, P., Baker, M., Blaye, A., & O'Malley, C. (1994). *The evolution of research on collaborative learning*. Retrieved from http://tecfa.unige.ch/tecfa-research//hm/ESF-chap5.text

Garcia, G. E. (2000). Bilingual children's reading. In M. L. Kamil, P. B. Mosenthal, P. D. Pearson, & R. Barr (Eds.), *Handbooks of reading research* (vol. 3, pp. 813–834). Mahwah, NJ: Lawrence Erlbaum.

Goodman, K., Shannon, P., Goodman, Y., & Rapaport, R. (2004). *Saving our schools: The case for public education. Saying no to "No Child Left Behind."* Berkeley, CA: RDR Books.

Hallahan, D., & Kauffman, J. (2000). *Exceptional learners: Introduction to special education* (8th ed.). Boston: Allyn & Bacon.

Halliday, M. A. K. (1975). *Learning how to mean: Exploration in the development of language*. London: Edward Arnold.

Hammerberg, D. (2004). Comprehension instruction for socioculturally diverse classrooms: A review of what we know . . . *Reading Teacher, 57*(7), 648–658.

Holdaway, D. (1979). *The foundations of literacy.* Portsmouth, NH: Heinemann.

Krashen, S., & Terrell, T. (1987). *The natural approach: Language and acquisition in the classroom.* Englewood Cliffs, NJ: Prentice Hall.

Ladson-Billings, G. (2001). *Crossing over to Canaan: The journey of new teachers in diverse classrooms.* San Francisco: Jossey-Bass.

No Child Left Behind Act. (2001). Conference Report to Accompany H.R. 1, Report No. 107-334, House of Representatives, 107th Congress, 1st Session.

Ovando, C., Collier, V., & Combs, B. (2003). *Bilingual and ESL classrooms: Teaching in multicultural contexts.* Boston: Hampton-Brown.

Pearson, P. D., & Gallagher, M. C. (1983). The instruction of reading comprehension. *Contemporary Educational Psychology, 8,* 317–344.

Piaget, J. (1955). *The language and thought of the child.* New York: Meridian Books.

Piaget, J. (1973). *To understand is to invent: The future of education.* New York: Grossman.

Piaget, J. (1977). *The development of thought: Equilibration of cognitive structures* (A. Rosin, Trans.). New York: Viking.

Ruddell, R. B. (1963). The effect of the similarity of oral and written patterns of language structure on reading comprehension. *Elementary English, 42,* 403–410.

Smith, T., Polloway, E., Patton, J., & Dowdy, C. (1998). *Teaching students with special needs in inclusive settings* (2nd ed.). Boston: Allyn & Bacon.

Standards for the English Language Arts. (1996). Urbana, IL: National Council of Teachers of English and the International Reading Association.

Thomas, W., & Collier, V. (1995). *A longitudinal analysis of programs serving language minority students.* Washington, DC: National Clearinghouse in Bilingual Education.

Tierney, R., & Shanahan, T. (2002). Research on the reading writing relationship: Interactions, transactions and outcomes. In R. Barr, M. L. Kamil, P. B. Mosenthal, & P. D. Pearson (Eds.), *Handbook of reading research* (vol. 2, pp. 246–280). Hillsdale, NJ: Lawrence Erlbaum.

U.S. Department of Education. (2002). *Fact sheet. The No Child Left Behind Act of 2001.* Retrieved from http://www.ed.gov/offices/OESE/esea/factsheet.html.

Vygotsky, L. S. (1978). *Mind in society.* Cambridge, MA: Harvard University Press.

Wells, G. (1990). Creating the conditions to encourage literate thinking. *Educational Leadership, 47*(6), 13–17.

Technology Resources

Educator's Reference Desk, language arts lesson plans:
http://www.eduref.org/cgi-bin/lessons.cgi/Language_Arts

Literacy Center Education Network: http://www.literacycenter.net/lessonview_en.htm#

part 2

Frameworks and Approaches to Teaching, Learning, and Assessing in the Language Arts

Part II of this text provides separate chapters for each of the language arts: reading, writing, listening, speaking, viewing, and visually representing. Throughout Chapters 3 through 9, you will become familiar with effective teaching, learning, and assessing strategies to nurture students in becoming literate persons and

effective users of language in many forms. Language arts strategies, literature that enhances instruction, technology resources, as well as opportunities for taking what is learned and applying it within classroom settings, are all valuable inclusions within these chapters

Chapter 8 frames language arts applications within content area classes such as math, science, and social studies as a means for assisting students in using the tools of language to more fully comprehend and appreciate content area learning. Chapter 9 details using a workshop approach to teach content and learning strategies in any subject area, using language arts as the key to tie content learning and communication skills together.

Reading and the Language Arts

Context Setting:

After reading this chapter, you will be able to

- Identify the developmental stages of learning to read
- Use standards to guide the teaching, learning, and assessment of reading
- Identify the various purposes of reading
- Identify the major components of reading
- Begin to understand the challenges of English language learner (ELL) students as they develop as literate persons

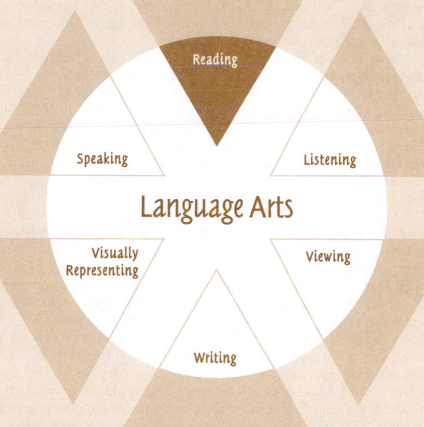

Before We Begin

- Think about your early experiences with reading. How did you learn to read? Was it a challenge for you? Was reading enjoyable? With what types of reading materials did you learn to read?
- Think about your perceptions regarding reading today. Do you consider yourself a reader? Do you read for pleasure on a consistent basis? What types of text do you enjoy reading?
- What do you believe is needed to teach children to learn how to read?

Reading is no doubt something you do on a daily basis and probably think little about how it is accomplished. Like many people, you most likely take for granted your ability to read as you peruse the menu in a restaurant or walk down the aisles of a grocery store looking for the items on your list or read billboards that you pass. You probably do not think about the complex process you are engaging in as you sit curled up reading the latest thriller novel or newspaper. However, if you do take time to reflect on all that you are doing as you read, you would be amazed at the complexity of the task. As a fluent reader, you have developed the ability to read with ease and use strategies for understanding text that is challenging to understand. At this point in your life it comes naturally to you. However, if you think about all that reading involves, you may wonder how you actually learned to partake in this awesome process. As a teacher, understanding reading and its processes is an important part of teaching language arts.

Reading is first making sense of what is read, that is, understanding and comprehending what is read. You will agree that reading includes the ability to decode and pronounce words, understand sentence structure and grammar rules, and put all these pieces together to read with fluency. However, if all of these components are present but a reader does not comprehend what he or she has read, is not it all for naught? As you saw in Chapter 2, reading includes the integration of all four cueing systems (graphophonics, syntax, semantics, and pragmatics or schema) simultaneously—a complex process that takes into account the meaning-making process of reading, or **comprehension.**

Beginning readers equate the squiggles on a page with meaning, for they see and hear fluent readers viewing those squiggles and telling stories and sharing information based on them. Without the meaning attached to the squiggle, that is all they would be—squiggles. Reading, then, is the making of meaning from a text. Text that can be read is not just in a written format, however. We use the term *text* with the understanding that it can refer also to a visual image, a musical piece, or a multimedia or visual presentation. If reading is comprehending text in a variety of formats and making meaning using one's background knowledge, then it is important to understand how this process occurs and how teachers can nurture children's development as readers of text in all forms. The remainder of this chapter will help you understand the developmental stages of reading, the major approaches to teaching reading, the variety of purposes for reading, and how to integrate the important process of reading into all language arts and content areas.

Stop to Think   If children read perfectly but do not understand anything they read, are they reading? If children stumble through reading but understand everything they have read, are they reading? How would you define reading?

Developmental Stages of Reading

Children pass through a number of stages in becoming fluent readers. Noting the characteristics of children's reading behaviors provides the teacher with an idea of what stage of reading development the child has reached, and the teacher can then design instruction to further development. The stages of reading and literacy development are aligned with general developmental stages as shown in Table 3.1. All children generally pass through the same stages, but they may progress at varying rates. Their interest in reading, the amount and quality of previous learning experiences, and their understanding of the reading process all impact how quickly the progression occurs.

Table 3.1

Stage of Literacy Development	General Age Range	Developmental Stage
Emergent/Early	3–7	Early Childhood
Early/Transitional	6–9	Middle Childhood
Transitional/Fluent	9–14	Early Adolescent

Following are some typical characteristics of reading at the various stages of development. Knowing these characteristics will assist you in understanding the natural progression readers go through.

Emergent Stage of Reading: Early Childhood, Ages 3–7

The emergent reader begins to explore print. During this emergent stage of reading development, the child

- Focuses attention on pictures and visual cues to tell a story
- Begins to identify letters of the alphabet and the corresponding sounds
- Memorizes and retells stories
- Realizes words are composed of sounds
- Begins to recognize rhyme
- Develops beginning phonemic awareness
- Understands that text has meaning

Early Stage of Reading: Middle Childhood, Ages 6–9

The early reader begins to focus heavily on print to tell the story and begins to use multiple strategies to gain meaning from print. During this stage of reading development, the child

- Develops sight words
- Predicts from pictures
- Identifies beginning and ending sounds
- Develops attention to meaning cues
- Rereads for meaning
- Uses prediction, context, and prior knowledge to infer meaning
- Focuses on phonics clues
- Begins to pay attention to punctuation
- Begins to self-monitor and self-correct reading
- Discusses what was read and shares opinion
- Develops an understanding of simple literary elements, including plot, and characters, setting

Transitional Stage of Reading: Early Adolescence, Ages 9–12

The transitional reader uses a variety of strategies to get meaning from print. During this stage of reading development, the child

- Becomes a more fluent reader, reading with accuracy and expression
- Infers information from text
- Pays increased attention to punctuation
- Expands sight word vocabulary
- Uses strategies automatically and in an integrated fashion
- Self-monitors and self-corrects flexibly
- Reads fluently with appropriate expression
- Becomes familiar with a wide range of genres

Fluent Stage of Reading: Early Adolescence/ Adolescence, Ages 9–14

The fluent reader uses strategies efficiently and automatically to get meaning from a wide range of text. During this stage of reading development, the child

- Effectively uses a variety of strategies to comprehend complex text structures
- Increases word meaning vocabulary
- Self-monitors and self-corrects with ease
- Shares responses to text orally and in writing

Initial Assessment of Student Development in Reading

We might be tempted to classify students as good, average, or poor readers, but designating students in this manner may not provide helpful information about how to guide instruction. Within every classroom, there is a wide range of reading ability. A review of grouping practices highlights the negative impact that grouping solely by reading ability may have on student self-esteem (Opitz & Ford, 2001). Some students may readily grasp the complexities of reading, while others need extended instruction before the process becomes meaningful. One of the first items on a teacher's list at the beginning of the school year should be to determine the stage of reading for each individual child in the classroom and what strategies the child is using to make meaning.

Teachers may use both formal and informal measures of reading progress. (See the Assessing Reading section of this chapter for a more in-depth discussion of assessment measures in reading.) Level of interest in reading and measures of reading fluency, strategy use, and comprehension are essential elements of any initial assessment process.

Students might be asked to select one or more books that they can read on their own without any assistance. Some children may need some assistance in selecting books at the appropriate level. While students are reading independently, the teacher may ask individual children to talk about what they are reading. This will provide a general sense of how well they comprehend what they are reading. Any initial samples of reading ability should be analyzed carefully. Children may be shy speaking with the teacher at the beginning of the year, and their responses may not be an accurate indication of their true stage of reading development. If children seem hesitant, the teacher might engage them in conversations about the book to put them at ease. The teacher might ask children to read a brief portion of the story aloud, providing the teacher with clues about the level of **fluency** (reading smoothly with accuracy and expression), the strategies being used, and comprehension. What do students do when they come to an unknown word? Do they glance at the picture or reread the sentence? If they read something incorrectly that changes the meaning of a sentence or passage, do they go back and self-correct? These are clues that illuminate the strategies being used by the reader. For example, if students self-correct errors that do not make sense with what they are reading or they use expression and proper intonation, this demonstrates how well the students are comprehending what they read. The teacher can ask a student if and how the story connects in any way to his or her life and experiences and also to predict what may happen next—this is another measure of how engaged students are with what they are reading. Older students who are struggling with reading may be reluctant to select books that are well below the materials being read by their classmates. Meeting privately with these students to determine their reading levels may relieve some of the anxiety they may be feeling.

A method for evaluating emergent readers is to determine whether they look only at the pictures or if they move their fingers along a row of print and "pretend read" or if they are actually reading. Do they seem interested in books? Do they hold books upright? Do they page through books from the beginning to the end? Can they talk about the pictures or story? These are indicators about how beginning readers view reading.

Asking students to respond to what they have read or what has been read to them is another way for teachers to gauge engagement with reading. Class discussions, drawings, retellings, journal entries, and dramatic reenactments are some activities that teachers may use. Anecdotal records and work samples can be used to document and supplement teacher observations.

Surveys of students' attitudes toward reading can provide valuable information about how much they enjoy reading or being read to and how they view themselves as readers. Older children might complete the survey on their own, and younger children might have the questions read to them and their responses recorded by an adult.

After initial data have been collected, teachers can make determinations regarding the developmental stage of reading each child is functioning at. These judgments should not be used to assign children to inflexible reading groups based on reading ability, but rather they should be used to note what children can already do with literacy and determine what types of experiences will aid their growth as readers.

Elements of Reading

A national reading panel was assembled through the U.S. Department of Education whose task was to review reading research and determine the effectiveness of the approaches used to teach children to read. The **National Reading Panel** (National Institutes of Health, 2000) established criteria for systematically evaluating the research with the goal of determining the methods that are most effective for reading instruction. To begin this laborious task, five areas of reading instruction and research were analyzed in depth: phonemic and phonological awareness, phonics instruction, reading fluency, comprehension, and vocabulary and word study. Understanding each of these elements will assist you in developing your knowledge of effective reading instruction. Each of these components includes numerous skills and methods for instruction.

Phonemic and Phonological Awareness

Phonemic awareness is the ability to distinguish the difference between the 44 sounds (or phonemes) within spoken language. **Phonological awareness** is the understanding that speech can be divided into words and sentences, including syllables, **onsets,** and **rimes.**

It is believed that possessing phonological and phonemic awareness is necessary for learning how to read and write and that having a strong foundation in phonemic awareness early on correlates highly with future reading success (Stahl, 2001). Some of the skills that readers use when they have phonemic awareness include blending words, segmentation or the capability to break words down into their individual phonemes, and substituting one phoneme for another to create new words.

Good readers and writers understand, though perhaps not consciously, that negotiating oral language involves both pulling sounds apart and putting sounds together. Teachers often use recitation of nursery rhymes and poetry to help children play with the structure and rhythm of language. One such example might be using the poem "Hickory, Dickory, Dock":

Hickory, Dickory, Dock,

The mouse ran up the clock.

The clock struck one,

Down he did run.

Hickory, Dickory, Dock.

Children recite the rhyme and clap out the rhythm. They stretch out "Hic-ko-ry, Dic-ko-ry, Dock." They might be instructed to listen for rhyming words as well. Children listen and learn about sounds and words. They recognize that *run* is a separate word with one syllable and three sounds /rŭn/ and *clock* is a separate, one-syllable word with four sounds /clŏk/. Other words such as *hickory* and *dick-ory* have more syllables and more sounds.

Graphophonics/Phonics

Graphophonics or **phonics** is the ability to understand the relationship between the sounds (phonemes) and the alphabet symbols of language. Skills related to phonics include understanding consonants (*C*) and vowels (*V*) (short and long), word families (*cat/bat/ fat/mat/sat*), and vowel patterns (such as open

(*CV*) and closed (*CVC*)). Beginning readers need repeated opportunities to develop these understandings, coupled with phonological and phonemic awareness, in order to develop as fluent and automatic readers (National Institutes of Health, 2000; Stahl, 2001).

Teaching graphophonics is never an end in itself. In Chapter 10, Kathi Glick highlights this point by stressing how she makes continual links between what the children are reading and the phonics that she teaches and reinforces. She recognizes that by teaching onset and rime (word families), students learn several new words at once, but they also learn to look for familiar patterns or chunks within words, an important strategy for beginning readers. This concept of patterns in words can be expanded from rhyming words to vowel patterns, word endings, consonant blends, and so on. The children apply what they know of letters and sounds in their reading and writing, and Kathi guides them in making these links.

Fluency

Fluency is the ability to read smoothly, with expression, and at an appropriate pace. Fluent readers do not read text word for word, but their reading process is a smooth progression. Reading at a smooth pace with appropriate expression and pitch does not ensure that one understands what is being read; however, to be fluent, comprehension must be apparent as well (Fountas & Pinnell, 2001). Think about reading a favorite novel. You will most likely be reading fluently because of your interest, your understanding of the vocabulary, and your ability to comprehend the plot. Contrast that with reading an astrophysics text. Although you may be able to read the words and read at a smooth pace, without comprehending the concepts and ideas you are not fluently reading the text.

Fluency is gained by reading and rereading text that is at the appropriate level of difficulty for the reader. Sandy Cabernathy in Chapter 11 understands that it is important to design purposeful opportunities for her second- and third-grade students to reread text to become more fluent readers. Therefore, she frequently has students prepare simple plays (reader's theater) from stories they've read. They also practice reading books they will share with their kindergarten reading buddies. As they rehearse for these activities, their reading becomes smoother and listeners can more easily follow the plot.

Comprehension

Reading is making meaning, and comprehension is the ability to make meaning of the concepts, ideas, and plot from text. Comprehension is a complex process that includes major factors that contribute to how a reader comprehends, including the reader himself or herself, the text, and the context of the reading situation. Imagine opening a book on a topic you have little background knowledge of or interest in reading. Your motivation to read would probably be low, and your ability to make sense of what you read would be impaired as well. If the text were designed in a reader-friendly manner, however, with such things as challenging content words defined within the context and numerous detailed visuals such as diagrams, photographs, and illustrations provided, your ability to comprehend most likely will be improved. Comprehension is an active meaning-making process that can be taught to students through a variety of strategies to use before, during, and after reading, including retelling, mapping, and the Know-Want to Know-Learned (KWL) strategy.

Paula noted that her sixth-grade students read quite well but had difficulty analyzing what they'd read. She selected the book *Holes* (Sachar, 1998) to read because she knew the controversial characters would grab the attention of the students. As they read, they debated the traits, feelings, and motivations of the various characters. They also made judgments about the characters' actions. In each of these activities, students were required to present evidence from the novel to support their assertions, providing Paula with authentic opportunities to guide students in developing predicting, analyzing, and inferencing strategies. She would refine these comprehension skills and add others in the next texts she selected for them to read.

Vocabulary and Word Study

In order to make meaning of what is read, an understanding of words and vocabulary is essential. Beginning readers must be able to quickly identify and read high-frequency words such as *the, he, what,* and *and* to be able to read quickly and fluently. Vocabulary instruction also includes teaching children words and their meanings so that comprehension is sustained through reading (Richgels, 2001).

Jackie's new words for the week are *don't, can't, I'm, sunny,* and *cloudy.* She selected three contractions because there are several contractions in the read-aloud books that she has been sharing with the class. She also determined that students are ready to focus on contractions in their writing. *Sunny* and *cloudy* were selected because the class is beginning a study of weather, and these are two key words in the unit. The new words are posted on a chart in the front of the room, and each morning Jackie leads students through activities to reinforce the words. They point to the letters and spell the words, match each contraction to the two words that it is composed of, and clap out the number of syllables in each word. They note the root words *cloud* and *sun* in *cloudy* and *sunny* and how the *y* at the end of each word sounds like /?/. As the students read and write during the week, Jackie helps them apply what they've learned. At the end of the week, the children will help her place the words under the appropriate letter on the word wall.

Major Approaches to Teaching and Learning Reading

Understanding the demands of helping students to meet reading standards and goals, you may be asking yourself, How does one teach reading in order for students to be successful readers? Selecting the "best" method for teaching reading has been a controversial issue for many decades. Some advocate for a more directed instruction approach (traditional model), while others support a more flexible means. Recently there has been a push for a more comprehensive and balanced approach (transactional model), which includes components of both ends of the continuum of approaches. The main purpose of this approach is to meet the needs of students with varied learning styles by using a variety of methods that best encourage achievement in reading. Let us look at both approaches and observe how components of each are included.

Traditional Model: Basal Reading Program

The traditional approach to teaching reading relies on heavy use of predetermined reading selections often in the form of basal textbooks, worksheets, whole class instruction, or grouping by ability and round-robin reading. This approach is highly structured, and often publishers of reading basal series supply detailed direction in implementing the content. This method of reading instruction concerns some teachers in that it often does not take into account individual students' literacy needs or backgrounds. For instance, consider a third-grade classroom where all students are required to read the same text selection from the same **basal reading textbook** about oceans and sharks written at an average third-grade reading level.

First, research shows that in today's typical diverse one-grade classrooms, there will be students functioning at a range of reading and ability levels—not all of them will be average third-grade readers. There will most likely be students reading at a second-grade level, those whose abilities lie more at a fourth-grade level, and probably some students reading at a first-grade and even a fifth-grade level. It is difficult to meet all students' reading levels with the exact text for each student, thus making the reading experience either too easy or too challenging for some.

Consider also the topic of the selection and how this affects a reading experience. If this third-grade classroom is located in the plains of Nebraska, children who have not experienced the ocean or have little knowledge of ocean life may find this text challenging, even if they are average third-grade or higher readers. Whereas if this third-grade classroom were located in Hawaii, where daily life consists of ocean living and shark sightings, this selection will be less challenging, even to less-than-average third-grade readers, because they can make connections between the text and their experiences.

There is much to consider when teaching reading in addition to the text selection. Not all children learn to read effectively using one method of reading instruction. The traditional approach relies on a largely prescribed method of teaching reading that can leave little room for individual design of learning experiences.

A more effective method would be to choose texts that closely match readers—in both reading and interest level—and plan reading strategies that could be taught and practiced using the text. This is not to say that students should not be challenged by a text, but instead, reading should be a meaningful, motivating experience, as motivation to read is a key aspect of being an effective reader, just as is possessing the necessary skills for reading. Amazingly, a longitudinal study done in 1988 found that 70% of the 54 first- through fourth-grade students, both poor and effective readers, preferred watching television to reading (Juel, 1988). Only 5% of effective readers preferred cleaning their rooms to reading, but 40% of poor readers would rather clean their rooms than read. Our goal as teachers is to help students view reading as an enjoyable process, and thus using teaching methods that make reading something children can and want to do is an ultimate goal of reading instruction.

Transactional Model: A Comprehensive/ Balanced Approach Reading Program

In the transactional model of reading instruction, reading is viewed as a transaction between the reader, the text, and the context of the reading situation. Therefore, this approach advocates that reading is a strategic process in which readers bring themselves to the task along with all of their experiences and background as an important part of making meaning of the text, in addition to using a wide range of decoding and meaning-making strategies. This is not only a transaction between readers themselves and a text but also a transaction with others in the environment. Children interact with others in the meaning-making process during literate experiences, and for genuine transactions to take place, using authentic texts and meaningful interactions with those texts and others are needed. To gain further understanding of this approach, the next section details the components of a comprehensive/balanced reading program, based on a transactional approach to teaching reading.

Components of a Comprehensive/ Balanced Reading Program

A reading curriculum that highlights modeling and support from a teacher and is designed to meet the needs of all students and allows them to become more independent as readers includes the components of **interactive read-aloud, shared reading, guided reading,** and **independent reading.** Interactive read-aloud is a highly teacher-directed, heavily modeled component, where the teacher provides scaffolded instruction and students are largely invited to listen actively and enter into discussion about the texts read. While reading aloud, teachers will do think-alouds, sharing the strategies that they use to read, and will stop at various points and encourage discussion about ideas and elements.

Shared reading is a whole-group instructional process where teachers are largely the model of effective reading but invite student participation in the meaning-making process, encouraging choral reading as the teachers read. Guided reading is a supportive instructional experience for small groups of typically two to six students that are temporary and formed based on students' reading needs and guided closely by the teacher. Independent reading is something even very beginning readers can do and allows them to apply the strategies learned during read-aloud, shared, and guided reading during independent experiences with books. A more thorough discussion of these components follows.

Interactive Read-Alouds

Reading aloud includes a proficient reader, usually the teacher, reading aloud to students as a way to model appropriate, fluent reading behaviors and strategies. There are a variety of ways to conduct read-alouds, from interactive read-alouds, where students are encouraged to discuss the text with the teacher, to read-alouds with little student interaction. A key to a successful read-aloud is having a fluent reader demonstrate how to read and comprehend a text while students are actively listening and enjoying. Some advocate sharing texts that are too challenging for students to read on their own as a way to expose them to quality literature that is beyond their independent or instructional reading level. However, this is not always necessary, as by reading texts to students that are at their level, they can see that reading is approachable, making meaning from the text is the key, and reading a wide range of texts at a range of levels and of a variety of genres is desirable.

Choose literature that you as a teacher enjoy and appreciate, as well as literature focused on a topic or theme in which you would like to expose students based on their interests and your curriculum. Teachers are the reading model during read-alouds, and if the text is not something teachers enjoy, they will portray this lack of enthusiasm, even if it is unintended.

Shared Reading

Shared reading is a participatory group experience that creates a supportive learning environment for readers, since all voices have the opportunity to be heard as students are encouraged to join in reading as they feel comfortable. Shared reading experiences include students having access to the text, in the form of a big book, chart story, individual texts, or an electronically projected medium such as a story shown on an overhead projector. Often the texts are chosen for their engaging nature and can include rhymes and chants that incorporate humor, repetition, and expression, stories with strong plot lines and characters with which students can identify strongly, as well as language that is rich and memorable. A key principle that guides shared reading is that the texts chosen are used for repeated readings as a means of investigating many aspects of a text and analyzing its features and content, as well as a means for applying new reading skills. As learners tend to move from whole to part in comprehending, the first reading allows readers to become familiar with a text, and in subsequent readings students are more comfortable to take risks in applying new skills.

Shared reading experiences offer many learning opportunities for students. At the emergent reader level, reading a big book can help them understand **concepts of print** such as **text directionality** (left to right), **return sweep, one-to-one correspondence,** and **letter recognition.** Older, more fluent readers can benefit from shared reading in that they can practice new skills, enjoy interaction with the reading process, and expand their literacy understanding (Fountas & Pinnell, 2001). Often teachers will decrease their level of support for older, more experienced readers, allowing the meaning-making process to come mainly from the students.

Guided Reading

Guided reading takes place with small groups of readers who are supported through the appropriate instruction and guidance of the teacher. Guided reading is a key component to a comprehensive/balanced literacy program, as it provides students with closely monitored instruction planned to meet each student's needs. It is through guided reading that teachers can gain much understanding of individual students as readers.

Guided reading includes flexible grouping practices, allowing the teacher to group and regroup students often on the basis of their skills, needs, and reading levels. It is important that a teacher frequently assesses students to assist in determining needs and group placement. Typically, guided reading groups meet for 15 to 25 minutes each session, with each child having a copy of the text being studied. The teaching of strategies that takes place during guided reading is then practiced during independent reading, where students implement what they have learned and experiment with a variety of texts.

Independent Reading

Imagine a group of 4-year-old students walking into a classroom for the first time and the teacher telling them to find a book and then sit down and read. Most children who have had access to books and adults who have read to them will know just what to do. Picture a child with this background experience choosing a book about dinosaurs from a display of books in the classroom library, sitting down on the carpet, and beginning to page through the book. The child begins quietly "reading," talking to himself or herself about the pictures on the page and what is being viewed. This *is* independent reading for a 4-year-old! It may look very different for a sixth-grade student, however, but the concept is the same— interaction, enjoyment, and practice with reading strategies as a student reads one on one with a text.

Reading for a Variety of Purposes

Think of all the types of reading that you do. You read for a variety of purposes, including personal reasons, for pleasure, to escape, and to learn about something you need to know. You read because you have to, to cope, to accomplish a task, or to get something you want, such as purchasing an item through the Internet. You read for pleasure or to fill your leisure time, such as while relaxing on the beach during vacation. We read for a variety of reasons, and we react to what we read as well. How you read also depends on the text you are reading. Understandably, you will read the comics section of the newspaper much differently than you will read a course textbook.

Transactional Theory of Reading Response

The transactional theory of responding to literature asserts that a reader connects with and interacts with a text and that it takes both a reader and a text to complete the reading process, that is, one cannot stand on its own without the other (Rosenblatt, 1938/1996). The process is not complete without the author and the author's intentions as the text was written, as well as the context in which the text is being read. How a reader approaches a text is important, because a reader can take on either an **aesthetic** or an **efferent stance** while reading as a means to gain pleasure from the experience or to gain knowledge or for a combination of purposes. Taking an aesthetic stance means that the reader is focusing on reading for enjoyment and appreciation of the text, whereas a reader taking an efferent stance is approaching a text for the purpose of gaining information or learning something. This is not to say that a reader cannot take on both stances at once, moving between the two, as reading is not a linear process. Envision a continuum with an aesthetic stance on one end, and on the opposite end, the efferent stance. While reading a text, a reader's stance can fall anywhere on that continuum, based on the text, one's purposes for reading, and the background one brings to the reading, and can even move back and forth throughout the reading process.

Take, for example, reading a book about hiking before planning an expedition as a way to gain more information about what to take and where to go. At the same time as reading for information, you could also be appreciating the rich descriptions of the landscape the text details in relation to the trails.

Theory Into Practice

Think about a book that you have enjoyed reading. Did you take mostly an aesthetic stance as you read? Were you involved in any efferent reading with this text? Think of a book that you read mainly to gain knowledge, such as a course textbook. Was your response to the text mostly efferent? Did you respond in any aesthetic ways as well?

Understanding reader response is important to teachers as they plan for reading instruction to assist in planning the objectives for the reading experience. Helping students think about the stance or stances they might take while engaging in reading can be useful to set a purpose for reading.

A View From the Classroom

Joelle Quimby begins her language arts class for her eighth-grade students with an interactive read-aloud for 15 minutes with the book *Stargirl* by Jerry Spinelli (2002). She uses the opportunity to stop at various points and ask her students for their ideas and responses to the text, asking such things as "What would you do in Leo's place as his fellow classmates begin to ostracize him and he grows closer to the outcast, strange new student, Stargirl?" Joelle's goal is to get her students to connect personally to the text and overall enjoy the listening experience. After the read-aloud, her students begin independent reading, and she meets with a small guided reading group of students who are reading a nonfiction text titled *Days of Jubilee: The End of Slavery in the United States* (McKissack & McKissack, 2003). Joelle's purpose is to assist this group of students with understanding how to determine a purpose for reading nonfiction texts. The students will read a section of the text from a chapter in the book. She teaches them the first stage of the **directed reading-thinking activity (DRTA)** (Stauffer, 1969) to help them better comprehend text and pull out the main

facts. There are three major pieces to the DRTA strategy before reading, during reading, and after reading. The first step is to establish a purpose for reading, and Joelle assists her students in doing this by asking a question that requires the students to predict what the section might be about. As the five students in the group suggest ideas, she writes them on a piece of chart paper to refer to later. She then instructs the students to read the predetermined selection silently to themselves while she will stop and ask each one to read aloud a portion for her. After all have independently completed the selection, they revisit the predictions they have made and add to and refine them, based on what they have read.

In the above example, we can see evidence of instruction in reading activity that requires students to take on both an aesthetic and an efferent stance while reading and respond accordingly. There are many opportunities within the language arts curriculum where understanding reader response theory can be helpful in planning for reading instruction and activity.

Integrating Reading Within the Language Arts

Language arts today is viewed not as a product but as a process that is a key to all learning, and reading is clearly a major key. It is difficult, if not impossible, for children not to be involved to some extent in language arts without using the skills and processes of reading. Throughout Part III of this text, you will see how reading is naturally integrated throughout the language arts curriculum as well as content area learning as you take a look into a first-grade, multigrade third/fourth-grade, and eighth-grade classroom.

Assessing Reading

Assessing student progress in reading and teaching students to gauge their own growth is essential in reading, teaching, and learning. However, simply gathering information about how well students are doing is only half of the assessment process. In the second half of the equation, the teacher uses the data to inform instruction and help students learn to set goals for the next steps in learning. Several formal and informal measures are available for teachers to note growth in reading on an ongoing basis. The following assessment tools and techniques are ideal for assessing reading; however, many of them assess other components of language arts as well. You can use this section of this chapter for models of assessing other components such as writing, listening, and viewing. Mention of these integrated uses will be made while discussing each tool.

Concepts of Print

Student understanding of concepts of print may be evaluated to determine which concepts of letter, word, sentence, and story emergent readers understand. First developed by Marie Clay (1972) as a screening instrument to select first-grade students in need of intensive literacy intervention, evaluating student understanding of these concepts has become a routine assessment tool in many schools. Some teachers use the formal instrument tools developed by Clay (1993), and others use a simplified checklist (as seen in Table 3.2) to monitor when these concepts are reflected in student reading behaviors.

Assessment of Strategy Use

Much has been made of student use of strategies to analyze unknown words and to take meaning from what has been read. **Word analysis strategies** include using picture, phonics, and context clues; use of prior knowledge; prediction; and summarizing. Comprehension strategies include rereading, summarizing, prediction, making inferences, and monitoring what was read to see if it makes sense. Each of these strategies can be taught directly and practiced by students in order to help them become effective, independent readers. In much the same way, effective use of strategic reading can be assessed directly. Assessment of strategy usage can be addressed through informal observation of independent or guided reading

Table 3.2 Checklist of Print Awareness

Name:			
Concept	**Date**	**Date**	**Date**
• Turns book right way up			
• Indicates front of book			
• "Reads" left to right and sweeps to next line of print			
• Starts to read on first page of story			
• Reads with one-to-one match of print to reading			
• Has concept of – Letter – Word – Sentence			

behaviors, **informal reading inventories (IRIs),** running records, checklists, conferencing, and student self-assessment.

Student Self-Assessment

In the end, the focus is not on which strategies have been taught but what strategy students use in their everyday reading. The more strategies that students can use effectively and the better they can integrate them into reading all genres, the more likely that students will become effective readers. When they are able to consciously use strategies to monitor comprehension and can describe how they used them, we have a glimpse of their metacognitive processes in the use of strategies. From very early on, students can be guided to name the strategies they use and to self-assess how well they use them while reading. Table 3.3 provides an example of a self-assessment for use with transitional readers. Figure 3.1 depicts a fifth-grade student's self-assessment based on his reading development.

Assessment of Response to Reading

Part of the assessment of student reading should include an analysis of student response to reading. Can students form opinions about the characters and plot? Can they relate what they have read to themselves (text-to-self connection), to other things they have read (text-to-text connection), and to the broader world (text-to-world connection) (Harvey & Goudvis, 2000)? Can they formulate opinions about how the author wrote the text (author's craft)? Students become true readers when they interact with the author on emotional and intellectual levels. Table 3.4 outlines

Table 3.3

Name: Date:

Title of book:

What is the book about?

This book was: Easy   Just Right   Challenging

Check the strategies you know how to use:

_____ Predict   _____ Think about what I know about this topic

_____ Use picture clues   _____ Skip a word and read on

_____ Use phonics clues   _____ Reread hard parts

_____ Use context clues

Name a new word you learned in this story: _____

How did you figure out what it was? _____

areas that students might self-assess as they think about how they respond to what they have read. Obviously, the categories outlined in responding to reading reflect student comprehension of text also. Anecdotal records may lend themselves well to recording student progress in this area. Review of dialogue journals, where students have responded to what they have read, may also be an effective measure in noting whether students are becoming more sophisticated in responding to literature. Samples over time may reflect growth in student reflection. Teachers will wish to note whether areas that were directly taught (for example, relating current text to another) are reflected in student responses. Areas that are not yet reflected will warrant additional focus either for the entire class or for small groups of students. Other written or electronic responses to reading, dramatic interpretations, projects, or discussions may also yield assessment information related to student response to the reading they do.

Reading Logs

Many teachers have students keep a record of what they have read, including the difficulty level of the materials, genre, and date completed (see Table 3.5). Reviewing these logs and having students monitor them as well provide a clear record of how much reading the student is doing; whether he or she is consistently reading books that are at the independent, instructional, or frustration level; and the variety of genres being read. Some teachers also have the students record whether they have just read the book, written about the book, or shared

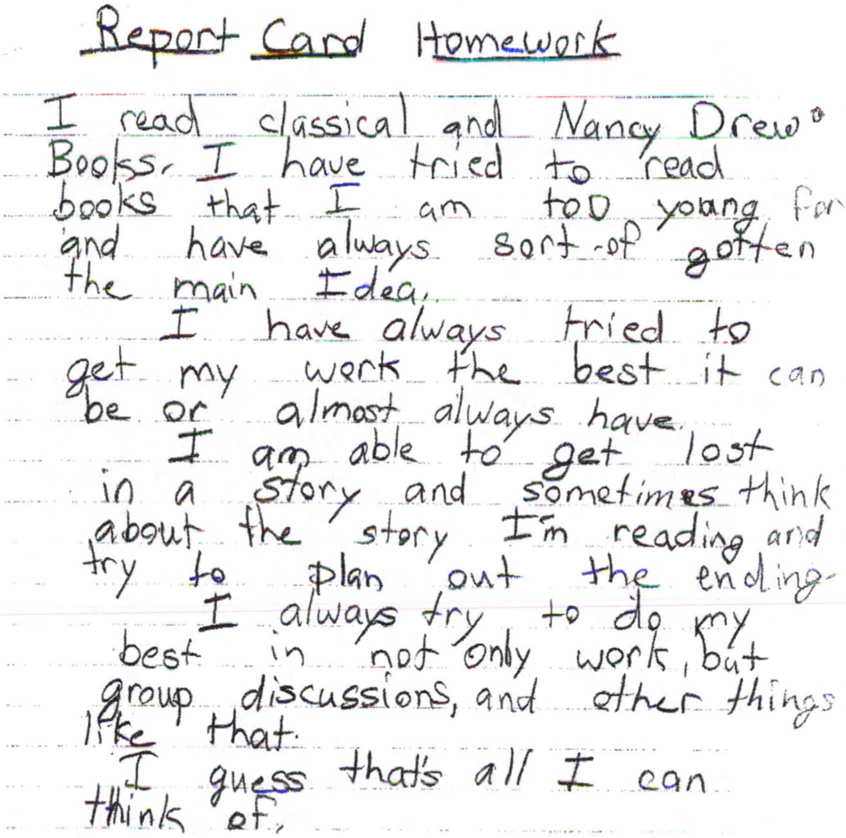

Report Card Homework

I read classical and Nancy Drew°
Books. I have tried to read
books that I am too young for
and have always sort-of gotten
the main Idea.
    I have always tried to
get my work the best it can
be or almost always have.
    I am able to get lost
in a story and sometimes think
about the story I'm reading and
try to plan out the ending.
    I always try to do my
best in not only work, but
group discussions, and other things
like that.
    I guess that's all I can
think of.

Figure 3.1 Reading Self-Assessment: Fifth-Grade Student

Table 3.4 Student Self-Assessment of Response to Literature

Name:			Date:
When I talk about what I have read, I can	**Well**	**Somewhat**	**With Difficulty**
– Summarize what I have read	___	___	___
– Form an opinion about whether or not I like the text	___	___	___
– Form an opinion about the characters	___	___	___
– Discuss the author's craft (how the author wrote the text)	___	___	___
– Relate the characters or plot to my own life (relationship to self)	___	___	___
– Relate this text to other things I have read (relationship to text)	___	___	___
– Relate this text to other things I know about (relationship to world)	___	___	___

Table 3.5 Reading Log

Title of book	Author	Date Started	Date Completed	Date Abandoned	Reading Level			Genre
					Easy	Just Right	Hard	

Name: Grade:

the book with someone. An additional category indicating whether the text was read independently or whether the student followed along with an audiocassette (listening comprehension) may be added for ELLs and/or students with reading challenges. A quick review of these logs lets the teacher know whether or not students need encouragement to read more by helping them find reading materials of interest or material at their instructional level rather than books that are too easy or too challenging. Some students may read literature exclusively from a single genre, folk literature, for example, and may need to be encouraged to expand their reading repertoire while continuing to enjoy a favorite genre.

Students can easily be guided to self-assess their independent reading behaviors and set goals for next steps. Geri had her fourth- and fifth-grade students chart the number of minutes they read at home each month. This provided them with a clear visual of reading time and assisted them in setting logical goals for the next month's reading. This also provided an opportunity for students to integrate math skills as they charted, graphed, and calculated averages and percentages of the amount of time read.

Informal Reading Inventories

As discussed earlier in this chapter, it is essential that teachers assess student reading ability at the beginning of the school year, as they will gain initial information about the range of reading ability in the classroom, students' attitudes toward reading, and skills and strategies students are able to apply to their reading. Assessing what the students *can* do rather than what they cannot do helps teachers approach reading from a positive perspective and helps students see their abilities rather than emphasizing what they lack. Informal reading inventories (IRIs), **running records,** parent/student surveys, and anecdotal records are measures that are commonly used at the beginning of the year to record baseline data and throughout the school year to periodically note progress.

A number of commercially prepared IRIs are available for use in schools (Flynt-Cooter, 2003; Johns, 1997; Leslie & Caldwell, 1995; Swearinger & Allen, 2000). The Flynt-Cooter is available in both English and Spanish.[1] An IRI is a "series of graded passages designed to measure a reader's overall ability as well as strengths and needs in word recognition and comprehension" (Cooper & Kiger, 2001, p. 571). IRIs are administered individually to students and provide general information about the estimated grade level at which students are reading, their comprehension of material read, and sight word/word analysis skills. They typically provide two or more reading selections at each level to avoid having students become overly familiar with one form or another. One form may be used for silent reading and the other for oral reading. In addition, one form may represent narrative text and another expository (Cooper & Kiger, 2001). IRIs also tend to have sample graded sentences that are used to determine the level at which students should begin reading the passages.

The teacher records each deviation children make from the actual text as an error (referred to as miscues) and later examines whether each miscue interferes with the meaning of the passage or whether it reflects students' concentration on what they are reading. Words and phrases that are substituted, omitted, inserted, reversed, repeated, and self-corrected are evaluated, and all miscues inform the teacher what strategies the students are using. Teachers pay special attention to self-corrections, as they indicate that students are attuned to errors while reading. Each passage is followed with a retelling of what was read or with a set of comprehension questions. Students are also asked to read graded lists of words in isolation to determine the estimated grade level at which they can identify sight words or correctly analyze words (see Table 3.6). Students continue reading more difficult word lists and passages until they reach certain error levels; students who struggle with the passages may move to easier passages.

Table 3.6

The following chart may be used to determine if specific texts are at the frustration level (too challenging), instructional level (optimal level for instruction), or independent level (can be easily read on one's own) of students.

A text is at the frustration level if students score

Below 85% word recognition (Grades 1–2)
Below 90% word recognition (Grades 3–8)
Below 50% comprehension (Grades 1–8)

A text is at the instructional level if students score

85%–98% word recognition (Grades 1–2)
95%–98% word recognition (Grades 3–8)
75%–89% comprehension (Grades 1–8)

A text is at the independent level if students score

99%+ word recognition (Grades 1–8)
90%+ comprehension (Grades 1–8)

Burns and Roe (1999) suggest that the instructional level for students in Grades 1–2 is reached when they attain 85% or higher in word recognition and 75% or higher in comprehension. The instructional level for Grades 3–12 is reflected by 95% or higher accuracy in word recognition and a score of 75% or higher in comprehension.

Results of the IRI provide teachers with a general sense of the range of reading abilities and the kinds of skills and strategies students already possess or will need to develop. A note of caution: some children become overanxious in testing situations, and others may be unfamiliar with the content of the passages or the structure of the comprehension questions. Teachers should examine the IRIs for bias and use the results only as samples to be included with other measures of reading progress.

Running Records

Running records (Clay, 1985) are quick and easy measures of student progress in reading. Literacy programs that highlight the use of guided reading (Fountas & Pinnell, 1996) use running records on an ongoing basis. In these assessments, the teacher listens to the child read a book or passage of about 100 to 300 words that is at the instructional reading level of the child. As the child reads, the teacher records a check mark for each word read correctly on a separate sheet of paper (see Table 3.7). The teacher also indicates miscues and self-corrections. Children may be asked to retell what they have read as a measure of comprehension. The teacher and the student may review the results of the running records to determine progress in difficulty of reading material, as well as use of reading strategies and improvements in comprehension.

In both IRIs and running records, it is important to balance reading fluency with comprehension of text. Some children read fluently but cannot retell or answer questions about what they have read. Conversely, other children may read in a very halting and inefficient manner but are able to demonstrate good comprehension. Teachers may gain useful information about the kinds of instruction to offer various groups of children from these assessments. Each of these measures, along with informal observation and conferencing with students, can yield insights into the kinds of strategies students use to support their reading and how effectively they use them.

Formal **standardized testing** will also comprise one component of reading assessment systems. Students in Grades 3–8 are required to complete standardized reading tests under the mandates of the No Child Left Behind (NCLB) legislation (2001). The results of these tests will be calculated, and students will be classified as having minimal, basic, proficient, or advanced ability in reading. The goal of this legislation is for all students to be reading at proficient or advanced levels by 2014. The **Reading First Initiatives** resulting from the NCLB designate specific areas of competence that states are to measure through standardized testing. In reading, these areas include phonemic awareness, phonics, fluency, vocabulary, and comprehension.

Table 3.7 Running Records Scoring Sheet

Text	Running Record	Analysis
Page 1:		
Mary came from Germany	✓ ✓ ✓ Gersey	substitution—distorts meaning
when she was just a child.	✓ ✓ ✓ ~~just~~ ✓ ✓	omission—does not distort
She remembered many things	✓ ✓ ✓ ✓	
about their trip to America.	✓ ✓ ✓ ✓ ✓	
Page 2:		
But her most vivid memory	✓ ✓ ✓ wonderful ✓	substitution—does not distort
was seeing the Statue of Liberty	✓ ✓ ✓ [State] ✓ ✓	self-corrects—does not distort
in New York Harbor.	✓ ✓ ✓ Heartland	substitution—distorts
Page 3:		
Many years later she returned to	✓ ✓ ✓ ✓ ✓ ✓ ^see	insertion—does not distort
New York Harbor with her granddaughter.	✓ ✓ Heartland ✓ ✓ ✓	substitution—distorts
The lady was just as magnificent	✓ ✓ ✓ ✓ ✓ [magical]	self-corrects—does not distort
as Mary remembered her.	<u>✓ ✓ ✓ ✓</u>	repeats—does not distort
Page 3:		
She rose from her seat, crying and	✓ got up ✓ ✓ ✓ ✓	substitution—does not distort
waving her hankie at the statue that	✓ ✓ hand ✓ ✓ ✓	substitution—does not distort
had welcomed her to this country	✓ ✓ ✓ ✓ ✓ ✓	
so many years before.	~~so~~ ✓ ✓ ✓	omission—does not distort

Standardized testing is used to develop macro-level snapshots of how well students in the United States are doing overall. School districts are ranked as to how well they performed on these measures, and the results are often made public. Decisions about funding and resource allocations are sometimes tied to how well districts perform, placing additional pressure on teachers and administrators to "teach to the test." Schools may find areas of deficiency as represented by the testing, but many schools have had to abandon curriculum plans that had great potential to enhance student learning in areas of critical thinking in order to meet the more skills-based demands of NCLB.

Anecdotal Records

Another type of student assessment in reading involves recorded teacher observations of student attitudes and abilities in the classroom. Anecdotal records provide more intimate and ongoing snapshots of student progress in literacy development to supplement formal types of assessment in reading. Anecdotal records are useful for monitoring application of emerging skills and strategies, attitudes toward reading, comprehension of text, and independent reading behaviors. Teacher observational notes are useful in evaluating both the overall effectiveness of the classroom reading program as well as noting reading behavior and progress for each student. The classroom is a busy place, and setting aside time to note the work of each child is a benefit of using anecdotal records, helping to ensure that student evaluations are accurate and not based on assumptions about student competence. Examining the entries over time provides teachers, students, and parents with a good indication of the child's progress. To show the growth of ELLs and/or students with learning challenges, anecdotal records, along with student work samples, can serve as helpful supplements to more formal reading measures. Table 3.8 reflects the sample anecdotal records taken by the teacher of a first-grade student who is an emergent reader.

There are two important considerations to make before undertaking the use of anecdotal records: determining what to observe and how to record information. Initially, teachers may need to experiment to determine the kinds of observations that will be useful in providing information to design instruction and to document and guide student growth. Teachers may wish to observe how well students are applying skills and strategies that have been previously taught and practiced by students. However, it is important to remain vigilant for additional information that

Table 3.8

Name: Antonio	Grade: 1
Sept. 10	Selected books during free time Tells story from pictures
9/17	Rereads predictable books from guided reading sessions Generally good one-to-one match between words and reading Recognizes a few sight words: *mother, father, birthday, and, the* Uses picture clues
9/24	Loves funny books Uses some initial letter sounds to guess new words
10/1	Reads big book to class, practiced first Used pictures, first letter cues well
10/8	Can retell stories—but elaborates on too many details Does not like to partner read—finds it hard to concentrate Beginning to use work chunking (saw *and* in word *stand*)
10/15	Often chooses books that are too difficult to read independently Loves books about fire trucks and firefighters

may be important but may not have been the focus for the observations. "With such record-keeping, you might find yourself noting surprising, puzzling, disturbing, or exciting events and breakthroughs for particular children" (Johnston, 1997, p. 255). It is important to give attention first to what the students *can do* and *are doing* rather than what they *cannot* do. Table 3.9 provides suggestions for areas to observe.

Table 3.9   Possible Areas to Observe in Student Reading for Anecdotal Records

✓ Attitude toward reading

✓ Perceptions of self as reader

✓ Application of recently taught skills and strategies

✓ Overall application of skills and strategies

✓ Links from what is read to self, other texts, and the world

✓ Ability to respond to literature

✓ Reading fluency

✓ Independent reading behaviors (materials selected, difficulty of materials selected)

✓ Interaction level during shared reading experiences

✓ Oral reading behaviors

✓ Types/genres of books read and/or enjoyed

Boyd-Batstone (2004) recommends a system of focused observations that he refers to as **Anecdotal Records Assessment (ARA).** ARA guides the teacher in maintaining a standards-based focus during observation of students. "The field of vision for observation is set by the verbs found in each standard. . . . Borrowing the key verbs from the content standard saves time with on-the-spot composing of anecdotal records" (p. 232). Obviously, the ARA assumes that either aspects of the standard have already been taught or the teacher is assessing background knowledge in a particular area before instruction. Notes should reflect observable and quantifiable information that can readily be analyzed for goal setting by teachers and students.

Many teachers record observations on a daily or regular basis, but they do not observe the entire class each time. Instead, they divide the class into groups of about five students each and focus on a single group each day of the week. If students have reading folders, they may be color-coded by observational group, for example, all of the students with red folders are observed or conferenced with on Monday. While students work independently or directly following guided reading sessions, the teacher records observations on this group of students. The observations are generally quite brief and focus on key aspects of reading development previously identified.

Many teachers have a notebook with one or more pages devoted to each child, while some prefer to use a clipboard with a sheet of blank address labels. Before the beginning of the literacy block, they write the date and the child's initials on several labels. Teachers may also prepare labels with the reading standard to be observed. (These can be typed and copied for each student's file.) As the teacher observes the child's reading behavior, the teacher records comments on the labels and later transfers the labels to the appropriate page of the notebook. Other teachers prefer to record observations directly into a notebook without using the labels. Table 3.10 reflects a series of anecdotal records for an emergent reader and a transitional reader.

Noting and compiling the observations is only half of the task. Teachers review the notes to determine how well the whole class is meeting standards and the attitudes, skills, and strategies they are developing for reading; instructional decisions can often be made based on this review. For example, if students are readily making connections between their reading and their own lives, it may be time to introduce them to making connections between books/materials they have read and their current reading. Conversely, if the teacher has spent a great deal of time teaching reading strategies but the students are not using them in their independent reading, it may signal that the teacher needs to focus on helping students apply what they have learned.

Reviewing records for individual children may reveal that they have or have not made significant progress over a specific period. If they have made good progress, the notes may indicate that more challenging learning experiences are warranted. The notes of struggling readers or unmotivated students may reflect trends that suggest needed background teaching or motivation. For example, it may become clear that some immigrant children in the class know many folktales from their home cultures but are unfamiliar with traditional folk literature in the United States being featured in a unit of study. Alternatively, it may be noted that a student who takes little interest in reading is very passionate about fire trucks and firefighters. In these cases, traditional folktales could be made available at the listening table for some students and books and magazines about firefighting for another.

Children who are more verbal may lead the teacher to believe that either all of the students understand very well or that the quiet students do not understand as well. Sometimes written work completed by students does not reveal the whole story about what students know and can do or how they learn. Anecdotal records that provide accurate information about each individual child's performance can be useful assessment tools.

Checklists

A less time-consuming (but also less informative) method of monitoring individual student progress is using checklists. These tools are especially useful for noting the acquisition and development of specific skills and strategies and can be

Table 3.10   Anecdotal Records Based on Standards

Name: Antonio   Grade: 1

Sept. 10   Selected books during free time
                           Tells story from pictures

Standard: Students apply a wide range of strategies to comprehend, interpret, evaluate, and appreciate texts.

9/17   Rereads predictable books from guided reading sessions
                           Generally good one-to-one match between words and reading
                           Recognizes a few sight words: *mother, father, birthday, and, the*
                           Uses picture clues

9/24   Loves funny books
                           Uses some initial letter sounds to guess new words

10/1   Reads big book to class—practiced first
                           Used picture and first letter cues well

10/8   Can retell stories—but elaborates on too many details
                           Does not like to partner read—finds it hard to concentrate
                           Beginning to use word chunking (saw *and* in word *stand*)

10/15   Often chooses books that are too difficult to read independently
                           Loves books about fire trucks and firefighters

Name: Seth   Grade: 5

Sept. 8   Listed Lemony Snicket books as favorites
                           Reads them independently during SSR

Standard: Students read a wide range of literature from many periods and many genres to build an understanding of the many dimensions of human experience.

9/15   Pointed out some aspects of historical fiction noted in reading
                           Listened attentively to first chapter of *Number the Stars*
                           Made logical predictions about what will happen next

Standard: Students apply a wide range of strategies to comprehend, interpret, evaluate, and appreciate texts (making inferences).

9/22   Found it difficult to infer why Anne Marie was not told everything
                           Response journal entry focused on the danger faced by Jewish neighbors
                           Excellent links to historical events in Germany at the same time

10/1   After group discussion, able to infer why Anne Marie's sister had died
                           Journal entry about bravery of the Gentiles in hiding their Jewish friends
                           Able to identify characteristics of historical fiction for new novel—*Roll of Thunder, Hear My Cry*

10/8   Shared an inference he had made in his independent reading
                           Made inferences about author's purpose in writing next book
                           Made interesting links about curtailed freedom in both books

adapted to match the level of academic achievement demonstrated by a child. Checklists can be shared with parents and used during conferencing sessions. Occasionally, checklists are publicly displayed in the classroom and observable to anyone entering the room. This is not good practice, as it makes learning competitive among students rather than encouraging motivation and goal setting for students as individuals. See Table 3.11 for a sample checklist.

Assessment Portfolios

Assessment portfolios may serve as informative vehicles for teachers and students in evaluating progress in reading and in setting goals for further learning. When goals and standards have been made public to students as a focus for teaching and learning, assessment measures should reflect progress toward the standard(s). Actual samples of student work, assessment rubrics, self-assessments, and reading logs might be effective portfolio pieces to use in demonstrating progress.

The teacher may require that students place certain pieces in their portfolios,

Table 3.11 Checklist of Reading Strategies and Attitudes

Name: _____					
Beginning Reading	**Date**	**Date**	**Date**	**Date**	**Date**
Word Recognition Strategies					
Uses phonics clues					
Self-corrects					
Develops sight word vocabulary					
Notes patterns in words					
Comprehension Strategies					
Uses picture clues					
Predicts with evidence					
Uses context clues					
Uses prior knowledge					
Meaning/Comprehension					
Reads for meaning					
Retells stories					
Relates reading to own life					
Attitudes Toward Reading					
Enjoys reading					
Chooses to read for enjoyment					

+ always, √ sometimes, − not yet

but others should be selected by the students to showcase their best work, work they struggled with, or what they learned from particular learning experiences. A reflection sheet may be attached to entries to indicate why students elected to include a particular piece and what it demonstrates about their learning (see Table 3.12).

Table 3.12 Portfolio Reflection Sheet

Reading

I included this piece in my portfolio because _____

_____

I have gotten much better at _____

_____

One or two goals that I have set for myself include _____

_____

Conferencing

After work samples and data related to students' reading growth and development have been accumulated, teachers and students should review the contents and prepare for a conference. Conferencing just before parent-teacher conferences is an ideal time to meet more formally with students; however, informal conferencing with students on a daily or weekly basis is important as well. All students can prepare for a conference by reviewing what they think they did well and what they need to work on in reading. Older students may write their responses in preparation for the conference. Students will not automatically know how to review their work, and teachers will need to model and guide students in using the process.

Portfolios are useful in student-led parent-teacher conferences, as they focus attention on what has been accomplished and indicates what will be worked on next. The evaluation comes from the perspective of the child and puts learning more squarely in his or her hands. Use of actual work samples and assessment instruments provide concrete evidence of student work, and parents and guardians will know what their children have been working on and how they might help them at home.

Numerous assessment options have been discussed in this section, and the management of classroom assessment may seem overwhelming to the new teacher. Determining connections between teaching, learning, and assessment goals will help clarify where you hope to take your students in terms of reading achievement. Establishing an assessment calendar or agenda will provide teachers with a clear overview of the comprehensiveness of their assessment plans. Table 3.13 highlights key components of an assessment agenda.

Table 3.13 Sample Teacher Assessment Agenda for Grade 6

Data Collection Format	Student Self-Assessment	Time Frame
Informal Reading Inventory		Beginning/Middle/End of Year
Standardized Reading Tests		One time per year
Running Records	√	One time per month
Skills Checklist	√	One time per month
Strategy Checklist	√	One time per month
Anecdotal Records		Weekly (5 students per day)
Review of Reading Response Journals	√	Weekly (5 students per day)
Independent Reading Logs	√	Review one time per month
Work Samples	√	1–2 in Portfolio per month

Data-driven instruction is currently very popular (Bernhardt, 1998; Gregory & Kuzmich, 2004; Guskey, 2000). The literature on the topic suggests that teachers and administrators use all of the above-mentioned measures to gather information about students' achievement and then design instruction and improve student learning. Table 3.14 highlights how assessment results might inform teaching and learning. We will learn about areas that we need to teach more directly, for example, how to select books at an individual's instructional reading level or how to relate material read to one's own experiences. There may be instances where we discover that students are not developing sophisticated responses to what they have read because we do not ask them to do so. Therefore, we may examine the types of questions we ask students to respond to and how well the learning experiences they engage in offer opportunities for students to develop critical thinking skills. In this way, we strive to continually make our teaching relevant to the needs and progress of our students.

Assessment instruments may be used to get a clear picture of each student's progress in reading. However, the bottom line of the evaluation of students' reading is to note and help them improve the development of problem-solving skills

Table 3.14 Evaluation Assessment Results

Assessment Result	Suggested Remedy	Teaching Plan
*Student reads most material at frustration reading level	– Teach book selection strategies	– Link interests to book selection – Teach five finger method[2] – Use retelling as comprehension criterion for book selection
*Student discusses what characters do but does not relate to own experiences	– Select books more closely matched to students' experiences	– Model how to draw comparisons between text/self
*Student responds with literal responses to reading	– Use more higher-level thinking activities to analyze character	– Ask more inferential questions – Develop more activities – Model use of inference strategy
*Student reads only fairy tales	– Conduct more book talks in different genres – Teach more about genres – Stock classroom library with more books of a variety of genres	– Teacher and students share favorite books

and strategies in reading and the development of higher-level thinking skills in responding to what has been read.

Reflection Journal 3.1

Which assessment tools do you feel you would be able to implement with confidence? Which tools do you want to learn more about and/or see in action?

Developmental Standards in Reading

The **International Reading Association (IRA)** and **National Council of Teachers of English (NCTE)** collaboratively designed academic standards for reading that provide a general map of literacy goals for students. They outline reading behaviors students must acquire to be successful readers both in and out of school. Most states interpret the standards more specifically and determine **benchmarks** (goals) students should strive to reach by Grades 4, 8, and 12. Many districts have further determined benchmarks for each grade level. Effective teachers align their teaching with the standards to make certain that individual students meet each of the standards and ensure a rigorous curriculum.

Reflection Journal 3.2

Examine the IRA/NCTE standards (on the inside cover of this text). Many include multiple components. Note the areas that have been considered essential for students to become proficient readers. They must be able to use a wide range of word analysis and meaning strategies, read for a variety of purposes, read and comprehend a wide range of genres, respond to what they have read, and make links between what they have read and other experiences. Highlight the components of each standard that you are already familiar with in one color. Highlight the components of each standard that you are not very familiar with in another color. You may wish to pay particular attention to the latter group and learn more about these components during this course.

In using the standards for curriculum planning, individual teachers and groups of grade-level teachers often meet to establish a hierarchy of reading behaviors to focus on during the school year. For example, they may determine one or two strategies to focus on at the start of the school year and subsequent strategies to develop after that. From here, they may select particular genres of literature that lend themselves to the development of the selected strategies. They will also determine which methods of responding to literature the students will be ready to undertake and ways they can guide students in making links to self, text, and world. This type of long-range planning enables teachers to make certain that they address the standards as fully as possible. It also enables teachers to guide students in becoming ever more sophisticated and knowledgeable readers.

Daily teaching rarely follows teachers' idealistic lesson plans for the week. It is often the case that by the end of the week, we have not gotten quite as far as we would have hoped. Some activities take longer than planned; sometimes students struggle with new concepts more than anticipated, and sometimes students have less prior knowledge about a topic than assumed and it is necessary to build background understanding. Of course, the opposite can be true as well. Children may need less instruction than anticipated, and it may be feasible to move along at a faster rate. It is all too easy to become immersed in the specific learning experiences we want our students to engage in and lose sight of our ultimate goals. The standards can be helpful in daily teaching, as they keep teachers focused on the bigger picture of what kind of readers we are guiding our students to be.

As we examine individual and whole-class progress in reading, the standards serve as fundamental guideposts to inform instruction. We can use this information about student progress to determine how effective our teaching has been. From here, we can set goals for our students and ourselves.

Schools have come to recognize the importance of reviewing student progress toward the standards at each grade level and for the school as a whole. Grade-level expectations comprise the horizontal component of progress toward standards. How well are the students doing at a particular grade level? Do classroom learning experiences provide students with opportunities to develop the standards? For example, if students are never asked to discuss what they have read or form opinions about characters or the writings of specific authors, they are unlikely to improve their ability to respond to reading. Are the learning experiences as rigorous as possible? In using the response to reading scenario once again, if students are only asked to write summaries of what they have read, they are unlikely to develop a sophisticated ability to analyze, synthesize, or evaluate what they have read. These could be areas teachers would want to work on with their students. The goal might be to guide students in analyzing and forming opinions about character motivation. Once goals have been set, teachers develop learning experiences that would be likely to help students reach the goals. Regular evaluation of progress toward goals and effectiveness of teaching, learning, and assessment plans will enable teachers to continually refine this process. It is important to set goals that match student needs and develop assessment practices that highlight their progress toward these goals (Rodgers & Rodgers, 2004).

Second Language Learners

Special considerations need to be made for ELLs, but you may not know exactly what their experiences are like. The scenario below places you in the shoes of a student who does not speak the language of the classroom as a way to help you understand what some of these students may be feeling through this experience. After reading A View From the Classroom below, view the CD companion that accompanies this text for a detailed analysis of what is happening in this scenario and numerous examples of how a teacher can assist second language learners.

A View From the Classroom

Imagine that your family has just moved to a non-English-speaking country. You do not speak the language, but you have just been enrolled in the third grade at your new school. Your mother brought you to school the first day, but she did not know what anyone was saying to her in the office. All she could say was "No hablo español." The secretary gave her papers to fill out, but she could not understand some of the questions so she had to leave them blank. Your mother gave you a quick hug and told you where to meet her after

(Continued)

(Continued)

school. One of the older students escorted you to your classroom.

The teacher tells you something, but you do not know what she said. She points to a desk, but you are not sure if she is telling you that this is to be your desk or not. You sit down and the teacher goes on with the lesson. You try hard to figure out what is going on but you cannot. The children begin to move into groups, but you do not know where you should go. The teacher says something to one of the children and he motions you to go with him to a table where the teacher and five other children are seated. The teacher hands each of you a reading book. Your heart sinks as you realize that you cannot make out one word on the first page. The teacher calls on each child to read aloud, and you hope that she will not call on you; thankfully, she does not. Instead, she moves her finger along the lines of print in your book as the other children are reading.

The teacher continues to do this for 2 weeks, and then one day she asks you to read too. By now, you recognize a few of the words, but you do not know what most of them mean. You say the words that you recognize but pause at the many that you do not know. The other children—some of whom are kind and others who are impatient at your slow progress in reading—call out the words, often before you get much of a chance to figure them out. The teacher smiles and says, "Muy bien." You hope that she does not ask you any questions about what you have just read, because you have no clue, but your luck seems to have run out. The teacher hands you the same assignment papers as the other children, and you have no idea about what you are supposed to

do with this vocabulary sheet. You make a couple of guesses but know that most of them will be wrong.

The teacher and the other students speak in Spanish all day long. You are beginning to understand words here and there, and you are beginning to understand the routine of the school day, but you tune out much of what is being said because you find it too challenging to understand what they are saying. It is tiring trying to keep up, and by lunchtime each day you are exhausted. You are very lonely in the classroom, but at least at lunch you can eat with the other girl from the United States and play with her at recess. She is from Kansas, and it is fun to be able to talk with someone at school and be with someone who understands the world more closely to your perspective.

Students will become conversationally fluent in another language in approximately 2 to 3 years. This means that they will be able to understand most of what is said to them in English and be able to respond appropriately. ELLs rely heavily on facial expressions and other cues to aid in understanding what is being said. Academic language takes far longer (7–10 years) for many children to acquire. Teachers who are not familiar with the process of second (or subsequent) language acquisition may be puzzled when children appear to speak English very well yet do not do as well as expected in their schoolwork. Language used in conversation or with friends on the playground is very different from language used in the classroom for academic learning. In fact, all students would benefit from development of academic language (analyzing, comparing/contrasting, inferring, drawing conclusions, etc.), but

ELLs in particular will need focused attention in this area.

Six Months Later

You are beginning to understand more of what is being said in the classroom. You can read at a first-grade level, though some of the words and stories do not make sense to you yet. Writing is much harder; you can write a little bit more each day, but it is still very short compared to your classmates. Many times, you are not sure of the word order, and you know the sentences do not sound right in Spanish. It is very frustrating, because you know what you want to write but cannot get the ideas down on paper. Your classroom teacher is very helpful. Rather than marking all of the mistakes on your paper, she chooses one thing to work with you on at a time. For example, this week she showed you how the adjective comes after the noun in Spanish (la casa blanca) rather than before it as in English (the white house).

You really enjoy going to the SSL (Spanish as a Second Language) classroom. It takes so much pressure off you to go there. There is only a small group of children. All of them are also learning Spanish, and the teacher is very nice. You feel much more comfortable trying to use Spanish there because no one will laugh at you if you make a mistake. Your classroom teacher tells the SSL teacher what you will be studying, and the SSL teacher introduces some of the concepts to you before you study them in the grade-level classroom. Your SSL teacher finds interesting and fun ways to help you learn about the concepts, including the vocabulary. You read simple texts about the topic and practice speaking and writing about the topic too. This is very helpful, because you will understand the concepts at least a little when you have to deal with them in the classroom.

Yesterday you were not able to go to school. You mother had a doctor's appointment for your little brothers, and she needed you to go with her to translate. You do not really speak very much Spanish yet, but because your mother has to stay home all day with the little ones, she can only say a couple of words in Spanish. You did not want to go along because it is very embarrassing to have to translate for your mother, and yet you want to help her. The doctor uses many complicated words at which you can only guess.

Home and School Links

Parental, guardian, or community reading events relating to reading to and with children extends the efforts of the school in many ways. Listed below are some of the benefits of reading at home or outside of school. Children who are read to frequently

1. View reading as an enjoyable experience

2. Develop favorite authors and/or stories

3. Note that there are different purposes for reading, for example, reading for pleasure and reading for information

4. Become familiar with book language and expect that it will be different than conversational language

5. Recognize that stories have characters, settings, and plots

6. Expand their vocabularies

7. Learn about a broad range of concepts, especially if they are exposed to a great deal of expository/informational text

8. Have models of fluent reading

9. Understand the structure of writing

10. Develop more ideas for writing

When family members read to children, they may do all of the reading and the children will enjoy listening, but increasingly the children can be encouraged to join in and read along (choral reading), or they may read one page and the family member may read the next. In this way, children are beginning to read on their own, but they do not have the burden of reading the entire text alone. Assure parents and guardians that stopping to discuss pictures, texts, or related ideas is a positive practice and actually extends reading experiences for their children.

Children of all ages enjoy being read to by an adult. Older children continue to develop their listening skills as they are being read to. Listening comprehension generally is more sophisticated than reading ability, so children may enjoy stories they could not yet read independently. They visualize the characters and anticipate the plot without the struggle of having to decipher text.

Learning to read is a complex activity that begins long before children come to school. As a teacher of language arts, reading is a key element in your curriculum. Understanding reading and its processes will assist you in designing appropriate language arts activity and learning for your students.

End-of-Chapter Reflection

- As you begin to think about your first teaching position, how will you go about setting up a program for reading development? What approach to teaching reading most appeals to you? Which components of a comprehensive balanced reading program do you feel would be most beneficial for your students? Which assessment methods do you believe would provide you with ample evidence of your students' reading abilities?

- What questions do you have about how to teach reading?

- What questions do you have about how to teach reading to ELLs?

Planning for Teaching

- Visit the teacher resource section at your school's library or resource center. Find a variety of reading-related assessment tools. Bring an example of a tool that you would find helpful to use in assessing reading in an elementary classroom. Be prepared to discuss the purpose and implementation basics of the assessment tool you choose.

Connections With the Field

1. Visit a school that aligns teaching, learning, and assessment to state or district standards. Interview one or more teachers to determine how they use reading standards to guide planning, instruction, and student learning in reading.

2. Visit a classroom and ask the teacher to describe what he or she does to evaluate literacy and especially reading skills at the beginning of the school year. What measure does the teacher use to determine the students' stages of reading? How does the teacher use the information? What reading stages are represented in the classroom?

3. Visit a classroom where the teacher uses anecdotal records to assess student reading ability and growth. Note the kinds of observations the teacher makes and how they are recorded. Interview the teacher about how the observations inform his or her teaching

OR

4. Visit a classroom during reading instruction. Select two students to observe during the session and listen to them read and engage in reading-related activities. Note the students' motivation toward reading activities, the level at which the children are reading, and the strategies they uses while reading or writing.

Student Study Site

The Companion Website for Developing Voice Through the Language Arts

http://www.sagepub.com/dvtlastudy

Visit the Web-based student study site to enhance your understanding of the chapter content and to discover additional resources that will take your learning one step further. You can enhance your understanding of the chapters by using the comprehensive Study Guide, which includes learning objectives, key terms, activities, practice tests, and more. You'll also find special features, such as the Links to Standards from U.S. States and associated activities, Children's Literature Selections, Reflection Exercises, Learning from Journal Articles, and PRAXIS test preparation materials.

Notes

1. Bilingual programs should preview translated materials very carefully to ensure that translations accurately represent the linguistic and cultural experiences of the children and represent quality translations.

2. Student raises one finger for each unknown word while selecting a new book. If all five fingers are raised by the end of the page, the book is difficult to read independently.

References of Children's/Young Adult Literature

McKissack, P., & McKissack, F. (2003). *Days of jubilee: The end of slavery in the United States*. New York: Scholastic Press.

Sachar, L. (1998). *Holes*. New York: Farrar, Straus & Giroux.

Spinelli, J. (2002). *Stargirl*. New York: Knopf.

References of Professional Resources

Bernhardt, V. (1998). *Data analysis for comprehensive school wide improvement*. Larchmont, NY: Eye on Education.

Boyd-Batstone, P. (2004). Focused anecdotal records: A tool for standards-based authentic assessment. *Reading Teacher, 58,* 230–239.

Burns, P., & Roe, B. (1999). *Burns/Roe informal reading inventory* (5th ed.). Boston: Houghton Mifflin.

Clay, M. (1972). *Sand: The concepts about print test*. Auckland, New Zealand: Heinemann.

Clay, M. (1985). *The early detection of reading difficulties* (3rd ed.). Auckland, New Zealand: Heinemann.

Clay, M. (1993). *Reading recovery: A guidebook for teachers in training*. Auckland, New Zealand: Heinemann.

Cooper, J. D., & Kiger, N. (2001). *Literacy assessment: Helping teachers plan instruction*. Boston: Houghton Mifflin.

Flynt, S. E., & Cooter, R. B. (2003). *Reading inventory for the classroom and tutorial audiotape package*. New York: Pearson Merrill Prentice Hall.

Fountas, I. C., & Pinnell, G. S. (1996). *Guided reading: Good first teaching for all children*. Portsmouth, NH: Heinemann.

Fountas, I. C., & Pinnell, G. S. (2001). *Guiding readers and writers grades 3–6: Teaching comprehension, genre and content literacy*. Portsmouth, NH: Heinemann.

Gregory, G., & Kuzmich, L. (2004). *Data driven differentiation: In the standards-based curriculum*. Port Chester, NY: National Professional Resources.

Guskey, T. (2000). *Evaluation of professional development*. Thousand Oaks, CA: Corwin Press.

Harvey, S., & Goudvis, A. (2000). *Strategies that work: Teaching comprehension to enhance understanding*. New York: Stenhouse.

Johns, J. (1997). *Basic reading inventory* (7th ed.). Dubuque, IA: Kendall/Hunt.

Johnston, P. (1997). *Knowing literacy: Constructive literacy assessment*. Portland, ME: Stenhouse.

Juel, C. (1988). Learning to read and write: A longitudinal study of 54 children from first through fourth grade. *Journal of Educational Psychology, 80*(4), 437–447.

Leslie, L., & Caldwell, J. (1995). *Qualitative reading inventory II*. New York: Harper-Collins.

National Institutes of Health. (2000). *Report of the National Reading Panel: Teaching children to read: An evidence-based assessment of the scientific research literature on reading and its implications for reading instruction*. Washington, DC: U.S. Department of Health and Human Services.

No Child Left Behind Act. (2001). Conference Report to Accompany H.R.1. Report No. 107-334, House of Representatives, 107th Congress, 1st Session.

Opitz, M., & Ford, M. (2001). *Reaching readers: Flexible and innovative strategies for guided reading*. Portsmouth, NH: Heinemann.

Richgels, D. J. (2001). Invented spelling, phonemic awareness and reading and writing instruction. In S. B. Newman & D. K. Dickson (Eds.), *Handbook of early literacy research* (pp. 142–155). New York: Guilford Press.

Rodgers, A., & Rodgers, E. (Eds.). (2004). *Scaffolding literacy instruction: Strategies for K–4 classrooms*. Portsmouth, NH: Heinemann.

Rosenblatt, L. (1996). *Literature as exploration*. New York: Modern Language Association. (Original work published 1938)

Stahl, S. A. (2001). Teaching phonics and phonological awareness. In S. B. Newman & D. K. Dickinson (Eds.), *Handbook of early literacy research* (pp. 333–347). New York: Guilford Press.

Stauffer, R. G. (1969). *Directing reading maturity as a cognitive process*. New York: Harper & Row.

Swearinger, R., & Allen, D. (2000). *Classroom assessment of reading processing* (2nd ed.). Boston: Houghton Mifflin.

Technology Resources

National Center for Family Literary: http://www.famlit.org
Electronic Journal of the International Reading Association: http://www.readingonline.org

Writing and the Language Arts

Context Setting:

After reading this chapter, you will be able to

- Identify the stages of writing that children pass through
- Use standards to guide lesson planning in writing
- Use process writing as a model for teaching, learning, and assessment in writing
- Integrate writing with the other language arts

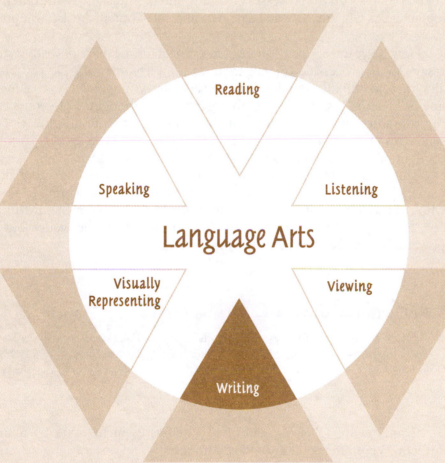

Before We Begin

- What kinds of writing do you do on a daily basis? What role does it play in your daily life? In your opinion, what characteristics do good writers possess?

Writing as a Language Art

Writing is a common occurrence in daily life and a critical skill in which to become proficient. Writing is used for myriad of purposes, from the automatic task of making a grocery list or jotting down a telephone message for a family member to more in-depth tasks such as writing a letter to the editor of a newspaper or writing in a school or business setting. Learning how to use the tools of writing, such as handwriting, spelling, and grammar, is important, but equally important are the content and thinking that go into a piece of writing. This chapter focuses on the processes of writing and the substance and content of writing, whereas Chapter 8, "Language Arts and the Content Areas," will present the tools of writing.

How do you feel when you need to create a formal piece of writing such as an essay? What process do you engage in to complete the task? Do you brainstorm all of the possibilities and details before actually writing, possibly making an outline or creating a semantic map to organize your thoughts? Do you sit down at the computer and just let the words flow? Do you try out a number of opening sentences focused on capturing just the right one? Do you agonize over the mere thought of writing, or do you approach it with enthusiasm?

The purpose of writing is to communicate with others. The more clearly and convincingly we convey our ideas, the more influence our writing has on people who read what we write. Everything from the legibility of our handwriting to correct spelling and grammatical usage has an impact on the reader, but it is the power of our words that actually carries the new message.

Reflection Journal 4.1

Think of someone's writing you particularly enjoy reading. What does the writer do to make his or her writing so compelling? What might you learn about writing from this writer?

Examine the following end-of-year self-assessment done by a first-grade student. What kinds of things do you notice?

Dis yer I lrnd meny tings.

Befor I did't use capatalls and now I do.

Befor I did't use pryods and now I do.

Befor I did't use diskrpshun and now I do.

While this is a very insightful self-assessment for a first grader, when asked what this evaluation revealed, many teachers only see the long list of errors in the child's writing. Perhaps you are thinking the same thing—that writing is either correct or incorrect. Or perhaps you are thinking that if teachers do not correct writing errors immediately, students will internalize incorrect spellings and never learn the "correct" way to spell words. While we strongly advocate for teaching spelling, grammar, punctuation, and handwriting as part of the writing process, it is essential to encourage students to first see themselves as capable writers who enjoy writing and can convey important messages through writing. Students who consistently use standard spelling and apply the grammar rules but who write life-less pieces only when required are not really learning to write in a way that will serve them well in their lives.

Think about and then discuss with your classmates the variety of experiences you all have had in relation to writing in school settings. What conclusions could you draw about the positive ways to encourage students to become writers?

Stop to Think

We must focus on guiding students to get their ideas on paper and not be overwhelmed when approaching a writing task. In minilessons and other learning experiences, you will teach the skills and strategies students need to continually improve their writing. We also focus on ways to teach these skills and strategies effectively.

Reflection Journal 4.2

Are you a good writer? Do you enjoy writing? Is it important for you to feel good about your writing if you are to be a teacher of writing?

Developmental Stages of Writing

From your study of theorists, such as Jean Piaget (1977), you know that although all children pass through the same stages in the development of cognition, they do not pass through these stages at exactly the same rate. This is the same with writing development. Some will have had experiences that are more meaningful with writing than others. Still others may be having their first experiences with learning to write in English. Of this latter group, they may fall anywhere along the continuum of very proficient to emergent writers in their first language.

Therefore, as teachers you will need to get a sense of where your students are in relation to the stages of writing and to design learning experiences that help move them forward. From there we repeatedly model good writing for students and nudge them to incorporate new things into their writing.

Numerous conceptualizations of the stages of writing have been developed by school districts, state departments of public instruction, and professional literacy organizations (IRA & NCTE, 1996). The number of stages of writing development identified by these organizations varies greatly, but each version begins with the most emergent (or beginning) level of writing and proceeds to fluent or standard writing in the target language. The most basic stages of writing development are portrayed in Table 4.1 to demonstrate the progression of development. You may wish to check with the schools where you have some connections to see how they have identified the stages of writing.

Table 4.1 Developmental Stages of Writing

Emergent Writers Generally

- Use a combination of drawings and scribble writing
- Understand that oral language can be written down
- Use random letters or print-like symbols in writing
- Use beginning and ending letters of words in English
- "Read" back own writing (note that although the earliest stages do not yield writing products that others might be able to read, they do reflect what children understand about the purpose of writing and how they view themselves as writers)

Beginning Writers Generally

- Distinguish between drawing and writing
- Use spaces between words
- Write phrases or short sentences
- Begin to accurately read what they have written
- Use temporary spelling with some phonetic elements
- Write with some conventional spellings (Mom, Dad, you)
- Use some uppercase and lowercase letters in appropriate places
- Begin to write a story with a beginning, middle, and end

Transitional Writers Generally

- Write stories with a beginning, middle, and end
- Use varied sentence patterns and lengths
- Use some descriptive detail and some elaboration of ideas
- Use more conventional than temporary spelling
- Write most high-frequency words correctly
- Use mostly correct capitalization and punctuation
- Begin to use paragraphs

Fluent Writers Generally

- Write with creativity and originality
- Use writing mechanics (punctuation, capitalization, spelling) correctly most of the time
- Use varied sentence patterns and lengths that develop and extend the topic
- Use rich, vivid vocabulary
- Use paragraphs consistently and appropriately
- Show a growing sense of audience

Figure 4.1   Four-Year-Old Writing Sample

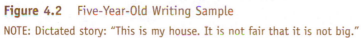

Figure 4.2   Five-Year-Old Writing Sample

NOTE: Dictated story: "This is my house. It is not fair that it is not big."

Daniel

would said of californium

fiv

I hav liesd

Daniel 6 years

Figure 4.3   Six-Year-Old Writing Sample

Developmental Standards in Writing

As in reading, standards for writing have been identified at the national, state, and district levels. Each school or district may have its own unique approach to how teachers are expected to represent the standards in their planning. For example, many building principals require that teachers submit weekly lesson plans with clearly identified standards to be focused on written at the top of each teaching/ subject area. In other schools, teachers meet in school- or grade-level groups to determine which standards to emphasize most fully.

Most standards are organized as benchmarks for Grades 4, 8, and 12. This is helpful if you teach at these particular grade levels. For example, if you teach seventh grade, you need to review the eighth-grade standards and determine where seventh-grade students would be on their way to reaching the standards by the end of eighth grade. If you do not, you will need to determine how students can work "toward" these standards at lower grade levels. Many school districts have already done this work and have established benchmarks for each grade from kindergarten through high school graduation.

For example, the Milwaukee Public Schools (2003) express the state standards as Learning Targets at each grade level. The Learning Targets for writing in Grades K–5 are identified in Table 4.2.

Table 4.2 Learning Targets for Writing From Kindergarten to Grade 5—Milwaukee Public Schools

Grade K

1. Express ideas using words and sentences
2. Participate in the planning, revising, and publishing components of the writing process
3. Demonstrate an understanding of the relationship between written symbols and the spoken word

Grade 1

1. Express ideas using basic sentences that are organized around a specific topic for a variety of audiences and purposes
2. Create various drafts of writing
3. Use words and punctuation marks to create sentences that express ideas

Grade 2

1. Communicate ideas in writing using complete sentences sequentially organized around a specific topic for a variety of audiences and purposes
2. Independently create multiple drafts of writing in a variety of situations
3. Correctly compose complete sentences

Grade 3

1. Organize sentences into paragraphs to create meaningful communication for a variety of audiences and purposes

2. Independently apply revision and editing strategies to create clear writing in a variety of situations
3. Employ standard American English, including correct grammar to effectively communicate ideas in writing

Grade 4

1. Prepare multiparagraph writing, adapting style and structure to suit a variety of audiences and purposes
2. Independently employ purposeful revision and editing strategies to improve multiple drafts of writing in a variety of situations
3. Identify various sentence forms and structures while applying the rules of Standard English to written communications

Grade 5

1. Compose detailed, multiparagraph, and organized writing to communicate for a variety of audiences and purposes
2. Independently produce and analyze multiple drafts of writing, using the writing process to create clear and effective writing
3. Produce various sentence forms and structures while applying the rules of standard American English in written communication

Not only do teachers need to plan teaching and lessons based on the school and district benchmarks, they also must focus on state and national standards. How do teachers make this all manageable so they know exactly what to teach and the students know exactly what is expected of them?

Applying the Standards for Writing: An Example

The sixth-grade teachers at Greenfield Elementary School, Paula and María, had multiple lists of what they were expected to accomplish in writing, oral language, and media technology with their students but needed to develop a framework that would relate everything in a meaningful manner in their planning. After reviewing the standards and learning targets and searching for logical connections, they decided to use writing genres as the organizer and to weave writing-related skills into this format. During the year, they were to focus primarily on persuasive, descriptive, and informational writing. Oral language and media technology standards were logical areas to link to writing.

Paula and María determined the skills and strategies their students would need while developing proficiency in each of the genres. They did this in two ways. First, they brainstormed and researched elements to be expected in good writing from each genre. Second, they examined their students' writing and discussed how they might organize teaching, learning, and assessment experiences to assist students in "approximating" quality writing in each of the genres. They determined what would be new for many students and where they might make links to already familiar areas. Several aspects of writing, oral language, and media technology emerged repeatedly in their planning, and these areas would receive special focus throughout the year. For example, "clarity" and "conciseness" were necessary elements for nearly every category they devised. Table 4.3 reflects Paula and María's initial planning efforts.

Once instruction actually begins, however, plans rarely evolve perfectly. It may take longer to teach certain areas than anticipated, students may struggle more than anticipated with certain concepts, and they may need more preliminary skill development than anticipated. The students will always be our real guide and their progress our ultimate standard.

Jay McTighe (1997) outlines "seven principles for performance-based instruction" that may also be used as an effective template in linking standards to instruction:

1. Establish clear performance targets

2. Strive for authenticity in products and performances

3. Publicize criteria and performance standards

4. Provide models of excellence

5. Teach strategies explicitly

6. Use ongoing assessments for feedback and adjustment

7. Document and celebrate progress

Numerous other lesson planning templates and frameworks are available for guiding teachers in aligning instruction and standards. Wiggins and McTighe (1998), Robert Marzano (2003), and Harris and Carr (2001) are some well-known resources on this topic.

Table 4.3 Paula and María's Planning Guide

	Writing Learning Target: Compose detailed, multiparagraph, and organized writing to communicate for a variety of audiences and purposes	Oral Language Learning Target: Apply effective skills and strategies to create, organize, and communicate oral presentations	Media-Technology Learning Target: Communicate using a variety of methods, such as word processing, graphics, and e-mail
Time Frames & Assessments	**Genre** / **Elements of Teaching & Learning**	**Elements of Teaching & Learning**	**Elements of Teaching & Learning**
Block I: 6–8 weeks **Summative Assessment:** Present descriptive essays along with digital photos	Descriptive / Use of adjectives; Creation of mental images in written form; Clarity of description; Conciseness of description	Oral presentation skills • Voice projection • Eye contact • Body language • Use of visuals	Digital camera skills • Light • Clarity • Angle • Distance Support description with digital images
Block II: 6–8 weeks **Summative Assessment:** Present oral presentation of position supported by computer-generated graphic organizer	Persuasive / Establish a position; Create an argument; Support for a position; Referencing; Fact v. Opinion	Create a mental image with words Presenting a position • Clear • Concise • Convincing • Presentation	Computer graphics to highlight position and outline argument • Select appropriate graphic • Label graphic • Relate graphic to position
Block III: 6–8 weeks **Summative Assessment:** Research report and PowerPoint presentation	Informational / Select a topic; Research topic; Outline report	Research report • Interesting • Informative • Sequential • Accurate	Computer PowerPoint presentation • Concise • Informative • Clear Add and delete content of a media product to improve focus and clarity for an intended audience

Major Approaches to Teaching and Learning Writing

There are two major approaches or methods for teaching and learning how to write. Historically, writing has not held a very prominent position in the curriculum, often being minimized or ignored altogether. If it was taught, teachers focused instruction mainly on writing skills and mechanics, including handwriting, spelling, and punctuation, with very little emphasis on how to write for creative purposes. This is considered the traditional approach to teaching writing.

Traditional Approach

Traditional approaches to teaching writing include teachers assigning topics that all students write about, despite their interest or knowledge about the topic. Students receive instruction related to handwriting, grammar, and punctuation skills, and then usually in one short period they produce a piece of writing that is grammatically correct and interesting. This is difficult for writers to accomplish well. This approach still is being used in some classrooms today; however, the other major writing approach, the process approach, is being used more as the method for teaching writing since the late 1970s.

Process Approach

The process approach to teaching and learning to write is based on the understanding that a writer works through a process in creating a written piece. This approach began in schools with the work of Donald Graves (1983) and others who worked with young children on creating writing from their own ideas and not through assigned topics by the teacher. Graves suggested that writing instruction should include creating an environment that is conducive to creative writing, emphasizing opportunities to move beyond the traditional approaches. Typically the process approach includes three major components or steps to the process: prewriting, writing, and postwriting.

Prewriting Stage

Usually one does not just sit down, begin writing at the top of the page with the first sentence, and continue until the piece is done and then present it to an audience. Most often there are thinking processes that a writer engages in to gather his or her ideas, try out various angles, do research related to the topic, talk with someone to further explore the topic—and this is only at the beginning of the process called prewriting.

Writing Stage

Writing begins after the context has been set and the ideas fleshed out. Then the writer begins with pen to paper or fingers to keyboard. This stage includes many of the same activities, such as thinking about where the piece is headed, fumbling to find the appropriate words, looking up information to keep the piece flowing, as well as many other activities. Writing does not stop once the words are placed on the paper, however, but also includes reading and rereading what was written, revising and editing the words and ideas, and tweaking the details so that the piece is clear and its message apparent to the reader.

Postwriting Stage

The postwriting stage consists of sharing one's writing with others in a variety of formats, including reading the piece aloud, posting it for all to read, or creating a book or other published document from the piece. Writers need response and feedback for their writing, and the postwriting stage is where this occurs, for example, as when students take turns sitting in the author's chair to celebrate their writing. Another piece of this stage is the goal setting that can take place as the writer reflects on what was learned about writing and what his or her next piece will encompass.

This authentic, meaningful method of writing is messy and includes a number of steps that are not necessarily followed in order. The process approach to teaching and learning writing is an involved yet natural and coherent way to write. Table 4.4 details the processes involved in each stage of creating a piece of

Table 4.4 Typical Processes Occurring During Each Writing Stage

Writing Stage	Writing Processes That Frequently Occur
Prewriting	• Observing • Free writing • Discussion • Reading for background information • Brainstorming • Outlining • Webbing and creating semantic maps
Writing	• Writing drafts • Conferencing with peers and teacher • Revising or "reseeing" (Murray, 1994) • Editing or correcting writing
Postwriting	• Publishing writing • Sharing in variety of ways and settings • Creating books • Setting goals for future writing

writing. The prewriting stage includes the planning, thinking, and preparations for writing. The writing stage occurs as the first and subsequent drafts are written, revised, and edited. The postwriting stage is the final step in the process, where the writing is celebrated and shared with others and future writing is planned.

Writing Workshop Framework

A framework that many teachers use for engaging students in process writing is the writing workshop framework. Writing workshop is typically done on a daily basis and lasts 45 minutes to an hour, creating a predictable time when students can plan on working on their writing. Writing workshop begins with a large group gathering where the teacher teaches a minilesson related to a writing skill, strategy, or management technique for which students have demonstrated a need. The group time is followed by independent writing time, where students work quietly on their writing in various stages of the writing process. The teacher does both informal and formal conferencing with students during independent writing time. Teachers circulate about the room while students are writing and ask them to talk about their writing. This is a good time for teachers to note what students are doing in their writing and nudge them to try new things. They could say, for example, "This is a very interesting story. Try to leave a space between each word so that you can read it more easily" or "You say that your mother is a police officer. I think your readers would like to know more about what kind of work she does." One of these examples focuses more on writing mechanics and the other on content. We can guide students forward in both areas during writing workshop. This may also be a good time to note when students are consistently misspelling a word and give them a Post-it note with the correct spelling that can be referred to as they write. Students may also have a spelling section of their journal where they enter words they are learning to spell.

After a period of time, depending on the age of the students, usually between 10 and 20 minutes, students can work together on revising, editing, and conferencing with their peers. The last component of a writing workshop includes a share time where, in a variety of formats, both small group and large, students will receive feedback and advice on their writing from their classmates. Although writing workshop has a predictable structure, it is a fluid process due to the fact that students are writing on a variety of topics and are at various stages in the writing and publishing process. It is important for teachers to stay in touch with students so that they can monitor the students' needs and writing development. Chapter 9 fully details the workshop format, including writing workshops and the stages involved in writing, including publishing writing using a variety of formats.

In order to understand more fully what encompasses each component of the writing process, looking at the stages in relation to Cambourne's (1988) eight conditions for effective learning can be helpful.

Immersion: During each stage, students are immersed in thinking about, planning, and engaging in creating writing. Teachers create an environment where writing is valued and takes place on a daily basis, and thus students are expected to immerse themselves in the process of writing.

Demonstration: The direct teaching of writing skills and use of the tools of writing through minilessons and conferencing encompasses the demonstration component necessary to learn to write effectively and creatively. The literature the students read and view in light of the writing style the author uses is an excellent demonstration of quality writing that can be used as a model for their own writing.

Expectation: When students are engaged in writing using the process approach, they know they will be writing on a regular basis. They know they are expected to be writers, taking on the many roles of a writer and looking forward to expanding their abilities.

Response: It is helpful for writers to receive response from others during all stages of the writing process. In the prewriting stage, students are encouraged to share their preliminary ideas and ask for feedback from their teacher and peers. During writing, students can share their pieces with peers and the teacher to assist with revisions and editing. In postwriting, getting response from others can serve as a celebration of writing and assist students in setting goals for future writing pieces.

Employment/Use: After being exposed to many models and demonstrations of effective and creative writing, students are expected to complete their own writing pieces that incorporate new skills and reflect understanding about the writing process.

Responsibility: Students are given and take on the responsibility to engage in the planning of their writing, trying out various methods and skills, and working with others. They have the responsibility for taking an idea to a completed or published draft.

Approximation: Students try out new ideas and skills in writing. They compare their work to writing rubrics to continually develop writing that resembles quality. Approximation is a key component of the writing process as students practice new understandings throughout all of the stages of writing.

Engagement: The process approach is a framework that requires student engagement. These classrooms are set up to encourage and value writing. When writing is valued, it is a central component of the curriculum and students are motivated to stay engaged in the learning.

Teacher as a Model of Writing

Teaching and demonstrating writing through shared experiences is an excellent way to model the many processes of writing. This typically occurs with the teacher as the facilitator leading the whole class or small groups of students who have the same writing needs. Two major experiences supply this kind of group support: shared writing and interactive writing.

Shared Writing

In a shared writing activity, the teacher does the writing with oral input from students. Shared writing experiences are good to use when the entire class wants to reflect on learning together, create a collaborative writing piece such as a thank-you letter, or use it as a means for recording classroom events. The teacher elicits ideas and response from students and models putting the ideas into a written format, demonstrating using Standard English, grammar, and writing mechanics. These experiences are often done using large sheets of chart paper on an easel or an overhead projector. It is important that the teacher openly receive students' ideas, encouraging oral sharing of their thoughts and giving credence to varied viewpoints as the first stage of beginning writing. In a shared writing experience, as teachers model correct usage and writing mechanics, it is beneficial if they do a **think-aloud,** describing why they are writing, spelling, and formatting in a particular manner. It is through these think-alouds that students are provided demonstrations of applying writing skills to use in their own writing.

Interactive Writing

Interactive writing is similar to shared writing in that creating a piece of writing is a collaborative activity. However, the difference is that both the teacher and the students share in the physical writing act. This activity should be conducted where all can view the writing, just as with shared writing, but the teacher offers the writing utensil to students at times to add to the writing piece. Often the teacher will have a black pen so that the teacher models are clearly delineated from that of the students, who may use a variety of colors. In interactive writing, students actually come up to the chart paper and do the writing as the teacher oversees and encourages while at the same time the teacher does more of the challenging writing (e.g., name of the company they visited as they are writing a thank-you to their tour guide). Both types of shared writing experiences are a beneficial way to demonstrate and model the many facets of composing a piece of writing and assist with scaffolding the students' growing knowledge and experience with writing.

Writing for a Variety of Purposes

Students are generally writing throughout the day when in school; they write stories and reports, reflect on their learning, take notes, make outlines, and much more. As language arts teachers, we want to make certain that they learn how to write for a variety of reasons, understand how to select the proper type of writing, and are able to self-assess the effectiveness of their writing. Following is a discussion of the three main purposes for writing with students: writing to learn, writing about reading, and personal writing. Each purpose has unique features and requires students to use a variety of skills and strategies.

Writing to Learn: Content Area Writing

Content area writing provides students with multiple opportunities to clarify and extend their understanding of concepts by exploring them through writing. Writing and note taking can serve as a good resource for students when they need to locate information or review for a test. By using a variety of graphic organizers and writing formats, students may be able to more easily determine relationships and components of concepts.

Students explore the genre of informational or nonfiction writing in their content area subjects. Most students have had extensive experience in writing fictional stories or personal narrative but are lacking in experience with informational writing. As students progress through the grades, the conceptual load of content area classes becomes increasingly complex, and teaching students to organize and extend their learning through content area writing will facilitate their progress with more in-depth learning.

Learning Logs

Learning logs are a record of what is learned and can be used in any subject or content area, including social studies, math, science, and language arts. Not only is it helpful for students to reflect upon what they learn, but it also serves as a helpful assessment tool for the teacher. A learning log can take many forms and include a variety of components. For a reading class, students can document their learning through keeping a list of books read during independent reading or literature circles and lists of favorite authors or genres they are interested in reading. In a math class, a learning log may contain reflections on how word problems were solved or lists of formulas to assist in solving mathematical problems. A science learning log can include the steps taken when completing an experiment as well as scientific hypotheses and observations that are made.

Learning logs used in a language arts class can include lists of grammar and spelling rules studied, topics and ideas for writing pieces, spelling words recently learned, elements of reading or writing genres, criteria devised by students to evaluate reading or writing experiences, and handwriting practice.

Another key aspect of learning logs is their reflective component. Writing one's goals and reflecting on what was learned in a learning log is an excellent self-assessment tool, allowing the student to assimilate all that was learned and to set goals for future learning on a topic or concept.

Writing Reports/Research Writing

Students of all ages can do research on a variety of topics in all subject areas. As teachers, we must understand the many steps in completing a research report and then guide students through the process in a way that is manageable. Long before students actually write a report, they must select a topic, find and review sources of information on the topic, compile and organize the information collected, and complete the actual writing of the report. In the writing, the audience must be determined, as well as a structure planned to make the report interesting, informative, and concise.

Research reports often serve as a way for students to extend their knowledge and understanding in content areas. When they have some choice in selecting the topic for their research, they can pursue their personal interests, enabling them to reflect their cultures and experiences.

Teachers can lead students to go beyond merely reporting what they have found in their research activities. Establishing criteria that engage students in using strategies such as applying, analyzing, and making inferences and having them reflect on how they met criteria helps to develop better critical thinking and self-assessment skills. More information regarding engaging students in doing research and the writing that accompanies research can be found in Chapter 8.

Double-Entry Journals or Two-Column Notes

Double-entry journals, like many other types of journals, can be used in various subject areas, including language arts. The student takes notes on content and information on one side of the page and places reflective comments and questions on the other side. The purpose of a double-entry journal is to allow students to make solid connections to the content of the subject matter and further their thinking or learning through reflection and questioning. Another method includes the left column as a place to record writing conventions and mechanics related to punctuation and the right-hand side of the page to detail the purpose and situation in which to use the conventions. For example, as readers encounter italicized print, in the left column they note the use of italics in a direct quote from the text, and in the right column they describe the purpose for this format. Table 4.5 is an example of a fourth-grade student's double-entry journal while reading *The Midwife's Apprentice* by Karen Cushman (1995), where the left column contains direct quotes from the text that caught her attention and the right-hand column reflects her personal response.

Sometimes it is not enough for students to merely read about new ideas. Journal responses can enable students to graphically display information in a way that helps them to make connections among concepts they may not see otherwise. For example, in a science journal, the left side of the journal page might contain drawings of the planets in order and the right side information about the distance of each from the sun and the differences in temperature. In a social studies journal, a map of the area surrounding the school might be on one side and drawings and/or descriptions of the community helpers needed in this area on the other side. In mathematics, the left side might contain a number line and several problems adding positive and negative numbers, and the right side might feature a listing of when this concept is used in real life.

Table 4.5 Double-Entry Journal Example

Pg. 15 "Beetle grabbed bottles off the shelf and bunches of dried herbs from the ceiling beams, surprised at how much she knew, how she could recognize the syrups and powders and ointments and herbs from their look and smell."	I am surprised she can remember the stuff she needs. Can imagine what this room looks like with all the stuff and herbs hanging and in jars.
Pg. 26 "Broken, by God's whiskers, broken" Pg. 67 "By the bones of St. Polycarp . . ."	I like the way the midwife talks with slang like this. I really feel like the book is in the medieval times with this talking.

Writing About Reading

Writing and reading can both be considered acts of composing (Tierney & Pearson, 1983). Writing clearly involves a great deal of composing, but you may not have thought about reading as an act of composing. However, when you consider that reading does not take on meaning until a reader reacts to it or forms an opinion, it clearly is an act of composing. Consider the book *The Da Vinci Code* by Dan Brown (2003). It seems that people are either completely intrigued by the cleverness of the mystery plot or are horrified by the license the author takes with aspects of Christianity. Are we not composing a response when we formulate our opinions and share them with others?

By having students formulate a response to what they read either verbally or in writing, we are encouraging them to think about what they have read. We might do this by asking them to analyze the author's craft, react to characters or plot, make comparisons with other books and authors, or relate what they have read to their own lives. There are a number of methods for encouraging student response and engagement with what they read, including using reading response journals and reading logs.

Reading Response Journals

A reading response journal is a place for readers to thoughtfully respond in writing to what they read, be it any genre, including fiction or nonfiction (Routman, 2000). Reading response journals, like many of the other types of journals, can be used when doing reading in all subject areas but are used frequently in language arts and reading classes. The purpose of a reading response journal is to highlight a reader's personal response and emotion to the content of what is being read. Similar to a double-entry journal, writers respond personally to what they've read, although they do not necessarily copy the quotation from the text.

Students are encouraged to respond both aesthetically and efferently. Aesthetic response is a very personal and emotive way of responding to what is read, similar to the example in Table 4.5 where the writer makes personal connections from her life and experiences to what she reads. Responding efferently is more matter of fact, focusing on analyzing the content of what was read, such as listing the characters' names and the specific setting from a novel.

Students can tape to the inside cover of their journals a list of prompts that could be referred to while deciding how to respond. There are generally three angles that readers take in responding to what they have read: personal reactions, links to own life and the world, and links to other things they have read. In reacting personally, the reader can discuss opinions about the characters and their actions:

> I am really beginning to like Harry Potter's friend, Ron. At first I thought he was just a clumsy boy who did things without thinking, but after reading about the chess match I think he is smarter than I thought. Maybe he really likes Hogwarts. He seems to be a very loyal friend, too.

In making links to one's own life, readers reflect on images and ideas the text makes them think of in relation to themselves or their own world. Helping students make these connections is an important step in ensuring that reading is meaningful for the reader. If we think about reading as a way to learn more about people and the world in which we live, then we need to take the time to encourage students to explore these connections.

> The main character in *Number the Stars* was so brave. When the boys were teasing Amalia last week about her new glasses, I told them to leave her alone.

> That was sorta brave, but I wonder how brave I would be when there was real serious danger. That makes me think about how dangerous it must be in Iraq.

In all of these areas, the more that students think about what they've read, the more they come to understand literature as they grow into becoming critical thinkers. This is especially true of making links to previous reading, as students become more alert to making these connections the more they are encouraged to think about their reading. They note similarities in authors' styles, character motivations, character types, plot developments, and so on.

> I just finished reading *Arthur's Eyes* by Marc Brown. All of his books are so funny. Arthur always has some problem to figure out. Lots of times he is not happy in the beginning but learns a lesson by the end. D.W. causes a lot of trouble for Arthur just like Fudge does for Peter in *Tales of a Fourth Grade Nothing*.

Reading Logs

Reading logs are generally used for students to think about what they know about and respond to what they read. These logs might be divided into several sections, such as lists of books read, reflections on reading processes and comprehension, vocabulary lists and definitions, and written and drawn reflections related to readings. Reading logs can become a helpful source of information when students are self-assessing their progress in reading or conferencing with their teacher.

It may seem strange to you at first if you have not done this before, but an important type of written reflection includes students reflecting on *how* they read. Part of our work as teachers requires us to teach students new content; another aspect requires us to teach students how to use strategies and think critically. This thinking about one's thinking is called **metacognition,** or the ability to analyze how one learns and communicates that understanding to others. This reflection may contain lists of what students believe they do well in reading and another of areas on which they want to work. For example, students may determine that they do well in using picture clues, making predictions, and rereading parts that are confusing. They may wish to improve reading fluency, thinking about what they already know when reading, and using context clues to figure out new words. Reflection on strategies used while reading and writing helps students self-assess how well they use the strategy at regular intervals. Some teachers have designed reproducible forms that students complete where they circle the strategies they use regularly and reflect on how well they understand what they read and set goals for what they will do to improve comprehension.

In one section of the log, students record the names and authors of books they have read (Cox, 2002), the genre of each, the level of reading difficulty (hard, just right, easy), and whether or not they enjoyed reading the book. Including the beginning and ending dates for reading each book enables students to evaluate the length of time they take to read a book, which may motivate them to try to read a bit more each month. These charts also provide a clear picture about whether they are reading widely or if their books come from the same genre or are written about the same topic. The teacher can use these lists during conferencing with students to assess their growth. If a teacher notices a student reading all mystery books, the teacher can nudge the student to try a different genre to expand reading interests and development. By using reading logs to reflect on what students know about reading and setting goals for future learning, students become partners in their language arts development.

Innovations on Text

Innovations on text is a way for students to create a "new" text, or an original version or portion of a text they read, either changing or extending the meaning of the text. An example comes from a second-grade classroom where the teacher read aloud *Charlotte's Web* by E. B. White (1952). The children rewrote the ending of the story so that Charlotte the spider's life moves in a different direction.

Their innovation focused on the sequence of events that might have occurred if she would have been able to see her many babies grow up. In order for the innovation to be authentic and believably created around the elements of the genre and not just a fanciful story created using the same characters, students must have solid comprehension of the events and underlying themes.

Innovations on a text are especially useful with emergent readers. Often the original story follows a pattern, as in *Brown Bear, Brown Bear, What Do You See?* by Bill Martin Jr. (1967). The pattern of the text moves in this way: "Brown bear, brown bear, what do you see." "I see a red bird looking at me. Red bird, Red bird, what do you see?" "I see a . . ." In creating the innovation, teachers may wish to link the content to other areas of study. For example, if students are immersed in a study of the ocean, sea creatures may become the focus of the new text. Instead of using the color of each creature, the teacher may focus on size words—small, medium, and large.

Together in a shared or interactive writing experience, the class would create the first innovation, with the teacher writing the pattern on a large sheet of paper: "_____ _____, _____ _____, what do you see?" "I see a _____ _____looking at me." The students might generate a list of sea creatures and their sizes and then complete the pattern for each one. For example, the first page might be "Little seahorse, little seahorse, what do you see?" Each student or pair of students would be given a page to illustrate from the story, and then all of the pages could be compiled to form a class book.

Through innovation on a text, students can more fully explore the structure of stories and how they are organized. When they are given a page of print to illustrate, it affords them the opportunity to try to read the print without pictures. Often teachers choose to make these class books on large sheets of paper to form big books that can be seen by the whole class in a group sharing session. Students enjoy rereading their own books, and because they created them, they are more likely to remember what they wrote.

Theory Into Practice

Collaborative learning is a teaching and learning method that helps students develop social and academic skills within a group. How might you have students use collaborative learning when engaged in writing activities such as the activities discussed within this chapter?

Writing Sequels

Sometimes students encounter books and characters they enjoy so much that they cannot get enough of them. Books like this can be good subjects for writing sequels. In writing sequels, students maintain the same characters and/or setting but incorporate their favorite characters in new situations to continue the action. To be effective, the sequels must be true to the personalities of the characters and the type of plot to be expected in these books. However, the writer has greater license to create them than in doing an innovation on a text.

Writing a sequel to a story is actually a fairly high-level activity for students, as it must be a logical extension of previous versions. Prewriting activities such as making character maps of the main characters that include traits that will need to be maintained in the sequel are helpful for planning. Students can outline the new story line and then evaluate whether it is parallel to the original version. Many opportunities for discussion can be built around this creative writing format. As with many new writing experiences, it may be beneficial to write a sequel as a shared writing activity first, as this provides a template for students on how to first plan and then collaboratively write a sequel before they are expected to write on their own.

Using Reading to Inform or as a Model for Writing

When students do a lot of reading, they can translate what they learn about the format or genre into their own writing. For example, students who read many fairy tales will pick up the format and may be inclined to write fairy tales themselves. Exposing students to varied examples of a genre of literature can help to create models for their own writing. Although any piece of quality literature can be used as a model for writing, a list at the end of this chapter provides suggested literature you can obtain for your classroom library that students can use as models for their own writing.

Using literature as a model for student writing can be done during the minilesson portion of writing workshop. If, for example, the teacher was doing a minilesson on how to write exciting opening paragraphs that hook readers and make them want to read on, the teacher may read the opening parts of books with good beginnings to illustrate the point. Some authors begin with a question, with a shocking statement, or may jump into the middle of an event, making the reader want to keep reading. After sharing a few samples, students might look through other books selected by the teacher or those they are currently reading independently to determine what authors do before trying on their own to write an effective beginning. In a later minilesson on writing a good ending, the teacher may use some of the same books, comparing the opening and closing paragraphs to illustrate how sometimes the final paragraph mirrors the opening paragraph in some way.

As you are becoming familiar with children's and young adult literature, can you think of other titles that you might use in your classroom to write about reading? You may want to begin a list of this type of literature for future reference.

Stop to Think

Personal Writing

In personal writing, students express their opinions and ideas on a variety of topics. A common characteristic of personal writing is choice and allowing students to use their own ideas for creating writing pieces.

Table 4.6 Literature With Openings That Hook Readers

Literature	Opening
The Midwife's Apprentice by Karen Cushman	"When animal droppings and garbage and spoiled straw are piled up in a great heap, the rotting and moiling give forth heat. Usually no one gets close enough to notice because of the stench. But the girl noticed and, on that frosty night, burrowed deep into the warm, rotting muck, heedless of the smell."
Morning Girl by Michael Dorris	"The name my family calls me is Morning Girl because I wake up early, always with something on my mind."
The Birchbark House by Louise Erdrich	"The only person left alive on the island was a baby girl."
Crash by Jerry Spinelli	"My real name is John. John Coogan. But everybody calls me Crash, even my parents."

Story Writing

In classrooms where teachers are successful in teaching writing, it is difficult to get students to stop writing. Part of this phenomenon is that not only have they gained confidence in themselves as writers, but they also understand that their writing can have an impact on people who read it.

Story writing can be complex; decisions need to be made regarding such things as characters, setting, and plot. Teaching students prewriting skills in planning these elements helps them to think ahead about what they will write. Relating the structure of stories they have read to the stories they are planning to write will help to make connections to the writing of published authors.

Some students, especially in the younger grades, dash off story after story in a relatively short period of time; others spend several days writing single, more involved stories. Allowing and encouraging them to carry writing over from one day to the next will provide time to develop stories more fully. Sharing finished stories with the class or small group provides an authentic audience. Using a writing workshop format on a daily basis in your classroom allows students to engage in all these processes of writing and to develop proficiency in skills over time.

Students enjoy creating classroom publications of their favorite stories. In these instances, they decide how much text to type onto each page and create illustrations to accompany the text. The pages can be bound in some way and placed in the classroom library to share with others. Some schools reserve a section in the library for student-authored books, and many of these books become very popular. See the list at the end of this chapter that includes resources for book making in the classroom.

Community Stories or Round-Robin Storytelling

In this entertaining writing activity, a group of students become the authors of a story, each writing at least one paragraph and then passing it to the next person. To create a story that is purely nonsense, the students fold over the portion written by others, only allowing their own writing to show for the next writer. Another method is to have the writer expose only the last line of his or her writing. The final student should be instructed to construct a conclusion paragraph. This is a fun writing experience that can be completed on a computer, where students hide the previous paragraphs by scrolling down and concealing them. Of importance to note, however, is that some basic ground rules should be set before beginning. Excluding such things as violence, unacceptable language, and the use of classmates' names often results in a humorous and often surprisingly coherent and flowing story.

Writing Autobiography

What could be more motivating than to write about something that you know so much about—yourself! Children are egotistical, and from age 0 to 5 feel that they are the center of the universe, or should be. Children ages 6–9 finally begin forming a more open mind to their peers and others and are less focused on themselves as they are trying to find their place within the realm of others. Middle school children again are back to being egotistical in nature. Although a child's life may not contain as many important milestones as that of an adult, they have many experiences about which to write. They may need some assistance to remember memories from their earliest years and understand that daily events in their lives are just as important as the big vacations, parties, or broken legs. The prewriting stage can consist of interviewing family members to help brainstorm the events from students' lives to include. Writing an **autobiography** can help a student understand his or her life and experiences in the larger scheme of things.

Personal Journals

Many teachers begin the day by having students write in personal or reflective journals, often selecting their own topics and writing independently for a specified period of time. Younger students generally enjoy illustrating their journal entries; in fact, emergent writers often compose their entries or stories by drawing a picture first. Being that they are concrete in their thinking at this stage, it is often easier for beginning writers to compose something after they have created a visual.

Personal journals can provide insights into students' interests and their lives outside of school. Cultural practices and values may also be reflected in the entries students make in their journals. Teachers can choose to read students' journals and respond to them in writing on a consistent basis, for example, each day of the week the teacher reads the same five to six students' journals. Allowing students to deem certain entries as private and not to be read by the teacher can encourage them to be truly reflective about personal issues but yet have an outlet for their thoughts.

Some teachers reflect a commitment to writing by writing with the students during these sessions and sharing what they have written during group share time. Students enjoy hearing about their teachers, and this serves as another model of writing for them.

Too often students write in journals as a classroom management tool, for example, when entering the classroom in the morning they often take their seats and write in their journals while the teacher completes morning routines such as taking attendance and collecting lunch money. This is productive if students are given some time to share what they have written with their classmates or conference occasionally with the teacher. Otherwise, students see this exercise as a time filler that holds little importance.

Dialogue Journals

Dialogue journals are often a favorite among students, as in this format they respond in writing to something that they have read. They discuss their feelings about the actions of the characters and make predictions about what might happen next, and so on. The teacher reads the entries and writes a response related to the ideas the students have about what they are reading but does not emphasize the errors that might be present. This is a personal and private conversation between the student and the teacher, and they enjoy the personalized attention.

After students have an understanding of how to effectively use dialogue journals, they may select a partner to journal with. Ground rules about respectfulness and content of the journal must be established up front so that students are clear on the expectations for their dialogue. Since students share different thoughts with their peers than they would with their teacher, this format can be insightful to both students and the teacher.

Dialogue journals are especially inviting for students who may be very shy and not very anxious to join in whole class discussions. They can also be very effective for struggling or English language learners (ELLs) who are beginning to write in English. These students can compose their thoughts and receive feedback from the teacher but not be uneasy about responding in front of the entire class.

Letter Writing

Communication between people in the written form has historically included writing letters. Today letter writing has evolved and includes communicating almost instantaneously by **telecommunicating** through the Internet and e-mail. There are two basic types of letter writing: friendly letters and business letters. A third type, telecommunicating with e-mail, instant messaging, and general Internet communication, is fast becoming a common and engaging mode of communication.

The format, content, and level of formality varies greatly between friendly letters and business letters, making letter writing a good opportunity for students to explore a variety of purposes for writing. The same considerations of format, content, and formality need to be taught in all three categories of letter writing, along with the technical use of the computer.

Friendly Letters

Writing letters to friends and family has built-in positive reinforcement for students in that they often get return mail. Teachers can engage students in shared or interactive writing activities during the year, thank-you notes to visitors to the classroom, class letters to invite parents to school events, and so on.

Sharing letters and e-mails that you write yourself and that are appropriate for the classroom will demonstrate the purposes for which we communicate with others via letters and messages. The informal style of friendly letters can be explored with students. Although letters are similar to talking, the need to explain what people cannot see and to explain these ideas concisely are two areas students can examine in sample letters and in reviewing their own letters.

Dear Cooks,

We are sorry to say that we are disappointed with the way you cook our food. For instance some of the meat is red on the outside such as mock chicken legs, hamburgers and ground beef. Also on Tuesday March 22, I Found a piece of tin foil in my spaghetti sauce! We would really appreciate it if you would be more careful in the preparation of our schools food. Please respond!

Sincerely,

Figure 4.4   Sample of Fourth Grader's Letter to the School Cooks

Students may brainstorm a list of reasons for writing letters to friends and family. Making available used and unused greeting cards that you have collected over time can be used to sort by their purposes and the recipient (mother, teacher, friend, grandfather) to teach about audience in letter writing.

In authentic writing activities, students should identify the person they wish to write to and the purpose of the letter. They select the appropriate medium to send the message, using the greeting cards or designing their own or selecting from an assortment of stationery available in the writing center. If possible, students should actually mail their cards and letters. When they receive responses, they may wish to share them with their classmates, as sharing correspondence keeps the interest level high in all writing activities.

Some schools have set up a post office to encourage letter writing where each hallway is given a city name and each classroom a street name. Students write their cards and letters, address the envelopes, and place them in "mailboxes" in the post office. On certain days, student "postal workers" sort the mail and deliver it to the various classrooms. Although this is an enjoyable way to keep students writing, guidelines need to be established regarding appropriateness of content, and consideration should be given to making certain that all students receive mail. One solution to this issue is to assign pen pals within the school or to pair older students with their "reading buddies" in earlier grades.

Business Letters

It is important for students to learn the format and tone of business letters. Without even considering the content, sending an informal letter to a company requesting a refund or to the principal asking to have a detention reconsidered may appear very inappropriate or rude and could elicit a negative response from the recipient. As with friendly letters, in first learning about business letters, students may brainstorm a list of those people we send formal business letters to and reasons for sending them. The class may compose business letters together before writing them on their own to assist them in learning the appropriate letter-writing format. For example, after a unit on nutrition and a review of the school lunch menu, they could compose a letter to the principal requesting less starch and more protein for the hot lunches. In a social studies unit where students each research a different state, business letters could be written to each state's chamber of commerce requesting information about the state.

Be aware of additional opportunities for students to send authentic business letters that are connected to units of study, classroom activities, or activities that include the community around the school. Using shared writing experiences, the class could write a letter of complaint if materials are purchased for the classroom and are defective. If funding for band or athletics is reduced, students might write letters to the editor of the local newspaper explaining why these programs are essential. If it is not safe for students to ride their bikes to school because there are not enough stop signs on busy streets, students might send letters to the city council and outline their concerns. To help students assess the effectiveness and/or appropriateness of business letters they compose, have them role-play receiving one another's letters and reacting to the contents as if they were the actual recipient of the letter.

Telecommunicating Through E-mail, Instant Messaging, and Other Internet Communication

Most students today are familiar with e-mail and instant messaging and use it regularly to keep in touch with friends. Students who do not have regular access to the Internet should be given special priority so they are not limited in the world of technology. Lack of access may put students at academic disadvantages in their education and later in life, when many jobs are not available to them because they require demonstration of computer literacy.

A key component of using e-mail is having keyboarding skills. These skills enable students to communicate with greater speed and competency, which may influence how often students wish to send messages and how much depth they include in each message. Using the hunt-and-peck typing method is very laborious, and students will not wish to continue in this manner for long periods. Other computer skills can also be taught as part of e-mailing messages, including accessing the Internet; using and storing e-mail addresses; replying to, deleting, and forwarding messages; and using proper netiquette (etiquette appropriate while using the Internet).

It is beneficial to make connections with teachers in schools in other cities or states so you can arrange for the students in both classrooms to pair up as pen pals or e-pals. World language teachers may do the same but arrange for students to exchange e-mails (or letters) in the target language. Discussing content for the first letter or e-mail will help students feel more comfortable writing to students they do not know. E-pals may be beneficial for ELLs who have few or no other classmates who speak their home language. Matching them with e-pals who speak their home language will provide them with opportunities to continue developing their L-1, or first language, literacy skills and will also provide the teacher with a sense of the literacy skills they have in that language.

E-mailing is fun for most students; they love to use the computer to send and receive messages. It may serve as a motivator for students who would balk at traditional letter writing activities. Table 4.7 outlines the types of letter writing, some skills that may be taught in letter writing, and the process of teaching students to write letters.

Table 4.7 Elements of Letter Writing

Types of Letters	Skills to Be Taught	Process of Teaching Letter Writing
Friendly	Letter formats	Share samples of well-written letters
Business	Purposes of letters	Model letter writing
E-mail	Computer skills	Shared/interactive letter writing
	Addressing envelopes	Critiquing letters
		Write and edit own drafts

Rules for Internet Writing

Students need to learn that there are rules for respectfully using the Internet and telecommunications. Although there are some similarities between written and oral etiquette when communicating, there are some differences. Table 4.8 is a sampling of rules to share with students; be sure to use a language level that they can understand.

Table 4.8 Rules for Internet Use and Online Telecommunication

1. Respect others' privacy and protect your own. Don't share your password or personal information (your phone number, address, parents' work phone numbers, or location of your school, etc.) with anyone else without a parent's or teacher's consent.

2. Don't write to others or respond to anything that makes you uncomfortable. Tell your teacher or parents if you receive any e-mail or messages that make you feel this way.

3. Avoid hurting someone else's feelings. It is sometimes hard to tell when someone is joking in e-mail or when instant messaging. Using smileys or emoticons:) can alleviate this.

4. Always try to look good on the Internet as you would in real life. Use standard spelling and grammar so you can communicate effectively, respect others' differences, and be friendly and helpful.

Integrating Writing Within the Language Arts

As previously discussed, the language arts by nature are interrelated. There are a variety of ways to think about connections that can be made between writing and the other language arts. The links between reading and writing are very logical; each area greatly reinforces the other. When examining student writing, it is often easy to identify students who spend a lot of time with books. Whether their parents or guardians read to them often, or whether they read a great deal on their own, these students have internalized large vocabularies from their reading that is reflected in their writing. They notice the patterns of words and punctuation in their reading and transfer that knowledge to their writing. The kinds of reading material that they have been engaged in is reflected in their writing in terms of the content, the types of characters, and the structure of stories.

Examining Authors' Craft

When students learn to examine an author's craft and then learn to apply these elements in their own writing, they will have an ongoing system in place for refining their own writing. In class discussions and activities, students may be asked to explore what authors have done to create stories or informational text that they found particularly interesting. For example, a story might be scary, and the students might note that what made it creepy was that it was very suspenseful. We might ask what the author has done to create suspense and then encourage students to find specific examples of the techniques the author uses. Students will not only become more proficient at evaluating quality literature through this process, but they will develop a better sense of how to structure their own writing. Table 4.9 provides two examples of examining author's craft as a way to assist writers in incorporating these characteristics into their own writing.

Table 4.9 Examining Author's Craft

Laura Joffe Numeroff has written a number of popular circle stories about a mouse that wants one thing, but when he receives it, leads to a string of additional requests and finally culminating with the original request. What does Numeroff do to make students want to read these stories?

Author's style

How does the author create humor in her book *If You Give a Mouse a Cookie*? In just one or two lines per page, she keeps the action moving. In this circle story, the plot ends up in the same spot it started. The mouse gets a cookie and then needs a glass of milk and on and on, and results in asking for another cookie on the last page.

What about the characters?

The mouse is an engaging main character. He is active and does many humorous things. The boy willingly caters to all the wishes of the mouse. He often looks surprised but never seems to get upset by the requests.

What about the illustrations?

Felicia Bond creates illustrations that really highlight the story and keep the action moving. She does an excellent job of creating simple humor that complements the story line of the book.

Think about the highly popular Harry Potter books. What is it that J. K. Rowling does that leaves children and adults alike unable to get enough of this world of wizards?

What about the characters?

The main characters are dynamic. They change over the course of the stories because they are put in adultlike roles and are charged with completing life and death tasks. There are some imaginary characters that are cleverly created and make the plot livelier.

What about the setting?

Certainly the setting is integral to the story. Hogwarts Academy is the perfect setting for wizards to be trained and prepared to take their roles in fighting evil.

What about the plot?

The plot is very well organized. "Good" is continually confronted by "evil," whether it is from the bad students of Slithering, the multiheaded monster guarding the Sorcerer's Stone, or the evils hidden in the Chamber of Secrets. The action is always connected to a dangerous task that must be completed. Good overcomes evil, thus bringing a pleasing conclusion to the stories.

Oral Language and Media Technology

As we saw in the planning example from the teachers Paula and María, there are also logical links between oral language and media technology. Once students write something either alone or with others, opportunities can be made available for them to share their writing in a variety of formats. Presentation skills, including voice projection, eye contact, body language, and use of visuals to support presentation, can be taught in conjunction with writing. A focus on the content of presentations based on student writing pushes students to more clearly demonstrate what they have learned. Additional work in this area will lead them to develop interesting formats for introducing, developing, and concluding their presentations.

Media and technology can also be easily integrated with writing. Paula and María use digital cameras, computer-generated graphics, and PowerPoint presentations to help their students support and expand the influence of their writing. Visual representations of student writing can be very powerful. Even exploring issues such as use of white/negative space and placement of writing on the page or writing surface can help students consider the effect and significance of their work.

Listening

Another link between writing and presentation relates to developing listening skills. As students listen to their classmates present their writing, they not only gain many new ideas for extending their own learning, but they also learn to critique their classmates' writing and develop effective and courteous ways to provide constructive feedback to aid their peers in refining their writing. Shared writing requires students to listen carefully to how the class writing project is proceeding and to offer appropriate suggestions to continue the piece.

Reflection Journal 4.3

You have just read about a few ways that writing can be integrated with the other language arts. What other links come to mind as you think about making these kinds of connections? Knowing what you do about students' development and interests, what are some ideas you have for incorporating writing into your teaching at the early grade levels? At the intermediate grade levels? In middle school?

Assessing Writing

Teaching and assessing logically go hand in hand with writing when students are being taught with and use a process approach. Through the process approach, assessment of writing is done during the prewriting and writing stages as a means for assisting writers through the process. Historically, using a traditional approach, the teacher assesses students' writing only at the end after the final draft is complete. At this point, the teacher "corrects" the writing, telling students what was done wrong, typically written in red. This, however, takes ownership away from the student as a writer and places revision and editing power in the hands of the teacher, rather than putting the onus on the student. As students engage in writing while using a process approach, there are numerous opportunities for feedback and writing assistance from teachers and peers. By getting help throughout the process of creating a piece of writing, students learn to practice their skills during actual writing time, rather than after they feel they have completed their writing. Following are some appropriate methods for assessing student writing in all stages of the writing process.

Conferencing

Working with students on an individual basis as they engage in all stages of the writing process will tell a teacher what students know about writing so that they can be assisted in their areas of need. One method for doing this is through conferencing. A short 2- to 5-minute conference with students can provide them with the amount of support they need or can teach a skill that they need at that precise point in their writing piece. Conferences should be both informal and formal in nature, planned and spontaneous, and should occur as students are engaged in various stages with a piece of writing. As students are working independently on their writing, the teacher should circulate around the room among them, checking on students' progress. In informal conferring, a brief stop at students' desks to ask "How are you doing? Do you need any help?" can go a long way in providing support just when it is needed.

Formal conferencing consists of brief periods of discussion with students but may last 5 to 8 minutes. Create a location in your classroom that is set apart from the students doing independent writing so that you can have a brief but uninterrupted time for conferences. A small table, with writing resources such as dictionaries, writing manuals, paper, pens, and highlighters stored nearby, works well for this purpose.

Use the few minutes you have with students conversing about their writing pieces and spending large amounts of time listening to students. In addition to general questions to get students talking about their writing, questions that are more specific can be broached as well to allow students to use metacognition and verbalize their thinking processes as well as to provide clarification of meaning in their writing. See Table 4.10 for suggested conferencing questions and prompts that can be used during formal and informal conferences to assist writers throughout the writing process as well as provide teachers with knowledge of students' progress and writing needs.

Table 4.10 Conferring With Students During the Writing Process

Prewriting Stage Prompts	• Tell me about your piece? What are your ideas? • Who is the audience for your piece? • What could I help you with?
During Writing Stage Prompts	• What is you piece about? • Show me a part that you like in your piece. Why do you like it? Is there a part where you are stuck? • What is going to happen next? What is the next part going to be about?
Postwriting Prompts	• Have you read your piece aloud? • What parts do you like best? Why? • What writing skills have you used well? • What were the hardest parts of writing this piece? • What do you think you'll write next?

Assessment and Record-Keeping Devices

Some of the record-keeping devices that can be used by both the teacher and students during conferencing and the writing process include anecdotal records, checklists of skills, and student record keeping of what was learned. Getting students involved in self-assessment of their own writing, even at a very young age, can prove to be beneficial in helping them set goals for their writing as well as improve their skills. During formal writing conferences, after learning or reinforcing a new skill, students could add to a list they have in their writing folders titled "Things I am working on in my writing" to document their learning (Table 4.11). Another list they could be taught to use is "What I know about writing" that can be created as the teacher provides feedback about the skills that are evidenced within writing pieces that students already have in place and are using successfully (Table 4.12). These types of record-keeping devices can be helpful during the revising and editing process, as students are encouraged to look over their "What I know about writing" lists and make sure that their current piece of writing adheres to what they know and already should have in place.

Checklists

Checklists are another device that can be used by both the teacher and students and can prove to be helpful "at a glance" assessment tools. To keep track

Table 4.11

Name: Maggie O
4th Grade

Things I Am Working On in My Writing

Date	Writing Skill
Oct. 24	I need to remember to put periods at the end of all of my sentences.
Oct. 29	Don't start all of my sentences with "The."

of when and how students use a writing skill that was taught, a checklist could be developed listing class names and columns for each skill. As the skill is witnessed in students' writing, the teacher would record this and any notations in relation to how the skill was used and in what context. Table 4.13 is an example of a teacher-created checklist developed to monitor third-grade students' use of recent writing skills taught within the prior 2 weeks. The teacher wanted to determine their appropriate usage of these skills and reintroduce those that students were not using or using incorrectly. After a quick check, the teacher can pull these students together to reteach or reintroduce that skill. Students can also keep lists of skills they learned and monitor their use of them with a checklist, similar to that of the teacher. There are many commercially produced checklists to assist in monitoring and assessing students' writing development, but we also suggest adapting those or creating checklists that will be helpful for you based on your teaching and your students' needs. Checklists can be a helpful tool in that they can be used quickly and can provide an overview of how students are progressing.

Table 4.12

Name: Maggie O
4th Grade

What I Know About Writing

Date	
Sept. 12	Ideas for pieces come from my own life.
Sept. 15	Every paragraph has a topic sentence.

Reflection Journal 4.4

Using your state standards for writing as a guide, brainstorm other possible checklists a teacher could use when keeping track of students' development and progress with writing. Sketch out a sample of one of the checklists. Share your list with a group of your classmates.

Table 4.13 Teacher-Created Checklist to Monitor Student Use of Recently Taught Skills

Directions: Note date and the writing piece the skill was demonstrated.

Student Name	Using Capital Letters	Using Paragraphs	Variety in How Sentences Begin
Samantha	10/12 dog story		10/10 dog story
Jaden		10/12 favorite things	
Jayme	10/11 trip to Disney	10/11 trip to Disney	
Randolph	10/15 food poem		
Keisha	10/11 my cat story	10/11 my cat story	10/18 park story

Anecdotal Records

Anecdotal records kept by the teacher are similar to checklists in that they can provide helpful information about students' progress and development but are not as structured as checklists. Anecdotal records or notes are brief written comments that teachers make as they observe students. These notes can come during **kidwatching,** an assessment method and concept described by Yetta Goodman (1978) that includes observing students as a way to gather information about them while engaged in learning and activities. Teachers naturally partake in watching students as an informal assessment tool, but Goodman suggests that this form of assessment should be systematic and valued, as much can be learned about students. A possible time to write anecdotal records is after a writing conference with a student as the teacher jots down notes related to the focus of the conference and what transpired (see Table 4.14). Keeping track of these encounters helps to monitor student writing and focus on areas that need development, especially during writing workshop, as each student is engaged in the process at different points and levels.

Student Self-Assessment of Writing

Students reflecting on what they know about writing and setting goals for themselves as writers can be a powerful learning tool. Having students reflect, either in writing or orally throughout the writing process, is helpful to them as well as the teacher in monitoring their writing development.

Table 4.14 Anecdotal Notes About Jaden (Third Grade)

10/1	Jaden asked for advice on starting his piece on the things he likes. Helped start a brainstorming list.
10/2	Began piece about his likes, started writing about each thing on list, writing a new paragraph for each.
10/8	Gave title to piece, "Favorite Things," signed up to share in author's chair.

Another assessment tool that students can use to monitor their use of standard writing skills is through an editing checklist. Developed by the teacher and with direct teaching of its use, an editing checklist can be helpful for improving a piece of writing after it has gone through the prewriting and writing stages. Used effectively in the postwriting stage, students should be taught how to use an editing checklist efficiently to analyze their writing based on the criteria it contains. See Table 4.15 for a sample editing checklist.

The sample editing checklist that follows is not all-inclusive of the skills teachers might expect their students to develop and use. The checklist should evolve throughout the year based on the skills that have been introduced or that students already use, and as new skills are taught and modeled on how to edit, they can be added to the checklist.

Portfolio Assessment

As students engage in process writing and writing workshop, they produce many pieces of writing over time. A portfolio that includes a sampling of students'

Table 4.15 Teacher-Developed Editing Checklist

Name: _____ Date: _____

Title of Piece: _____

Reread your piece. Check off each skill after you are sure you have completed it in your writing piece.

____ I have used capital letters at the beginning of my sentences.

____ I have used correct punctuation at the end of my sentences (periods, exclamation points, question marks).

____ I have checked the spelling of the words I am unsure of.

____ I have used paragraphs.

____ I have read my writing to a partner for feedback.

writing can demonstrate the range of skills and abilities they possess as well as help teachers determine what still needs to be learned. At specified intervals, both student and teacher should lay out all of the writing that the student has done and assess the strengths and needs evidenced. Making lists based on what is observed can be helpful, such as a list of types of writing done, topics of the student's writing, skills demonstrated within the pieces, things to work on, and goals in future writing projects.

Author's Chair

Part of effective literacy learning is receiving response and feedback in relation to one's development from others such as teachers, parents, and peers (Cambourne, 1988). This is especially true with writing, as many students welcome an audience for their pieces. Using an "author's chair" is an effective way to build in this component of the writing process (Graves & Hansen, 1983). An author's chair is a designated chair (or stool or podium or rocking chair) where the student author sits and orally shares his or her writing with peers. After the reading, the peers provide feedback, making comments on what they liked, compliment the writing in general, and suggest ways to make the writing clearer. Sharing one's writing and receiving feedback is an important stage in the writing process and allows students to celebrate their success.

Holistic Writing Assessments and Writing Rubrics

Writing rubrics are scoring guides that use levels of quality to assess students' ability in writing. The descriptors of abilities for writing include assessing such things as the ideas that a piece of writing contains, the organization, the mechanics, and voice.

A popular writing rubric, called the 6+1 Traits of Writing, can be used to assess and guide student writing. It is based on determining the extent to which seven common traits of writing are incorporated into a piece of writing. Developed by the Northwest Regional Education Laboratory (NWREL), the 6+1 Traits of Writing rubric includes ideas, organization, word choice, sentence fluency, and conventions, with the "+1" being presentation. This rubric is an effective assessment tool but also helpful for students to understand how their writing can progress to more advanced levels.

When using a rubric, it is suggested that students discuss the quality of a piece of writing at each level to make the rubric a meaningful tool for students and to assist them while engaged in writing. See Chapter 8 for examples of writing rubrics that can be used to assess as well as assist in improving student writing.

There are many effective methods for assessing students' writing development. Table 4.16 suggests the variety of assessment tools that can be used during a writing workshop and other writing activities.

Table 4.16 Assessment Tools to Use During Writing Workshop

Writing Stage	Teacher-Assessment Approaches	Self- and Peer-Assessment Approaches
Assessment in the **Prewriting** Stage	• Checklists • Anecdotal records— detailing writing topics/ideas	• Self-assessments
Assessment in the **Writing** Stage	• Checklists of writing skills demonstrated	• Editing checklists
Assessment in the **Postwriting** Stage	• Portfolio assessment— collection of pieces written over time, list of pieces written • Writing rubrics—(e.g., 6+1 Traits of Writing)	• Written self-assessments for each completed piece • Author's chair— verbally sharing writing

A View From the Classroom

Earlier in this chapter you were introduced to Paula and María, sixth-grade teachers. The following is an account of their planning for assessing student writing development using standards and benchmarks as their guide.

The teachers outlined plans for how they would introduce, reinforce, and assess progress toward the standards in their next steps in planning. The Holdaway (1979) model of teaching was strongly evidenced in their teaching process. First, Paula and María would introduce each genre and ask students to speculate on its purpose and would share quality samples of writing in that particular genre. After students were able to confidently identify elements of each genre, the teachers would work with students to create a set of criteria for quality writing in the genre.

With the newly created set of criteria in hand, students would review additional writing samples and use the criteria to judge whether they were weak or strong examples. This enables students to develop a good sense of writing expectations before they are required to write their own drafts. While writing their first drafts, students keep the criteria in mind, and when the draft is complete, they use them to review their own work. They highlight areas that were well done (met the criteria) in one color and areas that were weak in another color. This would help them evaluate their work when they went back to review their writing during the editing/revising process.

María and Paula determined the minimum number of pieces they would require

(Continued)

(Continued)

students to write in each genre and how they would develop flexible grouping situations to teach students who needed additional assistance in certain areas. They also looked for ways to link each writing genre to the content areas. For example, descriptive writing would work well in completing reading and science logs, research reports would become a component of the social studies curriculum, and persuasive writing would very logically be linked to issues raised in health education.

Since the teachers had decided to link oral language and media technology standards to writing, they brainstormed effective ways to extend writing experiences to include these additional areas. For descriptive writing, the students would use digital cameras to take a series of photographs around a theme in science. They would write descriptions of the photos and take these descriptions through extensive editing and revisions to ensure that they were creating clear and concise mental images that would be highlighted by the digital photos. In a summative assessment, they would select their best description and photo combination to share with the class. Prior to the presentations, students would learn and practice effective presentation skills for this type of activity, such as voice projection, eye contact, and pacing.

In persuasive writing, students would develop a list of controversial issues that have relevance and interest for them. They would identify their position on the topics and develop a set of arguments to support their positions. The oral language area would entail position statements where students present an argument and defense on a particular topic. The media technology component would involve the selection and development of a

computer-generated graphic organizer to support the student's position. A research report accompanied by a PowerPoint presentation would link writing, oral language, and media technology for informational writing and serve as the final assessment for this genre as well.

María teaches in a fifth-grade Spanish-English bilingual classroom. In her classroom, the students write in both languages. They may be writing at or above grade level in their dominant language and well below that level in their second (or subsequent) language. With intense practice and support, María expects that many students will develop quite comparable writing skills in both English and Spanish. She plans her L-2 (Language 2 or second language) writing instruction a bit differently than her L-1 (Language 1 or first language) instruction. In addition to learning about descriptive writing in English, for example, her Spanish-dominant students are expanding their adjective vocabularies in English. Some of the adjectives will have cognates (words from different languages derived from a common original form) in Spanish (cómico and comical, for example), but many will not. Study of figurative language and the use of idioms may also become essential components to explore during the persuasive writing segment.

However, the important idea to note is that although María teaches the students about good writing and the skills and strategies good writers use in only one of the languages, it will be understood for use in both languages. Cummins (2001) has provided evidence for the concept of Common Underlying Proficiency (CUP), in which most of what students understand in one language is available to them in their other language(s) as well This notion is often represented as a pair of interlocking triangles (see Figure 4.5). The fringes represent learning that can only be expressed in one of the languages, for example, mathematical tables or religious rituals. The remainder of the figure represents common understanding regardless of language.

Paula, on the other hand, is a monolingual teacher, but many of her students are fluent speakers of Spanish. At the end of the current school year, she sets goals for her teaching for the next school year, many of them related to supporting Spanish literacy development for her bilingual students. She plans to offer opportunities for students to complete writing assignments in Spanish and will collaborate with María in evaluating their work. She also plans to stock her reading corner with more books in Spanish so that students have access in both languages.

This level of planning will provide Paula and María with a solid template for instruction throughout the year. When they are ready to add additional genres of writing, they reevaluate their students' development and design learning

experiences that will build on what they can do well. Aspects of individual and collaborative groupings with students will also need to be figured into the mix. For example, during the descriptive writing lessons, different students may struggle with writing a description that creates a mental image. Others may need help with forming sentences. Still others may not be motivated to write at all. Paula and María will determine which students need help in each of these areas and establish grouping configurations for them. They will form flexible groups that stay together only as long as they need help in a particular area. In this way, students will work with a variety of their classmates throughout the year on those skills in which they need extra instruction.

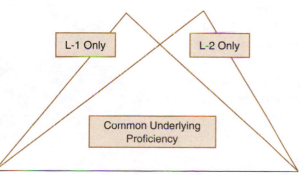

Figure 4.5   Common Underlying Proficiency: Learning in More Than One Language

Home and School Writing Connections

Many of the suggestions for reading can also be made for writing. In many classrooms, students keep logs of their work. Parents or guardians may be invited to make occasional entries in their logs about their children's work. Encouraging them to find authentic ways for students to write at home, for example, "Leave Dad a note to remind him to meet us at the soccer game tonight," "Make a list of what you'd like to get at the grocery store," "Send Grandma a thank-you note for the birthday gift she sent you." Asking students to share stories or reports they are writing with the family or posting them on the refrigerator highlights the importance of the child's effort to the family.

With older students, parents can encourage them to keep a record of their videos, video games, music CDs, and so on, creating a rating system that includes written comments. Suggest to parents that they discuss current issues with their adolescent children and encourage them to write letters to the editor (alone or as a shared family writing experience) voicing their opinions.

Suggest that parents have writing and drawing materials (such as pens, pencils, crayons, markers, various types of paper, note cards, and staplers and tape) easily accessible for their children so that they can use them to express themselves when so inclined. As with much teaching and learning, modeling all kinds of writing tasks is a powerful tool a teacher or parent can use to motivate and encourage student writing for authentic purposes.

🏠 A View From Home

Eleven-year-old Randy enjoys reading about and watching nature and animal shows on television. After watching a program on penguins, he wanted to learn more, as he was left with a few unanswered questions. Motivated, he visited the Internet and completed a brief search to find all the locations in the world where penguins live. He also wondered how many different kinds of penguins there are and what they are named.

He decided to compile his knowledge from the show with what he learned from his research and write up a "data page," as he called it, about penguins, including illustrations and charts. Upon showing his father, he suggested that Randy create a whole booklet of data pages about all the animals he has an interest in. Randy liked the idea and immediately began work on his second page related to wombats.

End-of-Chapter Reflection

- When thinking about teaching and assessing writing, what questions or clarification do you still need? With which aspects do you feel comfortable? Which aspects do you feel you need more examples?

- What goals do you need to set for yourself related to teaching and assessing writing with elementary-aged and middle school students?

Planning for Teaching

1. If you are a writer, find some of your own writing that students will enjoy (and that is appropriate) to read to them. What writing skills are represented within your writing that you could use as a model?

2. Keep the business letters that you send or receive for a period of time. Bring them to class to analyze the range of purposes for business letters. Determine if some of them would be useful examples to use in demonstrating how to write business letters. Consider having copies made of these letters for the class.

Connections With the Field

1. Visit a preschool classroom or center. Read a short but interesting story to the children and ask them to "write" something about the story for you when you finish. Bring the writing samples to class and compile them. Arrange the samples from early emergent to the highest level of writing represented. Discuss what these children understand about writing. Discuss what these samples show you about the range of writing ability for this age group.

2. Visit a classroom, preferably one where you already know the students to some degree, and make arrangements to read a short selection to the group. Select something that is interesting, funny, or surprising that the students will find captivating. Ask them to complete a writing activity based on the book. Collect the writing samples and examine them.

   a. What do the samples tell you about what these students know and can do in writing?
   b. What stages of writing are they at?
   c. How varied are the writing abilities of the class?
   d. What suggestions do you have for extending the writing abilities of this group?
   e. How do these suggestions correspond to Piaget's stages of development for the level(s) being examined?

3. Interview an ELL teacher. What languages does the teacher work with? How does the teacher teach the students to write in English? Why is it important for the students to focus on oral language development before beginning to write extensively in English?

4. Visit a bilingual classroom. Ask the teacher how he or she teaches writing in L-1 and L-2. If visiting a classroom above Grade 2, note the literacy skills of the students in both languages.

Student Study Site

The Companion Website for Developing Voice Through the Language Arts

http://www.sagepub.com/dvtlastudy

Visit the Web-based student study site to enhance your understanding of the chapter content and to discover additional resources that will take your learning one step further. You can enhance your understanding of the chapters by using the comprehensive Study Guide, which includes learning objectives, key terms, activities, practice tests, and more. You'll also find special features, such as the Links to Standards from U.S. States and associated activities, Children's Literature Selections, Reflection Exercises, Learning from Journal Articles, and PRAXIS test preparation materials.

References of Children's/Young Adult Literature

Blume, J. (1972). *Tales of a fourth grade nothing.* New York: Dutton.

Brown, M. (1979). *Arthur's eyes.* Boston: Little, Brown.

Cushman, K. (1995). *The midwife's apprentice.* New York: Harper Collins.

Dorris, M. (1992). *Morning girl.* New York: Hyperion.

Erdrich, L. (1999). *The birchbark house.* New York: Scholastic.

Lowry, L. (1989). *Number the stars.* Boston: Houghton Mifflin.

Martin, B., Jr. (1967). *Brown bear, brown bear, what do you see?* (Eric Carle, Illus.). New York: Holt.

Numeroff, L. (1985). *If you give a mouse a cookie.* New York: HarperCollins.

Rowling, J. K. (1998). *Harry Potter and the sorcerer's stone.* New York: Scholastic.

Rowling, J. K. (1999). *Harry Potter and the chamber of secrets.* New York: Scholastic.

Spinelli, J. (1996). *Crash.* New York: Knopf.

White, E. B. (1952). *Charlotte's web* (G. Williams, Illus.). New York: Harper & Row.

References of Professional Resources

Brown, D. (2003). *The Da Vinci code.* New York: Doubleday.

Cambourne, B. (1988). *The whole story: Natural literacy and the acquisition of literacy in the classroom.* New York: Ashton Scholastic.

Cox, C. (2002). *Teaching language arts: A student- and response-centered classroom* (4th ed.). Boston: Allyn & Bacon.

Cummins, J. (2001). *An introductory reader to the writings of Jim Cummins* (C. Baker & N. Hernberger, Eds.). Buffalo, NY: Multilingual Press.

Goodman, Y. (1978). Kidwatching: An alternative to testing. *National Elementary Principals Journal, 57,* 41–45.

Graves, D. H. (1983). *Writing: Teachers and children at work.* Portsmouth, NH: Heinemann.

Graves, D. H., & Hansen, J. (1983). The author's chair. *Language Arts, 60,* 176–183.

Harris, D., & Carr, J. (2001). *Succeeding with standards: Linking curriculum, assessment, and action planning.* Alexandria, VA: Association for Supervision and Curriculum Development.

Holdaway, D. (1979). *The foundations of literacy.* Portsmouth, NH: Heinemann.

International Reading Association (IRA) and National Council of Teachers of English (NCTE). (1996). *Standards for the English language arts.* Urbana, IL: NCTE; Newark, DE: IRA.

Marzano, R. (2003). *What works in schools: Translating research into action.* Alexandria, VA: Association for Supervision and Curriculum Development.

McTighe, J. (1997). What happens between assessments? *Educational Leadership, 54*(4), 6–12.

Milwaukee Public Schools. (2003). *Learning targets.* Milwaukee, WI: Author.

Murray, D. (1994). *The craft of revision.* Portsmouth, NH: Heinemann.

Piaget, J. (1977). *The development of thought: Equilibration of cognitive structures* (A. Rosin, Trans.). New York: Viking.

Routman, R. (2000). *Conversations: Strategies for teaching, learning and evaluating.* Portsmouth, NH: Heinemann.

Tierney, R. J., & Pearson, P. D. (1983). Toward a composing model of reading. *Language Arts, 60,* 568–580.

Wiggins, G., & McTighe, J. (1998). *Understanding by design.* Alexandria, VA: Association for Supervision and Curriculum Development.

Other Children's Literature Resources

Literature Models for Reflective Personal Writing

Baylor, B. (1986). *I'm in charge of celebrations* (Peter Parnall, Illus.). New York: Scribner.

Literature Models for Journal Writing and Learning Logs

Fitzhugh, L. (1964). *Harriet the spy.* Boston: Houghton Mifflin.

Krull, K. (1997). *Wish you were here: Emily's guide to the 50 states.* New York: Doubleday.

Leigh, N. (1993). *Learning to swim in Swaziland: A child's-eye view of a Southern African country.* New York: Scholastic.

Matthaei, G., & Grutman, J. (1987). *The ledgerbook of Thomas Blue Eagle.* West Palm Beach, FL: Lickle.

Literature Models for Letter Writing

Ada, A. F. (1997). *Dear Peter Rabbit* (L. Tryon, Illus.). New York: Aladdin.

Brisson, P. (1989). *Your best friend Kate* (Rick Brown, Illus.). New York: Bradbury.

Cherry, L. (1994). *Armadillo from Amarillo.* New York: Harcourt Brace.

James, E., & Barkin, C. (1993). *Sincerely yours: How to write great letters.* New York: Clarion.

Parks, R. (1996). *A dialogue with today's youth.* New York: Lee & Low.

Yevisher, A. (2002). *Dear Papa.* Cambridge, MA: Candlewick Press.

Literature Models for Autobiography and Memoir Writing

Ashabranner, B. (1990). *The times of my life: A memoir.* New York: Penguin.

Greenfield, E. (1992). *Childtimes: A three-generation memoir* (B. Pinkney, Illus.). New York: Harper Trophy.

General Writing Models

Ada, A. F. (1993). *My name is Maria Isabel.* New York: Atheneum Books.
Asher, S. (1987). *Where do you get your ideas?* New York: Walker.
Bauer, M. D. (1992). *What's your story?* New York: Clarion.
Christelow, E. (1995). *What do authors do?* New York: Clarion.

Literature About Writers

Cooney, B. (1992). *Emily* (Barbara Cooney, Illus.). New York: Doubleday.
Lester, H. (2002). *Author: A true story.* New York: Houghton Mifflin.
Nixon, J. L. (1995). *If you were a writer* (B. Degan, Illus.). New York: Aladdin.
Pulver, R. (2005). *Author day for Room 3T* (C. Richards, Illus.). New York: Clarion.
Rau, D. M. (2003). *Dr. Seuss.* New York: Childrens Press.
Whitely, O. (1994). *Only Opal: The diary of a young girl* (Barbara Cooney, Illus.). New York: Philomel.

Picture Books

Henkes, K. (1996). *Lilly's purple plastic purse.* New York: Greenwillow.
Martin, B., Jr. (1991). *Polar bear, polar bear, what do you hear?* (Eric Carle, Illus.). New York: Holt.
Myers, W. (1997). *Harlem* (Christopher Myers, Illus.). New York: Scholastic.
Numeroff, L. (1985). *If you give a mouse a cookie* (Felicia Bond, Illus). New York: HarperCollins.
Ringgold, F. (1993). *Dinner at Aunt Connie's house.* New York: Hyperion.
Say, A. (1993). *Grandfather's journey.* Boston: Houghton Mifflin.
Wise Brown, M. (1947). *Good night moon* (Clement Hurd, Illus.). New York: Harper.
Wood, A. (1996). *The napping house* (Don Wood, Illus.). Minneapolis, MN: Red Wagon.

Poetry

McKissack, P., & McKissack, F. (1995). *Redtail angels: The story of the Tuskegee airmen of World War II.* New York: Walker.
Nye, N. (Ed.). (2000). *Salting the ocean: 100 poems by young poets* (Ashley Bryan, Illus.). New York: Greenwillow.
Wise Brown, M. (1990). *The important book.* New York: HarperCollins.

Resources for Book Making in the Classroom

Bohning, G., Phillips, A., & Bryant, S. (1993). *Literature on the move: Making and using pop-ups and lift-flap books.* Englewood, CO: Teacher Idea Press.
Irvine, J. (1992). *How to make super pop-ups.* New York: Morrow Junior Books.
McCarthy, M., & Manna, P. (2000). *Making books by hand.* Gloucester, MA: Rockport Publishers.
Stowell, C. (1994). *Step-by-step: Making books.* New York: Kingfisher.

Technology Resources

See questions from some favorite young adult authors:
   http://www.ipl.org/div/kidspace/askauthor
Reference for teen writers and a place to submit their writing:
   http://teenwriting.about.com
Using Weblogs to promote literacy in the classroom:
   http://www.firstmonday.org/issues/issue9_6/huffaker/index.html
Epals, largest online community for students:
   http://www.epals.com/communityKidPub: http://www.Kidpub.org/kidpub

Language, Word Study, and the Tools of Writing

Context Setting:

After reading this chapter, you will be able to

- Describe the relationship between word study and reading
- Detail the relationship between word study and writing
- Identify a problem-solving approach to spelling and grammar
- Explain various philosophies on handwriting

Before We Begin

- What do you think is the best way for teachers to teach and students to learn spelling, grammar, and punctuation? What do your suggestions reflect about your philosophy of word study (studying words and their syntax, origin, etc.)?

What Is Word Study?

"When I come to a word that I don't know, I _____." If you would automatically fill in the blanks of this statement with "sound it out" because you had heard this many times while learning to read, your teacher probably used an approach that focused heavily on graphophonics or phonics. Sounding words out, or using phonics, becomes an end in itself in too many reading programs. There are three concerns with overemphasizing the teaching of phonics: (1) it detracts from focusing on reading to gain meaning from text or to communicate with the author; (2) readers are not relying on the other cueing systems of semantics, syntax, and pragmatics, three of the four essential systems an effective reader uses (as discussed in Chapter 3); and (3) English is not a very consistent language, and less than half of all words can be sounded out.

If the main purpose of using phonics is to help students gain meaning from text, word study and phonics instruction become somewhat tricky. How do we study "about" words and still keep them connected to meaningful text? One way to do this is to start with text and draw word study or word analysis from the text. For example, a group of first-grade children just finished reading the story about puppies featured in Table 5.1.

In this simple pattern story, there are many concepts that we might teach. We might focus on the things this playful puppy does and discuss how much fun it is to have a new puppy. We could focus on the story pattern and on the fact that only one word changes in each sentence, while the last sentence changes to end the story. We could teach the sight words *my*, *puppy*, and *can*, along with the use of picture clues or picture clues plus the first letter of each word to figure out what the puppy can do on each page. Or we might teach words that rhyme with *can*.

All of these teaching opportunities help children become better problem solvers when reading and writing. We want them to have as many tools for learning as possible at their disposal to assist them in building on what they know and

Table 5.1

My Puppy
My puppy can run.
My puppy can eat.
My puppy can play.
My puppy can jump.
My puppy can sleep.
I love my puppy.

are able to do on their own. The key is to begin with a meaningful piece of text that makes sense.

Rather than focusing on whether the child read all the words correctly when reading or spelled all the words correctly when writing, the main emphasis is placed on the question, "What is the author trying to tell me when I'm reading, and will someone be able to read what I wrote and know what I meant?" In both instances, the child needs to have well-developed word knowledge skills. Instead of merely learning to read and write words correctly, students problem solve to make reading and writing meaningful. In classrooms that are based on this belief, we repeatedly hear questions like "How did you figure that out?" "What would make sense here?" or "What could we do next?" Children learn to think about their learning (metacognition) and to evaluate their problem-solving efforts in these classrooms.

In the early childhood classroom, children learn about letters and the sounds they represent. The reciprocal nature of reading and writing can be made evident to young learners. They are guided to use what they know of writing to inform their reading and what they know of reading to inform their writing. "Children who have developed phonological awareness recognize that words rhyme, can begin or end with the same sound, and are composed of **phonemes** (sounds) that can be manipulated to create new words" (Ericson & Fraser Juliebö, 1998, p. 4). In other words, as children learn to read and write, they need to have awareness that speech and print are composed of words, words are composed of sounds, and new words can be formed by changing one or more sounds in a word.

Reflection Journal 5.1

Reflect on your experiences learning spelling, grammar, and punctuation. Was it (and is it) an easy process for you? What challenges did you have? What challenges do you still have today?

Phonemic Awareness

As you learned in Chapter 3, phonemic awareness is having an awareness of letter sounds and the ability to blend sounds together (What sounds do you hear in /cat/?) or take them apart (If you put the sounds /k//a//t/ together, what word would you have?). Therefore, teaching and assessment of phonemic awareness is done orally. Table 5.2 provides a sample of the types of items used to measure phonemic awareness on emergent reading screening instruments (Milwaukee Public Schools, 2000).

Table 5.2   Measures of Phonemic Awareness

Early Emergent Level

1. **Word Awareness**

   The child listens to a sentence, repeats the sentence, and indicates the number of words.

   I ride my bike.   (4)

2. **Rhyme Awareness**

   The child listens to pairs of words and indicates whether or not they rhyme
   me   car   (no)
   hat   sat   (yes)

3. **Initial Sounds**

   The child listens to a word and indicates the initial sound.
   bike   (b)

Upper Emergent Level

4. **Final Sounds**

   The child listens to a word and indicates the final sound.
   car   (r)

5. **Onset/Rime**

   The child listens to a pair of words and indicates the sound that is the same in both words.
   hand   stand   (and)

6. **Blending Phonemes**

   The child listens to a string of letters
   and blends them together to form a word.
   /r/   /u/   /n/   (run)

7. **Segmenting Phonemes**

   The child listens to a word and identifies the sounds in the word.
   bike   (/b/ /?/ /k/)

SOURCE: Milwaukee Public Schools (2000).

Children need to develop this conceptualization of sounds in words and words in sentences as they begin to read and write. In reading, they will use this understanding to blend sounds together (blending phonemes) as they learn to analyze new words. In writing, segmenting phonemes will be very important as they say words to themselves and attempt to write what they hear. Some experts (Allington, 1997; Goodman, Shannon, Goodman, & Rapaport, 2004; Routman, 2000) claim that 85% of children develop phonemic awareness without special instruction, and they question the efficacy of spending large amounts of time teaching and testing phonemic awareness directly. However, federal grants linked to NCLB (Reading First, 2001) have emphasized more direct teaching and assessment of phonemic awareness. Some researchers criticize organized instruction of phonemic awareness, and after an extensive review of research on this topic,

Table 5.3

Concept	Activities
Rhyme	Songs, nursery rhymes, poems
Alliteration	Riddles, guessing games
Initial/final sounds	Letter and object matches, picture sorts
Segmenting phonemes	Shared writing, journal writing, songs Ex: "B-I-N-G-O

Krashen (2004) concluded that phonemic awareness occurred as the result of knowing how to read but was not the cause of it.

Whether referred to as phonemic awareness or not, most kindergarten and Grade 1 teachers provide very rich instruction in this area as part of a precursor to developing reading and language arts ability. "It has been my experience that children easily develop phonemic awareness in literacy-rich environments through experimenting with and enjoying rhymes, poems, chants, and songs, and through such activities as 'clapping' syllables, exposure to alliteration, frequent repetition of classmates' names, and regular talk about words" (Routman, 2000, p. 101). Table 5.3 outlines some interactive learning experiences for developing phonemic awareness (Bear, Invernizzi, Templeton, & Johnston, 2003).

An effective means to evaluate what students understand about phonemic awareness is to examine their writing. They can only write what they understand about sound and spelling patterns. For example, if only the first letter of each word is present in a child's writing, we know that the child has developed an understanding of initial sounds in words and has not yet mastered medial sounds. This might be reflected in a student writing "wwtm" to stand for "We went to McDonald's." Another student who writes "I LV MY GMR" for "I love my grandmother" demonstrates an understanding of initial, medial, and final consonants.

Word-Solving Skills:
What Do You Notice?

Phonemic awareness, as we've seen, relates only to oral understanding of how sounds and words function in spoken language. How print and sounds interact is referred to as graphophonics (grapho = written, phonics = sound), often called phonics. Graphophonics relates to more than just the individual sounds represented by letters. It also provides the reader with important details concerning word identification and meaning. The child may "provide phonological identities for letters, digraphs, clusters, syllables, prefixes and suffixes, root words, phrases, and nonlanguage strings" (Clay, 1993, p. 290).

Graphophonics is one of the cueing systems (syntax, semantics, graphophonics, and pragmatics or prior knowledge) discussed earlier in Chapter 3. It is an important cueing system that readers use to facilitate gaining meaning from print. Failing to teach children how to use graphophonics deprives them of an important resource in reading effectively and efficiently. An overemphasis on teaching phonics or the exclusive use of graphophonics in isolation can be just as harmful. Reading programs that place a heavy emphasis on phonics instruction and promote the use of reading materials that primarily reinforce word patterns, rather than meaningful content, are more likely to produce readers who recognize a high percentage of words but may have poor comprehension of what they read. This phenomenon highlights the fact that good readers do not rely on a single cueing system as they read. Instead, when they encounter difficulty while reading, they automatically think about (a) what would make sense here?—semantics, (b) what type of word (noun, verb, etc.) should be used here?—syntax, (c) what do I know about this topic that could help me here?—pragmatics, and (d) what letter/sound relationships and clues can I use to help me put this all together?—graphophonics. This process happens in a fraction of a second and is done automatically by good readers. We need to teach graphophonics but also need to keep its usefulness linked to the other cueing systems to help children take maximum meaning from print.

Emergent readers generally begin learning letter names and sounds before they enter school, and most children know them well by the middle of Grade 1. There are many games, activities, and songs available for teaching letters and sounds, but it is important to link all word analysis and word study activities to use in actual reading and writing. For example, if the letter *B* and the /b/ sound are being learned, select poems and short books that naturally feature words that begin with *B*. After the story or poem has been read and enjoyed, ask students to find and frame *B* words. Later, some of the simpler words could be written on cards and used to develop sight word vocabularies.

If we begin asking children "What do you notice?" in relation to what they've read or noted in print, we guide them to develop good observational and analytical skills. These skills may focus not only on word study areas but also on meaning and literary elements. Many emergent-level teachers make good use of children's names while they are solidifying letter/sound recognition skills. With the students wearing name tags, the teacher might ask, "Whose name begins with *B*?" The children identify Beto and Bonnie. But when asked "Do you notice anything else?" one student notes that "Roberto" has *B* in his name but it is in the middle. Another student notices that the same is true of Abdul's name, and a third states that if the *B* is at the beginning of a name, it is an uppercase *B*, and if it is in the middle of a name, it is a lowercase *b*. The students continue the conversation after the teacher finishes a reading of *Bread, Bread, Bread* (Morris, 1989), which supplies additional opportunities to reinforce the letter *B* and the /b/ sound.

Alphabet Books

During this phase, children may be exposed to numerous alphabet books, and they may make their own. Alphabet books may be developed in relation to a theme under study in the classroom. For example, family is often the theme for social studies in Grade 1. A family big book may be compiled by the class, beginning with "A is for Aunt, B is for Brother, C is for Cousin" and so on, with pictures from home of family members. Table 5.4 provides a listing of some alphabet books that are available for emergent readers. Older students in exploring a certain topic may also make alphabet books, for example, fifth-grade teacher Lori had her students do a Civil War alphabet book as a culminating activity.

Table 5.4   Alphabet Books for Emergent Readers

Graeme Base	*Animalia*
Jane Bayer	*A, My Name is Alice*
C. L. Demarest	*Firefighters A to Z*
Lois Ehlert	*Eating the Alphabet*
Tana Hoban	*A, B See!*
Bert Kitchen	*Animal Alphabet*
Arnold Lobel	*On Market Street*
Bill Martin Jr. and	*Chicka, Chicka, Boom, Boom*
John Archambault	
L. Rankin	*The Handmade Alphabet*
Maurice Sendak	*Alligators All Around*
G. Shannon	*Tomorrow's Alphabet*
Chris Van Allsburg	*The Z Was Zapped*

A View From Home

Shelby, a 5-year-old kindergarten student, became enamored with the alphabet as she learned about the letters and the sounds they made. Her teacher made available and encouraged her students to read a wide range of alphabet books on a variety of topics. Over the weekend at home, Shelby used her crayons and paper to make her own alphabet book about the things that she likes, and included, for example, "A for animals, B for Baby Marissa [her doll], I for ice cream (bubble gum flavor), and S for swimming." Her mother helped her to spell the words and supplied some photos of objects she included in her book such as her dog Ziggy (Z) to accompany the hand-drawn illustrations she drew for her text.

Literacy Centers

A number of interactive center or activity ideas can also be used to reinforce letter recognition and sounds. Supplying students with sponge letters and containers of objects, for example, having them sort the objects and place them under the correct initial letters, provides a kinesthetic approach to learning. Being able to physically manipulate the materials helps many children make links between the object, the initial consonant, and the initial sound of the object's name. The same could be done with picture cards or magnetic letters and cookie sheets to sort letters and objects. Links can also be made between strategies students are learning in literacy-related activities and other content areas. For example, they can sort initial sounds in word study and sort living and nonliving objects in science.

Word Sorts

Word and picture sorts are often used to practice word patterns. The sorts are conducted using word cards with which children are already quite familiar. There are two general types of **word sorts.** The first type is a "closed sort," in which word cards are sorted into a predetermined category. For example, "Show me all the cards that rhyme with the word *hen.*" All of the word cards may be placed in a row, and the children may read the resulting list of rhyming words.

An "open sort" allows one person to make a display of several cards that all have something in common (*jump, run, hop, walk*). The other participants try to guess the common underlying organizer (all are ways to move). Both types of sorts can be used in small group and large group settings and provide opportunities for students to hone problem-solving skills while reinforcing recognition of words and patterns. Some common types of sorts include rhyming words, double vowel patterns, nouns, verbs, adjectives, adverbs, concepts (such as colors, people, animals, mammal/nonmammal), and words with a specified number of syllables.

Table 5.5 provides a list of suggested graphophonics skills that might be taught at various reading levels. It is important to determine the skills that students already possess and can use confidently, rather than assuming that students are all at the same level. It would not be a good use of a student's time to spend several months studying the letters of the alphabet when the child already knew them before the school year began.

Integrated Word Study

It is easy to assume that because some children are very far behind their peers (struggling learners or English language learners, ELLs), heavy doses of skills practice (often referred to as "drill and kill" in this context) will provide these students with the background they lack and enable them to quickly catch up to their peers. Not surprisingly, the opposite generally occurs. Students concentrate on completing more skill activities, which results in less time for actual reading of meaningful text. They study skills in isolation but are not given the opportunity

Table 5.5   Possible Word Study Themes

Emergent Readers Concept	Teaching/Practice Ideas
Letters of the alphabet	Making words
Consonant sounds	Letter-picture sorts
Vowel sounds	Rhyming words
Onset & rime—Level 1	Links to books, poems, songs
	Word wall
	Letter/sound games/software

Transitional Readers	
Onset & rime—Level 2	Making words
Spelling patterns—vowels	Word games/word sorts/software
Endings—*s, ed, ing*	Shared writing
Plurals	Phonics wheels
R-controlled words	Links to books, poems, songs
Making spelling pattern rules	Wall charts featuring word patterns
Blends	Word wall
Homophones	Relate to writing
Root words	

Early Readers	
Affixes	Links to print
Syllables	Wall charts, featuring word patterns, rules
Synonyms/antonyms	Relate to writing
Content area words	Software use
Contractions	
Digraphs/diphthongs	

Fluent Readers	
Word meaning	Links to print
Latin/Greek roots	Dictionary activities
Affixes	Relate to writing
Content area vocabulary	Software use

to see how these relate to actual reading. Furthermore, they learn about fewer books and stories in which they might become interested. It is difficult to become enthusiastic about learning to read when it only involves paper or electronic drill without the enjoyment of being exposed to quality literature.

Instead, it would be more beneficial to surround all students with quality reading materials that match their interests and reading level. Rich discussions and opportunities to respond to reading also fire students' desire to interact with text. Allowing students to listen to tape recorded versions of a story they are interested in (listening comprehension level), but may struggle to read independently will permit them to join their peers in discussing literature. Along with this immersion in quality literature, a teacher may focus on teaching the most essential skills students need assistance with and continually guide them in applying these skills to text.

Activities dealing with the use of patterns are especially prevalent in prekindergarten through Grade 1 but certainly could extend to all grades. In mathematics, children replicate and create object, color, and number patterns. In science, they sort and classify by identified properties or characteristics. In social studies, they note patterns in how families go about their days. This concept can certainly be extended to literacy development, especially in relation to word study.

Use of onset and rime (word families) is a very effective starting point for word study with emergent readers. They can learn a word (*cat*) whose rime (*at*) can be used to form many new words; students quickly expand the number of words (*bat, fat, hat, mat, Nat, pat, rat, sat*) they are able to recognize just by changing the onset. Linking these words to poems or stories to be read and reread many times by students provides them with the multiple practice opportunities necessary to begin internalizing sets of rhyming words. Shared and independent writing activities are appropriate avenues to use in guiding students to apply rhyming patterns they have learned to their own writing. "You want to write the word /bat/ here. *Bat* is one of our /at/ words. Can you remember how we write that? You can look at our list of /at/ words on the chart to help you."

In shared writing, the teacher or one of the students writes what the students dictate. The teacher may ask the students to spell along as he or she writes the message; patterns that have been studied already can be highlighted as the writing develops. If the teacher does this frequently during the day—"Spell the word *Dear* along with me for the beginning of our letter"—they are learning about and practicing spelling and phonics throughout the day.

The goal of all graphophonics instruction is for the decodable patterns to be recognized quickly and added to the child's sight word vocabulary. **Sight words** are recognized automatically and do not require word analysis. The less short-term memory that must be devoted to word analysis leaves more available for concentration on understanding and enjoying what was read; therefore it is desirable for children to develop a large repertoire of sight words.

Making Words

Making Words© (Clay, 1993) is an effective activity for guiding students to explore patterns in word formation. A set of letter cards needed for the day's word study is prepared for each child. Each card has an uppercase letter on one side and its lowercase counterpart on the other. The letter cards may be used to reinforce onset and rime patterns, for example, /at/ words. In this case, each student would have the following set of letters: *a, t, b, c, f, h, m, p, s*. Or they may receive the letters *s, t, a, n, d*. In the latter case, they would be asked to use the letter cards to spell the following words: *a, at, an, tan, Dan, Nat, sand*, and *Stan*. The children use all of the letters in forming the final word, *stand*. Manipulating the letter cards is a kinesthetic activity that allows students to physically explore word patterns. If students have difficulty spelling the word, they are encouraged to do as much on their own as they can and then look at their neighbors' work for additional help. Often the teacher has a chart to display the finished words and provide another source for students to use in checking their own work. Students spell the words together and individually, clap out the number of word parts, and divide the word into syllables.

At the transitional level, students are generally quite comfortable with basic word patterns, and they can use a word study booklet instead of letter cards. At this point the students would draw a dash to represent the number of letters in a specific word. A teacher saying, for example, "Our first word has four letters. Draw four dashes on your first line and write the word *same*. 'Your name is the *same* as mine.' We are using the 'e-marker rule' in this word. When a word ends with a silent *e*, the preceding vowel is long or 'says its name.'" Additional e-marker words might also be used in this lesson (*game, take, late, ride, nine, woke*) to further reinforce the concept. The same set of words is used for a number of days in a row until the children can readily form the words. Links between using e-marker words in reading and writing are then reinforced. Children point out when they find e-marker words in their reading and note how they decoded them. The teacher may point out when children misspell these words in their writing and guide them in making corrections.

Table 5.6 contains the 37 most basic rimes in English (Routman, 2000). It is important to make certain that students know how to use these patterns in their reading, but it is not advisable to spend large amounts of time on each separate rime. Once students know a few rimes, they often quickly acquire other similar patterns.

Table 5.6 The 37 Most Basic Rimes in English

ack	ank	eat	ill	ock	ump
ail	ap	ell	in	oke	unk
ain	ask	est	ine	op	
ake	at	ice	ing	ore	
ale	ate	ick	ink	ot	
ame	aw	ide	ip	uck	
an	ay	ight	it	ug	

Word Analysis

By the end of Grade 2, the majority of the general phonics patterns are automatic for most students, and attention moves to focusing more on word analysis in relation to meaning. In the transitional stage, students work with more complex onset and rime patterns. They also learn more about blends (*st, br, sl*, for example), root words (*eating = eat + ing*), simple word endings and plurals (*s, ed, ing*), and simple syllabication rules. More irregular spelling patterns and previously studied patterns in need of review might be included in Grades 3–4. Grades 5–8 focus most fully on word meaning, including exploration of word derivations. Study of affixes (prefixes and suffixes) becomes more predominant in relation to determining word meaning. See Table 5.7 for a list of commonly used affixes (prefixes and suffixes).

Table 5.7 Commonly Used Affixes

Prefix	Meaning	Example	Suffix	Meaning	Example
anti-	against	antihero	-able	capable of	comfortable
bi-	two, twice	biannual	-ful	full of	wonderful
circum-	around	circumference	-graph	writing	biography
ex-	out, from	exhaust	-ism	action/practice	feminism
in-	not	inconsistent	-less	without	worthless
inter-	between	interface	-logy	study of	biology
quad-	four	quadrangle	-ment	state/quality	agreement
pre-	before	pregame	-ness	state/quality	forgetfulness
re-	again	renew	-ous	full of	studious
sub-	under	submarine	-sion/tion	state/quality	suspension
un-	not	unable			

At each level it is important to select word study areas that students need and to continually relate word study to actual reading. Intermediate and advanced students focus on more complex vowel/consonant patterns, such as (a) consonant digraphs, where two consonants combine to form a new sound (*ch, th, sh*), (b) vowel digraphs (two vowels represent a single sound, as in *rain*), (c) vowel diphthongs, such as *oi* in *coin, oy* in *boy* (the sound of the first vowel glides into the second), (d) more complex plural formations, and (e) syllabication rules. As at other levels, students explore relationships between word parts and meaning through word study activities. They internalize these skills most fully when asked to relate what they have studied to their reading and writing. Older students extend their vocabularies through an understanding of affixes, as well as relating known words to synonyms and antonyms. Teachers may systematically study particular affixes as they appear in reading material and point these out to students. Word study book-lets, where students record their study of word parts and word meaning, are help-ful. They might record words they encounter in their readings that reflect affixes, synonyms, antonyms, homographs, and such, including the sentence where it is found. The booklets may also include areas of study that need review by the student, for example, determining when to double the last consonant before adding an ending.

Reflection Journal 5.2

Many times our preservice teachers provide interesting glimpses into the kinds of experiences they had as part of their own literacy development. Sometimes they even bring a tattered writing workshop folder from the fifth grade or favorite novels they wouldn't dream of parting with—even at age 20. Unfortunately, we never hear these kinds of responses when a study of teaching grammar is next on the syllabus. Why do you think that is true? Do you think we could make learning grammar less painful, maybe even fun? What are your experiences and thoughts about grammar?

Grammar

"Children intuitively learn the structure of the English language—its grammar, as they learn to talk. . . . They have almost completed [this understanding] by the time they enter kindergarten. The purpose of grammar instruction, then, is to make this intuitive knowledge about the English language explicit and to provide labels for words within sentences, parts of sentences, and types of sentences" (Tompkins, 2005, p. 568).

A problem-solving approach to learning grammar is a way to make it more useful and interesting for students, studying grammar to improve communication with one another. What students seem to object to most is the completion of page after page of workbook drill of grammar concepts. Often there is insufficient transfer of this knowledge to the students' writing because it is not relevant to what they are writing or issues they face in their writing. Students who understand how language is structured are able to manipulate it more effectively in making meaning clear. Languages have sets of rules for standard usage. Children may speak a dialect of English or use regional variations of Standard English, and these are acceptable methods of expression with regular patterns of usage. However, we do children a very big disservice if we do not make certain they are able to use Standard English as well (Delpit, 1995). Students should not be excluded from later educational or job opportunities because they are not well versed in the formal use of English. There will be many instances when each of us will be judged by how well we express ourselves, and our students need to understand this.

There are four general areas that are generally associated with the study of grammar: parts of speech, capitalization and punctuation, sentence structure, and types of sentences. Instructing children in these areas as they become essential for improving their speaking and writing skills provides them with an authentic purpose for learning grammar concepts. For example, if students are writing strings of short, choppy sentences, it may indicate that they are ready for instruction in combining sentences to form one sentence that is smoother and more interesting to listen to or read.

Assessing student speaking and writing is a beneficial way to determine instructional areas to focus on in grammar. If there are many areas that need attention, the teacher will need to prioritize and select a specific area to begin with. As students gain expertise in the first area, a new one may be added, and so on. Some comprehensive language arts and/or grammar series have been published, such as *Write Away* (Kemper, Nathan, Sebranck, & Elsholz, 1994), and teaching children to use these texts as resources to support speaking and writing may serve a better purpose than completing endless drill exercises in traditional grammar texts. Grammar can be taught and reinforced all day long in any content area class. Like spelling, grammar concepts that have already been taught can be reinforced in shared writing or reading and individual conferencing with students.

To ignore grammar issues with ELLs would be a mistake. Without specific instruction, some students do not move to full fluency in English (Wong-Fillmore, 1985). However, this is often a delicate line to walk for teachers. Over time, ELLs learn a great deal of English merely by being immersed in the language. Overemphasis on grammar forces students' attention on the form of language rather than the use of language to communicate effectively. Selecting one area at a time needing particular attention, and teaching and practicing this concept to mastery, is more effective than marking all errors on a student's writing.

Parts of Speech

The parts of speech is one area of grammar study that is relatively easy to teach and helps students learn how language is organized. Even the youngest of students can learn to identify nouns and verbs and the jobs they do in a sentence. Poetry can work well for teaching and learning parts of speech because it uses language so succinctly. Teachers may search for poems that emphasize nouns, verbs, adjectives, or adverbs. Students will enjoy the poems first and learn about the parts of speech a bit later. The rhythm, cadence, and/or lyrics of the poems may help students make links between specific poems and parts of speech. For example, in studying prepositions, poems might be used in which each line begins with a preposition, as in Table 5.8. Similarly, poems highlighting adverbs may lead students to note that most words that end in *ly* are adverbs. In other scenarios,

Table 5.8   Preposition Poem

In the dark

Down the street

With his brother

They sneak

Across the yard

Up the porch and

Into the house

Without getting caught

Out too late

By their mother

having poems on overheads and asking children to circle or highlight specific parts of speech may be effective ways to develop understanding of specific parts of speech. Students may also create charts or big/little books to document parts of speech. Other parts of speech minilessons might include sharing children's books that address specific parts of speech, and for younger children movement activities that dramatize verb action or impersonate nouns can be helpful.

An efficient way to practice parts of speech is to have students relate them to their own reading and writing. Asking students to circle all the verbs they used in a piece of writing and evaluate how descriptive they are will help them make their writing more interesting and precise. In preceding minilessons, the teacher could have highlighted the colorful use of verbs by certain authors or poets or asked the students to brainstorm more descriptive words for common verbs such as *said* or *went*. Students then complete independent work to either evaluate an author's use of parts of speech or focus on them in their own writing. With these types of activities, it would be logical to introduce the use of the thesaurus and have students consult them in their own writing. These activities link grammar and vocabulary as students explore the use of different parts of speech. At this point, students may try their hand at writing their own poetry, using the poetry studied as samples. Sharing sessions that focus on discussions of how, for example, descriptive verbs and adjectives were used to create more vivid images helps students explore parts of speech more fully. In these sessions, students demonstrate how well they are able to identify parts of speech and describe their functions in sentences.

Numerous games can be developed for students to identify, sort, and use parts of speech. Software is also available for the same purposes. Care must be taken to evaluate these materials to make sure they teach valuable skills and are related back to their use in reading and writing.

Table 5.9   The Importance of Capitalization and Punctuation

Which message is easier to read?

1. how important is capitalization and punctuation in writing do we really need to teach it it would save a lot of time if we could just skip it

2. How important are capitalization and punctuation in writing? Do we really need to teach it? It would save a lot of time if we could just skip it!

Capitalization and Punctuation

Use of capitalization and punctuation to enhance writing and appropriately interpret text is another area of grammar that students need to gain experience using. Table 5.9 highlights the importance of punctuation and capitalization in clearly communicating ideas.

Minilessons on capitalization may focus on beginning sentences with capital letters and capitalizing proper nouns. Punctuation may begin simply with an emphasis on using periods, question marks, and exclamation points appropriately. As students write, they are encouraged to capitalize the first word of each sentence and to use proper punctuation at the end of the sentence. As teachers circulate about the room while students are writing, they may offer individual guidance with these concepts. Self, peer, and teacher assessment and editing provide students with additional opportunities to solidify these skills. Providing students with rubrics for completing and revising writing provides guidelines for their work.

Many schools emphasize the use of daily language drills as a way to improve the correct use of spelling and grammar. In this type of activity, one or more sentences containing errors are written on the board or overhead transparency, especially in an area that is being studied in language arts. Students rewrite the sentences on their papers correctly. This is followed by a class discussion of the errors, with a student or the teacher making corrections on the board. Although these drills are widely used, teachers are often frustrated that these exercises do not transfer to student writing. Requiring students to correct errors in their own writing may be much more effective in helping them to internalize spelling and punctuation patterns.

Lessons for more advanced writers may include a review of the use of commas and minilesson demonstrations on when or how to use semicolons and colons. These concepts might be highlighted in texts the students are reading, along with explanations about how these areas of punctuation clarify meaning. When students begin writing more complex sentences, a need to use these structures will become apparent. As often can be the case in literacy development, the students' emerging skills will guide us in knowing what to teach. Either teaching what they already know or expecting them to master concepts they are not ready for does little to promote student learning. Instead, it will be important to look at what they manage easily and determine how best to move to the next step.

Sentence Structure

Sentence structure, as its name implies, focuses on how written communication is organized at the sentence level. A beginning level of sentence structure instruction may be designed to explore how sentences can be divided into subjects and predicates. In this way it becomes clear who the actors are and the actions they are involved in. Identifying subject and predicate helps readers interpret authors' ideas and helps writers clarify their own message.

Again the question becomes not merely can the children identify subjects and predicates correctly, but can they use this in their own reading and writing as a strategy to tease out and create meaning. It is meaningful to use the children's own reading and writing to teach this concept. However, it is important to use simple sentences initially because many sentences from children's and young adult literature are complex and have many clauses, prepositional phrases, and complex structures that may confuse students. Take, for example, this sentence from *Three Monks, No Water* by Ting-Xing Ye (1997). "Once upon a time, there was a mountain; on the mountain, there stood a temple; and in that temple, all alone, lived a young monk" (p. 1). The sentence takes many twists and turns and would require a teacher to do a lot of explaining as a grammar study. Sentences of this intricacy, however, may be appropriate for students studying complex sentences and punctuation. Sentences like "We can't find our cat" or "Mommy and Daddy bought a new car" are more manageable for the beginning study of subjects and predicates.

Table 5.10 highlights identification of subjects and predicates in sentences from the book *First Day in Grapes* by L. King Pérez (2002).

Minilessons that teach subjects and predicates and what they are and why it is important to be able to identify them can be followed by opportunities for students to practice identifying them on their own. In cases like this, perhaps a worksheet or two would be acceptable merely for students to learn the concept. Teachers may also use examples of student writing (from previous years) and teach students how

Table 5.10   Subjects and Predicates

Chico // never could decide if California reminded him of a fruit basket or a pizza.
Subject   **predicate**

His family // traveled from one migrant camp to another, picking fruits and vegetables.
Subject   **predicate**

They // had arrived at a camp in grapes last night.
Subject   **predicate**

to identify clearly written versus ambiguous sentences. Students could be given opportunities to make suggestions for clarifying the ambiguous sentences. For example, a child's sentence written as "Not find the cat" could be clarified to read "We can't find our cat." The change clarifies who can't find the cat and the cat's owner. Chart stories or overheads used for other purposes may also be analyzed to practice identifying subjects and predicates in sentences. Encouraging students to approach the study of grammar as detectives out to investigate how language is put together may help foster positive attitudes about grammar.

Once students understand subjects and predicates, a logical next step would be to move on to other structures within sentences. For example, prepositional phrases clarify the predicate more fully and provide information for making meaning and comprehension. Earlier examples, from *First Day in Grapes* (Pérez, 2002), highlighted the following sentences: "His family traveled *from one migrant camp to another,* picking fruits and vegetables" and "They had arrived *at a camp in grapes* last night." Each prepositional phrase provides more information about the verbs *traveled* and *arrived.* Since there are many prepositions, students should have access to a list of them that may be kept in their word study booklets or displayed on a chart in the classroom. Minilessons can be designed to teach the use and structure of prepositional phrases as well as games and learning activities used to reinforce their identification. As a final phase, students should look at the use of prepositional phrases in their own writing and self-assess how well they clarify the intended message.

Dependent and independent clauses are intended to clarify meaning but can be confusing for students. Guiding students in separating clauses from subject and predicate may be another strategy they can use in gaining meaning from print. Clauses are also evident in the sample sentences. "His family traveled from one migrant camp to another, *picking fruits and vegetables.*" And "Chico never could decide *if California reminded him of a fruit basket or a pizza.*" "[P]icking fruits and vegetables" further clarifies the work done at migrant camps and lets the reader know a bit more about what to expect in this story. This phrase would be an incomplete sentence on its own and therefore is classified as a dependent clause.

A clause within a sentence that could stand on its own as a separate sentence (e.g., has a subject and predicate) is called an independent clause. The sentence from the text *Three Monks, No Water* (Ye, 1997) contains two independent clauses. Punctuation is crucial in setting dependent and independent clauses apart from the rest of the sentence and presents a good opportunity to link grammar and punctuation. Minilessons that highlight how dependent and independent clauses are used in children's and young adult literature may be followed by opportunities to create such clauses in students' own writing.

Sentence Types

An examination of sentence types leads children to recognize that there are simple sentences, "Our cat is lost," and complex sentences, "We called our friends to come and help us because our cat is lost." One way to study sentence types is from the perspective of asking what makes writing interesting. Does it sound better to say "My grandmother came to visit. My grandfather came with her. My cousins are coming to visit tomorrow" or "My grandparents came to visit today and my cousins are coming tomorrow"?

Children's writing often resembles the former example early in their writing development. Exploring the writing of favorite authors can help them determine what they as writers might do to hold a reader's interest. Many factors influence good writing, such as creative plots, descriptive language, and interesting characters, but certainly another aspect involves the flow and rhythm of the language. Varied use of simple and complex sentences is part of what creates that language cadence.

There are numerous aspects of grammar that might be studied. Some will be important to your students' reading and writing development, and they will emerge as areas in which students need to gain expertise. These are areas that should definitely be taught. Other areas, especially those covered in students' grammar or language arts texts, are often too complex for students and do not enhance their literacy development; these areas could be safely eliminated from study.

As suggested, grammar can be made instructional and interesting for students if we make it relevant and select interesting learning experiences. A workshop approach may be a good format to use in teaching grammar concepts through minilessons, providing opportunities for practice and linking assessment to application of grammar to improve writing and reading.

Spelling

Reflection Journal 5.3

From what you remember, how did you learn to spell? Are you a good speller? What helped you become a good speller? Do you struggle with spelling? What would have helped you become a better speller? Write about your own feelings and experiences related to spelling.

Approaches to Teaching and Learning Spelling

The purpose of spelling correctly is to make writing more comprehensible to readers. Schools have different philosophies about how to help students become competent spellers. One philosophy is linked to the basal approach to reading, as described in Chapter 3. In this approach, each student has a spelling workbook or "speller" that features weekly lists of words and activities designed to provide practice in learning to spell these words correctly. Word lists are prioritized and begin with the simplest words and word patterns, for example, *the, can, pan, cat,* and *hat,* and continue with increasingly complex lists of words across each grade level.

The teaching format for spelling is quite standard and may sound familiar to you if you learned to spell using this approach. Each set of words is generally taught on a 5-day cycle, beginning with a pretest on Monday, word practice activities on Tuesday through Thursday, and culminating with a posttest on Friday. Word practice activities often consist of completing workbook pages, writing each word several times, defining words, and putting words in alphabetical order.

The basal method of teaching spelling is attractive to schools that believe learning to read and write involves mastery of a hierarchy of reading and writing skills. It is manageable and ensures that students receive an organized focus on spelling. However, there are drawbacks to teaching spelling in this fashion. For starters, what of the students who receive 100% on the pretest and another grade of 100% on the posttest? How has their spelling ability been extended or challenged if they could already spell the words correctly on Monday? Have we met the needs of those students? What of a student who receives a grade of 30% on Monday and 40% on Friday? We are asking him or her to work at the frustration level every week. How have we met those students' needs? Obviously, we could vary the word lists for each of our students or groups of students, and this would represent an improvement. However, there is another concern with this approach. Teachers frequently report that they do not see sufficient transfer from the spelling units to the students' independent writing. In essence, students learn the words to perform well on the test but do not transfer that learning into spelling those words correctly in their own writing.

Sharon Schmerhorn developed a response to the traditional spelling program that worked well for many of her students.

A View From the Classroom

Sharon Schmerhorn's Spelling Class

Javier did well in school and enjoyed everything except spelling. Each week his fourth-grade class received a list of 15 words to study. His heart would sink during the pretests, when he knew he'd misspelled most of the words. All week long he studied the words at school and then practiced with his mom at night. By Friday, he could remember how to spell a few of the words, but he got so nervous during the posttest that he mixed up many of those words too.

When Javier went to the fifth grade, he was lucky enough to have Sharon as his teacher. Sharon recognized that each student had reached a unique level in his or her spelling development, and she devised an individualized spelling program that enabled each student to work at his or her instructional level. Now Javier selects 10 words from his own writing that he has trouble spelling correctly. He knows that Sharon will help him if he's not sure which ones to select. She also adds a few words for the whole class. These words include the name of the month, four or five content area vocabulary words, and two or three words related to special upcoming events. Javier feels more comfortable with the new spelling program and is learning to spell words correctly that he had been struggling with for a long time. For example, he had spelled *they* as *thay* since second grade.

Javier has a partner that he works with for 20 minutes each day. They have a list of games and activities they can use to practice their words together. They like to play "word scramble" and "guess my word and write it." On Friday, Javier and his partner give each other a spelling test and correct the results. Each word that is spelled correctly comes off the list. Words that are not spelled correctly stay on the list until they are mastered. Because

Javier has only a few difficult words to learn each week, he doesn't feel overwhelmed by spelling class. He and his partner often come up with mnemonic devices or word chunks to help them spell the more challenging words. All of the students keep a log of their spelling activities along with their spelling tests, enabling Sharon to monitor their progress. Parents and students may also review progress in the transfer of spelling words to everyday writing.

In other classrooms, teachers do not approach spelling as a separate subject but integrate spelling with the teaching of writing. They use word study sessions in lieu of traditional spelling programs (Fountas & Pinnell, 1996, 2001). The activities mentioned earlier (Making Words, word sorts, onset and rime, word wall, and spelling rules) take place during the language/word study portion of the reading block. There are several advantages to using this approach to teaching children to improve their spelling ability. First, the content of the word/language study matches the instructional level of the students. A commercial program presents a "one size fits all" sequence of spelling development that may not be consistent with the needs of students. In the language/word study approach, teachers analyze student writing as one source in developing word and language study units. They also select words and patterns that relate directly to the learning experiences of the students. Second, a word study approach to spelling encourages students to explore word patterns and word structure more fully and to develop their own explanations for these patterns and structures. Word walls, word charts, and word study booklets can be used as resources to support language/word study. Third, because the material for word study comes directly from the writing and classroom experiences of the students, it is easier to help them link their word study back to their own writing. Students who misspell words already studied may be reminded to use the word wall, classroom charts, or word study booklets to check their work. Finally, students develop a better sense of learning about words and language in this format. "Have-a-go sheets" (Bolton & Snowball, 1993), for example, allow students to explore the spelling of words they are struggling to spell correctly. Students try out two or three different spellings of a word before they confirm the correct spelling by asking someone or using an outside resource, such as a dictionary or word study booklet (see Table 5.11), promoting reflection on how words are structured. Bear and colleagues (2003) offer a wide range of word study suggestions in their book *Words Their Way: Word Study for Phonics, Vocabulary, and Spelling Instruction*.

Table 5.11   Have-a-Go

Misspelled Word	Have-a-Go	Have-a-Go	Correct Spelling	Copied Spelling
skol	skool	scool	school	school
theef	theif	thief	thief	thief

Spelling Frequently Used Words

High-frequency words are listed in Table 5.12. As the name suggests, these are the 100 most frequently used words in the English language. Teachers make certain that these words first become sight words for their young readers and later become words they spell correctly in their independent writing. Some high-frequency words may be added to personal word lists and to the word wall each week.

Once words are added to a word wall, students can be held responsible for spelling them correctly because there is a reference available to check their spelling. Early in the school year and throughout the remainder of the year with younger students, it would be advisable to assess which high-frequency words students can spell correctly and on which they need to work. This information can be used to group students at similar spelling levels or prepare individual word lists if a more formal spelling class format is to be used. If the word study format is used in lieu of this, then progress in daily writing will be the gauge of student progress in the correct spelling of high-frequency words.

Learning Spelling Words

Gentry (1987), an expert on spelling, suggests some simple but effective ways for students to visualize and practice new spelling words. During the pretests, students should listen to and then write the new words. Immediately following this activity, they listen to the correct spelling of each word, pointing to each letter of their spellings, and make the necessary corrections. In this way students can identify how close they have come to the conventional spelling of the words.

Table 5.12 High-Frequency Words

a	friends	lot	their
about	from	make	them
after	fun	me	then
all	get	more	there
and	go	my	they
are	good	no	things
as	got	not	this
at	had	of	time
back	has	on	to
be	have	one	too
because	he	or	up
big	her	other	us
but	him	our	very
by	his	out	want
came	home	people	was
can	house	play	we
could	I	said	went
day	if	saw	were
did	in	school	what
didn't	is	see	when
do	it	she	will
don't	just	so	with
down	know	some	would
every	like	that	you
for	little	the	your

A five-step approach to learning to spell the words is recommended. Students look at a word, spell it while pointing to each letter, close their eyes and create a mental image of the letters and their organization, write the word, and check for correctness. Younger children might use word boxes (Clay, 1993), in which they draw boxes for the number of letters in a word and write one letter in each box. To practice spelling the word, students use a game chip that they move from letter to letter as they practice spelling the word. If applicable, a picture cue can be added to the activity. "Notice in the segmenting sounds activity that students see the letters and words (visual), hear the sounds (auditory), and touch (tactile) and move (kinesthetic) the magnetic counters to experience a multisensory approach" (Bender & Larkin, 2003, p. 55). This approach may be useful for students who struggle with spelling and writing (Atkinson, Wilkite, Frey, & Williams, 2002).

Teele (2004) has experimented with students with high ability in spatial reasoning in learning to spell. Her work indicates that asking students to draw a picture to represent words they are studying and write the word several times within the drawing is helpful. "I asked them to look at their picture and take a snapshot of the picture in their brain and to study the spelling of the word" (p. 132). Many students using this method were more successful than with more traditional spelling techniques.

Theory Into Practice

Many teachers incorporate word walls into their classrooms and have students complete activities using the word wall words. A method for helping students visualize the word as they learn and use it is to cut closely around the letters so that the tall letters and the letters that fall below the line stand out. Seeing the "shape" of words is a helpful visual for some learners.

Spelling Within the Writing Process

Making the transfer from spelling words to independent writing is difficult for some students. Asking them to make an attempt to write on their own is a first step. Using temporary or developmental spelling allows students to think about what they already know about how words are structured. As teachers circulate about the room, they may work briefly with individual students to assist them in (a) listening for beginning, medial, or ending sounds; (b) thinking about word chunks; (c) thinking about whether they've seen the word before; (d) linking the word to similar words; or (e) looking for root words, prefixes, or suffixes. Self- and peer editing were discussed earlier in relation to reviewing written work in terms of grammar and punctuation. The same can be done with spelling. On writing pieces that students wish to take to publication or make public in any way, the writing should be proofed for spelling. They may be able to correct some misspellings independently; for other errors, they may circle words they believe they have not spelled correctly. Have-a-go sheets (Bolton & Snowball, 1993) may be useful for students to explore conventional spellings, and asking a peer to edit the writing may help students determine other words that need to be edited. The peer may also provide some assistance in helping the author correct misspelled words. A final editing by the teacher will catch any additional spelling edits that need to be done. The actual editing process would primarily focus on the content and clarity of the message and use of language, but for the purposes of this discussion, only spelling is highlighted here.

Dictionaries may prove useful during the editing stage. Minilessons conducted prior to this point will prepare students with age-appropriate dictionary skills so that they are able to use this resource efficiently and effectively. Selecting dictionaries appropriate for the age and reading level of the students will also help avoid frustration. Older students can learn how to use pronunciation keys, word origin information, and other features in their word studies. Having students look words up in the dictionary, copy the definitions, and use them in sentences, however, is not a good use of the dictionary as a tool and represents busy work.

Spelling is an important component of writing. Conventional spelling helps the writer communicate more fully with the reader. Whether spelling is taught through a formal program or as part of ongoing word study, students' progress in spelling should be monitored and supported. Most important, spelling should always be linked to actual writing. Table 5.13 provides an overview of the components of effective spelling instruction. Teachers support student development in spelling all day long when they highlight how words are structured and used in all content areas (Fountas & Pinnell, 1996).

Table 5.13   What Does Good Spelling Instruction Look Like?

Good spelling instruction

- Is developmental in nature
- Is linked to student writing
- Encourages students to explore word patterns and chunks
- Provides multiple, interesting opportunities to practice word spelling
- Occurs at the instructional level of the child
- Is multisensory, especially for young children, students with learning difficulties, or students who are learning English

Handwriting

If the purpose of writing is to communicate with someone, then attention must be placed on developing quality penmanship. Handwriting that is legible is easy to read. Generally, young children learn manuscript (printing) writing first and later switch to cursive writing in about the third grade. Manuscript writing is often considered easier to master. Straight lines, half circles, and circles are used to form all of the letters in the Zaner-Bloser approach to manuscript handwriting, an approach that is widely used in U.S. schools (Hackney, 2003). "Manuscript handwriting is considered better for young children because they seem to lack the necessary fine motor control and eye-hand coordination for cursive handwriting. In addition, manuscript handwriting is similar to the type style in primary-level reading textbooks" (Tompkins, 2005, p. 601). A sample of traditional manuscript handwriting can be found in Table 5.14.

Table 5.14   Traditional Manuscript Handwriting Sample

A B C D E F G H I
J K L M N O P Q R
S T U V W X Y Z

a b c d e f g h i
j k l m n o p q r
s t u v w x y z

A more recent philosophy regarding handwriting has taken a different view with regard to penmanship. The d'Nealian (Thurber, 1986) style examines the level of difficulty that children face in transitioning from the manuscript to the cursive style of writing and strives to make links between the two types of handwriting. In this approach many lowercase letters have tails at the end of the letter to mimic cursive writing. The letters are not yet connected, but it is an easy transition when students begin cursive writing. Table 5.15 provides a sample of lowercase d'Nealian manuscript writing.

Table 5.15   D'Nealian Lowercase Alphabet Letters

a b c d e f g h i
j k l m n o p q r
s t u v w x y z

Traditionally, teachers spent a great deal of time having children complete daily handwriting exercises that methodically focused on the formation of each letter of the alphabet and required the completion of a series of practice sheets. Young children were encouraged to use "fat" pencils and were reprimanded to "stay in the lines" of prelined penmanship paper. However, when we look at the size of children's hands at the early childhood level, it quickly becomes obvious that their small hands could much more easily manipulate thinner writing instruments than wider ones. If we also examine their fine motor skills, it is obvious that paper without any lines at all might be more suitable for our youngest writers. Crayons, markers, chalk, and so on also make fine writing instruments and pique students' interest in handwriting.

Practicing Handwriting

When practicing and learning new words such as working with spelling, students can practice handwriting skills at the same time as learning their spelling in a meaningful manner. Another time to practice handwriting in an authentic way with younger students is while working with word wall activities. While many word wall activities are done orally, a teacher may ask students to write the words in addition to the oral component while at the same time practicing correct handwriting methods, for example, asking students "What are the words on the word wall that have *ing* endings?" After orally reciting them, the students could be instructed to write them using correct penmanship modeled by the teacher.

Pencil grip is an aspect of handwriting that should also be addressed. While children are writing, teachers may wish to note how children hold their pencils and make adjustments as needed to produce legible writing. It is much easier to assist children in making changes in pencil grip as early as possible. Students who have adopted a nontraditional grasp of their pencils may find it difficult to change their habit later.

Assessing Handwriting

Even though classroom teachers do not currently devote the same amount of time to handwriting as they once did, it is an important skill for children to develop. Children do need to learn how to form letters correctly, and the legibility of their writing needs to be monitored. Using small chalkboards or dry erase boards, younger students may practice formation of letters. The handwriting of older students may be evaluated to determine what improvements need to be made. Small group sessions may be advisable at this age level if there are only a small number of students who struggle in this area. Having students assess their own handwriting periodically may be an effective way for them to monitor improvements in this area. They may also compare handwriting from earlier samples to determine how much progress they have made. Table 5.16 contains a sample of self- and peer assessments of handwriting.

Table 5.16   Rubric for Assessing Handwriting

Self-Assessment of Handwriting	Peer Assessment of Handwriting
As I look at my handwriting	I am assessing _____'s handwriting
– I can easily read what is written	– I can easily read what is written
– It is large enough to easily see	– It is large enough to easily see
– The handwriting slants to the right	– The handwriting slants to the right
– All of the letters are correctly formed	– All the letters are correctly formed

Stop to Think

Some people believe that in today's technological world, which incorporates word processing, learning "proper" and legible handwriting is unnecessary. What do you think? How will you discuss this issue with parents who have a differing viewpoint than you do related to handwriting instruction and practice?

Adaptive materials are available for students who have physical difficulty in grasping a pencil. For some students who are not able to master the art of handwriting for one reason or another, keyboarding may be a very effective alternative. These students may be allowed to type all of their work rather than writing it in long hand.

All students need to learn keyboarding skills from a very early age. Many schools have computer labs where children learn and practice keyboarding and computer skills. Some are even lucky enough to have a computer teacher who works regularly with the students in the school. Sufficient opportunities to practice will help make this skill more automatic for students. Desktop publishing and use of graphics can also greatly enhance student motivation, as well as the appearance of their writing.

The topics of this chapter—spelling, grammar, punctuation, and handwriting—do not focus directly on the art of writing. They do, however, enhance the clarity, precision, and legibility of student writing. Learning skills in this area will certainly help students become more proficient readers and writers.

End-of-Chapter Reflection

- Reflect briefly on how you could teach spelling effectively in an eighth-grade classroom, a fourth-grade classroom, and a first-grade classroom. Reflect as well on how you could effectively teach grammar at these same levels.

- What would you say to a seventh-grade student who stated, "I don't have to have good handwriting, I do all my writing on a computer"?

- Many parents are familiar with traditional basal approaches to teaching and learning spelling. How would you describe your rationale for using more meaningful methods?

Planning for Teaching

1. Evaluate a child's writing. Create a chart to identify which graphophonic patterns the child has control of and uses correctly, which ones are nearly correct, or which are not yet under control. Examine the second column, "nearly correct" (instructional level), and recommend word patterns on which this child appears ready to work.

2. Visit the educational materials center in your college library or a teacher supply store to review the resources that could be used for word study activities with students. What are the characteristics of the best resources you found that make them good learning tools for the classroom? Design a set of criteria for selection of quality word study materials.

3. Make a list of approximately 10 words that you struggle with in spelling. Analyze your word list. Which words are irregular spellings *(subpoena, pneumonia)*, homonyms *(there, their)*, and so on? Try out some of the teaching suggestions from this chapter for learning to spell these words automatically. Which ones work best for you? Why do you think they were effective? Consider your learning style, ease of use, and so on.

4. Write a note to a friend. Print three sentences and write in cursive for three sentences. Compare your sample to the model in this chapter. Has your writing become very stylized? Practice writing the note over using the handwriting models provided.

Connections With the Field

1. Visit a Grade K–8 classroom. Examine the kinds of activities the students engage in for word study. How does the teacher link these activities to actual reading? Are there additional activities that you would use in this area?

2. Visit a classroom to observe word study or spelling. What kinds of activities are used? How does the teacher monitor progress? Are individual students' needs being met? In a small group, compile the information about the different approaches to spelling that were observed. Are there certain activities or approaches that appear to be more effective than others? Why?

Student Study Site

The Companion Website for Developing Voice Through the Language Arts

http://www.sagepub.com/dvtlastudy

Visit the Web-based student study site to enhance your understanding of the chapter content and to discover additional resources that will take your learning one step further. You can enhance your understanding of the chapters by using the comprehensive Study Guide, which includes learning objectives, key terms, activities, practice tests, and more. You'll also find special features, such as the Links to Standards from U.S. States and associated activities, Children's Literature Selections, Reflection Exercises, Learning from Journal Articles, and PRAXIS test preparation materials.

References of Children's/Young Adult Literature

Morris, A. (1989). *Bread, bread, bread.* New York: Harper Collins.

Pérez, L. K. (2002). *First day in grapes.* New York: Lee & Low Books.

Ye, T. (1997). *Three monks, no water.* Toronto, Ontario, Canada: Annick Press.

References of Professional Resources

Allington, R. (1997). *Balanced reading instruction.* Speech given at the annual meeting of the International Reading Association, Atlanta, GA.

Atkinson, T., Wilkite, K., Frey, L., & Williams, S. (2002). Reading instruction for the struggling reader: Implications for teachers of students with learning or emotional/behavior disorders. *Preventing School Failure, 46,* 158–162.

Bear, D. R., Invernizzi, M., Templeton, S., & Johnston, P. (2003). *Words their way: Word study for phonics, vocabulary, and spelling instruction.* New York: Prentice Hall.

Bender, W., & Larkin, M. (2003). *Reading strategies for elementary students with learning difficulties.* Thousand Oaks, CA: Corwin Press.

Bolton, F., & Snowball, D. (1993). *Ideas for spelling.* Portsmouth, NH: Heinemann.

Clay, M. (1993). *An observation survey of early literacy achievement.* Portsmouth, NH: Heinemann.

Delpit, L. (1995). *Other people's children: Cultural conflict in the classroom.* New York: New Press.

Ericson, L., & Fraser Juliebö, M. (1998). *The phonological awareness handbook for kindergarten and primary teachers.* Newark, DE: International Reading Association.

Fountas, I., & Pinnell, G. S. (1996). *Guided reading: Good first teaching for all children.* Portsmouth, NH: Heinemann.

Fountas, I., & Pinnell, G. S. (2001). *Guiding readers and writers grades 3–6: Teaching comprehension, genre and content literacy.* Portsmouth, NH: Heinemann.

Gentry, J. R. (1987). *Spel . . . is a four-letter word.* Portsmouth, NH: Heinemann.

Goodman, K., Shannon, P., Goodman, Y., & Rapaport, R. (2004). *Saving our schools: The case for public education: Saying no to "No Child Left Behind."* Berkeley, CA: RDR Books.

Hackney, C. (2003). *Handwriting: A way to self-expression.* Columbus, OH: Zaner-Bloser.

Kemper, D., Nathan, R., Sebranck, P., & Elsholz, C. (1994). *Write away: A handbook for young writers and learners*. Wilmington, MA: Write Source.

Krashen, S. (2004). *The power of reading* (2nd ed.). Portsmouth, NH: Heinemann.

Milwaukee Public Schools. (2000). *On the mark*. Milwaukee, WI: Author.

Reading First. (2001). *Put reading first: The research building blocks for teaching children to read*. Jessup, MD: National Institute for Literacy.

Routman, R. (2000). *Conversations: Strategies for teaching, learning and evaluating*. Portsmouth, NH: Heinemann.

Teele, S. (2004). *Overcoming barricades to reading: A multiple intelligences approach*. Thousand Oaks, CA: Corwin Press.

Thurber, D. N. (1986). *D'Nealian home/school activities: Manuscript practice for grades 1–3*. New York: Scott Foresman.

Tompkins, G. (2005). *Language arts: Patterns of practice*. Upper Saddle River, NJ: Pearson.

Wong-Fillmore, L. (1985). When does teacher talk work as input? In S. M. Gass & C. G. Madden (Eds.), *Input in second language acquisition* (pp. 17–50). Rowley, MA: Newbury House.

Other Children's/Young Adult Literature Resources

Alphabet Books

Base, G. (1987). *Animalia*. New York: Abrams.

Bayer, J. (1984). *A, my name is Alice* (Steven Kellogg, Illus.). New York: Dial.

Compestine, Y. (2006). *D is for dragon dance* (Y. Xuan, Illus.). New York: Holiday House.

Demarest, C. L. (2002). *Firefighters A to Z*. New York: Simon & Schuster.

Ehlert, L. (1989). *Eating the alphabet: Fruits and vegetables from A to Z*. New York: Harcourt.

Hoban, T. (1982). *A, B See!* New York: Greenwillow.

Kitchen, B. (1984). *Animal alphabet*. New York: Dial.

Lobel, A. (1981). *On Market Street*. New York: Greenwillow.

Martin, B., Jr., & Archambault, J. (1984). *Chicka, chicka, boom, boom*. New York: Simon & Schuster.

Rankin, L. (1991). *The handmade alphabet*. New York: Dial.

Sendak, M. (1962). *Alligators all around*. New York: Harper.

Shannon, G. (1996). *Tomorrow's alphabet*. New York: Greenwillow.

Van Allsburg, C. (1987). *The Z was zapped: A play in twenty-six acts*. New York: Houghton Mifflin.

Winter, J. (2006). *Calavera abecedario: A day of the dead alphabet book*. New York: Voyager Books.

Literature Appropriate for Language/Word Study

DeGross, M. (1998). *Donavan's word jar* (C. Hanna, Illus.). New York: Harper Trophy.

Gwynne, F. (1988). *A chocolate moose for dinner*. New York: Aladdin.

Heller, R. (2000). *Fantastic! wow! and unreal! A book about interjections and conjunctions*. New York: Putnam.

Frasier, D. (2000). *Miss Alaineus: A vocabulary disaster*. New York: Harcourt.

Juster, N. (1961). *The phantom tollbooth*. New York: Knopf.

Leedy, L. (2003). *There's a frog in my throat: 440 animal sayings a little bird told me* (P. Street, Illus.). New York: Holiday House.

Terban, M. (1993). *It figures! Fun figures of speech*. New York: Clarion.

Turner, P. (1999). *The war between the vowels and the consonants* (W. Turner, Illus.). New York: Farrar, Strauss & Giroux.

Technology Resources

Guide to grammar and style: http://andromeda.rutgers.edu/~jlynch/Writing

Guide to grammar and writing: http://grammar.ccc.commnet.edu/grammar

Strategies for Listening, Speaking, Viewing, and Visually Representing

Context Setting:

After reading this chapter, you will be able to

- Identify the components of listening, speaking, viewing, and visually representing
- Analyze how these areas of the language arts are integral to learning
- Design learning experiences that assist students in developing strategies for listening, speaking, viewing, and visually representing
- Design learning experiences that provide students with opportunities to use listening, speaking, viewing, and visually representing to develop higher-level thinking skills
- Develop assessment plans for measuring student progress in listening, speaking, viewing, and visually representing

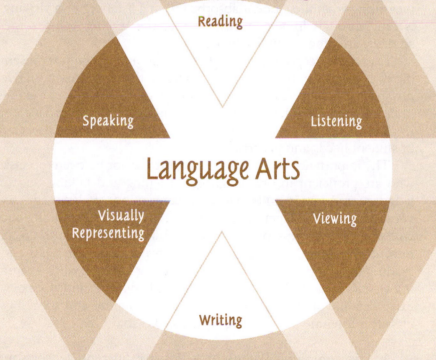

Before We Begin

- Would you consider yourself a good listener? How do you feel about your ability to speak clearly and with a purpose? Do you consider yourself a competent viewer? What skills do you use when you view? What about your ability to represent something visually; can you do this clearly and accurately?

The Integration of Listening, Speaking, Viewing, and Visually Representing

In this chapter, we explore listening, speaking, viewing, and visually representing as components of the language arts and how they impact literacy development. These areas of the language arts are closely integrated, as well as with reading and writing. Therefore, it is difficult to look at each area in isolation. We attempt to do so for the purpose of discussing the components and development of each area but also highlight how these language arts complement one another in strengthening overall literacy growth.

Listening and viewing are **receptive language functions** in that the listener and viewer receive information from the environment. Speaking and visually representing are **expressive language functions** in that some type of response is given. Receptive language functions place less burden on the receiver, but they are more difficult for the teacher to determine progress, as there is no way of directly measuring what the student absorbed from a listening or a viewing experience. It is only through indirect measures that the teacher gains some idea of how students are progressing in these areas.

Expressive responses through speaking and visually representing are more direct and provide the teacher with more firsthand information. Even in this area, however, students' responses are limited to their ability to express themselves orally or graphically. Judgments of student progress based on a composite of work in all of the language arts over time will often provide the most accurate picture of student needs and progress.

The importance of these language arts cannot be overemphasized. "Children who are proficient in oral language—listening and talking—use more complex language and better understand the conventions of language, score higher on vocabulary and intelligence tests, and perform better in reading and writing, than students who are less proficient in oral language" (Cox, 2005, p. 159). Louise Rosenblatt (1985, 1991) differentiated between taking an aesthetic stance when reading (reading for pleasure) and an efferent stance while reading (reading for information), and Tompkins (2005) and Wolvin and Coakley (1985) have expanded and applied similar categories to listening and speaking. Miller (2000) classified listening into the five types listed below:

1. **Discriminative listening:** the listener differentiates the sounds that make up the message and begins to attend to what is being said

2. **Purposeful listening:** the listener attends to the message to complete a task

3. **Creative listening:** the listener uses input from the message to develop a unique response

4. Critical listening: the listener analyzes and evaluates input and formulates an opinion or response

5. Appreciative listening: the listener listens for enjoyment or pleasure

Table 6.1 represents an expansion of these models to include viewing and visually representing.

Table 6.1   Types of Receptive/Expressive Language Functions

	Receptive Listening and Viewing	Expressive Speaking and Visually Representing
Discriminative – differentiate elements of message	Differentiates sounds and visuals	_____
Purposeful (efferent) – to complete a task	Attends to and responds to information, directions, or visual information	Determines oral or visual response
Creative (aesthetic) – use input to develop a unique response	Appeals to listener's/viewer's emotions and imagination	Expresses reactions or feelings orally or visually
Critical/Efferent – to analyze and evaluate input	Analyzes, evaluates, and forms opinions	Informs, persuades, represents opinion or position on issues
Appreciative (aesthetic) – to express pleasure or enjoyment	Listens or views for enjoyment or pleasure	Speaks or visually represents for enjoyment or pleasure

Listening

Reflection Journal 6.1

How well do you learn by listening? Are you an effective listener? How do you know? How might you improve your listening skills?

"**Hearing** is a physical act that involves the reception of sound waves through minute vibrations in the outer, middle, and inner portions of the ear. Listening, on the other hand, is a mental process; it involves the active conversion of sound waves into meaningful information in the brain" (Yellin, Blake, & DeVries, 2004, p. 146). We constantly receive and interpret *auditory cues* from our environment, and although listening is a receptive language function, it is not passive. Listeners react to what they hear in a variety of ways.

Receiving auditory stimuli is the first step in listening. Has the listener accurately heard what was said? The next step involves the level to which the listener comprehended what was said, which might be represented on a continuum ranging from "completely misunderstood message" to "fully understood message." The third step highlights the complexity of the skill of listening, for example, has the listener accurately interpreted the message? Students with impaired **auditory acuity** may find it more challenging to receive auditory stimuli, and/or students with processing difficulties may find it more difficult to interpret auditory stimuli. These students may rely more on additional visual and tactile cues to supplement the auditory information they receive.

Social and cultural differences in communication patterns may cause a mismatch in listening and interpreting messages. Anyone who has traveled extensively and tried to communicate in a language other than his or her own can probably relate to this statement. Level of cognitive maturity may also be involved. For example, parents and children alike might find humor in a *Sesame Street* skit, but for very different reasons. The creators of this show recognize that parents often watch the show with their children, so they design commentary that children interpret literally and parents enjoy for the inference or play on words their little ones are not yet ready to appreciate.

After a message has been received, comprehended, and interpreted, the listener must determine whether a response is expected and what the response might be. Young students seldom think consciously about this aspect of listening, and their responses are generally quite automatic. They clap their hands or jump up and down when they hear something exciting, respond openly and honestly to questions, and share their opinions about what they have heard. Older students become more thoughtful in their responses and consider more options before they respond. Table 6.2 outlines the components of the listening process.

Table 6.2   Components of the Listening Process

Components	Child Response
Physically Receives Message	Did the child hear the message?
Comprehends the Message	Did the child understand the message?
Interprets the Message	Did the child interpret the significance of the message?
Responds to the Message	Did the child determine whether/how to respond to message?

Listening as a Learning Tool

Since listening is a receptive language art, it is only when students respond to what they have listened to, through oral and visual responses, that teachers can gain an understanding of how well they listen and comprehend. Why is it of such critical importance for students to become good listeners? How does listening become integrated with the other language arts?

Students may learn about new concepts by listening to teachers, or other experts provide presentations or demonstrations, or they might listen to audio or video recordings. Additional opportunities to listen and respond to discussions, presentations, and/or recordings assist students in clarifying their understanding of concepts. This is reflected in Vygotsky's (1986) theory of the zone of proximal development in that students are able to revise or expand their personal schema surrounding a particular concept or emotion, as they have more opportunities to listen to and react to what they hear.

As students learn to listen critically, they begin to formulate judgments about what they hear, moving beyond **passive listening** to interpret and evaluate what they have heard. Critical listeners dissect a message carefully and think about each of its components. They judge the quality and truthfulness of the message as well. By listening and responding carefully to what they have heard, students can become well-rounded critical thinkers.

Purposes for Listening

Table 6.3 provides a sampling of the kinds of listening experiences that third grader Mary Vann was exposed to in the course of a single day, indicating a wide variety of purposes for listening. The purpose for listening will determine how

Table 6.3   Third Grader Mary Vann's Listening Experiences

Listening Experience	Type of Listening (Miller, 2000)
Talk to classmates	Creative Listening
Listen to story read by teacher	Appreciative Listening
Respond to questions about story	Purposeful
Directions for day's work	Purposeful
Word study (Sound)	Discriminative
Group work (Reading)	Creative/Purposeful
Math (Make measurement game)	Creative/Purposeful
Social studies (Role of community helpers)	Critical
Science (Directions for experiment)	Purposeful

students attend to auditory input. If they are engaged in word study and have been asked to match rhyming words, students will listen for ending word sounds that are alike. If the teacher is giving directions for the day's work, the students will listen to determine the work they need to accomplish. If they are asked to listen to and compare several versions of *Cinderella,* they may think about the version they know best and listen for details that vary from that norm. In addition, if they are listening to a debate about whether a date should be set to bring the soldiers home from Iraq, they will listen to and gather information from both sides of the argument to use in forming their own opinions.

Teaching students the different purposes for listening may help them be more aware of the many ways we learn through listening. It is evidenced from the examples above that purposes for listening are also determined by contexts for listening. A context may be social when friends are chatting, or it may be interactive (or purposeful) when students are working in a group. Listening may also be an individual and solitary experience, as when students listen to a read-aloud or a book on tape and form opinions about whether or not they like the story.

From our own experiences, we know that it is much easier to attend to auditory stimuli when it matches our interests; we pay closer attention and follow along more attentively. You may find your education-related classes more fascinating than some of your general education courses. If you have prior knowledge of a topic, you probably also find it easier to listen carefully because you bring a better understanding of the topic to the experience. In these circumstances, you may find that your attention wanders less and you gain more from the session. The same will be true for your students.

Listening Strategies

Teaching students to become effective listeners is something that can be done consciously and directly. Helping students recognize that they listen for a variety of purposes may be a first step in guiding them to an awareness of how much learning takes place through listening. They may keep a listening log for 1–2 days in which they record, either in written or graphic format, everything they hear during that period. Older students could work in small groups to put the information on cards and classify different purposes for listening. Younger students might do the same with cards that have both words and pictures. After the cards have been grouped, students identify the listening purpose for each set of cards; categories will generally revolve around "listening for enjoyment/pleasure" (aesthetic) and "listening for learning" (efferent).

Several strategies related to listening may help students focus more specifically on what they are listening to. For example, when students predict what will happen next in a story, they are more likely to think about what they have already heard and concentrate on what is read next to check for the accuracy of their predictions. This activity may be expanded to the use of the DRTA or directed reading-thinking activity (Stauffer, 1975). In using the DRTA, students predict what will happen next as they listen to a read-aloud. After reading to a predetermined point, teacher and students review the predictions that were made and indicate if each was accurate, somewhat accurate, or inaccurate. New predictions are made for the next listening segment and the process is repeated.

An **anticipation guide** (see Chapter 8 for an example) might be used prior to reading expository passages to serve the same general purpose. As students listen to oral texts and review and discuss the accuracy of their predictions, it is likely they will become more careful listeners and base predictions on clues and inferences.

A similar strategy for guiding students to listen to both main ideas and important details is to have students create visual images in their minds as they listen to text. Discussing or drawing their visualizations enables them to clarify their thinking and model their ideas for their peers. Rereading passages to students allows them to self-assess the accuracy of their listening visualizations. Rereading is also an effective method for students to monitor their own listening skills.

Asking students to summarize what they have listened to provides teachers with a good indication of how well students listened and understood what they heard. One way to do this may be to have students record main ideas and supporting details, either while they are listening or after they have finished. Or students may practice taking notes during the listening experience and note key ideas in sequence. Students self-assess how well they are able to retain and organize oral information by comparing their notes to those shared by the class.

Leading students to think about what they already know about a topic, before a listening activity, provides them with the opportunity to activate prior knowledge that may enhance understanding. Creating a web of student ideas will result in a visual that may also help students note how ideas are connected. Listening to new sources may enable students to expand or revise their understanding of how concepts are related.

Drawing student attention to how paralinguistic or supporting cues enhance understanding provides another strategy to gain meaning from listening experiences. Supporting visuals used by speakers or as part of video presentations such as overhead transparencies, electronic slide shows, or posters can clarify topics for listeners. Demonstrating the impact of presentations with and without visuals may exemplify this point for students. Tone of voice, facial expressions, and gestures can be explored in a similar way. Providing many opportunities for students to discuss and self-assess their attention to **paralinguistic cues** would help students continue to utilize this strategy.

A different purpose for listening is represented by phonological awareness (Adams, 1990) and word study types of activities. In these situations, students listen for similarities and differences in word structures and meanings and can become adept at listening to and discriminating among specific sounds and patterns. Learning experiences for students who have difficulty discriminating among sounds, however, may need to include more emphasis on visual cues and word patterns.

Table 6.4   Listening Strategies

Strategy	Learning Activity	Listening Skill Developed
Prediction	Anticipation Guide	Establish purpose for listening
Visualization	Drawing, Discussing	Create mental images
Summarization	Note Taking	Determine main ideas, sequence
Make Connections	Mapping, Discussing	Active prior knowledge, clarify understanding
Expand Meaning	Discuss, Journal, Draw	Active prior knowledge, clarify
Use Paralinguistic Cues	Self-assessment	Assessment of listening skill

Table 6.4 outlines a variety of listening strategies that could be utilized in teaching students to become effective listeners.

Listening Activities in the Classroom

Students listen all day long in the classroom, but do they capitalize on and improve their listening skills? Can they discuss how they listen or what they are working on to become better listeners? Introducing students to a variety of purposes and strategies for listening will provide them with the tools to learn effectively through listening. Because students are exposed to so much stimuli that are visual and interactive, listening skills may be less well developed than in listeners of previous generations. In addition, because curriculum and testing demands are ever increasing in content and expectations, students benefit from integrating learning in every way possible.

Conscious listening instruction and assessment help students develop in this area. Daily read-alouds provide opportunities for students to listen for both pleasure and information. A variety of purposes for listening can be introduced, modeled, and reinforced. Follow-up discussions and activities allow students to reflect on both the content and development of listening skills. Discussions, written activities, movement, art, music, and dramatic representations may be used for students to clarify and interpret what they have taken in auditorally. English language learners (ELLs) and students with learning challenges may find these kinds of experiences especially helpful, along with rereadings. Care should be taken to select interesting listening pieces that are of the appropriate length and complexity for students, especially for students with special educational needs or ELLs. Materials that are clearly presented at the appropriate volume and pace will be most meaningful to students.

Many classrooms have books on tape available in the listening center, and students frequently filter through this center as part of their balanced literacy block. Merely having students listen to a text on tape without any emphasis on purpose for listening or listening strategies is not likely to significantly improve listening competence. Students may view videos and presentations as additional methods of enhancing listening skill and be followed up by answering questions about them as a means to focus student attention as well. Students who participate in writing workshops often share their writing with their classmates, providing another venue for listening, as the audience listens carefully to completed pieces being shared in order to give feedback to the author. The author must listen carefully to the comments in order to interpret feedback for improving his or her writing.

ELLs and students with auditory impairments may benefit from measures to support listening, including the use of visuals, movement activities, gestures, and **graphic organizers.** Preparation for listening can be accomplished by activating prior knowledge, reviewing the purpose for listening, and previewing concepts and vocabulary. Listening activities for these students should be designed to meet their academic needs but should be as rigorous as possible. ELLs who are not yet ready to verbalize their understanding of listening material may be given opportunities to express themselves through movement, drama, art, or interactive activities. As in all learning situations, students progress more fully and with greater self-assurance in a nonthreatening learning environment.

A View From Home

After school one day, Marcus's mother came in to speak to his teacher, Jim Michaels. She profusely thanked him for the work he was doing with the students in his sixth-grade class related to listening. She said, "Since you've been teaching our kids about the different ways and reasons to listen, Marcus has really improved how he listens at home. He says he's just doing his homework by practicing listening to me, but I am so thankful. It's like I have a different son who listens when I speak!"

Assessment of Listening Progress

Student growth in listening cannot be measured directly. We cannot actually see how students listen or make sense of what they hear. However, we can use indirect measures related to how students respond to what they have heard to note progress in listening. To judge their progress, listen to the comments and questions they make and review the written, dramatic, and artistic interpretations they create. Anecdotal records may be used, along with checklists, as in Table 6.5, to note use of listening strategies and/or higher-level thinking skills.

As students are introduced to listening purposes and strategies, they will benefit from self-assessing these areas. Tables 6.6, 6.7, and 6.8 provide some examples of listening self-assessments.

Table 6.5   Listening Skills Checklist

Student Name: **Anecdotal Comments:**

_____ Listens attentively

_____ Responds appropriately to questions and prompts

_____ Makes logical predictions

_____ Identifies main ideas

_____ Accurately summarizes

Table 6.6   Listening Self-Assessment—Narrative Text

When I listen to stories, I can	Usually	Sometimes	Rarely
– Visualize the story	_____	_____	_____
– Identify the setting	_____	_____	_____
– Follow the action of the story	_____	_____	_____
– Identify the main characters	_____	_____	_____
– Predict what may happen next	_____	_____	_____

What I could do to be a better listener: _____

Table 6.7   Listening Self-Assessment—Expository Text

When I listen to informational text, I can	Usually	Sometimes	Rarely
– Identify the most important ideas	_____	_____	_____
– Keep the ideas separate	_____	_____	_____
– Identify supporting details	_____	_____	_____
– Summarize what I've heard	_____	_____	_____

What I could do to be a better listener: _____

Table 6.8   Listening Self-Assessment Listening Strategies

I use the following strategies when I listen:	Usually	Sometimes	Rarely
– Predict what will happen next	_____	_____	_____
– Visualize what I hear	_____	_____	_____
– Make connections to what I already know	_____	_____	_____
– Expand what I already know	_____	_____	_____
– Interpret visuals, gestures, facial expressions	_____	_____	_____

What I could do to be a better listener: _____

_____

_____

Viewing

Another receptive language arts area is viewing. "Viewing refers to the communication processes involved when students view videos, computer simulations, and computer games; comprehend book illustrations, and interpret charts, tables, maps, and other print media" (Yellin et al., 2004, p. 4). This language mode is growing in importance, due to the types of technological advances we are experiencing. "Language-based literacy is still necessary, but it is no longer enough for the kinds of literacy practices that already characterize and will continue to be developed in the information age of the twenty-first century" (Pappas, Kiefer, & Levstik, 2006, p. 28). This is consistent with brain research that suggests that students learn best when they are immersed in a wide range of learning experiences that encompass many learning modes and modalities (Sousa, 2005).

A broad range of visual materials and experiences broadens students' experiences and awareness of the world around them. Knowing the backgrounds and interests of students should also be a factor in selecting materials that are culturally and socially relevant for them. Students need to see themselves represented in the curriculum and also to learn about students and adults who lead different lives.

Purposes for Viewing

Students view a wide range of **visual media** both inside and outside the classroom. The overall purpose of teaching **visual literacy** is twofold: (1) to interpret and (2) to evaluate visual input in learning more about the world. In the first instance, students analyze the elements of what they are viewing and determine how to use those elements to gain meaning. Evaluating visual input helps students use the information to further critical thinking on a topic, taking the information gained to draw conclusions, infer, synthesize, and make judgments.

When teachers lead students in analyzing the purpose for visual representations, the students soon realize that actors, authors, and artists have specific reasons for creating and/or presenting ideas in a particular manner. Illustrations in a student's book might be designed to both entertain and teach. For example, in *The True Story of the 3 Little Pigs* (1989), Jon Scieszka and Lane Smith want students to laugh at the hilarious antics of the wolf, but they also raise the question of considering diverse points of view.

Visual media might be used to recount or summarize, as in a timeline or a social studies play that provides a dramatic interpretation of a historical event or time in history. It might also serve the purpose of explaining or reporting what something is like or how it works. A major purpose of visual media in the classroom is to instruct and expand student understanding of the world. With the onslaught of the use of visuals in advertising, a major purpose of advertisements is to persuade viewers to value certain products and lifestyles. Therefore, it is important that students gain expertise in critically evaluating the purpose of advertising from a variety of sources and viewpoints. A second purpose is to guide students in making judgments about whether to accept or reject claims and insinuations made in ads.

Visual media are often designed to evoke an emotional response from viewers. Students can learn to identify the response that is intended and how it is portrayed. Possessing these types of skills makes students better educated and informed consumers of information both in and out of school. Table 6.9 reflects the range of visual learning experiences that third grader Mary Vann is exposed to on a regular basis.

Viewing Strategies

Determining Purpose

As with listening, there are a number of strategies that students can acquire to help them gain meaning from visual learning experiences and lead them to understand that these materials may be used for a variety of purposes and that visual literacy is an integral part of most learning experiences. Materials may be developed that entertain, explain, instruct, recount, report, and persuade. After some practice, students may begin to identify the purpose independently or select visual materials and experiences that match their own objectives in learning experiences. In content areas, such as mathematics, social studies, and science, it is important for students to explore the purpose of text features that will support learning. Maps, tables, charts, and graphs are used extensively in many texts and trade books. Providing opportunities for students to determine the purpose of each helps them interpret the information in a meaningful manner. For example, is a timeline being used to highlight growth over time, a sequence of events, patterns and connections, or to summarize a certain period of time? Is a table being presented to record or organize information, demonstrate patterns, or reflect a schedule (Moline, 1995)?

Table 6.9   Third Grader Mary Vann's Visual Learning Experiences

Viewing Experience	Setting	Purpose
Textbooks	School	Inform, Instruct, Report
TV ads	Home	Persuade
Internet	Home/School	Entertain, Inform, Persuade
Videos/CDs	Home/School	Entertain, Inform, Persuade
Novels	Home/School	Entertain, Instruct
Comic Books	Home	Entertain
Class Handouts	School	Instruct, Inform

Previewing

Previewing materials or gaining background information about a play or a video is a good strategy for students to use prior to a reading or viewing experience. Glancing over pictures, maps, and other graphics to get a general feel for the content before reading a section of social studies text is an example of previewing visual materials. Reading and discussing a novel before seeing a play of the same title might be a suitable preview experience before a performing arts experience. Reading books and viewing video segments before students visit a dinosaur exhibit at the museum could extend the viewing experience overall. The previewing strategy is closely linked to making predictions. As students preview visual experiences, they set expectations for what they expect to view or experience. Discussion of how well clues were used to make predictions may be useful in helping students refine their skills in making accurate and informed predictions.

Predicting

After discussion, reading, or other viewing experiences but prior to examining visuals, students might be asked to predict what the visuals might depict, allowing them to make links and set purpose. Some examples include the following: "We are going to read a new Chris VanAllsburg book. What do you think the illustrations will be like? What key elements do you expect to see on this timeline?" "Given what you know about Mexican history, what would you expect to see in Diego Rivera's murals in Mexico City?" "Since you have read the book *Because of Winn Dixie,* what do you think the movie will be like?"

Selecting Key Information

Selecting key information in viewing may not be as straightforward as it sounds. In a play or video, for example, students may get caught up in the antics of one or more characters and miss the gist of the show. In visual materials, attention may be drawn to isolated pieces of information, and connections or relationships neglected. Some Internet sites, for example, are replete with information and directions, and students need practice in sorting through and knowing how to identify key points. **Skimming** and **scanning** are two strategies that will assist in selecting key information. Chapter 8 provides more information on using graphic materials in the content areas.

Understanding the Design of Visuals

Perusing visual information to interpret tone or purpose is a major strategy in viewing. The layout of information is instrumental in establishing the tone, purpose, clarity, and ease of use. A clearly organized article about how crayons are manufactured that includes clear, interesting, and informative photos would more likely hold students' attention than one with unsequenced, dense information covering the entire page, with only a few photos or graphics to clarify the process. The use of color, font, type size, artwork, headings, and bolding may further enhance or detract from the viewers' ability to obtain meaning from the visuals. Use of white space, boxes, columns, and so on to direct attention and emphasize importance of concepts is another measure students may examine.

Evaluating Bias

Even at a young age, students may begin evaluating visual materials for bias by asking questions such as "Whose point of view is represented in these illustrations?" "Why did the illustrator make the adults so large and the students so small; what message is being presented?" "The characters of color in these illustrations never look directly at the viewer, but the Anglo characters do. How do you feel about that?" Students need to be taught how to ask questions of the visuals they view as a beginning step for identifying and analyzing bias.

Evaluating Tone and Mood

Students may begin by exploring illustrations in picture books to get a sense of how a variety of illustrators convey meaning through their illustrations. How do they use color, line, and shadow to create mood? (See Chapter 7 for a discussion of these elements.) How do they portray emotion? How do the visuals enhance the text? After picture storybooks, students may begin to evaluate informational text and Internet sources to determine how effectively graphics are used. Evaluations can be made of both the quality of the visuals—Do they portray important and interesting concepts?—and the clarity—Do they clearly represent intended concepts? Becoming discriminating evaluators of visuals will not only help students select and interpret materials and experiences more critically but will also provide them with a set of strategies that can be used in designing their own work. The same process can be used in discussing videos and plays through asking questions such as "Did the setting enhance the play?

Were there too few or too many props? Were the costumes appropriate for the story? What are your thoughts on the transitions from one part of the story to the next? Could you follow the plot easily enough? What would improve the performance?"

All of these elements combine to reveal the mood in visuals, and asking such questions as "Are the visuals, the videos, the play, the artwork, and so on playful or sullen? Is the topic simple or complex?" will assist students in determining these elements. Students may also explore and interpret biases the creators of the pieces may have held. Culture or gender statements, for example, may be reflected in how characters are portrayed or the roles they are assigned. Who is portrayed as being most knowledgeable or most powerful? Who is in the foreground and who is in the background? How are color, shadow, and white space used to express the characters' personalities, and how they are viewed?" Pappas and colleagues (2006) discuss "interactive meanings," or the interactions between producers and viewers of images. They have identified several dimensions that may be reflected as part of this interaction. Two of the dimensions may be especially pertinent in exploring bias in graphic media:

1. **Visual demands** and **visual offers:** Character shots in which the character seems to be looking directly at the viewer are "demands" and suggest a relationship between the character and the viewer. "Offers" portray characters that do not appear to gaze at the viewers and do not suggest a relationship.

2. **Power:** "If represented participants are seen from a high angle with the viewer looking down on them, then these participants are seen as if the viewer has power over them. In contrast, when they are represented from a low angle, the participants are depicted as if they have power over the viewer. Eye-level angle depicts an equality between represented participants and the viewer." (p. 266)

Making Personal Connections

The final strategy encourages students to make links between elements of visuals and prior knowledge. When students think about what they already know or have experienced and what they are viewing, they are more likely to bring greater meaning and understanding to the viewing experience than if they approach it as an isolated event. When viewers keep the purpose for viewing in mind, they are able to focus more directly on relevant aspects of the visual stimuli, and if they are able to make links between the visuals and related text, it is likely that more connections will be made between the two media. Table 6.10 highlights a variety of viewing strategies.

Table 6.10 Viewing Strategies

Strategy	Learning Activity
Determine Purpose	Review texts, plays, movies for different purposes
Preview	Preview costumes, props, stage setup before viewing play
Predict	Predict how play will be portrayed, after reading book
Select Key Information	Discussions, overheads, Internet sites—circle key words/phrases
Interpret	Introduce effects of color, white space, font, type size, and critique in several mediums
Evaluate Tone and Bias	Select a variety of paintings on a single topic and evaluate for bias and point of view

 **Stop to Think** When have you used these viewing strategies in your own life? Where do you encounter visuals? How astute are you in interpreting and analyzing them in an educated manner?

Assessment of Viewing Progress

Student progress in viewing may be evaluated in a number of ways. Informal observations about student selection of visuals will inform teachers about how well students are able to match materials to objectives. For example, if students were instructed to select and print an advertisement from the Internet that was aimed at influencing students to behave in a certain way, did they select an appropriate ad? Small group discussions might reveal how well students are able to articulate the impact of color, shadow, white space, and so on in creating mood. The teacher may also note evidence of "strategies in using and relating major and minor text (captions, labels, keys, etc.)" (Pappas et al., 2006, p. 388). Tables 6.11, 6.12, and 6.13 are examples of self-assessments for viewing that encourage students to evaluate what is being portrayed and the message it conveys.

Using visual materials extensively is especially helpful for ELLs. ELLs who are able to scrutinize and interpret visual information and cues are able to supplement developing English language skills to clarify meaning. Viewing visuals or videos prior to learning experiences with the whole class provides ELLs with an opportunity to develop background information that they may bring with them.

Table 6.11   Self-Assessing My Use of Visuals

List the visuals you used: _____
_____

Yes	Somewhat	No	
_____	_____	_____	The visuals made my project clear. Describe: _____
_____	_____	_____	I made good connections between my visuals and my topic.
_____	_____	_____	The visuals were appropriate in size for my purpose.
_____	_____	_____	I made good use of color or black and white in the visuals I used.
_____	_____	_____	I had an organized layout.
_____	_____	_____	My visuals were accurate.

Table 6.12   Assessing What I Viewed

Media I viewed:	_____ TV Show	_____ Play/Drama	_____ Movie	_____ Presentation
	_____ PowerPoint	_____ Internet	_____ Painting	_____ Photographs

I viewed this because _____.

I learned _____.

The components of the visual that were done well include _____.

I would suggest the following improvements to what I've viewed: _____.
_____

Table 6.13   Assessing for Bias

Was everyone treated fairly? If not, who was not and why?

Who is powerful in the viewing situation?

    How do you know?

Who has little or no power?

    How do you know?

Who is quiet or not heard from?

Rate this viewing for bias: No Bias   Some Bias   Serious Bias

Speaking

Like all of the language arts, speaking or talking is interactive in nature. As an expressive language art, speaking is also social. Whether engaged in an informal chat with another person or as a more formal presentation to a larger audience, an effective communicator continually adjusts his or her speech to meet the purpose of the situation. Therefore, the speaker may speak louder if listeners appear to be straining to hear or explain an idea in different words if the listener appears confused. The social nature of language is often evident in how students make friends or resolve conflicts. Obviously, a child's personality, level of shyness, and so on also impact the level of success in this area. However, paying special attention to these areas and helping students develop effective interaction skills may assist students.

There is a wide range of speaking situations, or **registers,** and students will benefit from practice with a variety of them. Students learn the difference between how speech differs when two students are speaking together versus when a child and a teacher are speaking together, the former being informal and the latter a more formal speaking situation. In other words, the purposes for speaking, for example, to explain, persuade, amuse, and so on, become linked to how people speak or what they say. Adjusting to the background of the listener plays a key role in selecting an appropriate register. For example, explaining the classroom routine to students will be different depending on whether or not the listener is familiar with, or has a prior knowledge base about, formal schooling in the United States.

Opportunities can be provided for students to develop speaking skills throughout the school day; however, this necessitates a major change in schools. Traditionally, classrooms have been relatively silent places, where the teacher talked and the students listened. A quiet classroom was equated with effective teaching and classroom management skills. A classroom where students are continually improving their thinking and speaking skills may not be quite so quiet. In order for this to happen, teachers must talk less and provide opportunities for students to talk more. These, however, must be carefully planned to ensure that the speaking activities engage students in the development and refinement of significant thinking and interaction skills, representing new ways for students to expand what they know and understand about specific concepts.

Speaking as a Learning Tool

🚚 A View From the Classroom

Bonnie is a second-grade teacher with several ELLs in her class. She understands that her students learn more about both English language structure and the science theme of habitats that they are studying if she gives them opportunities to explain the concepts to one another. Therefore, Bonnie plans to divide the class into two groups: one group will watch a video about predators in a forest habitat and the other group will view a PowerPoint presentation about predators in a desert environment. The segments and pacing are relatively brief and slow, and the concepts are clearly presented, making this material suitable for ELLs. Both groups will take notes and draw pictures about their topic. Later, Bonnie will pair students with one student from each group.

In this **reciprocal teaching** activity, where students teach one another, they take turns sharing what they know about predators in their assigned environment. The students are then directed to create a visual depicting how predators in the two environments are similar or different. Finally, the pairs will share their findings with another pair. Bonnie circulates among the pairs and encourages them to explain their ideas as fully as possible and offers suggestions when meaning is confused.

In the scenario presented in View From the Classroom above, students are using speaking to clarify their understanding of concepts. As suggested by Vygotsky's (1986) zone of proximal development, students build from what they have heard in the presentations and in conversations with a partner to make the concepts clearer for themselves. Bonnie recognizes that the more fully students are able to discuss their topics through words and drawings, the more in depth they understand the concept overall. She has been surprised to note, however, that her English-dominant students have also improved their understanding of concepts since she started using this reciprocal teaching format in science.

The language arts are rarely used in isolation, and Bonnie's scenario provides an example of their integration. Students listen to and view presentations before meeting with a partner. The pair then verbally exchanges information, visually represents information on a graphic, and presents their findings to another pair. The redundancy built into the learning experiences enables students to clarify understanding.

Purposes for Speaking

Reflection Journal 6.2

Keep a list of every time you speak for one or two full days. Sort your list by similar purposes for speaking. Reflect on the variety of purposes for speaking that students may encounter and the variety of skills needed for each purpose. How might you best assist them in becoming more effective speakers?

When students engage in casual conversation with one another or as part of a small or large group, there is usually a give-and-take pattern of one person speaking and another person responding. There are some things that students could use to more effectively evaluate their listening when participating in a conversation, including such questions as

- Does the speaker express ideas clearly?
- Does the respondent follow the conversation or change to a new topic?
- Who does most of the talking/listening?
- Are there leaders/followers in the conversation?
- Are some people excluded from the conversation? Who? Why?

In other words, students can learn about the dynamics of communication, how to be more inclusive, and how to identify the effects of conversations. They may also learn to determine how the context of a conversation may differ depending on the venue. For example, the way students speak to one another in the classroom with adults present may be very different from the way they speak to one another on the playground. These types of understandings might be related to dialogue and verbal interactions among characters in books, films, or dramatic presentations. Understanding more about verbal interactions may give students better insights into what they are reading, listening to, or viewing.

Classroom speaking experiences may be formal or informal. During formal learning experiences, students may do oral or dramatic presentations where they prepare and practice their speaking in advance and share their work with an audience. Often students use props or visuals to clarify their presentations or make them more realistic. During informal classroom speaking experiences, students may engage in discussions that activate background knowledge before a learning experience, or they may stop at intervals to discuss what they have read or studied. Answering questions posed by the teacher or classmates is often an integral component of their discussions. All of these experiences may be linked to the development of critical thinking skills; students may use oral language to inform or persuade one another, or they may express opinions and provide evidence to support their positions. They may also focus on using oral language to draw conclusions, make inferences, describe, evaluate, or make connections to prior knowledge.

Speaking Strategies

Speaking strategies can be clearly identified and taught to students to help them examine how effectively they communicate and to make improvements. Table 6.14 outlines some key strategies related to speaking.

Determining Purpose

As with the other language arts discussed in this chapter, it is important for students to understand that there are different purposes for speaking and that

Table 6.14   Speaking Strategies

Strategy	Learning Activity
Determine Purpose	Keep a log of all speeches heard during 2 or 3 days and chart purposes
Respond to Audience	Role-play audience reactions and brainstorm possible adjustments
Use Prior Knowledge	Discuss how prior knowledge influenced what was said/understood
Organize Ideas	Use outline to prepare oral presentation
Express Ideas Clearly	Rehearse presentation with small group and evaluate feedback
Develop Presentation Skills	Review video of speaking and self-assess volume, eye contact, and pacing
Select Appropriate Register	Role-play a situation through a variety of registers

different purposes dictate different ways of speaking (registers). Students might brainstorm all the different reasons they can think of for why people speak. For example:

- My mother calls me to get up in the morning.
- The teacher asks questions and we answer questions about the story we heard.
- The news announcer tells us what happened in the world today.
- Cartoon characters on TV make us laugh.
- The gym teacher tells us how to be safe while we do flips on the trampoline.
- Kids get into fights and yell at one another on the playground.

Each scenario might then be outlined according to who is speaking, why they are speaking, and how they are speaking, as a way to help students recognize that different purposes dictate different ways of speaking.

Responding to an Audience

Speaking is a fluid language art. Good speakers notice how their audience responds to what they say. They make adjustments when needed to keep their listeners engaged. To help students learn this strategy, they might view brief video clips that are good and poor examples of this phenomenon and then analyze them to determine whether or not the speaker has appropriately adjusted to the listener(s). Perhaps the speaker goes into detail and the audience begins to yawn or fidget. Alternatively, the speaker may be animated about the topic or have visuals that clarify the topic. Once students have a good understanding of what to look for in monitoring audience response, they may begin to judge how well they adjust to the audience in their own presentations and discussions.

Using Prior Knowledge

Students will bring greater clarity and more information to their oral responses if they integrate their prior knowledge into discussions on new topics. In this area, students might focus on the depth of information in their oral communication. Do they make brief, shallow comments, or do they carefully analyze ideas and make connections with other ideas? Again, students might view and analyze video clips to determine the level of thinking represented by the oral responses and construct a set of criteria that might be used in a speaking rubric. In videotaping their own speaking, they may begin to make connections to the level of thinking represented in their responses and self-assess themselves using the rubric they helped create.

Organizing Ideas and Developing Presentation Skills

Another speaking strategy is to organize and present ideas fully and sequentially as either a mental or a written exercise. Even as students are informally chatting with one another, they might focus on the organization of their ideas. One way to do this is to monitor the response of the listener(s) and to adjust as needed, as suggested above. Videos of student presentations are often very instructive for students, especially if they have a set of criteria against which to judge their work. Part of this self-assessment might include an evaluation of volume, pacing, and eye contact.

Selecting Appropriate Register

Selecting the appropriate register for speaking is generally something students have some experience with. They talk differently to the principal than they do to their younger siblings. They may know this intuitively, but it is important for them to recognize that there are different registers of speech and to know when and how to use each. Factors affecting selection of a particular register might be gender, age, racial/ethnic heritage, geographic region, and social group (Cox, 2005). Brief video clips from a number of movies might highlight the variety of **speech registers,** though care should be taken to avoid the development of stereotypes and to demonstrate that there may be great variety even within groups. Many students speak a nonstandard dialect of English. Students' dialects should be respected, and they should not be penalized for the language of their home and community. However, students must learn and gain access to Standard English in school.

Speaking Activities in the Classroom

Group work enables students to hone oral communication skills and use them for a variety of purposes. Students complete tasks while working in groups, but they might also evaluate how well they communicated their ideas or used oral language to complete their work.

Many types of discussions take place in a classroom on a daily basis, and teachers might evaluate these to determine if students are provided ample opportunities to refine their oral language skills. If questioning is used, are students expected to give only one-word or short-phrase responses to closed questions with a correct answer? Or are students also provided numerous opportunities to respond to open-ended questions? Are additional probes used to help students respond more fully, or does the teacher quickly move on to listen to another child's response? Both teachers and students might make improvements in this area. Responses to literature might begin with questions from the teacher and evolve to more student-led discussions. Students may be encouraged to take notes or mark entries in text to share in preparation for literature discussions.

Drama is an effective way for students to improve their speaking skills. In some instances, a script is already prepared and students can concentrate on eye contact, voice projection, and character portrayal. In other cases, students develop their own scripts. Storytelling with puppets or props may also be useful. Reader's theater enables students to improve both reading and speaking skills as they prepare for and present favorite stories and characters. ELLs generally find these kinds of activities less threatening if they are given the appropriate level and amount of material to prepare and present. They should also have sufficient time and support to practice before being asked to share with a larger group. Often they will be more likely to use newly developing language skills in a smaller, supportive group. The use of PVC plastic elbow pipes that look like telephone receivers enables students to hear themselves better as they rehearse. The use of props or visuals, perhaps with key vocabulary or phrases attached, may serve as helpful scaffolds.

Assessment of Oral Communication Skills

Varieties of rubrics now exist for assessing oral communication skills in students. Many states include standards in this area as well. Rubrics should be shared with students prior to work involving the development of speaking skills to ensure that they understand and focus on specific areas that will be assessed later.

Informal and anecdotal assessments of oral communication skills will provide teachers an idea of student strengths and weaknesses. As suggested earlier, video recordings of student presentations and discussions can be used for teacher, peer, and self-assessment of speaking. As students become more aware of oral communication skills, they might compile a list of Characteristics of Good Speakers and then use these criteria to self-assess their own progress. Assessments for ELLs should focus on content, with separate measures for English language development. Progress should be measured against previous performances rather than compared to native speakers of English.

Visually Representing

🚗 A View From the Classroom

The students in Mrs. Bodine's second-grade class are working on descriptive writing. As a prewriting activity, students are informed that they will not plan their writing with written words but instead will go to nearby Sandy Beach Park armed with crayons, markers, and sketch pads. Mrs. Bodine guides the students in brainstorming individual writing topics about the park, for example, children playing in the park, the play equipment, and how the community uses the park. The students draw as many details as possible about their particular topics. They are informed that later they will write a description and draw pictures related to their topic for a display celebrating the park's 100th anniversary and hang them in the public library.

In learning through visually representing, "[s]tudents create meaning through multiple sign systems such as video productions, Inspiration, and other computer programs, dramatizations, story quilts, and illustrations on charts, posters, and books they are writing" (Tompkins, 2005, p. 34). Authentic visual representation incorporates several of the multiple intelligences, providing students with a variety of learning experiences to develop understanding. Spatial, bodily-kinesthetic, musical, and interpersonal intelligences are more easily integrated in visually representing learning than in more traditional classroom learning experiences.

The array of learning experiences that might be included as part of visually representing is broad and limited only by the level of creativity of the teacher. Movement activities may be used, especially with the youngest students, in both learning new concepts or demonstrating understanding at the conclusion of a unit of study, for example, singing and acting out "head, shoulders, knees, and toes" to review body parts. A variety of art media might be used, including paint, chalk, and sculpture. Graphics, such as maps, charts, graphs, and graphic organizers, are often valuable references for students as they work. Drama generally incorporates movement and provides yet another opportunity for students to express themselves, often on an emotional level. Multimedia choices continue to expand, and students could create CDs, I-movies, PowerPoint presentations, digital photo slide shows, or Web pages.

A View From the Classroom

Ms. Kim and her fourth-grade students engaged frequently in movement activities. When the local art museum was holding an exhibit of Faith Ringgold's quilts, and after extensive study of this well-known author/illustrator and artist and quilter, she took her class on a field trip. In preparation for their visit, they studied her art and created paper quilts of their own, borrowing Ringgold's style. While viewing the exhibit, Ms. Kim helped her students see the movement represented within Ringgold's quilts and encouraged the students to allow the quilts to suggest movement within them. Since the students felt comfortable with movement activity in a variety of formats and contexts, many of them allowed the quilts to inform movement of their bodies and began to move about in front of the quilts in free flowing actions. Upon returning to school, the class discussed their movement responses and some students chose to reflect in writing how the quilts encouraged them to visually represent their emotions and responses to the art through moving their bodies or parts of their bodies. Ms. Kim felt that this experience helped students see the many facets of art and use art and integrated language arts to appreciate this traditional art form.

Learning done through representing visuals can be readily integrated with the other language arts, as noted in the examples above, because this area generally serves as a reflection of what students have learned. In other words, students must develop background understanding before they are able to represent what they have learned through a particular medium. They listen to and read for information, view many materials and perhaps select some to use in projects, write scripts and rehearse plays or reader's theater productions; and very often create oral presentations to describe and explain their work.

Visual Representation as a Learning Tool

While visually representing is an excellent way for students to depict what they have learned and what they understand, it serves another equally important role. While creating graphics, sculptures, or dramatic presentations, students clarify and extend their understanding of concepts, often needing to consult resources to confirm information or write scripts that enable them to construct their ideas visually. Visually representing generally involves making connections between new concepts and prior knowledge. If students are preparing graphics to represent the changes in a character throughout a story, they might connect this to what they learned previously about **dynamic characters.** This might help them search for factors that influenced the character's transformation. This example might also be used to highlight how representing through visuals may be used to express one's understanding but also feelings and emotions as well.

The use of visuals can be instrumental in developing critical thinking skills. This does not occur when students merely create art projects, graphics, or dramatic presentations. It does occur when students use these creations to think more fully about their learning as they describe, analyze, or evaluate concepts.

Purposes for Representing Visually

Visual representations can be used for a variety of purposes, and linking these purposes to teaching/learning standards and making them clear to students is essential. Students develop skill in visually representing when they share information, explain a process, demonstrate how something functions, express an opinion, depict an emotion, or make a statement. Reflecting personal interpretation of ideas or concepts can be enhanced with visuals. Generating enthusiasm, curiosity, or questions can be developed in a variety of ways. Higher-level thinking skills such as making connections or inferences may also be developed through a variety of visual representations. As with the other language arts discussed in this chapter, identifying the purpose for representing learning visually is a critical strategy.

Visual Representation Strategies

Once students have established a purpose, they will have guidelines that can facilitate the selection of appropriate materials and the creation of meaningful materials or presentations.

Selection of an appropriate medium is a key strategy. Can understanding best be demonstrated through a PowerPoint presentation, a poster display, or a movement activity? Knowing the options available and how to determine what is most appropriate for the learning experience is an important component of this strategy, as is creating visuals that are appropriate for the topic and the learning experience. Are the visuals clear? Do they depict concepts fully? Students might determine the criteria that make visuals or performances aesthetically pleasing and complete and then use these criteria in designing their own work.

Do the experiences using visual representations demonstrate understanding? Is an important message conveyed? Is the content expressed accurately? Teaching students to self-assess and revise their work in this area helps them to look for deeper meanings. In a related strategy, students learn to draw on their prior experiences and knowledge to make connections with what they already know. Table 6.15 outlines strategies related to visually representing.

Table 6.15   Visually Representing Strategies

Strategy	Teaching/Learning Activity
Determine Purpose	Review examples of representing through visuals and brainstorm purposes
Select Appropriate Medium	Introduce a new medium for each activity, then choose own
Design Visually Appealing Materials	Conduct a series of lessons focused on designing visual representations
Represent Understanding	Students conference with teacher to explain work and set goals
Make Connections	Create a graphic for students to map out connections

Activities in the Classroom Focused on Representing Through Visuals

After students have been exposed to a range of ways to expand and represent their learning through visual representations, providing them with choices in selecting the medium to best reflect understanding allows maximum creativity of expression. When students are comfortable with artwork or drama, for example, they are able to focus more on the content of what they are trying to convey. Guiding them to explore new avenues of expression will expand their development of the multiple intelligences.

Students may work individually or in groups, but group work is often appropriate in visually representing learning experiences. Students may learn a great deal from one another's strengths. Those who are strong in a particular area may learn how to more effectively demonstrate or explain to others what they do. Students also learn to problem solve in negotiating meaning while they are completing projects with partners.

As teachers plan units of study, they determine which areas to build into each unit that encompass representing ideas visually. For example, one unit may focus on the use of drama while another includes use of technology with a PowerPoint presentation. Several of the lessons are related directly to teaching students how to use visual representations, and they are given opportunities to incorporate these areas into their work and to self-assess their progress.

Sketch-to-stretch (Harste, Short, & Burke, 1988; Whitin, 1994, 1996, 2002) is an effective learning activity in which students use visual representations in expanding their analysis of what they have read. Students read and discuss (or complete journal entries) about what they have read and then draw pictures to reflect what the text meant to them or to depict the theme of the story/chapter. They may share their drawings and explanations with the whole class or in small groups. Sketch-to-stretch provides a meaningful tool for students to learn about using symbolism to represent ideas or emotions. They develop analytical and inference skills in determining the tone or theme of the text and representing these aspects visually.

Theory Into Practice

Sketch-to-stretch is a good strategy to encourage students to use their viewing and visual representation skills as they create a visual that must include clear information for others to view competently. Using this strategy in all content areas, not just language arts, can be beneficial to students.

Assessment of Visual Representation

While creating visual representations may be enjoyable to students, using them to assess significant learning and progress toward standards is always the bottom line. Providing students with opportunities to relate their work to rubrics or a set of criteria helps them to make those connections. Visually representing lends itself well to student self-assessment, as students have tangible products or videotapes of their work. They can judge, for example, whether the timeline created for a book they just completed includes the most significant events to explain how the story ended as it did. Or in illustrating a story that follows the pattern used by Jan Brett of using side panels to predict events, students might review their work against criteria for the project, including whether or not the side panels provide clear clues as to what will happen next in the story. In these instances, criteria would need to be included to cover both the content and areas of visual representation as in Table 6.16.

In some instances, a separate rubric might be applied for the medium being used. For example, if students are learning to use PowerPoint, the rubric might ask them to evaluate how well they were able to select background, arrange information, and organize a slide show. In using role-playing to demonstrate character conflict, they might self-assess whether they selected appropriate actions and words to convey the conflict and whether the desired emotions were portrayed.

Table 6.16   Content and Visually Representing Rubric

Rate yourself from 1 (low) to 5 (high) on each of the criteria below:

_____ Illustrations provide clear story clues as to what may happen next. Evidence:_____
_____

_____ Voice is clearly developed. Evidence:_____
_____

_____ The story is very well organized. Evidence: _____
_____

_____ Writing mechanics are used accurately. Evidence: _____
_____

A View From the Classroom

Even the youngest of students are able to use visually representing to self-assess their level of understanding. When 3-year-olds in an inner-city preschool were given the task of explaining the metamorphosis of the butterfly, one teacher designed an ingenious yet simple kinesthetic assessment (Lawrence, 2005). Students were given a string and a set of beads. As they strung the beads, they explained that the first white bead represented the egg from which a caterpillar would hatch. The next red bead represented the head of the caterpillar and the three green beads its body. The clear bead went on next, representing the chrysalis. The students explained that the caterpillar wrapped itself in the chrysalis and began to change. The final bead was shaped like a butterfly, and the students indicated that when the chrysalis opened, the caterpillar had changed into a butterfly. Students used a thumbs-up/down/middle show of hands to indicate how well they thought they had explained the metamorphosis. The string was made into a bracelet, and students wore them home and explained the process to their families, providing further reinforcement of the concept.

English Language Learners and Listening, Speaking, Viewing, and Visually Representing

ELLs and struggling students may often have a level of understanding of concepts but not have the oral language to express their thoughts. Representing ideas through visual opportunities often enables the students to demonstrate and expand their learning. Adaptations can be made to accommodate their level of English language development. For example, graphics and models might include labels or pictures rather than longer written explanations. Students might demonstrate how something was put together while another student narrates the process, adding to the oral communication when possible. Smaller speaking parts might be given to ELLs with more limited English language skills as well, allowing them to represent their ideas more often through visuals.

Listening, speaking, viewing, and visually representing are important areas of language arts, and combined with reading and writing, they form a comprehensive package for literacy development. They are more often integrated with one another and seldom stand completely alone.

Listening and viewing are receptive language functions, while speaking and visually representing are expressive functions. However, all of these areas are dynamic in the sense that there is a relationship between sender and receiver of information, and the receiver makes a response, whether efferent or aesthetic, to what was experienced.

ELLs and struggling students are provided with additional avenues of expressing understanding through viewing and visually representing. Accommodations can be made in listening and speaking in all areas of the curriculum to make input more comprehensible and to provide students with greater opportunities to expand their learning.

End-of-Chapter Reflection

- What role do you think listening, speaking, viewing, and visually representing play in helping children become literate? How do these language arts integrate with reading and writing? Support your position information from this chapter and/or other sources.

- Analyze your own strengths and weaknesses as a literate person in the areas of listening, speaking, viewing, and visually representing. How will these strengths or weaknesses impact your teaching in the area of literacy development? What might you do to strengthen areas that you want to develop more fully?

Planning for Teaching

- Review lessons that you have already taught or that you prepared for your classes. What types of listening, speaking, viewing, and visually representing experiences, if any, were included? In what ways could you add or enhance learning activities related to these areas of the language arts? What strategies might you emphasize?

Connections With the Field

- Observe in a K–8 classroom. Dialogue with the teacher about how he or she views the listening that students do in the classroom. What purposes are identified for listening? What kinds of opportunities are students given to develop higher-level listening, speaking, viewing, and/or visually representing skills?

Student Study Site

The Companion Website for Developing Voice Through the Language Arts

http://www.sagepub.com/dvtlastudy

Visit the Web-based student study site to enhance your understanding of the chapter content and to discover additional resources that will take your learning one step further. You can enhance your understanding of the chapters by using the comprehensive Study Guide, which includes learning objectives, key terms, activities, practice tests, and more. You'll also find special features, such as the Links to Standards from U.S. States and associated activities, Children's Literature Selections, Reflection Exercises, Learning from Journal Articles, and PRAXIS test preparation materials.

References of Children's/Young Adult Literature

DiCamillo, K. (2001). *Because of Winn Dixie*. Cambridge, MA: Candlewick Press.
Scieszka, J. (1989). *The true story of the 3 little pigs* (L. Smith, Illus.). New York: Penguin.

References of Professional Resources

Adams, M. (1990). *Beginning to read: Thinking and learning about print.* Cambridge: MIT Press.

Cox, C. (2005). *Teaching language arts: A student- and response-centered classroom* (5th ed.). Boston: Pearson, Allyn & Bacon.

Harste, J., Short, K., & Burke, C. (1988). *Creating classrooms for authors: The reading-writing connection.* Portsmouth, NH: Heinemann.

Lawrence, L. (2005). *Self-assessment of the Learning Project with three-year old kindergarten students.* Presentation to P-5 Steering Committee. Milwaukee, WI: Milwaukee Public Schools.

Miller, W. (2000). *Strategies for developing emergent literacy.* Boston: McGraw-Hill.

Moline, S. (1995). *I see what you mean: Children at work with visual information.* York, ME: Stenhouse Publishers.

Pappas, C., Kiefer, B., & Levstik, L. (2006). *An integrated language perspective in the elementary school.* Boston: Pearson, Allyn & Bacon.

Sousa, D. (2005). *How the brain learns to read.* Thousand Oaks, CA: Corwin Press.

Rosenblatt, L. (1985). Viewpoints: Transaction versus interaction: A terminological rescue operation. *Research in the Teaching of English, 19,* 98–107.

Rosenblatt, L. (1991). Literature: S.O.S. *Language Arts, 68,* 444–448.

Stauffer, R. (1975). *Directing the reading-thinking process.* New York: Harper & Row.

Tompkins, G. (2005). *Language arts: Patterns of practice* (6th ed.). Upper Saddle River, NJ: Pearson Merrill Prentice Hall.

Vygotsky, L. (1986). *Thought and language.* Cambridge: MIT Press.

Whitin, P. (1994). Opening potential: Visual response to literature. *Language Arts, 71,* 101–107.

Whitin, P. (1996). Exploring visual response to literature. *Research in the Teaching of English, 30,* 114–140.

Whitin, P. (2002). Leading into literature circles through the sketch-to-stretch strategy. *Reading Teacher, 55,* 444–450.

Wolvin, A., & Coakley, C. (1985) *Listening* (2nd ed.). Dubuque, IA: William C. Brown.

Yellin, D., Blake, M., & DeVries, B. (2004). *Integrating the language arts* (3rd ed.). Scottsdale, AZ: Holcomb Hathaway.

Other Children's/Young Adult Literature Resources

Lester, H. (1997). *Listen, Buddy* (L. M. Munsinger, Illus.). New York: Houghton Mifflin.

Choral Reading and Reader's Theater Suggestions

Angelou, M. (1978). *Life doesn't frighten me.* New York: Stewart, Tabori, & Chang.

Braun, W., & Braun, C. (1996). *A reader's theater treasury of stories.* Calgary, Alberta, Canada: Braun & Braun.

O'Neill, M. (1961). *Hailstones and halibut bones.* New York: Delacorte Press.

Sierra, J. (1996). *Multicultural folktales for feltboard and reader's theater.* Westport, CT: Greenwood.

Viorst, J. (1981). *If I were in charge of the world and other worries: Poems for children and their parents.* New York: Aladdin.

Technology Resources

Online rubric creator: http://rubistar.4teachers.org/index.php

Using digital cameras in the classroom: http://www.educationworld.com/a_tech/tech147.shtml

Many ideas for using digital cameras in classrooms:

http://www.wacona.com/digicam/digicam.html

7 Children's and Young Adult Literature as a Tool for the Language Arts

Context Setting:
After reading this chapter, you will be able to

- Identify the role of children's and young adult literature in the language arts curriculum
- Identify the use of multicultural literature to represent and expand student experiences and understandings
- Describe how knowledge of literary elements and genres may enhance student interactions with literature
- Analyze the role of technology in children's and young adult literature

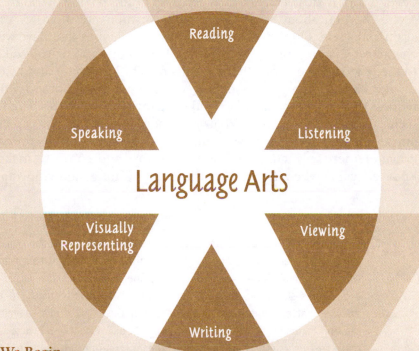

Before We Begin

- Krashen (2004a, 2004b) examined the correlation between the number of books available to children, either in the home or the community, and found overwhelming evidence that the more books children had access to, the better they did in school. This held true regardless of race, ethnicity, educational background of parents, and level of income. In your opinion, how important is children's literature to the academic success of students? Explain your answer.

Children's and Young Adult Literature in the Language Arts Curriculum

There are references to a number of specific children's and young adult books in this volume, many of which relate to the use of literature in the classroom. This chapter, however, focuses on children's and young adult literature itself, exploring the identification of quality literature, literary elements, and genre and determining how to use these aspects to effectively develop enjoyment, appreciation, and learning from literature.

A key consideration in the use of children's literature is that students be surrounded with quality reading materials in the classroom. "A good book is one created by a knowledgeable and skilled author where the elements of literature measure up under critical analysis. . . . Those elements may include the following: style and language, character, plot, setting, theme, tone, point of view, illustrations, mood, pacing, design and layout, and accuracy" (Jacobs & Tunnell, 1996, p. 15). A steady diet of mediocre and uninteresting literature does little to excite children about books and reading or motivate them to read the books again and again. On the other hand, books of all types that have well-developed characters, exciting plots, interesting information, and/or ear-catching rhythm to the language are books that students delight in reading and listening to on a regular basis. Often parents of very young children report that their children request that certain books be reread so many times that the parents are able to recite them from memory. What is it about the book that the child finds so attractive? In this chapter, we examine what we might teach students about **literary elements,** language of literature, genre, and so on to make them more knowledgeable when it comes to using, appreciating, and enjoying literature.

Stop to Think

The assistant director of an after-school reading project for children struggling with literacy development remarked that she was off to a rummage sale where children's books were to be sold. She stated that she would buy whatever books she could find. "These children are just learning to read, so it doesn't matter what books we give them. Once they have developed some reading skills, we'll get higher-quality books for them." How would you respond to the assistant director's philosophy regarding reading materials for children?

A second consideration in a discussion of children's and young adult literature has to do with the reader's or listener's taste in books. Being an award-winning publication of even the highest literary quality does not guarantee that all children will enjoy it. Since reading involves communication between the author and the reader, readers' preferences and past experiences will influence their choices in books. It is not surprising, then, that children are occasionally drawn to books that make us scratch our heads and try to figure out why they find particular books interesting or satisfying. It may be that a book, though poorly written or with uninspiring illustrations, strikes a chord with the experiences of the child.

A View From Home

When Jonathan was 3 years old he insisted that his parents reread the Perkins book *Hand, Hand, Finger, Thumb* (1969/1997) many times each evening. The parents could understand that the rhythm of the words, along with the colorful illustrations depicting the antics of a number of energetic monkeys, made the book so enjoyable to him. They were less sure why a relatively dull book about firefighters on their way to put out a fire also caught his attention. Perhaps it was due to the fact that Jonathan was a "Grandpa's boy" and was inseparable from his grandfather.

Grandpa was the chief of a volunteer fire department, and Jonathan often sat in the trucks pretending to drive. In this instance he may have taken pleasure in the book because it reminded him of adventures with Grandpa rather than because of its literary merit.

Generally, however, the selection of award-winning books is a safe way to ensure that quality literature is made available to children. The best-known awards are the Randolph Caldecott Medal, for most distinguished illustrations in a picture book, and the John Newbery Medal, for best written children's book. The Coretta Scott King Awards "are presented to authors and illustrators of African descent whose distinguished books promote an understanding and appreciation of the 'American Dream'" (Mitchell, 2003, p. 58). There are other literary awards that are given to quality children's and young adult literature as well. See the student Web site that accompanies this text for more information.

Purpose of Literature in the Curriculum

The purpose of using quality children's literature in the language arts curriculum first and foremost is to cultivate enjoyment and appreciation of reading. Keeping this in mind enables us to use children's and young adult literature and design learning experiences to nurture children's love of books and reading.

Lifelong Habits of Reading

Supporting the creation of lifelong reading habits and the ability to link what is read to other experiences guides students to comprehend and appreciate more fully and think more critically about what they read. Students who like books will be more likely to read, as will students who find literature that matches their interests and their reading levels. By doing so, students are more likely to develop lifelong habits that ensure they will read often and widely. Some children will already possess this habit when they come to school, and others will begin to develop it at school.

Making Connections to Oneself (Text-to-Self)

Harvey and Goudvis (2000) stress the importance of readers making connections from themselves to the text as a way to build comprehension and appreciation for what they are reading. "Students need to feel that they are accomplishing meaningful tasks and finding something out—not just plodding from story to story or book to book, answering questions and filling out worksheets without trying to make connections or see what literature has to do with understanding life. Meaning and the impact of the literature must be at the center of what we do with students" (Mitchell, 2003, p. 111). Children's and young adult literature has the potential to guide students to reflect on who they are and how they live their lives by reading about other children's experiences. Sometimes they realize that characters act in the same way as they do or possess the same traits, and other times they reflect on how different their experiences are or how different they are from characters. The Ramona books by Beverly Cleary (1977, 1980, 1981), for example, may comfort first graders who also misinterpret what adults say or who make decisions without clearly thinking through the consequences. They may come to understand that they are also impetuous like Ramona, and even though she may aggravate her parents and teachers, they still love her and care about her. Reading about Jess in *Bridge to Terabithia* (Paterson, 1977) may make certain preteen students think about whether or not they are imaginative, how far they go to be popular at school, or whether they would strike up a friendship with a member of the opposite sex.

Students might also reflect on how similar or different the experiences of the characters in books are from their own. Sometimes they relate very closely to the characters, and other times they experience situations from a different perspective. Selecting a book for classroom use where the main character is bullied, for example, might guide students in exploring the motivations of the bully and the reactions of the tormented students. Discussion could help students understand the motivations of children who harass their peers and guide them in developing effective reactions to bullying. In this sense, literature provides students with opportunities to explore character motivation and perhaps even lead to changes in behavior based on realizations gained from reading about the experiences of others.

Reading, discussing, and appreciating books about a variety of cultures and lifestyles expands students' horizons. The more students know of the world, the greater appreciation they are likely to bring to encountering people who are not exactly like them. For example, in *Spitting Image* by Shutta Crum (2003), "[t]welve-year-old Jessie accepts her lot in life, living in a poverty-stricken community where toddlers roam the streets and enter houses for food, until two social workers visit on behalf of President Johnson's war on poverty, leading her to question her life and environment" ("Top Shelf Fiction," 2003). This might be an excellent book for students to begin exploring poverty in the United States. Day (1994) suggests making comparisons between events from one culture to another as represented in children's literature to help students explore how different events might be interpreted in different ways depending on the culture. For example, discussions of cakewalks are found in both *Family Pictures/Cuadros de Familia* (Garza, 1990) and *Mirandy and Brother Wind* (McKissack, 1988).

Day also offers numerous suggestions for children to evaluate books for bias, discrimination, and stereotyping in literature. In *Reading, Writing and Rising Up: Teaching About Social Justice and the Power of the Written Word,* Christensen (2000) chronicles experiences in guiding students to critically analyze societal stereotypes and how they are represented in literature. She also focuses on how students learn to use literature and writing to understand themselves and the world around them.

Reading widely can also enable students to explore the range of possible human emotions and behaviors. Analyzing the restraint or lack of restraint demonstrated by characters in a variety of situations allows readers to step back and reflect on their own behaviors in similar situations. Such reflection may provide them with insights into their own thoughts and reactions to certain circumstances.

Making Connections to Other Texts (Text-to-Text)

It could also be the case that students are just drawn in by the characters or the plot of what they read. They may see links to other books they've read, or they may analyze characters or plots in books by the same author. In much the same way, similarities in style, setting, point of view, and so on can be studied either in books by the same author or by a variety of authors.

An important component of "text-to-text" connections (Harvey & Goudvis, 2000) is that students be guided to make observations and comparisons about similarities and differences between what they are currently reading and what they have read previously. In first-grade classrooms, a wide range of Eric Carle books can generally be found. Encouraging students to think about what they believe Eric Carle likes, as judged by the kinds of books he writes, may yield the following observations:

Eric Carle likes

- Bright colors (paint and tissue paper)
- Bugs
- Folded pages
- Holes in pages
- Kids

The Harry Potter books by J. K. Rowling may fascinate older students. In this series they might look at how the author builds suspense and adventure that draws readers in and makes them keep reading. The Red Wall series by Brian Jacques is a great example to use in exploring the author's use of personification in bringing the lives of forest rodents to such a level of intensity. Aspects of the creation of fantasy could be compared across several books or series to enable students to explore why these books are so attractive to them.

Text-to-text connections make readers better consumers of what they read. They look beyond the immediate story and expand what they know about how stories are constructed and about the authors' craft. They become good critics of what they read and continually expand their critical thinking skills.

🚐 A View From the Classroom

Mr. Ransic's fifth-grade class recently read *Number the Stars* by Lois Lowry (1989) set in Denmark during World War II and studied the effects of a country and people being occupied during wartime. Mr. Ransic deliberately chose *When My Name Was Keoko* by Linda Sue Park (2002), set in 1930s Korea when the country was occupied by Japan, to read next so that his students could make comparisons of the effects on people and the courage they can show during wartime. His students readily and enthusiastically made numerous links between the two texts and wrote comparison and contrast papers as a way to explore the many similarities between the texts.

Making Connections to the World (Text-to-World)

We often hear that the whole world is available to people who read, and indeed it is. Reading enables students to explore worlds and situations very different from their own. From these experiences, they are able to draw conclusions about the many ways in which we are all alike. For example, after reading several books about families, students might conclude that families exist everywhere in the world and generally the ties among family members are very close. Parents and guardians go to great lengths to protect their children and provide a good life. However, they might also note that parental expectations of children differ from one group to another and gender roles may be in opposition from one culture to another or from one historical period to another. In *The Breadwinner* by Deborah Ellis (2000), the only way for some families to survive the cruelness of the Taliban in Afghanistan was for girls to impersonate boys and obtain jobs in the marketplace. The reader comes to understand that females under this regime were not accorded the same rights and freedoms as are enjoyed by females in the United States. The reader also gets a sense of what it might be like to lose one's freedom and live in fear of a country's rulers.

Books of this nature, about both national and international themes, are effective in giving voice to traditionally silenced groups. Students who exclusively read literature with mainstream plots and characters are denied the richness of the world around them. Majority students do not come to challenge issues of "white privilege," and minority or nontraditional students may feel as though they are never represented in literature. Such omissions may lead them to question how they are valued by society. For these reasons, it is important to seek out quality literature that reflects the ethnicity and experiences of one's students as well as other cultures. Teachers who are committed to expanding the horizons of their students strive to build well-rounded collections of literature that represent a wide range of experiences, cultures, and perspectives.

To make connections to the world through reading does not always require an international setting. Rural students can learn about urban living and vice versa. Learning about other lifestyles in the same community can be enlightening for students as well. Experiences that cannot be had directly can be explored vicariously through reading.

Exploring the Social and Cultural Aspects of the World Through Literature

Beyond simply knowing more about the world through reading, analysis of what has been read can help students expand their views of events and lifestyles. It may lead them to understand actions that are different from their own. They may be more likely to suspend judgment when encountering different points of view or different ways of living because they have learned that they need to more fully understand the social and cultural values represented by the actions of others. In other words, reading may go a long way to help students develop tolerance for differences.

Literature that deals realistically and sensitively with sexual orientation is one such avenue for building tolerance and understanding. Children with same-sex parents, for example, need to see themselves represented and respected in children's and young adult literature. The other students benefit from being exposed to quality literature with memorable characters that happen to be homosexual or bisexual. Readers of this literature learn the issues encountered with sexual orientation, as they learn that nontraditional families and lifestyles may lead to very rich and rewarding lives.

In discussing the book *Am I Blue? Coming Out From the Silence,* edited by Marion Bauer (1994), which features famous children's authors discussing gay and lesbian issues, Diana Mitchell (2003) reminds us how critical it is to help students understand their worlds as fully as possible. "In the introduction, Bauer expresses the concern of many when she speaks of the significant number of teenagers who attempt suicide because of fears associated with their gay or lesbian sexuality" (p. 193). Inclusion of literature in this area may be a concern to some teachers and parents. Parents should always have the option to remove their children from learning experiences that do not align with their beliefs and values. However, it is important that the role of exposure to build tolerance and understanding also be considered. A listing of some quality children's and young adult books dealing with sexual orientation can be found at the end of this chapter.

Multicultural literature opens the door to a variety of lifestyles and perspectives. Teachers may periodically review their classroom libraries to determine how much variety is represented in their collection. They can ask themselves the following questions:

Which cultural groups are represented? Which are not?

Can these books be classified as quality literature?

Are there any racial, gender, or socioeconomic biases or stereotypes in these books?

Could my students be able to broaden their horizons by reading and reflecting on these books?

Reflection Journal 7.1

Review the collection of children's and young adult literature you currently have or are familiar with. What is the quality of this collection? What would you like to add before you start teaching? Using this text and other resources, begin a wish list of at least 10 quality texts you would like to include in your classroom and curriculum.

Differing **points of view** can also be explored in literature, providing students with greater insights into why people might develop differences of opinion. *The Pain and the Great One* by Viorst (1974) is a good book to use in guiding younger students, because in this story, a younger brother (the Pain) gives his impression of how his sister (the Great One) acts and treats him. In the second half of the book, the sister provides her own impression of her little brother. From the accounts of each sibling, it is clear that they have misinterpreted one another's feelings and actions.

Literature and Its Influence on Language Arts Development

Along with developing lifelong reading habits and learning to make connections, the language of literature is another avenue through which students develop an appreciation and enjoyment of reading (Cullinan, 1987). The most obvious aspect of language that is impacted during reading is vocabulary. Children who continually read quality literature, rich in the use of descriptive and expressive language, expand their sight word and meaning vocabularies. Students who are read to regularly at their listening comprehension level (which is generally well above the level at which they can read independently) develop **receptive vocabularies** that are also enhanced by the vocabularies to which they are exposed.

Authors use language that highlights and gives voice to a range of human emotions. Often animals portray these emotions to make it seem a little safer for children. They may discuss how the author made them feel and what emotions a story evoked. Having them share actual passages that brought out these emotions helps them focus on how the author uses language and the true power of language.

For example, consider this passage from *If You Come Softly* by Jacqueline Woodson (1998):

> Every [*sic*] since he was a little boy, his father had always warned him about running in white neighborhoods. Once, when he was about ten, he had torn away from his father and taken off down Madison Avenue. When his father caught up to him, he grabbed Miah's shoulder. *Don't you ever run in a white neighborhood,* he'd whispered fiercely, tears in his eyes. Then he had pulled Miah toward him and held him. *Ever.* (p. 143)

The language of the passage evokes the sheer terror of the father in protecting his son from what he does not yet understand.

Literal language can create vivid images for readers. Levels of analysis and inference might be required, but the language is generally more straightforward and easy for students to follow. "Young readers find books accessible if the language is natural for the text and for them" (Mitchell, 2003, p. 16). A balance between narrative and dialogue must be struck for the story to both convey its message and the action to move along at an appropriate pace. Obviously, good writing is at the heart of all quality literature for children.

Figurative language can take literature to new levels of imagery. If presented clearly and concretely through examples they are already familiar with, students can understand simile, metaphor, and personification. While more instruction may be warranted for students to understand figurative language, it will certainly add to their appreciation of literature.

Opportunities to Appreciate and Enjoy Literature in the Classroom

Many suggestions for cultivating an appreciation and an enjoyment of literature are highlighted throughout this text. Teachers create a classroom climate to appreciate good books when they set aside time daily to read and discuss books for enjoyment and demonstrate an eagerness to do so. An atmosphere for literary appreciation is developed when a comfortable and inviting space is arranged for children to relax and savor the read-aloud. Later they may discuss their response to the story and/or characters and make predictions and connections to themselves and other books. A wide variety of genres should be shared as read-alouds, enabling students to gain an appreciation of both **narrative** and **informational literature.** They learn the differences between the genres, especially if this is part of the discussion, and come to anticipate what each will have to offer.

Read-Alouds

Read-alouds are an excellent way to expand the listening comprehension of students. Unencumbered by the challenges of actual reading, students are free to settle back, listen, and let the story play out in their minds. Some students have been read to since birth, and others may need practice before they can visualize what they are hearing. Asking children to share their reactions and impressions of what they have listened to or to draw pictures of images from the read-alouds will expand their understanding of literature as they learn from the responses made by their peers.

Book Talks

There are many ways to entice children to expand their reading habits, all of which center around matching children to books they can readily read and that are of interest to them. Daily time for independent reading gets children in the habit of reading and provides regular time to read for enjoyment. Modeling **book talks,** short commercial-like introductions to books, will prepare students to excite one another about good books they have read. Teachers and librarians share book talks also, but peer recommendations carry a great deal of influence in the classroom. Time set aside for book talks signals that reading is an important component of the curriculum. Requiring students to read at least 15 minutes at home sends a message to both parents and children that reading outside of school is an important habit to cultivate. When students maintain a personal log of their reading, they are able to make judgments about how much and how widely they are reading. Some classrooms may even keep a log of all the books they have shared throughout the school year.

Illustration Study

Sharing illustrations during read-alouds can enhance the reading experience for students and may be a great way to hook children on books. Some children scour the illustrations and note every detail of an illustrator's work. Often they will point out details or clues that teachers or parents never noticed. There is more information on illustrations in children's literature later in this chapter.

Author and Genre Study

Author or **genre studies** provide students with in-depth opportunities to examine literature. Regular visits to the library get children in the habit of searching for books and magazines they may enjoy. It also is a good opportunity for students to get practice in learning how to locate particular books and to select materials at the appropriate level of difficulty. Bulletin boards and book displays may be used to further entice students to read.

There are a number of ways to extend student enjoyment of favorite literature. Reader's theater or puppet shows can be quick and easy ways to supplement rereading of literature and enable children to deepen their understanding of character, setting, and plot. Videos or DVDs are available for many stories. Asking students to compare the book and the video often results in students deciding that they find the print version richer. Generally, teachers share the electronic version following a reading of a book, though watching segments prior to reading may make stories more comprehensible for English language learners (ELLs) or students who struggle with reading and/or comprehension.

Teachers make sure they have students read or listen to age-appropriate stories that will be presented as plays by local theater groups. Children are anxious to see these live productions where they nearly feel as though they are part of the drama. These activities and many others are designed to get students hooked on reading children's and young adult literature.

Developing Strategic Readers Using Authentic Texts

Quality literature lends itself well to the development of **strategic readers.** Because characters are vivid or plots provocative in good books, it makes it easier for students to learn and use strategies that support reading development. For example, there is a rich story line in *The Mulberry Project* by Linda Sue Park (2005), and students naturally feel compelled to predict what will happen next. In the same book, the reader is led to infer that the main character's mother must face her prejudices against African American people and Julia must come to grips with the Korean side of her heritage.

In the novel *If You Come Softly* (Woodson, 1998), quoted earlier in this chapter, the author narrates, "Jeremiah didn't know they had been looking for a man. A tall, dark man. If he had known, he would have stopped when the shout came from behind him. But he was tangled up inside his thoughts" (p. 170). The **foreshadowing** from the first passage leaves a dread in readers' minds that makes them hope their predictions will not be borne out. The writing is vivid and emotional, and students can easily find evidence to support their prediction.

The plot of *If You Come Softly* challenges many assumptions and stereotypes that both the characters and the reader might hold. As such, students have opportunities for developing their skills of analysis and inference in rich discussions of the book and race relations in the United States. They are led to formulate opinions and make judgments they will have to defend.

Novels of this nature are excellent tools for children to explore the **author's craft.** Woodson made Jeremiah (Miah), who is African American, the son of a famous movie producer, and Ellie, who is Jewish, the daughter of a doctor and a mother who has abandoned her family on three separate occasions. Having students explore how the author developed the characters' personalities, how she revealed issues of race through the characters' actions, and what she does to create intensity in the plot is also a step toward analyzing an author's style.

Quality children's literature for very young readers can also support development of reading strategies. The illustrations in quality literature do a great deal to enhance the effective use of **picture clues** in reading. *Snowballs* by Lois Ehlert (1995) provides vivid drawings that match the text on each page. Pictures at the beginning and end of the book depict all of the materials that could be used to build the snowmen. Repeating plot elements, where a family of snowmen are created one by one, enable children to predict and use picture clues and context clues to support their reading.

In much the same way, Barbara Reid uses plasticine relief illustrations to chronicle the first hours of life of Buttercup's new calf in *The New Baby Calf* by Edith Newlin Chase (1984). The illustrations not only highlight the text on each page but also serve to build background understanding for children who are not familiar with life on the farm. For children who know farm life, the illustrations can be used to help them make connections to their own experiences and anticipate the text. The language is lyrical and creates an image of the wobbly new calf:

> The new baby calf took
> A very little walk,
> a teeny little walk,
> a tiny little walk.
> His skinny legs wobbled
> When he took that little walk,
> and the new baby calf fell down.

Students can begin to develop an awareness of how authors use language to create an image by studying it in books such as this. Recognition of repeating words and phrases and context clues could also be strategies to emphasize when reading this text. Obviously, these understandings often become reflected in students' writing as well.

Reading for Information Using Authentic, Meaningful Text

Informational books, also referred to as concept books or nonfiction, can expand students' curiosity about the world. Some students are intrigued with a single topic, such as dinosaurs, gymnastics, dogs, or car racing; they will read every book or magazine they find on the topic. It is often surprising to find a 6-year-old who can pronounce the multisyllabic names of numerous dinosaurs and provide incredible detail about their sizes, predators, and physical capabilities. Other children sample a wide variety of topics they find interesting and enjoyable. Books that have accurate information formatted in an interesting and easy-to-read manner will be more attractive to students. Information presented in a manner that matches the reading and conceptual level of the reader is most manageable for students.

Informational books can go a long way in activating or expanding children's curiosity. They can be instrumental in leading students to develop questions about the world around them that they hope to answer. Awakening a curiosity about the world in students is an important step in developing a classroom full of critical thinkers. In some instances they are led to action by what they read. They may attempt to make changes or improvements in their school or community, or they might start collections, construct things, or attempt new activities because of what they read.

Students might be interested in topics that correlate with what they are studying in the content areas and bring greater background knowledge to the classroom learning experience. They may be invited to serve as the "expert" in such instances and share their understandings, proving to be positive opportunities for children who are shy or who struggle to gain positive feedback from their peers. Children's interests may also inform what they study in school. For example, an avid collector of baseball cards may understand fractions and decimals well because of her fascination with batting averages. She may demonstrate to classmates how the batting averages work and how they apply to an understanding of fractions and decimals.

Teachers may also cultivate student interests through trips to libraries. Knowing how libraries are organized and how to find particular reading material surely expands student access to books and magazines that will be appropriate and interesting. It follows the understanding that the more children access informational literature, the more familiar they will become with the organization and components of this genre (index, glossary, graphics, maps, etc.) and the more easily they will gain meaning from the text. See Chapter 8 for a more in-depth discussion of the elements of informational literature often used in content area study.

As students read and enjoy informational books, the better they become at evaluating quality literature in this area. They will quickly put down a book that does not measure up but may pore over a book with new and interesting information for extended periods of time.

Learning About and Through Literature

The Development of Visual Literacy

We live in a highly visual world, and students are constantly inundated with visual images. It is important for them to develop skill in interpreting and appreciating visuals in order to function and communicate effectively. Visual literacy can be viewed as the ability to understand, interpret, appreciate, and clearly communicate the meaning of visual messages and produce visual messages using basic principles and concepts of visual design. Children's literature, in the form of picture books especially, is an effective medium for helping students develop visual literacy skills, as books are an important part of young children's lives as they learn about their world and the basics of reading through "reading" both the pictures and stories within them. Picture books provide students with a convergence of text and illustrations that are highly connected. This allows analysis and appreciation of the visual components, guiding students to develop skills that help them develop their visual literacy, a much needed element in their literacy learning.

Theory Into Practice

Research done by Chesner (2000) found that 5-year-olds used and learned a variety of visual literacy skills through exposure to picture books as they read them themselves or listened to them being read by their teacher. They used the following skills: noticing details, distinguishing between fact and fantasy, being aware of an illustrator's artistic style, evaluating illustrations, using imagination to add to or understand illustrations, questioning and understanding the illustrator's intent, making personal connections, and playing visual games with the illustrations. Picture books are an excellent tool for developing visual literacy skills not only in young children but to further enhance these skills in older students. Learn more about visual design and visual literacy as it relates to picture books through these books—*Looking at Picture Books* by J. Stewig (1995) and *The Potential of Picture Books* by B. Kiefer (1995)—and apply this to your future use of picture books in the classroom.

Literary Elements

The previous section discussed the purposes for weaving quality literature into the language arts curriculum. High-level appreciation and enjoyment of literature arises when students are able to understand and analyze what they have read. Students need to develop the tools to make these kinds of analyses. The role of the classroom teacher comes into play in guiding students to make connections and develop opinions about what they read. An understanding of literary elements and the components of the various genres adds to students' knowledge of what literature has to offer.

Characters

"**Characterization** is the art of creating people out of words on the page. When a writer has done a good job of characterization, readers feel as if they have gotten to know another person. How does a writer achieve that?" (Temple, Martinez, Yokota, & Naylor, 1998, p. 35). Answering this question is at the heart of studying characterization.

We come to know characters in books by what they look like, how they act and react, what they say, what others say about them, and how they relate to others. Every time a book is shared with students, these ways of revealing a character can be presented and reinforced in subsequent book conversations. Charts could be prepared, as in Table 7.1, to help students monitor their learning about characters. Younger children might create visuals of what the characters look like and add single words or phrases to describe them. Illustrations from the text may be helpful in identifying the characters.

Identifying the main and secondary characters is another skill students will need to learn how to use. Establishing the main character(s) guides the reader in determining who will receive the most attention in the story and around whom the plot will most likely be developed. The role of minor characters in advancing the plot may be examined, especially by older readers. In *Off to School* (Battle-Lavert, 1995), Wezielee is obviously the main character, but Papa and Mama are important in informing the reader that she is persistent about wanting to go to school and willing to take the risk of disobeying Papa to sneak off to school.

Sometimes the author allows us to learn about characters by placing them with contrasting characters with different personalities. "[T]he characters come to life through a sort of comparison and contrast: A character is like the group in

Table 7.1   How a Character Is Created in a Book

Story Summary: *Off to School* (Battle-Lavert, 1995)

Wezielee's family members are sharecroppers and move from state to state harvesting crops. It is Wezielee's turn to stay home and do the cooking. After the harvest, the children will go off to join their Caucasian classmates at school. However, Wezielee cannot wait that long and makes several attempts to sneak off to school, with disastrous effects on the family's meals.

What the Author Tells Us About Wezielee	What We Learned About Wezielee
Youngest, long-legged, strong, girl, black	Wezielee:
What she says: "Why can't I go to school now?"	is impatient
"I can't stay long, I got some cooking to do"	loves school
"Oh, Papa, I didn't mean to."	is persistent
What she does: Doesn't pay attention to cooking	takes risks
Sneaks off to school	
What others say: "Baby girl, be more careful tomorrow."	
"Child, just wait on time."	
"Child, don't go sassing me."	
How relates to others: Obeys Papa—"sort of"	

some ways, but strikingly different from it in some particular way" (Temple et al., 1998, p. 36). For example, Sarah in *Sarah, Plain and Tall* (MacLachlan, 1985) is from the East Coast and has never been to the Midwest. She does things differently and thinks differently. Her character is revealed as she strives to get acquainted with her new family. As a mail-order bride, she is unsure if she could live so far from her family and from the sea. She discovers amazing similarities between the two parts of the country, as well as fulfillment in forming a new family with Jacob and his children.

Once students are able to identify the traits of characters, they may move on to the characters' goals and motivations and how these may lead them to certain actions. Uncovering how the author lets readers know this can be interesting for students. Is it through the actual words of characters, through their actions, or through the words and actions of others that we learn most about the characters?

Plot

"**Plots** unfold when a character is drawn toward a significant goal. The goal is almost always related to *conflict,* either within the character, between the characters and some rival person, between the character and nature, or between the character and the expectations of society" (Temple et al., 1998, p. 38). Mapping plot development may provide students with insights into the way stories are organized. Did the plot rise to a climax and culminate in the **resolution?** In these instances, students identify the problem or "conflict," then follow the attempts of characters to resolve the problem, and note the final resolution of the story. Or was the book a series of "episodes" that the characters were engaged in?

The Circuit by Francisco Jimenez (1997) is a good example of an **episodic novel** (patterns of episodes or stories within a larger story). As the family stops at various migrant worker camps, the main character, Francisco, relates the experiences of himself and his family. In *Brave Irene* by William Steig (1986), there is a very definite conflict that must be resolved. Irene, the mouse, must deliver a very important gown for the ball. When she encounters a blizzard in the forest, we are unsure if Irene will be brave enough to complete the mission.

As a component of the study of plots, teachers may guide students to evaluate how well the author created the story. Mitchell (2003) suggests some questions or criteria that might be useful in evaluating plot in realistic fiction:

Do the strands of the plot work well together?

Does anything seem too coincidental?

How is the conflict presented—subtly or all at once?

What effect does this have on the story?

Other questions might be added, such as

Did the plot hold your attention? Did you enjoy it?

Is there sufficient detail?

Do the illustrations, graphics, or photos enhance the plot?

Are there any biases or stereotypes reflected in the plot? (p. 272)

The same type of evaluation might be done with characters. Did you learn enough about them? Were their actions consistent with the portrait the author painted of them? As with a study of characters, studying plot might take place through discussions, dramatic activities, creation of graphics, comparison charts, journal entries, and so on.

Setting

The setting refers to the time and place of a story. In some genres, folk literature, for example, the setting is described in a vague and succinct manner, "Once upon a time, in a land far, far away . . ." Other settings require much more description for the reader to get a sense of the time and place of the story. *Jacob Have I Loved* (1990) by Katherine Paterson has a setting that the author says is **integral** to the story, as its Maine locale carries the plot of sibling rivalry between two sisters. Often historical fiction requires setting elaboration. Generally, however, the opening paragraph or two or chapter will make the setting of a story clear.

Sometimes the setting is very crucial or "integral" to the plot. In these instances, the story could not take place somewhere else and still have the same impact. Hogwarts School is integral to the Harry Potter (Rowling) stories. A setting other than a mythical school of wizardry and witchcraft could not allow the same plot to unfold. *The Polar Express* (Van Allsburg, 1985) is another such book where the setting plays an important role in how the plot develops on a crisp Christmas Eve night in a cold climate and the North Pole.

In other stories the setting is not crucial to the development of the plot and serves merely as a **backdrop** to story events. The setting in *The Wednesday Surprise* by Eve Bunting (1989), in which a young girl teaches her grandmother to read, is unimportant to the plot. There is nothing about the setting itself that enhances or detracts from the surprise the girl and her grandmother are planning.

Discussions of setting and whether or not they were integral to the story will draw attention to the role that setting plays in a variety of plots and genres. The impact of the setting on the actions of the characters could also be explored. Does Harry Potter's attendance at Hogwarts School influence the young adult he becomes?

As students become more aware of how authors create and use setting in literature, they may develop their own criteria to evaluate how effectively each author has done this. They may include questions like the following:

Is the setting believable in this story? Provide some examples.

Is this a good setting for this story? Why or why not?

Is the setting clearly developed? Provide some examples.

Is the setting important to the development of the plot? Where is this evident?

Theme

Books that have a solid **theme** leave readers with something to think about. They may lead readers to ponder the following questions (Mitchell, 2003):

Is this something that will help me think about issues within myself?

What did I learn about people and society or myself?

What kinds of connections to people and society did this book give me?

Did this book show me possibilities and make me critical about thinking further about issues? (p. 34)

Sometimes fictional stories are **didactic** in nature and strive to teach a specific lesson. Folk literature often "teaches a lesson" as the primary purpose of the story. Nevertheless, as the questions above suggest, more often a well-written story is one that makes readers engage in reflective thinking and make connections to themselves or the world.

Themes are explicit when the author states them directly in the text. In *The Story Bag,* a Korean folktale in the book *Korean Children's Favorite Stories,* retold by Kim (2004), a rich child loves stories and keeps all of them tightly packed in a cloth sack for several years. On the eve of his wedding, a "faithful old servant" hears the captured stories plotting revenge on the young man for keeping them hostage and uncomfortable for so long. The servant rescues his master, and the story concludes with an explicit statement of the theme. "That is why when stories are heard they must never be stored away to become mean and spiteful, they are passed from one person to another so that as many people as possible can enjoy them" (p. 15).

The theme of friendship is implicit in *Bridge to Terabithia* (Paterson, 1977). Jesse and Leslie become neighbors, and despite vast differences in their family circumstances, they befriend one another. "Jess . . . is more sensitive than the rest of his farm family; his friend Lesley is more down-to-earth than her idealistic professional family. They are more like each other than their own kin" (Temple et al., 1998, p. 36). The theme of friendship slowly emerges as the plot unfolds.

Once a book falls into readers' hands, it is up to those readers to determine the meaning the book holds for them. Sometimes the reader will come away from the reading pondering the issues the author had in mind in writing the text. At other times, the reader may reflect on issues the author never even thought about while writing. The experiences and schema of the reader definitely impact what a person takes away from the reading.

What is critical for students is to, first, determine what the reading makes them think about, and second, to reflect on how the author led them to think about particular issues. They may focus on whether the theme is implicit or explicit. If the theme is implicit, how did the author reveal the theme? Was it through the plot, or was it through the characters' own words or actions, or was it through what was said or done by others?

Discussions of theme generally encourage the use of higher-level thinking skills. Students need to analyze, infer, synthesize, and evaluate. They must form opinions and be able to support them with evidence. Part of the analysis of theme might also include what Temple et al. (2006) refer to as "reading against the grain." Students reflect on the portrayal of various characters in a text as members of a particular group, for example, gender, race/ ethnicity, social class, age, and mental/physical capabilities, and determine how they are depicted in the text. An examination of the portrayal of the "faithful old servant" from *The Story Bag* might fall into this category. How is the servant treated? Why does he remain loyal to his master? They may also be asked to consider how the plot might have been altered if characters from a different group took their places, for example, a male became the main character replacing a female. This is an effective activity to use in having students examine books for stereotypes.

Certain recurring themes can often be found in children's and young adult literature. In books for children, themes often center on concepts that are important to them, such as family, friendship, humor, adventure, social reality/issues, personal issues, and animal themes (Anderson, 2006). Students might keep a running list of books they've read, noting the theme of each. Occasionally they could analyze their data and determine which themes continually recur in the books they have been reading. In this way they may become more aware of this phenomenon and look more closely for theme in their reading.

Style

Style relates to the way authors write. How do they use language to develop the plot? Do you have a clear visual image of what is taking place in the story? How does the author use language to evoke emotion? Do you feel like you are there? Do you feel like you know the characters? When children are disappointed by the movie version of a book they've read, it serves as a compliment to the author's writing. With words alone the author was able to create more powerful images than can be replicated by stage or cinema. This speaks to the style of the language and writing the author uses.

The tone or the attitude an author takes is part of the style. Some authors write in a single tone for all their works, and others use a variety of tones depending on the topic, theme, and setting of the text. "Some examples of tone used in children's books include serious, humorous, moralistic, hopeful, sympathetic, wondrous, longing, loving, satirical, and nostalgic" (Anderson, 2006, p. 38). Older students in particular, or students who read primarily a certain genre or many works by the same author, may become adept at identifying an author's tone.

Reflection Journal 7.2

Select a children's author who writes primarily in one of the tones mentioned above. Analyze what the author does to create this tone. How would you describe the author's voice? How would you go about teaching children to analyze an author's tone or style?

For example:

Serious Tone

- Shiloh Trilogy by Phyllis R. Naylor
- Books by Byrd Baylor
- Novels by Mildred Taylor

Humorous Tone

- Amber Brown books by Paula Danzinger
- Junie B. Jones books by Barbara Park
- Books by Roald Dahl

Examining voice in various authors' writing is helpful for students as they strive to develop their own voice. "Voice in literature has to do with the way an author comes across—from folksy to impersonal, from bold to timid, from expert to unreliable" (Temple, Martinez, Yokota, & Naylor, 2002, p. 52). Voice may be impacted by use of language, point of view, and tone. Choice of characters, settings, and plots also influences an author's voice. Many authors have developed a very distinctive style or voice in their writing. Discussions and reflections on authors' voice are certainly an important component in teaching children to appreciate and enjoy literature.

Genres of Children's and Young Adult Literature

One way to expand students' understanding of literature is to show them how books can be classified by characteristics they have in common, that is, by genres. Each genre has its own style, form, and content. Many books may fit into more than one genre, but knowing the general characteristics of the various genres enables students to bring a greater knowledge of what to expect in their reading.

When students begin reading books from a particular genre, they might create a chart of the characteristics they expect to find in that genre. As they read more widely in the genre, additions or modifications may be made to the listing. Students often have a sense of these characteristics, but asking them to analyze texts and verbalize the kinds of characters, settings, and plots they expect to find makes them more aware of how literature is organized. Table 7.2 provides an overview of the general characteristics of several genres of children's and young adult literature. Students develop a wide variety of reading strategies when they read from a broad range of genres, as different genres require them to think in different ways and to expect different outcomes (Wiencek & O'Flahavan, 1994).

Picture Books

Picture book is a broad classification of literature for younger readers. Many books from this genre are classified in other genres as well. The predominant feature of the picture book is that the illustrations and the words work together to convey the story and/or the information of the book. Picture books provide an opportunity for children to focus on how well the illustrations complement the book and to learn about how color, line, and size of illustrations create an impact. The books of Caldecott Award Medal winners (an award conferred annually for the most distinctive illustrations in a book for children) could be studied, and students could nominate and defend their own favorite illustrators.

Any literature meant for young children that uses illustrations to highlight and expand the text can be classified as picture books. As such, the characters could be real or fantastic people or animals. The story could be set anywhere in the world. Generally, the plots are related to children's interests, and many will

Table 7.2 Characteristics of Various Narrative Genres of Children's Literature

	Picture Books	Folk Literature	Realistic Fiction	Historical Fiction	Modern Fantasy	Mystery
Characters	*Real or fantastic people or animals	*Royalty *Villagers *Talking animals *Contrasting characters (good vs. evil)	*Real people or animals—no special powers or characteristics	*Real historical figures *Believable fictional character from time period	*Real or fantastic people, animals, or objects *Ghosts *Aliens *Creatures	*Detective *Suspects *Victims *Assistant to detective
Setting	*Anywhere in the world	*Long ago *Once upon a time *Forest *Castle *Village	*Modern times *Actual locations *Anywhere in the world	*In the past *Could be any place or any past time frame	*Present, past, or future *Real or fantastic settings *Other worlds *Supernatural elements	*Anywhere *Anytime *Real setting *Clues/motive as part of setting
Plot	*Related to children's interests *Ordinary children dealing with problems *Illustrations and words tell story *Little text per line	*Magic *Sorcery *Good conquers evil *Evil characters are tricked *Humble characters triumph *Events in threes *Live happily ever after	*Real-life situations *Range of topics *Happy or sad ending *Main character finds a way to cope with problem	*Stories of famous historical figures *Ordinary people in important historical events *Ordinary lives in the past *Themes of war, power, social issues	*Survival in the future *Often humorous *Sometimes scary *Good vs. evil	*Clever detective to figure out clues *Series of clues *Mystery solved as clues are revealed *May be surprise twist or ending
Strategies Developed	*Picture clues *Link illustrations to text	*Determine moral/lesson	*Make personal connections	*Make historical connections	*Draw conclusions *Suspend judgment	*Make deductions *Make inferences

Table 7.3   Picture Books

Brett, J. (1989). *The mitten*. New York: Putnam.

Brown, M. (1947). *Goodnight moon* (C. Hurd, Illus.). New York: Harper.

Bunting, E. (1994). *Smoky night* (D. Diaz, Illus.). San Diego, CA: Harcourt.

Cherry, L. (1990). *The great Kapok tree: A tale of the Amazon rain forest*. San Diego, CA: Harcourt.

Dorros, A. (1991). *Abuela* (E. Kleven, Illus.). New York: Dutton.

Ehlert, L. (1990). *Feathers for lunch*. San Diego, CA: Harcourt.

Henkes, K. (1996). *Lilly's purple plastic purse*. New York: Greenwillow.

Henkes, K. (2004). *Kitten's first full moon*. New York: Greenwillow.

Keats, E. (1962). *The snowy day*. New York: Viking.

Lehman, B. (2004). *The red book*. Boston: Houghton Mifflin.

Lobel, A. (1979). *Frog and toad are friends*. New York: Harper & Row.

Martin, B., Jr. (1967). *Brown bear, brown bear, what do you see?* (E. Carle, Illus.). New York: Holt.

Martin, B., Jr. (1989). *Chicka chicka boom boom* (J. Archambault, Illus.). New York: Simon & Schuster.

Polacco, P. (1993). *The bee tree*. New York: Philomel.

Say, A. (1996). *Emma's rug*. Boston: Houghton Mifflin.

Sendak, M. (1963/1989). *Where the wild things are*. New York: Harper & Row.

Van Allsburg, C. (1985). *Jumanji*. Boston: Houghton Mifflin.

Williams, S. (1992). *Working cotton* (C. Bayard, Illus.). New York: Harcourt.

be about ordinary children dealing with real everyday problems. There is often larger-size type and limited text per page, and typically they are 32 pages in length. See Table 7.3 for a listing of some well-known picture books.

Folk Literature

Folk literature, often referred to as "traditional literature," is an inclusive genre containing the body of stories and poems that have been handed down orally from generation to generation and whose original authors are typically unknown. As such, this genre includes myths, fables, fairy tales, folktales, legends, myths, epics, and porquoi and trickster tales. Many of the works from this body of literature were intended as tales that would teach a lesson or pass values from one generation to the next. Many of the characters are flat because their purpose is not for the reader to get to know them but to consider what they represent. The characters often include royalty, especially kings, queens, princes, and princesses. There are often characters that demonstrate opposite personalities; common or defenseless characters generally wage battle against more powerful, evil characters that plan to do them harm.

Magic and sorcery abound, though clever characters survive by their quick-witted thinking and actions. Good conquers evil, or true intentions vanquish trickery in most plots. Evil characters are often tricked by their own dastardly intentions, and humble characters often triumph over powerful oppressors. Events frequently happen in threes: three wishes, three pigs, three bowls of porridge. Conflicts are resolved in a satisfactory manner, and the final line is often "and they lived happily ever after." Fables might end with a statement of the lesson that was to be learned. Table 7.4 provides a listing of some traditional literature for children, followed by a listing of Cinderella stories from around the world.

Realistic Fiction

A large proportion of children's and young adult literature falls into the category of **realistic fiction.** As the name implies, all of the books in this genre must include characters, settings, and plots that can be found in reality. The characters are real people who have no supernatural powers or abilities. Animals may be characters in this genre, but they must act like actual animals. People may ascribe personality traits to them or speculate about what they are thinking, but the animals themselves cannot speak or think for themselves. The time frame must be modern times, and the setting may include any place in the world, but it must be a location that could actually exist.

The plot in realistic fiction literature must include only real-life situations but could include a very broad range of topics. The ending may be happy or sad, though the main character usually finds a way to solve the problem or conflict of the story. See Table 7.5 for a short listing of well-known, well-written realistic fiction literature you may be familiar with.

Historical Fiction

Like realistic fiction, **historical fiction** is also based in reality. The characters must either be actual historical figures, whether well known or not, or they may be fictional characters placed in a particular historical period. All of the characters must be portrayed as believable participants from the historical era being represented. "In a historical novel, the details of the setting may go a long way to satisfy young readers' curiosity about a place that is far removed in time" (Temple et al., 2002, p. 34).

Historical fiction often portrays themes related to war, power, social issues, immigration, and so on. The lives and feats of famous historical figures may be the subject of the plot, or it may feature ordinary people participating in important historical events. Other pieces of realistic fiction may focus on the era itself and

Table 7.4   Traditional Literature

Aardema, V. (1981). *Bringing the rain to Kapiti Plain: A Nandi tale* (B. Vidal, Illus.). New York: Dial. [African]

Galdone, P. (1973). *The little red hen.* New York: Seabury Press. [British]

Hamilton, V. (1985). *The people could fly: American black folktales* (L. & D. Dillon, Illus.). New York: Knopf. [African American]

Hutton, W. (1994). *Persephone.* New York: McElderry. [Greek]

Isaacs, A. (1987). *Swamp angel* (P. Zelinsky, Illus.). New York: Dutton. [North American]

Kellogg, S. (1988). *Johnny Appleseed.* New York: Morrow. [North American]

Lester, J. (1996). *Sam and the tigers* (B. Pinkney, Illus.). New York: Dial. [African American]

Martinez, A. (1991). *The woman who outshone the sun/La mujer que brillaba aún más que el sol* (F. Olivera, Illus.). San Francisco: Children's Book Press. [Latino]

McDermott, G. (1972). *Anansi the spider.* New York: Holt. [African]

McDermott, G. (1994). *Coyote: A trickster tale from the American Southwest.* New York: Harcourt. [Native American]

San Souci, R. (1998). *Fa Mulan: The story of woman warrior* (J. Tseng & M. Tseng, Illus.). New York: Hyperion. [Chinese]

Taback, S. (2000). *Joseph had a little overcoat.* New York: Viking. [Jewish]

Wells, R. (1993). *Max and Ruby's first Greek myth: Pandora's box.* New York: Dial. [Greek]

Wisniewski, D. (1996). *Golem.* Boston: Houghton Mifflin. [Jewish]

Xiong, B. (1989). *Nine-in-one. Grr! Grr!* (N. Hom, Illus.). San Francisco: Children's Book Press. [Hmong]

Cinderella Tales From Around the World

Climo, S. (1996). *The Korean Cinderella* (R. Heller, Illus.). New York: HarperTrophy.

Climo, S. (1999). *The Persian Cinderella* (R. Florczak, Illus.). New York: HarperCollins.

Hickox, R. (1999). *The golden sandal: A Middle Eastern Cinderella* (W. Hillenbrand, Illus.). New York: Holiday House.

Hooks, W. (1987). *Moss gown* (D. Carrick, Illus.). New York: Clarion. [Appalachian]

Jaffe, N. (1992). *The way meat loves salt: A Cinderella tale from the Jewish tradition* (L. August, Illus.). New York: Holt.

Pollock, P. (1996). *The turkey girl: A Zuni Cinderella story* (E. Young, Illus.). New York: Little, Brown.

San Souci, R. (1997). *Sootface: An Ojibwa Cinderella story* (D. San Souci, Illus.). New York: Bantam.

Table 7.5   Realistic Fiction

Children

Allard, H. (1985). *Miss Nelson is missing* (J. Marshall, Illus.). Boston: Houghton Mifflin.

Danzinger, P. (1997). *Amber Brown sees red* (T. Ross, Illus.). New York: Putnam.

English, K. (2004). *Hot day on Abbott Avenue* (J. Steptoe, Illus.). New York: Clarion.

Hoffman, M. (1991). *Amazing Grace.* New York: Dial.

Look, L. (2004). *Ruby Lu, brave and true* (A. Wilsdorf, Illus.). New York: Simon & Schuster.

Rylant, C. (1986). *The relatives came* (S. Gammell, Illus.). New York: Simon & Schuster.

Viorst, J. (1971). *The tenth good thing about Barney* (E. Blegvad, Illus.). New York: Macmillan.

Young Adult

Alphin, E. (2003). *Picture perfect.* Minneapolis, MN: Carolrhoda Books.

Banks, K. (2003). *Walk softly, Rachel.* New York: Frances Foster Books/Farrar Straus Giroux.

Bredsdorff, B. (2004). *The Crow-Girl.* New York: Farrar.

Cleary, B. (1983). *Dear Mr. Henshaw* (P. Zelinsky, Illus.). New York: Dell.

Codell, E. (2003). *Sahara special.* New York: Hyperion.

Coulloumbis, A. (1999). *Getting near to baby.* New York: Putnam.

Creech, S. (1994). *Walk two moons.* New York: HarperCollins.

Curtis, C. (1995). *The Watsons go to Birmingham.* New York: Delacorte.

Gardiner, J. (1980). *Stone Fox.* New York: HarperCollins.

Henkes, K. (2003). *Olive's green.* New York: Greenwillow.

Johnson, L. (2002). *Soul moon soup.* New York: Front Street.

Naylor, P. (1991). *Shiloh.* New York: Atheneum.

Paterson, K. (1978). *The great Gilly Hopkins.* New York: Crowell.

Paulsen, G. (1987). *Hatchet.* New York: Bradbury.

Woodson, J. (2003). *Locomotion.* New York: Putnam/Penguin.

highlight the lifestyle of people from a variety of social stations. Table 7.6 provides some examples of historical fiction for children and young adults.

Modern Fantasy and Science Fiction

In the genre of **modern fantasy,** characters often have supernatural powers. They may be ghosts or aliens, or they could be talking animals or objects. Fantasy literature goes beyond the known world and creates a new or transformed world.

Table 7.6   Historical Fiction

Children

Bunting, E. (1996). *Train to somewhere* (R. Himler, Illus.). New York: Clarion.

Dorris, M. (1992). *Morning girl.* New York: Hyperion.

Hopkinson, D. (1993). *Sweet Clara and the freedom quilt* (J. Ransome, Illus.). New York: Knopf.

Houston, G. (1988). *The year of the perfect Christmas tree* (B. Cooney, Illus.). New York: Dial.

Levitin, S. (1996). *Nine for California* (C. Bowman Smith, Illus.). New York: Orchard.

Micheaux, V. (2003). *Almost to freedom* (C. Bootman, Illus.). Minneapolis, MN: Carolrhoda Books.

Polacco, P. (1994). *Pink and Say.* New York: Philomel.

Turner, A. (1987). *Nettie's trip south* (R. Himler, Illus.). New York: Macmillan.

Yolen, J. (1992). *Encounter* (D. Shannon, Illus.). San Diego, CA: Harcourt Brace.

Young Adult

Barrett, T. (1999). *Anna of Byzantium.* New York: Delacorte.

Bradley, K. (2003). *For freedom: The story of a French spy.* New York: Delacorte.

Choi, S. (1991). *The year of impossible goodbyes.* New York: Dell.

Cushman, K. (1994). *Catherine, called Birdy.* New York: Clarion.

Cushman, K. (2003). *Rodzina.* Boston: Houghton Mifflin.

Donnelly, J. (2003). *A northern light.* New York: Harcourt.

Hesse, K. (1997). *Out of the dust.* New York: Scholastic.

Lowry, L. (1989). *Number the stars.* Boston: Houghton Mifflin.

McCully, E. (1996). *The bobbin girl.* New York: Dial.

Naylor, P. (2002). *Blizzard's wake.* New York: Atheneum.

Park, L. S. (2001). *A single shard.* New York: Clarion.

Park, L. S. (2002). *When my name was Keoko.* New York: Clarion.

Rinaldi, A. (1992). *A break with charity: A story about the Salem witch trials.* New York: Harcourt.

Taylor, M. (1990). *Mississippi bridge* (M. Ginsburg, Illus.). New York: Dial.

Taylor, M. (2003). *Roll of thunder, hear my cry.* New York: Dial.

The setting could be in the present or the future, in a realistic or a fantastic setting. Characters could be realistic in another world setting, or they could be otherworldly characters in a real or fantastic setting. Time travel may be a component of modern fantasy as well.

Modern fantasy is often humorous or adventurous in nature, though some plots may be frightening for some readers. Children often have to suspend expectations and think in new ways about characters, settings, and plots when reading fantasy. Science fiction themes often feature survival in the future after an environmental disaster, survival on a new planet or in a new universe, or coping with other forms of life. Good generally triumphs over evil. See Table 7.7 for some examples of modern fantasy for children and young adults.

Table 7.7   Modern Fantasy

Children

Alexander, L. (1992). *The fortune tellers* (T. Schart Hyman, Illus.). New York: Dutton.

Brett, J. (1996). *Berlioz the bear.* New York: Putnam.

Lionni, L. (1995). *Little blue and little yellow.* New York: HarperTrophy.

Meddaugh, S. (1994). *Martha speaks.* Boston: Houghton Mifflin.

Munsch, R. (1999). *The paper bag princess* (M. Martchenko, Illus.). New York: Scholastic.

Ringgold, F. (1992). *Aunt Harriet's underground railroad in the sky.* New York: Crown.

Salinas, B. (1998). *The three pigs/Los tres credos.* San Francisco: Piñata Books.

Scieszka, J. (1996). *The true story of the 3 little pigs* (L. Smith, Illus.). New York: Puffin.

Wells, R. (1985). *Max's breakfast.* New York: Dial.

White, E. B. (1974). *Charlotte's web.* New York: HarperTrophy.

Willems, M. (2003). *Don't let the pigeon drive the bus.* New York: Hyperion.

Young Adult

Babbitt, N. (1975). *Tuck everlasting.* New York: Farrar.

Collins, S. (2003). *Gregor the Overlander.* New York: Scholastic.

Dahl, R. (1961). *James and the giant peach.* New York: Knopf.

DiCamillo, K. (2003). *The tale of Despereaux: Being the story of a mouse, a princess, some soap, and a spool of thread* (T. B. Ering, Illus.). Cambridge, MA: Candlewick Press.

Ferris, J. (2002). *Once upon a marigold.* New York: Harcourt.

Gaiman, N. (2002). *Coraline* (D. McKean, Illus.). New York: Harper Collins.

Howe, J., & Howe, D. (1979). *Bunnicula* (L. Morrill, Illus.). New York: Atheneum.

Jacques, B. (1987). *Redwall.* New York: Philomel.

Jacques, B. (1991). *Muriel of Redwall.* New York: Philomel.

And others in the series

Jarvis, R. (2002). *Thorn ogres of Hagwood.* New York: Harcourt.

L'Engle, M. (1962). *A wrinkle in time.* New York: Farrar, Straus & Giroux.

Lowry, L. (1993). *The giver.* Boston: Houghton Mifflin.

Rowling, J. (1998). *Harry Potter and the sorcerer's stone.* New York: Scholastic.

Mystery

A detective, victims, suspects, and occasionally an assistant to the detective are the usual characters in mystery stories. The settings are realistic, though there may be elements that make them appear fantastic in some way. The mystery often takes place in the present and can occur in any location; the site of the mystery is often dark or mysterious and evokes an aura of suspense and intrigue. Clues often found in the setting lead the reader to speculate about "who done it."

In a mystery story, generally a clever detective is engaged in working on solving the mystery. In young children's mystery books, there is seldom a crime but more often an object that is missing or some phenomenon that cannot be explained. The detective, often a child or young adult character, is presented with, or uncovers, several clues that he or she must follow up on in finally solving the mystery. Occasionally, clues and suspects turn out to be false leads, and the reader and/or the detective must puzzle through available evidence to draw new conclusions in solving the mystery.

The genre of mystery can be interactive for readers as they link clues to suspects and make deductions about how to solve the mystery. See Table 7.8 for some examples of children's and young adult mystery books that are sure to engage readers.

Table 7.8   Mystery

Children

Adler, D. (1987). *Cam Jansen and the scary smoke mystery*. New York: Viking. [Part of the Cam Jansen mystery series]

Base, G. (1988). *The eleventh hour: A curious mystery*. New York: Viking Kestrel.

Pageler, E. (1994). *The market stake-out mystery*. Novato, CA: High Noon Books. [Part of the Riddle Street Mystery series]

Sobol, D. (1968). *Encyclopedia Brown solves them all* (L. Shortall, Illus.). New York: Scholastic. [Part of the Encyclopedia Brown series]

Young Adult

Bunting, E. (1992). *Coffin on a case*. New York: HarperCollins.

Hamilton, V. (1968). *The house of Dies Drear*. New York: Silver Burdett Ginn.

Nixon, J. (1996). *Search for the shadowman*. New York: Delacorte.

Raskin, E. (1978). *The westing game*. New York: Dutton.

Sachar, L. (2003). *Holes*. New York: Yearling.

Informational Literature and Concept Books

Informational books are organized in a different format from other genres in that they focus on a particular topic, and rather than a story line, information is organized in a particular manner. This genre need not necessarily be read cover to cover, especially if the reader is interested in looking for particular information in the text. "Authors of informational books employ an expository style of writing to explain, inform, and describe. Biography and autobiography are examples of informational books. Expository writing uses various organizational patterns to present information, such as description, chronological sequencing, explanation, comparison/contrast, defining with examples, and problem-solution" (Temple et al., 2002, p. 401). Children can expand their critical thinking skills a great deal by reading extensively in this genre. Chapter 8 focuses more fully on information literature as part of an exploration of the role of language arts in content area courses.

Informational books for young readers are referred to as **concept books**. These books are designed to teach basic concepts to children and often contain colorful, large illustrations that play an important role in teaching about the concept. Print is large and minimal in books for the youngest children. Alphabet, counting, colors, and daily routines such as dressing or eating make up the themes for a large number of these books. See Table 7.9 for some examples of informational books for children.

Table 7.9 Informational Books for Children

Cha. D. (1996). *Dia's story cloth: The Hmong people's journey of freedom* (C. & N.T. Cha, Illus.). New York: Lee & Low.

Freedman, R. (1997). *Eleanor Roosevelt: A life of discovery*. New York: Clarion.

Fritz, J. (2001). *Leonardo's horse* (H. Talbott, Illus.). New York: G. P. Putnam.

Gerstein, M. (2003). *The man who walked between the towers*. Brookfield, CT: Roaring Brook Press.

Hoyt-Goldsmith, D. (2001). *Celebrating Ramadan* (L. Migdale, Photographer). New York: Holiday House.

Jenkins, S., & Page, R. (2003). *What do you do with a tail like this?* New York: Houghton Mifflin.

Martin, J. B. (1998). *Snowflake Bentley* (M. Azarian, Illus.). New York: Houghton Mifflin.

Montgomery, S. (2004). *The Tarantula scientist* (N. Bishop, Photographer). New York: Houghton Mifflin.

Morrison, T. (2004). *Remember: The journey to school integration*. New York: Houghton Mifflin.

Murphy, J. (2003). *An American plague: The true and terrifying story of the yellow fever epidemic*. New York: Clarion.

Pringle, L. (2003). *Whales! Strange and wonderful* (M. Henderson, Illus.). Honesdale, PA: Boyds Mills Press.

Sis, P. (2003). *The tree of life*. New York: Farrar Straus Giroux.

Poetry

There is a wide range of what can be included in the genre of poetry, including everything from nursery rhyme to free verse. "Poetry is multifaceted; it can tell a story, describe something in a fresh and novel way, make a comment on humanity, draw a parallel to aspects of your life, or make you laugh" (Anderson, 2006, p. 303). Children generally love the lyrical and often playful tone of much of the poetry for young people.

Poetry is an effective genre for children to explore the power of language. Few words are used to convey strong images and ideas. The rhythm of the language is accented by the arrangement of words on paper. It also provides an authentic opportunity to teach about figurative language, including simile and metaphor.

As teacher Kathi Glick demonstrates with her first graders in Chapter 10, a large part of teaching about poetry is exposing children to a wide variety of poetry to develop appreciation and enjoyment. Beyond that, they learn about types of poetry, including narrative and lyric, and poems with specific forms, such as limerick and haiku, concrete poetry, and free verse.

Students generally enjoy the freedom they find in writing poetry. Often ELLs or struggling writers are able to express poignant ideas and emotions in poetic form that they are not able to easily convey in conventional narrative writing. Some poetry sources can be found in Table 7.10.

Technology and Literature

Not surprisingly, with continual advances in the development of CD-ROM capabilities and the ever-expanding use of the World Wide Web, technology is impacting the field of language arts and children's and young adult literature as well. Although much technology is available, selecting appropriate and quality materials that match the interests and learning needs of the students remains a challenge. Technology, in and of itself, is not a panacea but requires careful and thoughtful planning by the teacher to use it wisely.

E-Books

"[E]Books are virtual **electronic books** that are displayed on a computer or handheld viewing device (Click-a-Word Talking e-Books). Interactive electronic books can be viewed online or downloaded from the Internet. Viewers have access to the library of a site and may download materials 24 hours a day. These electronic books use hypertext technology to organize information and provide options for readers" (Tompkins, 2005, p. 66). One page of text is displayed on the screen at a time, and students may click on a button to listen to the text, or they may read along with the text that is highlighted as it is being read. They may opt

Table 7.10 Poetry for Children

Alarcón, F. (1999). *From the bellybutton of the moon and other summer poems/Del ombligo de la luna y otras poemas de verano* (M. C. Gonzalez, Illus.). San Francisco: Children's Book Press.

Bruchac, J., & London, J. (1992). *Thirteen moons on the turtle's back* (T. Locker, Illus.). New York: Philomel.

Delacre, L. (1989). *Arroz con leche: Popular songs and rhythms from Latin America*. New York: Scholastic.

Fleischman, P. (1988). *Joyful noise: Poems for two voices* (E. Beddows, Illus.). New York: Harper.

Harrison, D. (2000). *Farmer's garden: Rhymes for two voices* (A. Johnson-Petrov, Illus.). Honesdale, PA: Boyds Mills Press.

Hughes, L. (1996). *The dream keeper and other poems* (J. Pinkney, Illus.). New York: Knopf.

Janeczko, P. (2001). *A poke in the I*. Cambridge, MA: Candlewick Press.

Meyers, W. D. (1993). *Brown angels: An album of pictures and verse*. New York: HarperCollins.

O'Neill, M. (1989). *Hailstones and halibut bones* (J. Wallner, Illus.). New York: Doubleday.

Poe, E.A. (2002). *The raven and other poems*. New York: Scholastic.

Prelutsky, J. (1984). *The new kid on the block* (J. Stevenson, Illus.). New York: Greenwillow.

Prelutsky, J. (1993). *The dragons are singing tonight* (P. Sis, Illus.). New York: Greenwillow.

Schwartz, A. (1992). *And the green grass grew all around: Folk poetry for children* (S. Truesdell, Illus). New York: HarperCollins.

Silverstein, S. (1974). *Where the sidewalk ends*. New York: Harper & Row.

Sneve, V. (1989). *Dancing teepees* (S. Gammell, Illus.). New York: Holiday House.

Wong, J. (2000). *Night garden: Poems for the world of dreams* (J. Poschkis, Illus.). New York: McElderry.

to read the text independently, clicking only on words they do not know to have them pronounced aloud.

Many of the books are accompanied by workbook-like activities. This is one area where teachers must be discriminating in determining if or how to use e-books. A question to keep in mind when previewing these resources for possible use in the classroom is whether the activities truly further the skills and comprehension of young readers. In addition, the quality of the stories must be reviewed, as many located on the Internet are of dubious quality, written by unknown authors. One company advertises, "Our mission is to provide electronic books without judging their content" (Globusz, 2006). A Web site at Iowa State

University includes a caveat about children's e-books that the e-books available online are those that are available due to the owner having legal copyright. That does not imply that the books are quality books, and indeed many of them are not. Therefore, a teacher must be wary of the quality of the e-books that are obtained.

Computerized readings may also be stilted or unclear. The text may be presented without illustrations and only as dense pages of text on the screen. Other sites feature books that are designed to teach phonics and have story lines that make little sense and are contrived merely to provide practice in sounding out particular phonics patterns. These resources frequently include music or sound effects, but children are seldom attracted to the literature component, as the story lines do not hold their attention for long.

When e-books feature quality literature, user-friendly technology, and good instructional teaching options, they can be very useful additions to a classroom library. Beginning readers, ELLs, and students struggling with reading may enjoy the additional support of electronic books. They receive instant feedback on words they do not know and have access to fluent reading of each page. Both fluency and sight word vocabularies may be improved in this way, and repeated readings along with support from illustrations may help enhance comprehension as well. However, use of these tools alone cannot guarantee reading success. Rich discussions of books along with careful instruction in skills and strategies are the primary instructional activities that promote literacy development. Resources such as electronic books may serve as good support materials to reinforce what has been learned in guided or shared reading sessions.

"Many electronic books include reading logs, word-identification activities, and other reading and writing activities. Scholastic WiggleWorks and Broderbund's The Living Books Framework are two of the best-known programs, and they use trade books written by well-known children's authors such as Mercer Mayer and Jack Prelutsky" (Tompkins, 2005, p. 66). Table 7.11 provides a listing of some e-book sites.

Other computerized software that encompasses the use of children's literature should also be evaluated critically to determine whether it promotes the development of lifelong reading habits for children. **Reading management programs**, for example, assign points to students after they have read a book and completed an electronic test on the contents of the book. Often teachers require that students must earn a minimum number of points each quarter. However, children may become disenchanted with reading when they are doing so only to earn points by completing multiple-choice tests rather than engaging in meaningful discussions and learning experiences centered on the book (Carter, 1996).

"[O]nline book clubs can help students explore their ideas through literary conversations. Many authors maintain websites. Students can learn about their favorite authors and even communicate with them through e-mail. . . . Because students can follow their interests by using hyperlinks, online books provide students with a refreshing change from the linear process of reading traditional text" (Cramer, 2004, p. 210). When students engage in authentic online discussions

Table 7.11   E-Book Web Sites

Brøderbund (The Learning Company): http://www.learningcompanyschool.com

Children's e-library: http://www.childrenselibrary.com/account_intro.php

Corner Stone Reading Comprehension: http://www.hart-inc.com/csrdg.htm

EBookJungle.com

eBooks.com: Children's books

eReader.com

Gamco Education Materials/Siboney Learning Group: http://www.gamco.com

ipicturebooks.com

Mind Like Water—Free children's e-books: http://www.mindlikewater.com/Directory/Free/ childrens_free _ebooks.html

WE READ—Literacy and Education for Life: http://www.weread.org

The Work E-Books—children's e-books: http://www.planetwide-exodus.com/Childrens Books.html

of books with peers and learn more about authors of books they are reading and listening to, the technology serves to enhance overall enjoyment and literacy development for them.

Living Books

Living Books are software programs that are developed based on children's literature. One of the most popular and first out on the market is *Just Grandma and Me,* written by Mercer Mayer (1998). Living Books software contains colorful graphics and clickable hotspots and text, allowing students to interact with the book. Students can choose to have the books read aloud to them through the software (text is highlighted as it is read so users can follow along) or can read it themselves, clicking on individual words to obtain correct pronunciation. Often Living Books software includes the ability to use it with a number of languages such as Spanish, French, or German.

Living books can help improve students' comprehension and appreciation of literature, and they can be helpful for ELL students because of the high level of reading support they provide. When choosing Living Books for use in your classroom, preview the software completely to determine appropriateness for your students. Some of the available quality titles for young children include the following:

Dr. Seuss, *Cat in the Hat*

Marc Brown, *Arthur's Adventure with D.W.*

Janell Cannon, *Stellaluna*

Virginia Lee Burton, *Mike Mulligan and His Steam Shovel*

Aesop Fable, *Tortoise and the Hare*

Digital Storytelling

"**Digital Storytelling** is the modern expression of the ancient art of storytelling. Digital stories derive their power by weaving images, music, narrative and voice together, thereby giving deep dimension and vivid color to characters, situations, experiences, and insights" (Rule, 2005). In some schools, digital storytelling has become a common curricular component where students take their written pieces and turn them into digital storytelling creations, adding visuals and their own voices narrating the story. Taking the power of the digital age and combining it with children's love of story and telling stories, a teacher can use this new medium for engaging children in literature and creating stories of their own. See the technology resources at the end of this chapter for more information on digital storytelling.

The more informed students are about literary elements, genre, and ways to make connections to what they read, the more likely they are to read with appreciation and understanding. Providing children with access to a broad range of quality literature may entice them to expand their reading interests and begin the development of lifelong reading habits that will serve them throughout their lives.

End-of-Chapter Reflection

- Many examples of children's literature were discussed throughout this chapter. Which books sounded interesting to you that you might want to explore for use with children in the future? Were there certain genres that intrigued you? Were there any genres that you typically do not read that you would like to explore in order to be more familiar with them?

- Explore the role of theme in children's literature. Note whether themes are explicit or implicit in children's books. How would you teach these two concepts?

Planning for Teaching

- Spend time in the children's area of a public library. Watch the children who are there. How are they choosing books? What types of books do they seem most interested in reading by their choices? If you are comfortable talking with some of them and you clear it with their parents/guardians, ask them about their choices. Why did they choose the books that they did? Be aware that some children may not be comfortable talking with you or may not have a lot to say if they have not have been taught how to discuss their reading choices.

Connections With the Field

1. Visit one or more K–8 classrooms. Ask students to write (or dictate) a list of their five most favorite books. Tally the responses and analyze the data. What do the results tell you about these students and their reading preferences?

2. Visit an early/middle childhood classroom where the teacher reads aloud to the students frequently. What are the children's favorite books? How do you know? Why do you think they are attracted to these particular books?

3. Visit a classroom where use of quality children's and young adult literature is emphasized. Note how literature is used during the day. How are books and reading materials organized and displayed in the classroom? How does the teacher promote the development of life-long reading habits?

Student Study Site

The Companion Website for Developing Voice Through the Language Arts

http://www.sagepub.com/dvtlastudy

Visit the Web-based student study site to enhance your understanding of the chapter content and to discover additional resources that will take your learning one step further. You can enhance your understanding of the chapters by using the comprehensive Study Guide, which includes learning objectives, key terms, activities, practice tests, and more. You'll also find special features, such as the Links to Standards from U.S. States and associated activities, Children's Literature Selections, Reflection Exercises, Learning from Journal Articles, and PRAXIS test preparation materials.

References of Children's/Young Adult Literature

Battle-Lavert, G. (1995). *Off to school* (G. Griffith, Illus.). New York: Holiday House.

Bauer, M. (Ed.). (1994). *Am I blue? Coming out from the silence.* New York: HarperCollins.

Bunting, E. (1989). *The Wednesday surprise.* New York: Clarion.

Chase, E. (1984). *The new baby calf* (B. Reid, Illus.). New York: Scholastic.

Cleary, B. (1977). *Ramona and her father.* New York: HarperTrophy.

Cleary, B. (1980). *Ramona and her mother.* New York: HarperTrophy.

Cleary, B. (1981). *Ramona, age 8.* New York: HarperTrophy.

Crum, S. (2003). *Spitting image.* New York: Houghton Mifflin.

Ehlert, L. (1995). *Snowballs.* New York: Scholastic.

Ellis, D. (2000). *The breadwinner.* Toronto, Ontario, Canada: Groundwood Books.

Garza, C. (1990). *Family pictures/Cuadros de familia.* San Francisco: Children's Book Press.

Jimenez, F. (1997). *The circuit: Stories from the life of a migrant child.* Albuquerque: University of New Mexico Press.

Kim, S. (2004). *Korean children's favorite stories.* North Clarendon, VT: Tuttle Press.

Lowry, L. (1989). *Number the stars.* New York: Houghton Mifflin.

MacLachlan, P. (1985). *Sarah, plain and tall.* New York: Harper & Row.

Mayer, M. (1998). *Just Grandma and me* (2nd ed.). Broderbund Software.

McKissack, P. (1988). *Mirandy and Brother Wind* (J. Pinkney, Illus.). New York: Knopf.

Park, L. (2002). *When my name was Keoko.* New York: Clarion.

Park, L. (2005). *The mulberry project.* New York: Clarion.

Paterson, K. (1977). *Bridge to Terabithia.* New York: HarperTrophy.

Paterson, D. (1990). *Jacob have I loved.* New York: HarperTrophy.

Perkins, A. (1997). *Hand, hand, finger, thumb* (E. Gurney, Illus.). New York: Random House. (Original work published 1969)

So-un, K. (2004). *Korean children's favorite stories* (K. Sim, Illus.). Boston: Tuttle Press.

Steig, W. (1986). *Brave Irene.* New York: Farrar Straus Giroux.

Van Allsburg, C. (1985). *The polar express.* Boston: Houghton Mifflin.

Viorst, J. (1974). *The pain and the great one.* New York: Bantam Doubleday.

Woodson, J. (1998). *If you come softly.* New York: Putnam.

References of Professional Resources

Anderson, N. (2006). *Elementary children's literature: The basics for teachers and parents* (2nd ed.). Boston: Pearson, Allyn & Bacon.

Carter, B. (1996). Hold the applause! Do Accelerated Reader & Electronic Bookshelf send the right message? *School Library Journal, 42,* 22–25.

Chesner, G. A. (2000). *Invitations for interpretation and appreciation: How five-year-olds construct meaning through response to picture book illustration and design.* Unpublished doctoral dissertation, University of Wisconsin–Milwaukee, Milwaukee, WI.

Christensen, L. (2000). *Reading, writing and rising up: Teaching about social justice and the power of the written word.* Milwaukee, WI: Rethinking Schools.

Cramer, R. (2004). *The language arts: A balanced approach to teaching reading, writing, listening, talking, and thinking.* Boston: Pearson, Allyn & Bacon.

Cullinan, B. (Ed.). (1987). *Children's literature in the reading program.* Newark, NJ: International Reading Association.

Day, F. (1994). *Multicultural voices in contemporary literature: A resource for teachers.* Portsmouth, NH: Heinemann.

Globusz. (n.d.). Retrieved on May 9, 2006, from http://www.globusz.com.

Harvey, S., & Goudvis, A. (2000). *Strategies that work: Teaching comprehension to enhance understanding.* Portland, ME: Stenhouse.

Jacobs, J., & Tunnell, M. (1996). *Children's literature briefly.* Englewood Cliffs, NJ: Merrill.

Kiefer, B. (1995). *The potential of picture books: From visual literacy to aesthetic understanding.* Englewood Cliffs, NJ: Prentice Hall.

Krashen, S. (2004a). *Children's literature: Very good news and very bad news.* Presentation at the Children's Literature Council of Southern California.

Krashen, S. (2004b). *The power of reading.* Westport, CT: Libraries Unlimited.

Mitchell, D. (2003). *Children's literature: An invitation to the world.* Boston: Allyn & Bacon.

Rule, L. (2005). Digital Storytelling Association. Retrieved from http://www.dsaweb.org.

Stewig, J. W. (1995). *Looking at picture books.* Fort Atkinson, WI: Highsmith Books.

Temple, C., Martinez, M., Yokota, J., & Naylor, A. (1998). *Children's books in children's hands: An introduction to their literature.* Boston: Allyn & Bacon.

Temple, C., Martinez, M., Yokota, J., & Naylor, A. (2002). *Children's books in children's hands: An introduction to their literature* (2nd ed.). Boston: Allyn & Bacon.

Tompkins, G. (2005). *Language arts: Patterns of practice* (6th ed.). Upper Saddle River, NJ: Pearson Prentice Hall.

Top shelf fiction for middle school readers. (2003, February). *Voice of Youth Advocates* (VOYA), 455.

Wiencek, J., & O'Flahavan, J. (1994). From teacher-led to peer discussions about literature: Suggestions for making the shift. *Language Arts, 71,* 488–498.

Literature Dealing With Sexual Orientation

Bauer, M. (Ed.). (1994). *Am I blue? Coming out from the silence.* New York: HarperCollins.

Bowles, N. (2001). *Cootie shots: Theatrical inoculations against bigotry for kids, parents, and teachers.* New York: Theater Communications Group.

Coville, B. (2001). *The skull of truth: A magic shop book* (G. Lippincott, Illus.). San Diego, CA: Harcourt Brace.

Garden, N. (1996). *Good moon rising.* New York: Farrar Straus Giroux.

Garden, N. (2000). *Holly's secret.* New York: Farrar Straus Giroux.

Gordon, S. (2000). *All families are different* (V. Cohen, Illus.). New York: Prometheus Books.

Greenberg, K., & Halibian, C. (1996). *Zack's story: Growing up with same-sex parents* (C. Halibian, Illus.). Minneapolis, MN: Lerner.

Herron, A., & Mason, M. (1999). *How would you feel if your dad was gay?* (K. Kovich, Illus.). Los Angeles: Alyson Wonderland.

Mastoon, A. (2001). *Shared heart: Portraits and stories celebrating lesbian, gay, and bisexual young people.* New York: HarperCollins.

Newman, L. (2000). *Heather has two mommies* (10th anniversary ed.) (D. Souza, Illus.). Los Angeles: Alyson Wonderland.

Rachel, T., & Costello, R. (Eds.). (2004). *Bend, don't shatter: Poets on the beginning of desire.* Brooklyn, NY: Red Rattle Books.

Reynolds Naylor, P. (2001). *Alice alone.* New York: Simon & Schuster.

Snow, J. (2004). *How it feels to have a gay or lesbian parent: A book by kids for kids of all ages.* Binghamton, NY: Harrington Park Press.

Valentine, J. (2004). *The duke who outlawed jelly beans and other stories* (L. Schmidt, Illus.). Los Angeles: Alyson Wonderland.

Wersba, B. (1997). *Whistle me home.* New York: Holt.

Woodson, J. (1995). *From the notebooks of Melanin Sun.* New York: Blue Sky/Scholastic.

Multicultural Children's Literature

African American

Coleman, E. (1996). *White socks only* (T. Geter, Illus.). Morton Grove, IL: Whitman.

Greenfield, E. (1988). *Grandpa's face* (F. Cooper, Illus.). New York: Philomel.

Greenfield, E. (1988). *Nathaniel talking* (J. Spivey Gilchrist, Illus.). New York: Thomas Crowell.

Hamilton, V. (1985). *The people could fly* (L. & D. Dillon, Illus.). New York: Knopf.

Hamilton, V. (1990). *Cousins.* New York: Philomel.

Hoffman, M. (1991). *Amazing Grace* (C. Binch, Illus.). New York: Dial.

Johnson, A. (2003). *The first part last.* New York: Simon & Schuster.

Lawrence, J. (1993). *The great migration: An American story.* New York: HarperTrophy.

Mathis, S. (1975). *The hundred penny box* (D. & L. Dillon, Illus.). New York: Viking.

McKissack, P. (1992). *The dark thirty: Southern tales of the supernatural* (B. Pinkney, Illus.). New York: Knopf.

McKissack, P., & McKissack, F. (2003). *Days of jubilee: The end of slavery in the United States.* New York: Scholastic.

Mitchell, M. (1993). *Uncle Jed's barbershop* (J. Ransome, Illus.). New York: Simon & Schuster.

Ringgold, F. (1992). *Aunt Harriet's underground railroad in the sky.* New York: Crown.

Ringgold, F. (1996). *Tar Beach.* New York: Crown.

Taylor, M. (1976). *Roll of thunder, hear my cry.* New York: Dial.

Taylor, M. (1990). *The road to Memphis.* New York: Dial.

Walker, A. (1974). *Langston Hughes: American poet* (D. Miller, Illus.). New York: Thomas P. Crowell.

Williams, V. (1992). *A chair for my mother.* New York: Greenwillow.

Williams, V. (1997). *More, more, more said the baby.* New York: Tupolo.

Williams-Garcia, R. (1995). *Like sisters on the homefront.* New York: Puffin Books.

Woodson, J. (2004). *Coming on home soon* (E. B. Lewis, Illus.). New York: Putnam.

Asian

Breckler, R. (1996). *Sweet dried apples: A Vietnamese wartime childhood* (D. Kogan Ray, Illus.). Boston: Houghton Mifflin.

Cha, D. (with Livo, N.). (1991). *Folk stories of the Hmong: Peoples of Laos, Thailand and Cambodia.* Westport, CT: Libraries Unlimited.

Choi, S. (1991). *Year of impossible goodbyes*. Boston: Houghton Mifflin.

Choi, S. (1993). *Echoes of the white giraffe*. Boston: Houghton Mifflin.

Lord, B. (1984). *In the year of the boar and Jackie Robinson*. New York: Harper.

Louie, A. (1982). *Yeh-Shen: A Cinderella story from China* (E. Young, Illus.). New York: Philomel.

Mochizuki, K. (1997). *Passage to freedom: The Sugihara story* (D. Lee, Illus.). New York: Lee & Low.

Say, A. (1993). *Grandfather's journey*. Boston: Houghton Mifflin.

Yep, L. (1975). *Dragonwings*. New York: HarperCollins.

Young, E. (1989). *Lon Po Po: A Red Ridinghood story from China*. New York: Philomel.

Latino

Ada, A. (1991). *The gold coin*. New York: Macmillan.

Ada, A. (1993). *My name is María Isabel*. New York: Atheneum.

Alvarez, J. (2002). *Before we were free*. New York: Knopf.

Alvarez, J. (2005). *Un regalo de gracias: La leyenda de la Altagracia* (B. Vidal, Illus.). New York: Dragonfly Books.

Anaya, R. (1995). *The farolitos of Christmas: A New Mexico Christmas story* (R. Sandoval, Illus.). New York: Hyperion.

Ancona, G. (1997). *Mayeros: A Yucatec Maya family*. New York: Lathrop, Lee & Shepard.

Cameron, A. (2003). *Colibrí*. New York: Frances Foster Books/Farrar Straus Giroux.

Casilla, R. (2003). *First day in grapes*. New York: Lee & Low.

Garza, C. (1990). *Family pictures/Cuadros de familia*. New York: Children's Book Press.

Jimenez, F. (1998). *The circuit: Stories from the life of a migrant child*. Albuquerque: University of New Mexico Press.

Mohr, N. (1990). *Felita* (Ray Cruz, Illus.). New York: Bantam Skylark.

Mora, P. (1997). *Tomás and the library lady* (R. Colón, Illus.). New York: Knopf.

Mora, P. (2005). *Un cuento de una mujer gigante con un gran corazón* (R. Colón, Illus.). New York: Dragonfly Books.

Soto, G. (1990). Baseball in April and other stories. New York: Harcourt.

Native American

Broker, I. (1983). *Night flying woman*. Minneapolis: Minnesota Historical Society Press.

O'Dell, S. (1970). *Sing down the moon*. Boston: Houghton Mifflin.

Technology Resources

International Children's Digital Library project is funded by the National Science Foundation (NSF) and the Institute for Museum and Library Services (IMLS) to create a digital library of international children's books. The goal of the project is to collect 10,000 books published in over 100 languages that are free to the public, especially teachers and students: http://www.icdlbooks.org

Kentucky schools have developed a digital storytelling center. View and listen to samples of students' storytelling as well as find valuable resources for engaging in digital storytelling yourself and for your students:

http://www.scott.k12.ky.us/technology/digitalstorytelling/ds.html

A resource and information for working with digital storytelling:

http://www.digitalstorytelling.org

A comprehensive Web site detailing digital storytelling in an educational setting and the procedures for beginning: http://www.coe.uh.edu/digital-storytelling

Digital Storytelling Association Web page: http://www.dsaweb.org

Scholastic Inc. has many videos that feature children's and young adult authors and illustrators: http://www.scholastic.com

Language Arts and the Content Areas

Context Setting:

After reading this chapter, you will be able to

- Conceptualize integrating language arts into content area instruction
- Teach children to read and interpret content area text
- Analyze skills and strategies in specific content areas
- Assess student progress in developing language arts content area skills and strategies
- Make content area/language arts teaching, learning, and assessment more accessible for English language learners (ELLs)

Reading

Speaking

Listening

Language Arts

Visually Representing

Viewing

Writing

Before We Begin

- Mr. Smith teaches Grades 5 and 6 science. His principal has initiated a set of professional development sessions for the school year, focusing on teaching reading, writing, listening, viewing, visually representing, and speaking in all the content areas. Mr. Smith is very upset about this and has stated, "I teach science, not reading!" How would you respond to this teacher if you were the principal?

Content area instruction refers to teaching, learning, and assessment in subject areas other than language arts, such as math, science, and social studies. Some teachers approach these as separate subjects and teach them independently. Others use an integrated approach by selecting a specific theme of study and combining relevant objectives from reading, math, science, social studies, art, music, drama, and so on to provide students with a more in-depth understanding of the topic. Although the primary focus in content area instruction is on the development of content knowledge in these areas, language arts elements need to be taught and emphasized to make the content learning easier to understand. The first part of this chapter analyzes how language arts skills and strategies can be developed as part of content area instruction. Specific language arts development in math, science, and social studies is discussed in the second part of this chapter

While many of the same skills are used to read and understand both **narrative** and **expository text,** they are used in different ways and for different purposes in each content area. Unlike Mr. Smith, effective teachers recognize the complexities of teaching, learning, and assessment in the content areas. They determine students' prior knowledge and build background where needed and help students make links to new learning. They teach their students about how expository (informational) text is organized and how text features can aid understanding. In conjunction with teaching concepts related to the content areas, they determine the **learning strategies** that will encourage their students to be critical thinkers. Textbooks and worksheets are not sufficient for these teachers; they seek out interesting and relevant materials that will excite students to learn about a particular topic. They engage them in active and authentic learning experiences to explore topics as fully as possible. Students in these classes learn how texts and materials differ from one subject to another, and they understand the kinds of skills and strategies required by each. Table 8.1 outlines some key elements that link literacy and content area instruction. Notice how language arts is an integral part of many of these elements. Each is discussed in depth in the following section.

Conceptual Development

Helping students learn new content requires a solid framework from which to integrate new information, and assisting them to develop **conceptual knowledge** requires some preteaching, preassessment, and preplanning on the part of the teacher.

Activate Prior Knowledge

The starting point for any instruction should include determining the background information or prior knowledge that students already possess on the topic being studied. Encouraging students to share what they know before instruction

Table 8.1   Elements Common to Content Area Instruction

1. **Conceptual Development**

   a. Activate prior knowledge
   b. Relate new concepts to known/real world
   c. Develop new schema

2. **Identifying Needed Information**

   a. Key vocabulary
   b. Key concepts
   c. Key information

3. **Content Area Skills and Strategy Development**

   a. Monitor comprehension
   b. Make connections
   c. Compare and contrast
   d. Make inferences
   e. Note taking
   f. Summarize

   g. Skimming/scanning
   h. Sequencing
   i. Monitor production
   j. Cause and effect

4. **Instructional Considerations**

   a. Selection of effective resources and materials
   b. Purposeful reading, writing, listening, speaking, viewing, and visually representing
   c. Active learning
   d. Development of critical thinking
   e. Assessment of content area learning

5. **Content Area Subjects: Mathematics, Social Studies, Science**

   a. Text features
   b. Content-area-specific skills and strategies

begins provides insights into what the class as a whole knows and understands. A positive aspect about this type of open discussion is that students who thought they knew little about the topic may have their **schema** activated and come to realize that they know more than they originally anticipated (Anderson, 1994; Pearson, 1993).

This may provide teachers with a sense of what the class knows as a whole, but they may also wish to consider how many students are responding; it may be that only three or four students shared a great deal of information and the rest of the class remained silent. Small group discussions or preliminary activities may provide additional information about what students seem to understand, because a class often includes some who are reluctant to share in a large group setting. Having students complete an activity, for example, classifying objects as living and nonliving, expands student understanding of the concepts and also provides the teacher with valuable information about whether they are ready for these concepts or whether more background understanding must be developed before plunging into the original teaching plan.

Relate New Concepts to Known/Real World

In any type of learning experience, it is important and helpful to relate the **concepts** being studied to the "real world." When students can see how the concepts are understood and used by people in their everyday or professional lives, they are more apt to invest the time and energy in their learning because they understand that they might need to be knowledgeable about these things themselves. The following vignette highlights this point.

🚗 A View From the Classroom

In an eighth-grade unit on geometry, the students questioned the necessity of learning about figures, angles, and measurements. Their attitudes quickly changed, however, when the teacher invited a pair of city planners as guest speakers to their classroom to share information about the many ways they use math in their daily work, geometry in particular. They especially piqued students' interest when they shared that they did as much to plan what went below the ground as what went above. These visitors engaged the students and convinced them that the study of geometry was indeed important to know beyond classroom learning.

Develop New Schema

Another aspect of conceptual development to consider when extending language arts into content areas in the curriculum is that the schema students already have developed about the concepts being studied will either be expanded or changed. It will be expanded if students already have a foundation and are now gaining a more in-depth understanding of the topic, enabling them to make more links with other concepts. Students' schema will be changed if they come to believe or understand something in a new way. Learning takes place when schema are expanded or transformed. For students who do not learn anything new in a unit, or students for whom the material is too challenging, little change in schema may take place.

It is important to determine the prior knowledge and background understanding ELLs bring with them. Some come with extensive educational or experiential background from previous educational experiences and lack only the language to express what they know and understand; some students may even be quite accelerated relative to U.S. standards. A graduate student from China recently lamented that what her seventh-grade daughter was currently studying in math in a U.S. school was content that she had mastered in China 2 years earlier. Other students may have had little experience in a particular content area and require greater support or scaffolding of learning.

A View From the Classroom

In a first-grade classroom, the students began observation of a tree outside their classroom window that continued throughout the school year. Students had the opportunity to hone their observational skills as they noted changes on a regular basis. While his English-dominant peers talked about how the tree had branches and leaves that fell off in the fall, Juan Carlos patiently colored his drawings of the tree. When the bilingual assistant asked him what he knew about trees, the response was quite surprising.

Juan Carlos began a long discussion of how trees are home to birds that use the trees' twigs and leaves to build their

nests. He talked about how trees provide shade when it is hot and can be used for firewood when it is cold. He described in minute detail how the trees were different in the United States from the ones on his grandfather's ranch in Mexico and that the leaves did not turn pretty colors and fall from the trees because it was warm all year round.

This View From the Classroom highlights the importance of learning about student schema. Without this encounter, the teacher and the educational assistant would not have known that Juan Carlos had had so many experiences that made him a careful observer of natural phenomena. Now they could build on his rural background and make opportunities available for him to expand his knowledge, especially in relation to science concepts.

Identifying Needed Information

Key Vocabulary and Key Concepts

Marzano et al. (2001) document the dramatic impact on learning that occurs when vocabulary is taught directly and systematically as a component of new content. Placing an emphasis on **key vocabulary** and providing multiple opportunities for students to learn and use this vocabulary grounds them in the concepts being studied. Defining key vocabulary, linking it to known concepts, and exploring the context in which it is used is helpful in guiding students to a deeper understanding of the concepts being studied.

Many content area textbooks highlight key vocabulary as it is introduced. The sentence in which the highlighted word is found generally provides a definition of the term. Guiding students to pay careful attention to these key vocabulary terms is an important step in assisting them to become more careful and critical readers. Many teachers arrange for students to have a notebook for each content area subject, divided into sections for vocabulary, notes, reflections, and so on. Students can be directed to write definitions or descriptions of terms in their notebooks for future reference.

It is also important for students to be able to locate **key concepts** in their textbooks or other class materials. Many textbooks list the key concepts at the beginning of the chapter or section and may indicate key content. Teaching students to preview these features before reading helps to establish expectations for their reading.

Key Information

Knowing how to find **key information** within reading material enables students to extend their learning with greater confidence and less frustration. Some authentic ways to help students do this might be to have students find needed information to complete a science experiment, solve a mathematical problem, or prepare for a debate in social studies. Teachers teach students to identify **text features** such as headings, subheadings, and bolded print as ways of determining where information might be found and to skim the material as a preview. Teaching **signal words,** such as *therefore, however, then,* and *later,* helps students interpret information. Scanning visuals and graphics helps to identify key information. Being able to ascertain what is being studied and the key components of that topic is a critical step in developing content area understanding.

There are numerous ways to guide students in analyzing key vocabulary and concepts in the content areas (Nagy, 1988; Nagy & Herman, 1985). The goal is not merely for students to be able to define key words but to be able to use them effectively in learning new concepts and in making connections to previous learning. Semantic maps, concept maps, sorting activities, and visuals may be very helpful in guiding students to internalize new terms and concepts.

Before initiating a new unit, a teacher may ask students to name everything they can think of related to the topic. Table 8.2A represents such a brainstorming exercise with first graders around the theme of money. Table 8.3A highlights a Grade 5 class sharing ideas about planets. Students may then be asked to sort and label the ideas, as demonstrated in Tables 8.2B and 8.3B. The latter table represents further sorting as students order the planets according to distance from the sun.

These models could easily lead to the development of a semantic feature analysis (Baldwin, Ford, & Readance, 1981; Johnson & Pearson, 1984). This graphic organizer "helps students discern the meaning of a term by comparing its features to those of other terms that fall into the same category. When students have completed a **semantic feature matrix** they have a visual reminder of how

Table 8.2A   Grade 1: Semantic Map

Credit card

Money to go a movie   Penny

Quarters   Bank

                          Coin collectors

Dime   Money   Buy food

Buy toys

                          Allowance

Dollars   Nickel

Put in wallet/purse   Lunch money

        Cash register

Table 8.2B   Sorting Ideas From Money Brainstorming Web

Names of Money Types	What We Use Money For	Where We Keep Money
Penny	Go to movies	Pocket
Nickel	Buy food	Wallet
Dime	Allowance	Purse
Quarter	Lunch money	Bank
Dollar	Buy toys	Cash register

Table 8.3A   Grade 5: Semantic Map

Jupiter   Pluto—furthest away

Space probes   Saturn—has rings

Uranus   Some have moons

Could be other planets   Travel around the sun

Earth—life   Planets   View at planetarium

Neptune   Mercury

Mars—red planet   View with telescope

Some are very cold   Don't twinkle

        Venus—closest to Earth

Table 8.3B   Sorting Ideas From Planet Brainstorming Web

Planet Names	Characteristics	Studying Planets
Jupiter	Travel around the sun	View at planetarium
Uranus	Don't twinkle	View with telescope
Earth—life	Some are very cold	Could be others
Neptune	Some have moons	Space probes
Mars—red planet		
Venus—closest to Earth		
Mercury		
Saturn—has rings		
Pluto—furthest away		

certain terms are alike or different" (Barton & Jordan, 2001, p. 58). At a glance, students are able to make comparisons and draw conclusions. See Table 8.4 for an example of a semantic feature map (Williams & Regan, 1986).

Graphic organizers may be helpful as a reference in writing projects related to the theme. One way to begin is to pose questions that enable students to use graphic organizers to find and interpret information. The following questions could accompany the planet semantic feature map in Table 8.4:

Which atmospheres do you think would be poisonous for humans? Why?

Why do you think Jupiter and Saturn have so many moons?

Why do you think Saturn and Uranus have rings? What are they made of?

Students can be invited to make additional observations about what they can deduce or infer from the graphics. These graphic organizers are helpful in developing concept and vocabulary knowledge in that they build students' schema.

Content area journals or **learning logs** can serve as tools for students to record what they are learning and are useful in applying, analyzing, synthesizing, and evaluating their understandings (Popp, 1997). Students may enter some of the information by hand, and other pieces may be handouts they include in their notebooks. For example, in the Grade 1 study of money, students may glue pictures of coins into their notebooks and write the values below. Other entries might include a comparison list of how children and adults use money, word problems, and coin equivalency charts. The Grade 5 unit on planets might include learning logs that contain visual representations of the planets with features described below, a map of the orbits of the planets around the sun, and analyses of the semantic feature map. **Vocabulary maps,** as in Table 8.5, are useful in making complex concepts more manageable for students in that various characteristics of concepts are explored. These kinds of visuals are especially helpful for ELLs and

Table 8.4   Semantic Feature Map: Planets

	Number of Moons	Atmosphere	Has Rings
Mercury	0	None	—
Venus	0	Carbon dioxide, sulfuric acid	—
Earth	1	Nitrogen, oxygen, water	—
Mars	2	Carbon dioxide	—
Jupiter	63	Hydrogen, helium, ammonia, methane	—
Saturn	34	Hydrogen, helium, methane, ammonia	Yes
Uranus	5	Hydrogen, helium, methane, miranda, ariel	Yes
Neptune	2	Hydrogen, helium, methane	—
Pluto	1	Methane	—

Table 8.5   Vocabulary Map

Word	Draw it
Describe it	Example of it

students with learning challenges. In social studies, **historical character maps,** as in Table 8.6, may assist students in identifying and analyzing the contributions of these figures (Doty, Cameron, & Barton, 2003). Historical character maps could be kept as part of an electronic learning log, enabling students to import pictures of their character and relevant information from the Web.

Table 8.6   Historical Character Map

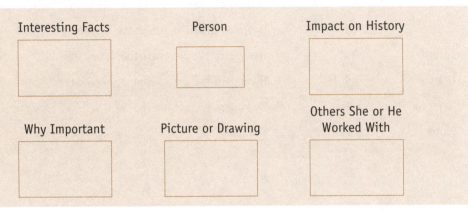

Interesting Facts   Person   Impact on History

Why Important   Picture or Drawing   Others She or He Worked With

Reflection Journal 8.1

Examine content area textbooks in mathematics, science, and/or social studies. Also, examine teaching guides and supplementary materials. Evaluate the positive and negative aspects of these materials for use with children at a specific grade level in terms of their layout and reader friendliness. How would you compensate for negative aspects? Would you recommend these texts? Why or why not?

Content Area Skills and Strategy Development

Although language arts learning strategies can be taught throughout the school day and within all content areas, there are several that are particularly useful for development in relation to content area instruction. Several of the strategies may be introduced in one subject and incorporated and practiced in other areas as well, with students coming to see the strategies as expansive and flexible.

It is recommended that the strategies be taught directly, that students have multiple opportunities to practice using them and are then taught to self-assess how well they have used them (Echevarria, Vogt, & Short, 2004). Often we assume that if we use a particular strategy with our students, they will understand it and be able to use it independently. However, it is only after our students can name the strategies they use and explain how they affected their learning that we have evidence that they have internalized them. Viewed in this manner, only four to five strategies need be taught in a single school year, but they would be studied in depth, from multiple perspectives, and in a variety of content areas. Each of the strategies described in Table 8.7 can be used in mathematics, science, social studies, and other content area curricula.

Table 8.7   Comprehension Strategies

Strategy	Application in the Content Areas Students should be able to
Monitor comprehension Reread unclear passages to clarify meaning Formulate questions to clarify meaning	– Stop at points to review level of understanding
Make connections Connect new learning to previous learning	– Connect learning to own experiences
Compare/contrast Determine differences among concepts/ideas	– Determine similarities among concepts/concepts
Make inferences	– Infer word meaning and concept understanding from available information – Make logical deductions from available information
Note taking	– Select key information to record – Retrieve information from notes for study and use in learning experiences
Summarize	– Highlight main ideas and supporting details
Skim, scan	– Use headings, subheadings, bolded terms, and graphics to determine where to search for needed information – Locate key information
Sequence	– Order ideas, concepts, or materials – Demonstrate or explain the rationale for the sequence
Monitor production	– Reflect on whether or not work meets learning goals – Determine how to edit, revise, or refine work
Cause and effect	– Determine what impact certain actions/events/ideas have

Instructional Considerations

There are some generic literacy considerations to take into account in planning, implementing, and assessing language arts learning in the content areas. Using the Holdaway (1984) model is effective in content area teaching and learning as well (teacher introduction of concepts, assisted practice, independent practice, and sharing of learning). Using this model as a guide, students have opportunities to continually refine and extend their learning but with scaffolded support as needed. Following are some considerations to think about when integrating language arts into content area learning.

Selection of Effective Resources and Materials

Prereading activities that activate prior knowledge and build necessary background serve to prepare and excite students about new learning. As mentioned previously, textbooks alone are rarely sufficient for learning in the content areas. The reading level of these texts is often well beyond the instructional level of many of the students (Barton & Jordan, 2001). It is imperative that students have access to materials that they can understand and learn from, thereby meeting the needs of all students, including those who are struggling and those who are advanced. When students are invited to preview materials they will be using and find materials that match their reading and interest levels, their curiosity may be further piqued.

Some commercial companies have begun designing graphic texts to support learning for students who struggle with reading and/or comprehension (Capstone Press, Saddleback Publishing Inc.). These materials feature a comic book format, with fast-paced but easy-to-read text. Topics in graphic novels range from biographies and historical events to classical novels.

María Godina Plans for Science

María Godina's third-grade students help prepare a display about sound. They put an easel and poster in place that reads "The Physics of Sound," containing a list of questions they will try to answer during this unit of study, including the following:

- What is a tuning fork and how can it be used to study sound?
- How does sound get from the object that made the sound to your ear?
- How does your ear work?
- Does your brain have anything to do with how you hear sound?
- Is sound louder in the air or under water?

A bulletin board is prepared for children to exhibit what they learn about sound as the unit progresses, including a display of themed books about sound. Since this is a dual-language classroom, María has located a variety of books in both English and Spanish. Some are uncomplicated and others are more advanced, but María has previewed the books and selected only those that fully develop the concept of sound. She did not include books that were too simplistic to meet the science standards she has selected for this unit of study.

A table in front of the book display contains many of the materials the students will use in their study of sound, including tuning forks, megaphones, stethoscopes, drums, a model of an ear, and wood blocks. The students peruse the materials, read the questions, and speculate about what they know about sound a few days before they actually begin work on the unit.

Where do you see an opportunity for students to use language arts (reading, writing, listening, speaking, viewing, and visually representing) in preparing and beginning work on the unit in María's class?

Stop to Think

Purposeful Reading, Writing, Listening, Speaking, Viewing, and Visually Representing

When students engage in reading activities in the content areas, setting a purpose for reading helps focus on key concepts and vocabulary, similar to what is done with narrative text. Instead of merely saying "Read pages 13–15," a more focused approach might be to provide the students with a prereading guide that includes the following:

Read pages 13–15 to find out what goods and services a community needs.

Do we need both goods and services? Why or why not?

Think about the goods and services of our community.

Students might engage in partner reading, with one student reading as they take written notes for discussion. Periodically they could stop to discuss the information and determine if the questions have been answered. Afterwards, the whole class discusses their findings. This could become a **jigsaw activity** if each pair reads a separate section and answers different questions or answers the same questions from different points of view, sharing the information from their assigned sections to teach one another what they have learned.

🏠 A View From Home

Jessica's mother is actively involved in helping her daughter gain as much knowledge related to the curriculum as possible. When Ms. Godina sent home a letter detailing the new unit of study related to communities and invited parents to share information, artifacts, and expertise, Jessica's mother gushed to her friend, "This teacher makes learning so much fun. I can't wait to find out what they are going to study next so I can learn along with Jessica."

Active Learning

Sai, a first-grade teacher, understands the importance of **active learning** as well. She has turned a corner of her classroom into a store. Parents and guardians have contributed empty food and merchandise packaging to "sell" in the store. Students engage in literate and content area learning activities as they pretend to be the shopkeeper or the customers, purchasing items and using language that one might hear in a store. Among other things, through these simulations students learn to count money and make change. Sai supplements this learning experience with money games, having students make entries in their math journals and using a few well-developed worksheets. Large posters hung in the area display pictures of coins and their values, and others highlight work students have done with money. Each morning, students count lunch money along with their teacher. They talk about their allowances and bring in advertisements that indicate how much things cost that they would like to buy. These activities help students make links between the classroom and the way money is used in the outside world, thus learning content in a meaningful manner.

Char's sixth-grade class is studying cells in science class. Because this concept is quite abstract and because she has several ELLs in her classes, she takes special care to scaffold learning of the content to make it more comprehensible. The text is complex, so she highlights key paragraphs for certain students to read and provides alternate reading material for her students who struggle the most. She selects materials that have a number of visuals and readable, clear text, making certain that key concepts and vocabulary are highlighted. As she plans, she ensures that all students will have an opportunity to make progress toward grade-level science standards by using their literacy skills in appropriate ways.

Students include drawings in their science journals along with written vocabulary and concept entries. They create large three-dimensional models of cells that simulate the shape of actual cell components. Later in the unit, some students will write lyrics to a song to highlight the function of a cell, and others will demonstrate their understanding through a dramatic reenactment. Field trips or visits to the classroom by experts can be very valuable to learning in the content areas. An excursion to a planetarium, for example, would be a great way to either introduce or supplement a solar system unit of study.

Development of Critical Thinking

María, Sai, and Char understand the importance of developing higher-level thinking skills with their students. María focuses on teaching her students to make inferences in their study of sound, Sai stresses classifying as students learn about money, and Char has her students compare and contrast plant and animal cells. They each believe it is important that students take not only factual information from one learning experience to the next but that they also develop one or more learning strategies that can be used in a variety of learning experiences. They understand that students need learning experiences that enable them to explore concepts as fully as possible, and since they recognize students learn much from each other, they incorporate opportunities for working in pairs and small groups regularly. Table 8.8 outlines some of the factors that may be taken into account in planning for the development of critical thinking skills.

Table 8.8 Designing Content Area Instruction

Learning Outcomes	Learning Experiences	Materials
Higher-level thinking skills	Field trips/guest speakers	Visuals
Active learning	Reciprocal teaching	Realia/models
Cooperative learning	Learning logs	Manipulatives
Use of learning strategies	Simulations/role-playing	Graphic organizers
	Games	Trade books
	Drama/art/music	Magazines
		Text

Assessment of Content Area Learning

Char has her students use the cell models in two other ways that help them and her assess their learning. Her class of 18 students is divided into three groups. Each group has a special focus. Group A is responsible for demonstrating the structure of plant cells, Group B the structure of animal cells, and Group C must demonstrate how cells divide. These are the "home groups." Each group is charged with making certain each member of the group is able to clearly explain the group's concept. Next, smaller "expert groups" of three students each are formed containing one member of each home group. The groups engage in reciprocal teaching, and each person of the group becomes the expert on his or her concept and must demonstrate either cell structure or cell division to the other two members of the group. Reciprocal teaching requires that students understand the concepts fully enough to be able to explain them to classmates and answer questions. Therefore, Char uses this technique only after students have had ample time to fully explore the concepts.

Second, Char uses the reciprocal teaching preparation and demonstration as an assessment tool as well. She listens as students explain the concepts to one another and notes how clearly they are able to explain work with cells and appropriately use vocabulary. This activity provides Char with one sample of student understanding, and she makes anecdotal notes related to student work and has them complete an oral self-assessment where they reflect not only on their understanding of concepts but also on how well they demonstrated them to their peers.

María emphasizes learning experiences that lead her students to make inferences and deductions about sound. They complete a series of experiments, and after each one, they complete learning log entries and science worksheets to record what they have learned. Whole class discussions focus on key questions:

How does sound travel?

Is sound louder in the air or in the water?

What does this mean?

Working in a bilingual setting, María uses many visuals and models the concepts as clearly and simply as possible. She provides many opportunities (like expert/home groups) for students to rehearse and use language in authentic learning experiences. Students compile their work on this topic and select key pieces that reflect their understanding of sound to place in their portfolios. Each student's portfolio has a page containing the science standards, and the work placed behind it demonstrates progress toward the standards. Students explain their entries to María as she conferences with them as a final assessment. Her students conduct student-led parent-teacher conferences and use their portfolios (which contain materials from all subject areas) to demonstrate their growth. This is the ultimate **summative** (or final) **assessment** of learning. María videotapes these conferences and reviews them with individual students to help them refine this process. She includes this video as part of her own professional development portfolio, as her students' ability to explain their understanding is a good measure of her own effectiveness as a teacher and helps her to reflect on her teaching and set goals for improvement.

Sai writes anecdotal records as her students play store. She notes the coins they are able to identify and how well they use them in buying items or making change. She understands that students who have been given experiences with money will be able to complete these activities easily, and those who have had little contact with money may find them more difficult. However, both groups need to progress as fully as possible. The students with little experience will learn through active engagement with their classmates in selecting coins to represent the value of an object. Students who already have an understanding of money will gain experience in making change. This is a good example of structuring **open-ended learning experiences** that enable students to enter at their own level of expertise and grow from that point.

Sai invites the kindergarten class to visit her first graders one afternoon and has her students prepare a demonstration about money. They write and illustrate the invitation, share books about money, create money posters, and demonstrate selecting appropriate coins to pay for items. In this example of reciprocal teaching, each first-grade student pairs up with a kindergarten student and buys items from the play store. Several other pairs serve as cashiers. Although the children are playing and having fun, they are using language skills and abilities and learning a great deal about the content as well.

Content Area Subjects: Mathematics, Social Studies, and Science

Text Features

Whether teachers use commercially prepared textbooks or not, there are differences between reading expository or informational text and narrative text. In addition, the *type* of content makes for a different emphasis in reading as well. For example, a math book is different from reading either a science text or a social studies book. Students who are aware of the features of a variety of texts are able to use them more effectively, which suggests the need for teaching about them directly.

Teaching students about text features can be linked to guiding students to monitor comprehension of what they read. For example, pointing out headings and subheadings and having students predict what a section will be about or use headings and subheadings to locate information can be tied to having students read and think about what they have read. Often when students have difficulty with content area subjects, they report that they cannot recall what they have read. Activities focused on making meaning from information or expository text will help improve comprehension.

As mentioned earlier, focusing attention on what the authors have done to highlight key vocabulary and concepts in the text also helps students grasp the content of the passage. It might be that key vocabulary is represented in bold font or perhaps highlighted in yellow. Knowing this helps students focus their attention on vocabulary that they should remember as they read for initial understanding and as they reread to complete additional learning experiences. Illustrations often highlight important concepts, and the accompanying captions explain what the pictures represent. Figures, tables, and maps further clarify what has been stated in the text, and critical data and information are often highlighted in these graphics. Teaching students to interpret visual features serves at least two purposes: (1) the graphics represent key ideas students are expected to take away from reading the text, and (2) they provide visual representations that clarify meaning for students. Students who have not learned to read critically often overlook these important pieces of information, reading only the main text and ignoring other useful aids.

Reflection Journal 8.2

Think about your own reading habits. When completing reading assignments for class, what strategies do you use to help yourself better comprehend the content? Do you preview the text first to get a sense of what the selection will be about? Do you use pictures, graphs, charts, and maps to fully understand what you read? Do you stop periodically to think about what you have read? Are there some areas you would like to develop more fully, so that you will be able to authentically model these for your students?

Students generally read narrative text by starting at the beginning and proceeding through to the end. Expository or informational text is often read in a more analytical manner, such as through reading a portion of text and then exploring relevant visuals and graphics. The material is often divided into subtopics, and readers may read some sections and not others, or they make reference from one section to another. Teaching students how to effectively read expository text might be done through modeling. Think-alouds, a strategy in which teachers read the passage aloud and think aloud how they use the visuals and what they learn from examining them closely, provide students with insights about how to maneuver effectively through expository text. The teacher may also model **monitoring comprehension** by stopping at certain points and summarizing what has been read and/or making links to other areas. Teachers can also focus on using the index, table of contents, and glossary as aids for locating information and clarifying meaning. Table 8.9 outlines a number of text features of expository text.

Table 8.9   Text Features of Expository Reading

Table of contents	Index	Key vocabulary & definitions
Glossary	Figures and tables	Headings and subheadings
Graphics	Pictures and captions	Key concepts
Examples	References to other pages	Explanations

Content Area Materials

While content area texts and teacher guides may represent neatly packaged teaching and learning programs, they are seldom complete in and of themselves. One of the most common complaints about using commercially prepared textbooks is that the reading level is often very challenging for students, often written at a higher level than the grade level for which they are intended. Another complaint is that the material is covered in a very cursory fashion, moving too quickly from one topic to another and not providing enough detail or background information for a solid understanding. Students are bombarded by many terms and bits of information, with few examples to ground them in the concepts. Therefore, it is generally necessary for the teacher to supplement the textbooks with many rich learning materials such as trade books (children's and young adult literature), software, guest speakers, realia, and field trips. Some teachers use the textbook primarily as a guide to determine which concepts, strategies, and skills to develop and choose to teach exclusively from materials they compile around a topic, including gathering a wide variety of reading materials for the unit, making certain they match the reading levels of the students. Books and magazines from school and municipal libraries can be obtained to supplement classroom collections. Realia materials, visuals, and manipulatives related to the learning experiences that are being planned can also be gathered from many sources. Letters describing the unit of study can be sent home to invite parents and guardians to send relevant materials to school or to serve as experts on a particular topic. Field trips are helpful in providing students with more in-depth understanding of a topic. Bringing in additional materials and learning experiences provides greater opportunities to meet the interests and learning level of the students.

The more thoroughly and authentically children study concepts, the more likely they will link what they already know to the new concepts and make comparisons and connections. Teachers should review the materials they wish to use for clarity, level of difficulty, and concept development to ensure a meaningful learning experience for their students. The following sections detail how a teacher might help students use language arts to learn content in social studies, mathematics, and science classes.

Content-Area-Specific Skills and Strategies: Reading Social Studies Text

As in any area of teaching, the first steps in social studies instruction are to determine the prior knowledge of students and to examine social studies standards for the district. The goal, of course, is to get all students to meet or exceed these standards. However, if they lack the necessary background, it will make little sense to move forward with grade-level material and require that children work at their **frustration level.** For example, if multiple maps are used but students have only limited map reading and interpretation skills, they will be ill equipped to use and interpret complex information from maps. In a situation like this, it would be necessary to focus on developing map reading and interpreting skills as one of the social studies objectives.

Students who have been schooled outside of the United States may have very different backgrounds in social studies relative to students born and raised in the United States. This may be especially true of older students who have little or no background in the history or geography of the United States. However, they may have a solid background in the history and geography of their own countries that may be tapped to expose the class to different perspectives and points of view.

Many social studies series have adopted common developmental topics spanning across the grade levels, with Grade 1 focusing on the broad theme of self and family, Grade 2 neighborhood, Grade 3 communities, Grade 4 state, Grade 5 U.S. history, and Grade 6 world history. Geography is integrated into each of these topics. Some schools find this progression useful, and others find it important for children to develop a worldview from a younger age. This is especially true of schools with a more ethnically diverse student population where children's background experiences and cultures are not similar.

Selecting key vocabulary and key concepts for each unit of study and making these clear to students direct their attention. Graphic organizers, such as concept and semantic maps that have already been presented in this chapter, can be helpful aids to assist children in understanding new concepts and vocabulary. Students might prepare word cards or make entries in their learning logs to highlight key vocabulary and concepts. Table 8.10 provides an example of a concept card developed as part of a Grade 4 study of how the economy of the Middle Atlantic states has changed over time (Boehm, Hoone, McGowan, McKinney-Browning, & Miramontes, 1997). Students write the vocabulary word in the middle of the front side of the card and surround it with relevant phrases that describe and clarify the term. The back side of the card contains one or more sentences directly from the text that clarify the meaning of the vocabulary word in context.

Another way of representing key vocabulary in social studies is to have students create cards or learning log entries that include both a visual

Table 8.10   Vocabulary/Concept Cards

Side A

Middle Atlantic States

Rich farmland	Along Atlantic coast

Coastal Plain

Produce (fruits & vegetables)	Truck farms

Side B

p. 167. "Much of the land in the Middle Atlantic states is part of the *Coastal Plain,* the low land that stretches along the Atlantic Ocean."

Table 8.11   Vocabulary Association Cards

New Term	Visual Representation
Definition	Characteristics What this term reminds me of

Table 8.12   Anticipation Guide

Mark each item below with *G* for Goods or *S* for Services that you might find in a community.

_____ school	_____ department store	_____ bakery
_____ grocery store	_____ car dealership	_____ bank
_____ church	_____ hospital	_____ fire department
_____ pharmacy	_____ toy factory	_____ police station

Define "goods" _____

_____

Define "services" _____

_____

representation and a personal association (Doty et al., 2003). Table 8.11 provides an example of this type of vocabulary or concept representation.

Teachers can also prepare anticipation guides as a way to determine what students know about a topic and to get them thinking about a subject or concept before they begin reading. Table 8.12 provides an example of an anticipation guide for a Grade 3 study of goods and services within a community. In this example, students begin to think about how to classify goods and services and the role they might play in a community.

There are numerous text features associated with social studies texts; Table 8.13 reflects several of them. As new features are presented in the text, they can be introduced to students, and their value in clarifying learning examined. This aspect of reading critically, that is, paying attention to text features, is likely to transfer to reading experiences in other subject areas. Making opportunities available for students to locate information or interpret a variety of visuals provides the practice they need to become proficient in reading and analyzing social studies text. Asking students to reflect on how well they used text features to understand concepts provides feedback to the teacher in terms of which features students are using effectively and which ones need additional emphasis.

Table 8.13   Text Features of Social Studies Textbooks

Features	Components to Teach
Maps	– Title, key, compass rose, scale, types of maps
Pictures and captions	– Historical information, locations, artifacts
Graphs and diagrams	– Comparisons, parts of whole, cross-sections
Headings	– Main ideas of sections, subheadings
Guiding statements	– Key statements or questions that reflect main ideas of sections
Biographical sketches	– Information about key historical figures
Information sources	– Table of contents, index, glossary, timelines

As mentioned earlier, reading in the content areas involves greater use of expository text. Teachers often have students compare narrative and expository texts to determine differences in purpose, format, and content. Table 8.14 highlights some of the differences. Students also come to understand that there may be overlapping features in some instances, for example, a narrative may contain factual information, or an informational text may include a biographical sketch.

When preparing units of study involving social studies concepts, many teachers take advantage of opportunities to supplement textbooks with other types of reading materials. In addition to collecting a wide variety of books on the topic that cover a broad range of reading levels, they provide relevant magazines, newspapers, maps, brochures, and so on for the students. Some students enjoy the variety of reading materials, which may motivate them to read more widely.

Table 8.14   Comparison of Narrative and Expository Text Features

	Purpose	Content	Format
Narrative Text	Entertain	Characters	Chapters
	Teach a lesson	Setting	Pictures portray action
	Portray emotion	Plot	Title portrays plot
	Evoke a response	Story line	One story per book
	Tell a story	Tone	
Expository Text	Inform	Information on a topic	Divided into sections
	Serve as resource for research	Pictures and captions	Pictures portray topic
	Build on prior knowledge	Graphics representing topic	Chapters
		Comparisons	Title portrays content

Learning Experiences in Social Studies

Obviously, the types of learning experiences that are developed by teachers greatly influence the level of interest students have for social studies. A social studies classroom that consists only in students taking turns at reading a paragraph of text aloud while the rest of the class follows along, answering questions at the end of each section, and taking a test at the end of the chapter is not sufficient. For these students, social studies is indeed dull. More important, these students have limited interaction with the concepts to remember or even to understand them. Students need to read for specific purposes, discuss what they have learned, and make connections to their own worlds and/or other historical events. They also benefit from organizing information with graphic organizers and analyzing the impact of current and historical events. In classrooms where social studies themes deal directly with historical content, it might prove advantageous to create a permanent timeline in the classroom, including the historical periods to be studied. As each era and important historical events are explored, students add key information to the timeline, along with relevant visual materials. The timeline becomes a major visual as the class moves through various historical periods of history and helps students draw conclusions and make connections among events.

Social studies themes lend themselves to role-playing and **simulations** as a way to comprehend content. Half of the students may be asked to read materials from one particular point of view and the other half from an opposing point of view. In a fifth-grade class, half of the students may read materials as if they were revolutionaries in 1776, for example, and the other half may take on the role of loyalists. Each group might then prepare arguments to present at a town hall meeting about whether to remain a British colony or declare independence.

Second graders might take on the roles of critical neighborhood helpers and then explore the role each helper plays in the neighborhood.

To understand the concept of community and how communities function and interact, third graders might build a village or neighborhood using cartons or blocks. This kind of project is often seen in classrooms but becomes meaningful when students explore significant concepts revolving around communities, for example, the goods and services that are essential for a well-run community, what makes a community efficient, and how people depend on one another in a community. Written and oral presentation activities can be built into these projects as opportunities for students to explore and reflect on concepts more fully and utilize their language arts skills.

A major emphasis in content area learning is reading, viewing, and listening to gain information and develop understanding of concepts. Students need multiple experiences within a wide range of contexts in order to be effective note takers. However, students do not automatically know how to take or use notes effectively. One way to begin teaching and learning note taking could be having students watch cartoons or newscasts and then discuss and write the main idea and details necessary to relay what was viewed. A brief passage can be projected and students asked to highlight important concepts by paraphrasing them in simple phrases. These notes could be written down and reviewed to determine whether they included the most important ideas and if any unnecessary details could be deleted.

A next step might be to provide students with sample notes from materials they would read for social studies and have them critique the notes. A set of criteria for effective note taking could be developed by the class to use in analyzing notes taken by others or by themselves. An example is available in Table 8.15. **Kidspiration** (Inspiration Software Inc.), software used for organizing ideas, provides a variety of useful outline formats that students might find

Table 8.15   Criteria for Taking Good Notes

Main Ideas

_____ stated clearly
_____ all main ideas are included

Supporting Details

_____ stated clearly
_____ only important details included
_____ details are written under the main idea they describe
_____ Notes are clearly organized
_____ Notes are in a logical order

helpful in organizing their notes (Helfgot & Westhaven, 2001). After these activities, students will be ready to practice taking notes on their own. The purpose for taking notes should be made clear to them. Are they taking notes to use (a) in studying for a test; (b) for presentations, projects, or research; (c) to reflect on what they have learned; or (d) for keeping track of learning? While they are learning to become effective note takers, the teacher may wish to work one on one or with small groups to guide development. After using their notes to study for a test or prepare a presentation, a review session could be held for students to reflect on the usefulness of their notes and how they could improve them in the future.

Social studies lends itself well to the development of several additional comprehension and concept development skills and strategies. The strategies that could be developed most fully are (a) compare and contrast, (b) cause and effect, (c) point of view, (d) generalization, and (e) drawing conclusions. Teachers may wish to select one or two strategies to focus on throughout a semester or school year and have students explore them in depth across several content areas and genres. As students read and do research in social studies, they need to be able to scan titles, headings, subheadings, and tables of contents to find relevant materials and then skim the pages to find the desired information. Obviously, a skill that is embedded in note taking is summarization. One must be able to select main ideas and supporting details in both areas. Sequencing of historical events is also an important skill in social studies that needs to be taught and practiced.

A beneficial strategy in helping students understand social studies concepts is that of **making connections.** The connections may be between the concepts and the students' own lives or from one historical event or historical figure to another. For example, creating a fictional community in third-grade social studies can set the stage for students to make comparisons to their own community. Present-day immigrants might see connections to immigration patterns in other historical eras or parts of the world.

Children's and young adult literature can be beneficial to use in social studies, as students may find history textbooks poorly developed and remote. Reading a story set in a particular time period makes the realities of that era come alive, and students gain a more in-depth understanding of historical events. For example, *When My Name Was Keoko*, by Linda Sue Park (2002), portrays a riveting story of a Korean family set in the early 1940s during the Japanese occupation of Korea. In the epilogue, Park describes the factual evidence she used in creating this novel. A novel of this type could be used as a first introduction to World War II and its implications on peoples around the world.

Historical fiction, biography, and folk literature are three genres that lend themselves well to social studies themes. The characteristics of each may be explored as students read and later use these genres in their own writing. Historical fiction sets the characters in a specific historical setting where all the characters and events are accurate. Biography enables students to explore the lives and accomplishments of various historical figures and informs students about important contributions of people from a variety of circumstances. For example, if a classroom is composed of predominantly African American students, reading biographies of important African American leaders will inform them about their many accomplishments and may be instrumental in helping to develop a sense of pride in their heritage as well as help other students gain a perspective of other cultures. Or in a classroom with many immigrants, students may explore the resettlement of others and compare them with their own experiences (Shea, 2003).

Folk literature can provide insights into the lifestyles and values of the people for whom these oral tales were passed down from generation to generation. These tales were often developed to ensure that certain events were preserved and were designed to teach a lesson as well (Temple, Martinez, Yokota, & Taylor, 1998). Virginia Hamilton (1985), for example, has compiled a contemporary collection of 24 American black folktales titled *The People Could Fly,* featuring stories of slaves and fugitives.

Research in Social Studies

Research can be tied to social studies themes where there are many opportunities to introduce students to the research process, accompanying skills, strategies, and resources. Even children as young as kindergarten or first grade are capable of engaging in simple research. General steps for completing research are outlined in Table 8.16.

Generally, research projects begin after a significant amount of study around a topic has already occurred. In this way, the research constitutes specific and

Table 8.16

The following steps constitute the research process:

1. Choose appropriate topic
2. Research a variety of sources for information
3. Organize a format for gathering information
4. Use an outline to arrange the information
5. Include appropriate information to make topic clear
6. Use own words except for exact quotations
7. List all sources completely and correctly

SOURCE: Milwaukee Public Schools (2003).

personalized expansion of a theme. For example, after reading and studying about labor conditions for children before the enactment of the child labor laws, one group of seventh-grade students chose to research what the conditions were like for children working in mines. They began by gathering information from the library, including Russell Freedman's book *Kids at Work* (1994). Because this school is located in a former mining area, the students plan to interview senior residents of the community who can provide firsthand information on working conditions in the mines. They have decided they will gather information to show why the child labor laws were necessary. They have selected three areas that they wish to research: "kind of work children did," "dangers the children faced," and "what kids missed out on." Information will be recorded on index cards and placed on a large chart divided into columns, labeled with the three areas. This will provide a visual of the information collected and enable them to arrange it in the desired order.

The teacher created a child labor **WebQuest** (Dodge & March, 1998), including a set of Web sites related to the topic that students could access. She helps this group determine which sites will be helpful to them, guiding them in determining how much information to put on the note cards. Each group of students will prepare a page of a newspaper dealing with child labor as the final product of their research, as the teacher previously introduced this format of writing in an earlier writing workshop.

After the group has compiled enough information for each of the three areas (kind of work, dangers, and things kids missed out on), they decide that the article should be an editorial that will lead easily to the oral presentation. To prepare, they review newspapers to learn the format for editorials. Discussing the organization, each student selects one of the three areas to write about and, using a computer, saves it on a disk. After the sections are completed, the group reconvenes to combine the pieces into a single file, editing the article and then writing a conclusion.

Each group also prepares an oral presentation of their work. The class has chosen to present the information as an informational seminar for parents aimed at outlining the importance of enacting the child labor laws, including posters outlining their position. The class has already practiced several **presentation skills** from earlier projects, and Table 8.17 highlights the skills focused on this year. For this project, they will include summarizing main ideas as part of the conclusion to their presentation.

The students in the group described above used a rubric to guide their work and now use it to assess their work and to set goals for future learning. They conclude that they did well on gathering and organizing information and are happy with the newspaper editorial, as they feel it clearly outlined their argument. They wish they had used more of the information they prepared for the oral presentation charts in the editorial. They also realize that the writing on the charts was too small for their audience to see during the presentation.

Table 8.17   Presentation Skills

I.   Presentation Skills
  a. Voice projection
  b. Eye contact (audience/camera)
  c. Sufficient practice
  d. Gestures and body language
  e. Use of visuals to support presentation

II. Content of Presentation
  a. Introduction (names, school, grade, topic, etc.)
  b. Shows/demonstrates what was learned
    i   Study of an important topic
    ii.   Description of research process
    iii. Discussion of what was learned
  c. Uses interesting format (possible suggestions)
    i.   Demonstration
    ii.   Role playing or drama
    iii. Interesting/surprising facts
    iv.   Begins with an interesting question
  d. Conclusion
    i.   Summarizes main ideas
    ii.   Relates importance of information/findings

SOURCE: Milwaukee Public Schools (2003).

It is clear that a teacher must plan in advance to prepare students for research projects. In the instance above, the teacher taught newspaper and presentation skills early in the school year. Students also already had skill in gathering and organizing information. The teacher prepared a WebQuest, gathered relevant materials, and informed the librarian of the project so he could be prepared to assist the students as well.

The students were given choices in their topics and methods for presenting their work that helped to motivate them and keep them focused. They clearly had already acquired the ability to work cooperatively and were ready to make decisions about how to accomplish their tasks. It is obvious that this teacher had a vision for what she wanted her students to accomplish by the end of the school year. A large part of teaching, then, is to determine our goals for our students, including the standards we want them to meet and the skills and strategies they will need to develop.

Content-Area-Specific Skills and Strategies: Reading Mathematics Text

Most state and district mathematics standards are influenced by the standards designed by the National Council of Teachers of Mathematics (2000). Many school mathematics programs are also guided by the development of the **problem-solving process.** The components of this process typically include selecting an appropriate strategy, organizing the information, solving the problem, and communicating mathematical understanding. Teaching mathematical concepts within the problem-solving process provides students with a framework for thinking mathematically and developing critical thinking skills.

As with any area of teaching, it is important to get a sense of what students already understand and a measure of their comfort level in math. Many students have a relatively high level of math anxiety, which means that priority should be given to helping students form a more positive attitude toward their ability in this area. Therefore, it is important that students are working at their instructional level and are able to manage the conceptual load to which they are being exposed.

Mathematical textbooks have become more language based than in the past. Barton and Heidema (2002) cite several challenging aspects of this phenomenon:

There are many reasons that the language and vocabulary used in mathematics challenge even able readers.

1. Conceptual density of mathematics text

2. Complex overlap between mathematics vocabulary and the vocabulary used in "ordinary" English,

3. Varied and large number of mathematics symbols and graphics (p. 13)

In relation to the first point, it is clear to anyone who has taken math courses that attention must be paid to every part of the page in a mathematics book. Often several concepts or variations within a concept are presented on a single page. To assist them, students could create a chart of all the new concepts they are to master during a certain time frame. The chart could be posted in the classroom or included in students' math logs.

New meanings for mathematical vocabulary may present a challenge when they differ from the way students are accustomed to using the words. "For example, the word *difference* could easily confuse the young student faced with the question, 'What is the difference between 4 and 7?' The student might answer, 'Four is even, but seven is odd,' when the intended correct response is 'three'"(Barton & Heidema, 2002, p. 13). These kinds of differences in language usage might be particularly confusing for ELLs or students struggling to learn mathematics.

The **conceptual load** for mathematics is further challenged because there are numerous symbols students must be able to interpret and use. Once learned and used effectively, these symbols may actually facilitate student learning, but time must be devoted to building an understanding of the symbols' meaning. Graphics also carry a great deal of information that students need to access and interpret. This also may challenge ELLs or struggling learners.

Given these challenges, along with the notion discussed earlier that content area textbooks are generally written at a level well above the grade level for which they are intended, we are provided with a good sense of the importance of directly teaching students to use language and text features to facilitate math learning. As in social studies, students might analyze overheads of textbook pages to highlight key vocabulary, key information, and statements that indicate the required task. Notes or charts might be compiled to highlight "signal words" that indicate the mathematical operation to be used. Table 8.18 provides a list of signal words for Grade 2 for addition and subtraction. Analyses of additional information or graphics that are intended to help students understand concepts may also be reviewed, such as sample problems, charts, tables, number lines, and so on.

Table 8.18   Signal Words

Words that tell me to add	Words that tell me to subtract
– how many in all	– how many are left
– how many altogether	– find the difference
– find the sum	– take away

Math journals may prove useful for students in organizing, reviewing, and evaluating growth with math concepts. Keeping a section focused on vocabulary in the learning log, or creating math vocabulary cards, can prove useful in helping students master this vocabulary. This in itself is insufficient for students to internalize and understand their meaning, but having students use their notebooks or vocabulary cards as references for math activities and games will facilitate their understanding of the concepts. Similar to the social studies model, four square vocabulary cards made by the students may clarify mathematical vocabulary for students, as seen in Table 8.19. Pictures, drawings, and graphic organizers may also be included to further clarify meaning.

A key to developing understanding in mathematics is to ensure that students can relate the concepts to everyday use. The teacher and students might bring in examples of the how the concepts they are studying are represented in everyday

Table 8.19   Mathematical Vocabulary Cards

A. Vocabulary Card Format		B. Sample Vocabulary Card	
Vocabulary Term	Examples	Factor	2 is a factor of 4, 6, 8, and all the even numbers 1, 2, 4, 8, & 16 are all factors of 16
Definition	Facts/ Characteristics	A factor is a number that can be divided evenly with another number	Use factors with arrays. The dimensions of each array are factors of the total number in the array

SOURCE: Adapted from Frayer, Frederick, & Klausmeier (1969).

life. For example, newspaper sale advertisements provide many examples of how people need to understand the concept of percentages. A single item might be examined in several different sales to determine which store offers the best deal. These kinds of materials might also be added to the learning log, where students use writing for a variety of purposes.

Discussions about text features, vocabulary, and ways to interpret math text may be helpful to students who would not have paid attention to these clues. The more these discussions are built into the math curriculum, the more likely that students will become critical readers of mathematical material. They can be guided to make connections, compare and contrast, and analyze mathematics concepts. The discussions will also facilitate students learning from others, and as they listen to one another, they will recognize that there is more than one way to solve a problem and communicate understanding.

Reciprocal teaching is especially appropriate for mathematics, as students with a good grasp of a concept will teach it to others who are still somewhat uncertain about how to apply it. Students who "teach" must review the material to make certain they are able to explain the concept clearly, provide examples, and ask questions. A teacher can model for students how to summarize, generate questions, clarify confusing text, and predict while reading a text selection aloud. It is important, then, to provide time to practice these skills (Barton & Heidema, 2002). All students can be given opportunities to either engage in reciprocal teaching in small groups, the whole class, or with a partner.

Focusing on problem solving in math may be used to guide students in the development of higher-level thinking and language development skills. Discussion of not only correct and incorrect answers but of the clues that are used to select strategies, the process of organizing information and visuals, evaluating the appropriateness of a solution, and communicating an understanding of the problem all require students to engage in serious and creative thinking. Learning logs or math journals are logical places for students to write about what they are learning in math, how well they understand concepts, and what they might do to become better mathematicians. Students are able to look back through their journals periodically, reflect on their progress, and set goals. Teachers may also use the logs to conference orally with students and during parent-teacher conferences. Used in this manner, the logs may become self-assessments of student progress and places to authentically use language arts skills.

With proper instruction, most students can develop a real enthusiasm for studying mathematics. Starting with the students' prior knowledge and linking math concepts to everyday use are two ways to make math manageable and useful for students. Teaching problem-solving skills that enable them to explore math texts and math assignments as an adventure to be puzzled through, analyzed, applied, and evaluated may make math learning more fun for both teachers and students.

Content-Area-Specific Skills and Strategies: Reading Science Text

Much of what has been discussed in relation to reading social studies and mathematics text also applies to reading science text. The reading level is challenging even for good readers; a large number of concepts are introduced and covered quickly and superficially, especially in the older grades. The features of text are similar to the other areas, though there may be more illustrations of models, steps in experiments, diagrams, and charts for recording data. Many school science programs focus on teaching science through the **scientific method.** Table 8.20 highlights the steps of this process (Harcourt Science, 2002, pp. x–xii).

In science, students are often called upon to compare and contrast, define concepts, describe, generalize, and determine cause and effect (Barton & Jordan,

Table 8.20   Steps in the Scientific Method

1. Observe and ask questions
2. Form a hypothesis
3. Plan an experiment
4. Conduct the experiment
5. Draw conclusions and communicate results

2001). It is helpful to not only provide students practice in using these strategies in their science work but also be able to name them and describe how they enhance science learning. Many of the skills and strategies of learning and applying science rely on the use of strong language arts skills (reading, viewing, writing, visually representing).

Some students experience a high level of anxiety with science, as they do with math. Making science interesting and applicable will help hold students' attention; linking science study to the outside world leads children to see the relevance of science in their lives. Selecting science materials that relate to the reading level and science background of the students will make science more meaningful and manageable.

One of the advantages of science is that it can become a hands-on content area to teach. Performing experiments or making observations in the environment provide students with clear examples of concepts. They also require students to pay careful attention to detail on several levels: reading for information, conducting experiments and observations, and writing records of observations or experiment results. These learning experiences create opportunities to directly teach how to read, explore, and write in a careful and detailed manner. Lab journals can be comprehensive records of vocabulary study, strategy development, experimental logs, and self-assessments of learning. Note taking for observations and experiments might focus on recording observable results and use of detail. Writing conclusions from experiments could be linked to making connections and generalizations based on evidence. As can be evidenced, there are many language arts skills being utilized within the elementary and middle-level science curriculum.

Group work is often built into science lab work, as students often have a lab partner with whom they must utilize speaking skills and cooperate to conduct experiments and complete lab reports. This could be very beneficial for ELLs and students who struggle with science. In any of the content areas, it is important to note that ELLs may have a range of background in the subject from substantial to limited. Students with a substantial background may be far ahead of the class in the content area and only lack English language skills to express that understanding. Conversely, students with limited content area skills must learn the language *and* the content.

Science also lends itself to active learning in other ways. Students can prepare oral or PowerPoint presentations to demonstrate learning. Models, experiment results, or displays can be created and explained in relation to the underlying science principles of the unit of study. Music, art, and drama are useful and enjoyable ways to demonstrate understanding as well. One middle school science teacher taught concepts of human body systems to the tune of "The Twelve Days of Christmas." During a test, quiet strands of the song could be heard throughout the room as students went through the lyrics until they were able to retrieve the information they needed. Through a dramatic reenactment, another class demonstrated an understanding of how a tsunami is created. As in the other content areas, learning logs can be used by students to focus in writing and through visuals on what they are learning and to set science goals for themselves. Reflecting on how effectively they use the scientific method helps students gauge how well they are beginning to think and act like scientists.

Essentially, teachers are teaching and reinforcing language arts and literacy skills all day long, including within content area learning. Teaching students to read informational literature as a genre with a set of unique characteristics will help students become more careful and critical readers and writers in the content areas. Using a variety of texts and trade books can serve to heighten student interest in reading informational literature and create a balance between use and understanding of narrative and expository text. This balance in the classroom will more than likely break down the fourth-grade literacy barrier many students face when they are exposed to more challenging conceptual loads in the content areas.

Integrated Units of Study

Many teachers recognize the importance of integrating not only the language arts but also the content areas. They select a theme or a learning standard and analyze relationships that could be developed across several content areas. Students are given the opportunity to make more links and connections than would be possible if the content areas were studied separately. When skills and strategies are taught as part of integrated units of study, students gain a better sense of how they can be used in a variety of situations.

Integrated units may be organized around a particular subject area, an author, or a major concept. Tables 8.21 and 8.22 provide examples of integrated units at various grade levels.

Table 8.21   Integrated Unit on Immigrants Planned Around Subject Areas

Grade 5

Theme: Immigrant Kids Yesterday and Today

Standards:

A.8.1   Students will use effective reading strategies (inference, predicting) to achieve their objectives in reading.

A.8.1   Students will use reasoning abilities to perceive mathematical patterns and identify relationships.

A.8.6   Students will explain the ways in which scientific knowledge is useful and also limited when applied to social issues.

B.8.12   Students will describe how history can be organized and analyzed using various criteria to group people and events.

Learning Outcomes:

- The students will compare and contrast the lives of immigrant kids in 1900 and 2000.
- The students will use inference and prediction in reading, writing, listening, and speaking about immigrant kids in 1900 and 2000.
- The students will gather and organize information to create an oral and visual presentation comparing immigrant kids from 1900 and 2000.

Science & Technology
- differences in technology
  between 1900 & 2000
  - communication
  - work
  - home
- impact on immigrants' lives

Writing
- journal entries
- interview questions and notes
- script for play
- letters/postcards home

Physical Education
games kids played

Social Studies
- jobs for immigrants
- ports of entry
- countries of origin
- reasons for immigration
- challenges
- immigration laws
- reader's theater/drama

Immigrant Kids Yesterday & Today

Assessments
- drama, art, music
- journal entries
- passport information
- conferences
- strategy evaluations

Mathematics
- comparisons of groups (census data)
  - number of immigrants
  - countries of origin
  - jobs
  - income
  - level of education
bar graphs, pie charts (reading, visually representing data)

Strategies
- note taking
- inference
- predicting with evidence
- compare and contrast

Language Arts
- genre
- reader response
  - context clues

Immigrant Kids
Esperanza Rising
Tangled Threads

Table 8.22   Integrated Unit Planned Around a Specific Author/Illustrator

Grade 1

Theme: Analyzing the Craft of Author—Eric Carle

Standards:

A.4.2 Students will read, interpret, and critically analyze literature (recognize and recall elements and details of story structure).

B.4.1 Students will create or produce writing to communicate with different audiences for a variety of purposes.

C.4.3 Students will participate effectively in discussion.

Learning Outcomes:
- Students will analyze the author's craft of Eric Carle; mapping out similarities of character, setting, plot, illustrations, and critique of artwork of the author/illustrator.
- Students will describe favorite Eric Carle books and justify reasons for selection.
- Students will prepare an oral presentation outlining a critique of the work of Eric Carle.

Author's Craft
- What makes Eric Carle a "unique" author
- Characterize Eric Carle books

Setting
- Where do the stories take place
- How do you know
- How are settings represented in art

Favorites
- Select favorite book
- Reasons for selection

Plot
- What are the stories about
- What problems do the characters run into
- How are problems solved

Eric Carle

Characters
- Identify characters

Web Site
- Critique Eric Carle site
- Write letter to author

Strategies
- Description (words/phrases)
- Elaboration
- Justifying
- Fluency
- Purpose for reading

Word Wall
- Words to describe

Art
- Medium
- Tissue paper
- Formats
- Colors
- Vividness

Assessment
- Critique the work of Eric Carle
  - Art
  - Characters
  - Settings
  - Plots

Reading: Read Eric Carle's books

Writing: Prepare book reviews, write about author's craft, letter to Eric Carle

Viewing: View Eric Carle video and Web site

Listening: Listen to Eric Carle books, ideas about author's craft, opinions about books

Speaking: Share opinions about books and characters, presentation about author's craft

Visually Representing: Replicate art style of Eric Carle, prepare visuals for presentation

End-of-Chapter Reflection

- Reflect on the notion that content area teachers are also literacy teachers. Provide some examples from what you have just read and may have experienced within a classroom setting.

- Reflect on how you plan to teach students to read and understand content area text. What methods and strategies did you learn that you feel will be effective?

- What ideas do you have to make content area materials comprehensible for ELLs or students with learning challenges?

Planning for Teaching

1. Examine social studies, science, and math standards for Grades 4 and 8. How could you integrate literacy goals with these content standards? Can you find literacy already integrated into the standards?

2. Preview social studies, science, and math texts. What are the unique features of texts from each content area? What considerations would you make in helping students read these texts effectively? In small groups, compile a list of signal words that could be pointed out to students to guide them in making sense of content area texts. For example, "however" signals an exception.

Connections With the Field

- Visit a content area class such as social studies or science. Observe and record all of the integrated language arts that takes place. Do students seem to be using language arts skills to learn and apply content? How so? Discuss what you have observed with your classmates.

Student Study Site

The Companion Website for Developing Voice Through the Language Arts

http://www.sagepub.com/dvtlastudy

Visit the Web-based student study site to enhance your understanding of the chapter content and to discover additional resources that will take your learning one step further. You can enhance your understanding of the chapters by using the comprehensive Study Guide, which includes learning objectives, key terms, activities, practice tests, and more. You'll also find special features, such as the Links to Standards from U.S. States and associated activities, Children's Literature Selections, Reflection Exercises, Learning from Journal Articles, and PRAXIS test preparation materials.

References of Children's/Young Adult Literature

Freedman, R. (1994). *Kids at work: Lewis Hine and the crusade against child labor*. New York: Clarion.

Hamilton, V. (Ed.). (1985). *The people could fly: American black folktales*. New York: Knopf.

Park, L. S. (2002). *When my name was Keoko*. New York: Clarion.

Ryan, P. M. (2000). *Esperanza rising*. New York: Scholastic.

Shea, P. D. (2003). *Tangled threads*. New York: Clarion.

References of Professional Resources

Anderson, R. (1994). Role of the reader's schema in comprehension, learning, and memory. In R. Ruddell, M. Ruddell, & H. Singer (Eds.), *Theoretical models and processes of reading* (4th ed.). Newark, DE: International Reading Association.

Baldwin, R., Ford, J., & Readance, J. (1981). Teaching word connotations: An alternative strategy. *Reading World, 21*, 103–108.

Barton, M., & Heidema, C. (2002). *Teaching reading in mathematics*. Aurora, CO: Mid-Continent Research for Education and Learning (McREL).

Barton, M., & Jordan, D. (2001). *Teaching reading in science*. Aurora, CO: Mid-Continent Research for Education and Learning (McREL).

Boehm, R., Hoone, C., McGowan, T., McKinney-Browning, M., & Miramontes, O. (1997). *States and regions*. Orlando, FL: Harcourt Brace.

Dodge, B., & March, T. (1998). WebQuest. Retrieved from http://www.ozline.com/webquests/intro.html.

Doty, J., Cameron, G., & Barton, M. (2003). *Teaching reading in social studies*. Aurora, CO: Mid-Continent Research for Education and Learning (McREL).

Echevarria, J., Vogt, M., & Short, D. (2004). *Making content comprehensible for English language learners: The SIOP model* (2nd ed.). Boston: Allyn & Bacon.

Harcourt Science. (2002). *Harcourt science, 4*. Orlando, FL: Harcourt School Publishers.

Helfgot, D., & Westhaven, M. (2001). *Kidspiration*. Portland, OR: Inspiration Software.

Holdaway, D. (1984). *The foundations of literacy*. Portsmouth, NH: Heinemann.

Johnson, D., & Pearson, P. (1984). *Teaching reading vocabulary* (2nd ed.). New York: Holt, Rinehart & Winston.

Marzano, R., Pickering, D., & Pollock, J. (2001). *Classroom instruction that works: Research-based strategies for increasing student achievement*. Alexandria, VA: Association for Supervision and Curriculum Development.

Henn-Reinke, K., Lawrence, L., Plicka, G., Skarich, N., Yemma, M., & Cooper, A. (2003). *P-5 assessment portfolio guide 2003-04*. Milwaukee, WI: Milwaukee Public Schools.

Nagy, W. (1988). *Teaching vocabulary to improve reading comprehension*. Urbana, IL: ERIC Clearinghouse on Reading and Communication Skills and the National Council of Teachers of English and the International Reading Association.

Nagy, W., & Herman, P. (1985). Incidental vs. instructional approaches to increasing reading vocabulary. *Educational Perspectives, 23*, 16–21.

National Council of Teachers of Mathematics. (2000). *Principles and standards for school mathematics*. Reston, VA: Author.

Pearson, P. (1993). Teaching and learning reading: A research perspective. *Language Arts, 70*, 502–511.

Popp, M. (1997). *Learning journals in the K–8 classroom: Exploring ideas and information in the content area*. Mahwah, NJ: Lawrence Erlbaum.

Temple, C., Martinez, M., Yokota, J., & Taylor, A. (1998). *Children's books in children's hands: An introduction to their literature*. Boston: Allyn & Bacon.

Other Children's/Young Adult Literature Resources

Brink, C. (1973). *Caddie Woodlawn*. New York: Macmillan.

Bunting, E. (1994). *Smoky night* (D. Diaz, Illus.). San Diego, CA: Harcourt Brace.

Carle, E. (1968). *1, 2, 3 to the zoo*. New York: Putnam.

Carle, E. (1970). *The very hungry caterpillar*. Cleveland, OH: Collins-World.

Carle, E. (1981). *The honeybee and the robber*. New York: Philomel.

Carle, E. (1985). *The very busy spider*. New York: Philomel.

Carle, E. (1986). *The grouchy ladybug*. New York: HarperCollins.

Carle, E. (1986). *The secret birthday message*. New York: Harper & Row.

Carle, E. (1987). *A house for hermit crab*. Natick, MA: Picture Book Studio.

Carle, E. (1990). *The very quiet cricket*. New York: Philomel.

Carle, E. (1991). *The tiny seed*. Natick, MA: Picture Book Studio.

Carle, E. (1992). *Today is Monday*. New York: Putnam.

Carle, E. (1993). *Eric Carle: Picture writer* [Videocassette]. New York: Philomel.

Carle, E. (1995). *The very lonely firefly*. New York: Philomel.

Coerr, E. (1977). *Sadako and the thousand paper cranes*. New York: Putnam.

Cole, J. (1989). *The magic school bus inside the human body* (B. Degan, Illus.). New York: Scholastic.

Cole, J. (1995). *The magic school bus inside a hurricane* (B. Degan, Illus.). New York: Scholastic.

Cole, J. (1998). *The magic school bus in the rain forest* (B. Degan, Illus.). New York: Scholastic.

Collier, J., & Collier, C. (1974). *My brother Sam is dead*. Portland, OR: Four Winds.

Curtis, C. (1995). *The Watsons go to Birmingham*. New York: Delacorte.

Cushman, K. (1994). *Catherine, called Birdy*. New York: Clarion.

Cushman, K. (1995). *The midwife's apprentice*. New York: Clarion.

Dorris, M. (1992). *Morning girl*. New York: Hyperion.

Fleischman, P. (1991). *The borning room*. New York: HarperCollins.

Freedman, R. (1987). *Lincoln: A photobiography*. New York: Clarion.

Freedman, R. (2001). *In the days of the vaqueros: America's first true cowboys*. New York: Clarion.

Hahn, M. (1991). *Stepping on the cracks*. New York: Clarion.

Hall, D. (1979). *The ox-cart man*. New York: Viking.

Hesse, K. (1992). *Letters from Rifka*. New York: Holt.

Hopkinson, D. (1993). *Sweet Clara and the freedom quilt.* New York: Knopf.

Houston, G. (1988). *The year of the perfect Christmas tree.* New York: Dial.

Jimenez, F. (1997). *The circuit.* Albuquerque: University of New Mexico Press.

Jimenez, F. (2001). *Breaking through.* Boston: Houghton Mifflin.

Lionni, L. (1974). *Fish is fish.* New York: Dragonfly.

MacLachlan, P. (1985). *Sarah, plain and tall.* New York: Harper.

McCully, E. (1996). *The bobbin girl.* New York: Dial.

Mockizuki, K. (1993). *Baseball saved us.* New York: Lee & Low.

O'Dell, S. (1970). *Sing down the moon.* Boston: Houghton Mifflin.

Patterson, K. (1973). *The sign of the chrysanthemum.* New York: Crowell.

Patterson, K. (1991). *Lyddie.* New York: Dutton.

Polacco, P. (1994). *Pink and say.* New York: Philomel.

Rinaldi, A. (1992). *A break with charity: A story about the Salem witch trials.* New York: Harcourt.

Ringgold, F. (1992). *Aunt Harriett's underground railroad in the sky.* New York: Crown.

Rosen, M. (1995). *A school for Pompey Walker.* New York: Harcourt.

Rylant, C. (1982). *When I was young in the mountains.* New York: Dell.

Shea, P. (1994). *The whispering cloth: A refugee story.* Honesdale, PA: Boyds Mill Press.

Speare, E. (1958). *The witch of Blackbird Pond.* Boston: Houghton Mifflin.

Speare, E. (1983). *The sign of the beaver.* Boston: Houghton Mifflin.

Taylor, M. (1977). *Roll of thunder, hear my cry.* New York: Dial.

Taylor, M. (1981). *Let the circle be unbroken.* New York: Dial.

Taylor, M. (1990). *Mississippi bridge.* New York: Dial.

Turner, A. (1987). *Nettie's trip south.* New York: Macmillan.

Whelan, G. (1995). *Once on this island.* New York: HarperCollins.

Williams, G., & Regan, D. (1986). *Adventures in the solar system: Planetron and me.* Los Angeles: Price Stern Sloan.

Yep, L. (1995). *Dragon's gate.* New York: HarperCollins.

Yolen, J. (1992). *Encounter.* New York: Harcourt.

Yoshiko, U. (1978). *Journey home.* New York: Atheneum.

Technology Resources

Inspiration Software Inc.: Award-winning software developed to assist users utilize visual and thinking abilities to plan, create, and organize ideas. Kidspiration is the K–5 version ideal for educational settings and purposes. Excellent use of graphic organizers and integration of the language arts, as well as other content area learning. A free trial download is available at www.inspiration.com.

Extensive library of Web sites of interest and for use by teachers and students categorized by subject, grade level, and format. Easy to search for topics and lessons using the Web site's advanced search feature: http://www.kn.pacbell.com/wired/bluewebn

Challenges for ELLs in content area learning. Part of the Everything ESL Web site that provides lesson plans, teaching tips, discussion topics, and resources for teaching ESL and

ELLs:http://www.everythingesl.net/inservices/challenges_ells_content_area_l_65322.php

Songs for Teaching Web site, based on the belief that music and song can assist learners in all areas of the curriculum. Web site includes lyrics, music clips, and teaching suggestions: http://www.songsforteaching.com/rationale.htm

WebQuest portal to locate WebQuests on a variety of topics/content areas, also integrated language arts: http://webquest.org

Online graph maker: http://nces.ed.gov/nceskids/createagraph

Capstone Press: www.capstonepress.com

Saddleback Publishing Inc.: www.sdlback.com

Workshops in the Language Arts Curriculum

Context Setting:

After reading this chapter, you will be able to

- Conceptualize reading, writing, and content area workshops
- Prepare the classroom for use of the workshop model
- Determine procedures for workshops
- Determine the format and content of workshops

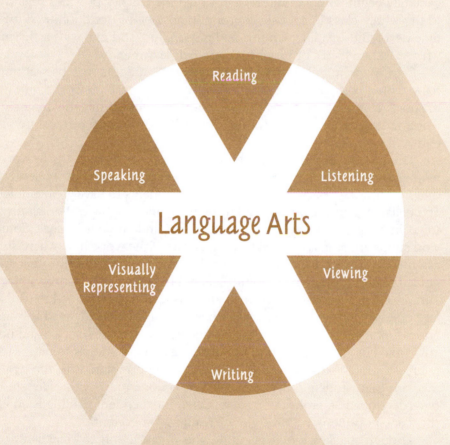

Before We Begin

- There is a lot of content to cover and many modes of learning to include in the language arts curriculum. What are your ideas for ways to organize your school day to meaningfully incorporate all these aspects of teaching, learning, and assessing language arts?

What Are Workshops in the Language Arts?

There is much content and activity that are a part of the language arts curriculum. It is important to think about ways for organizing language arts instruction and activity in order to ensure inclusive and comprehensive teaching, learning, and assessing. A workable format for organizing instructional time is through using the **workshop model.** Reading, writing, and language are the most commonly used content areas for workshops, although, as will be seen later in this chapter, workshops can be a beneficial format for content area learning as well. Workshops generally begin with a minilesson in which the teacher provides brief instruction to the whole class or to a small group in an area of need, followed by blocks of time devoted to reading, writing, and responding, and end with a sharing session where all share work or insights about their learning.

During the middle portion of a workshop, students may be working individually, with a partner, or within a small group. The teacher works with individuals or small groups in guided reading or writing activities while the other students are working independently. Individual or small group **conferences** are an integral part of the workshop.

The workshop model provides time and space for students to work through writing and reading processes in a variety of groupings, independently and with others. Using a workshop framework allows students to have greater independence and collaborate more during reading, writing, and language. Workshops are structured in a variety of ways based on teachers' and students' needs. Some reading workshops encompass guided reading as part of the workshop, where students are assigned to groups based on their level of reading progress. In other workshops, guided reading is designed around sets of books that may, for example, reflect an author, a genre, or a theme. A small group is formed or assigned to read a particular book, participate in book discussions, and/or complete related learning experiences. Upon completion of the sets of books, new sets are selected and new groups are formed or assigned. A third use of a reading workshop is to have each student read a separate text as an individualized reading program, with the teacher working with each student independently. This is done more with older students who have developed as proficient readers. Often independent reading is an element of the workshop, along with the guided reading component.

Though it takes much planning and organization to establish a workshop model in a classroom, the benefits are numerous. Students learn to work collaboratively in a well-run workshop. They recognize that they are able to do more together and share a greater variety of ideas than when they work exclusively on their own. A great deal of pressure is taken off English language learners (ELLs) and students who struggle with literacy development, as students are encouraged to use the students who have mastered the content and strategies in specific areas, thus having other sources of help besides the teacher.

Benefits and Challenges of a Workshop Framework

Students develop independence in reading and writing workshops through opportunities to work independently and make choices in their work. Due to the individualized conferencing and feedback they receive from the teacher and peers, expectation in a workshop should be that students would accept greater responsibility for their own progress.

Teachers have flexibility with their time using a workshop model. While the students work independently, the teacher moves about the classroom assisting individuals or small groups as needed. The teacher can note student work that represents a breakthrough for the class or the individual and invite these students to share at the end of the workshop or participate in teaching part of the minilesson for the next day. Because students are making choices about their learning and because their work is more individualized, they often tend to take greater responsibility for it in a workshop format. Many begin exploring their writing more as a craft that they are developing, and they read more as something to make connections with and critique rather than just as assigned work. The nature of the workshop provides students with encouragement and freedom to try new things and then step back to examine their attempts, leading them to be more reflective about their efforts.

There are some challenges with using workshops in the classroom. Because students are expected to work independently, the teacher must teach about expectations and provide them with opportunities to practice. Not only do students need to be more independent in the amount and quality of their work but also in managing materials and self-assessing progress. Students may be expected to work cooperatively or collaboratively. These skills must also be taught and practiced, and using modeling and minilessons are ways to do achieve this.

Although it may take students longer to learn the workshop format and become familiar with the expectations, the benefits far outweigh the challenges. Students become engaged in their work because they have internalized learning for its own sake and they begin to grow more reflective, continuing to develop as critical thinkers.

The Workshop Format

Generally, the workshop model consists of three parts: **minilesson, work session, and sharing session**. This format provides students with a framework during which to learn something new, try it out in their own work, evaluate how well their efforts went, and share with others.

Minilessons

Minilessons are typically brief introductions or reinforcements of a procedure, a skill, or a strategy, often completed in 5–7 minutes but occasionally may run longer for more complex topics. "Some of my mini lessons are mini: a five-to ten-minute lecture on a single, highly-focused topic . . . Other lessons are longer and interactive so students and I can generate ideas and build a theory together, or so I can demonstrate some of my understanding as a writer and reader" (Atwell, 1998, p. 153). The purpose of the minilesson is to provide students with a quick lesson in a specific area where many students demonstrate a need. It provides students with just enough information and practice to apply the concept to their activities in the workshop. For example, if students are not using capital letters in their writing, one or more minilessons might focus on capitalization rules.

Often minilessons are taught as whole-class learning experiences. However, they may be conducted with small groups when only a few students need or are ready to learn the concept. When presented to the whole class, minilessons will have varying impact on the students, depending on their experiences and level of development. Some students will be ready to apply the concepts immediately to their work, others will understand the concept but not be ready to apply it, and still others will need additional instruction or support with the concept at a later time.

Minilessons might relate to skills, strategies, procedures, or study skills related to the type of workshop being conducted, for example, reading, writing, or content area workshop (see Table 9.1 for examples). Early in the school year, minilessons may focus primarily on procedures and expectations for participating in workshops. After the workshop framework has been established, the focus may shift to deal with skills, strategies, and in-depth examination of aspects of the area of study. The topic of minilessons is a specific concept or part of a concept that can be briefly and concisely introduced or reinforced with students and then applied to the day's work. Larger concepts are broken down into manageable parts and presented developmentally to students.

Selecting appropriate topics for minilessons is of critical importance in creating a successful workshop. There are several main considerations in the selection process:

- Determine the standards students must meet or work toward by the end of the semester or year
- Evaluate student work to ascertain current level of functioning in relation to standards

Table 9.1   Examples of Workshop Minilesson Topics

Skills	Strategies	Procedures	Study Skills
Writing mechanics	Self-assessing work	Use of materials	Completing work
Text features	Prediction	Following the schedule	Quality work
Research	Analysis	Peer collaboration	Working toward goals
Reading mechanics	Inference	Conferencing	Pacing

- Determine short-range and long-range goals for student progress in the workshop
- Break goals into a series of brief developmental lessons that will lead students ever closer to the standards

In A View From the Classroom that follows, we see how Carol uses the standards and her understanding of student needs to conceptualize a reading workshop plan for her students.

A View From the Classroom

Carol would like her students to meet the following standard in reading: students apply a wide range of strategies to comprehend, interpret, evaluate, and appreciate texts. As she observes her students' reading and discussing what they've read, she notices that many read fluently, rarely stumble on a word, and are able to summarize what they read fairly well. However, they find it difficult to make connections to what they have read. Therefore, Carol plans to develop a series of minilessons that focus first on teaching students to make connections between what they've read and their own experiences (**text-to-self connections**). She'll use books that feature the experiences of characters that are similar to those of her students to facilitate making text-to-self connections. After the students have a good sense of how to make connections to their own experiences, Carol plans to present additional minilessons that relate what students are currently reading to what they have read previously (**text-to-text connections**) and to the world around them (**text-to-world connections**). Following is an overview of her plans to structure this

series of minilessons. The number of minilessons will depend on how quickly students learn to make connections in each area.

Planning Minilessons Related to Making Text-to-Self Connections, Text-to-Text Connections, Text-to-World Connections

Definition and purpose (students put in notebooks)

Model reading and making connections to self using read-alouds

Students listen to short story/piece of text and note connections to self

Students share self-to-text links from own reading

Carol has a number of ELLs in her class, and she would like to create minilessons that are as visual and interactive as possible to maximize learning for the whole class, but especially for these students. Therefore, she will have students find experiences that they can identify with and act out the characters' experiences and then compare what happened to them that was similar. On

(Continued)

(Continued)

other occasions, Carol will place copies of illustrations from the book on posters, and in pairs students will draw what the illustrations made them think of in their own lives. She also plans to take three or four major events from the story, draw large circles to represent each event, and label them on a large sheet of paper. Students will place Post-it notes in each circle where they have had the same experience as the characters. Discussions of how these connections help relate more fully with the author and the characters will be emphasized throughout the minilessons.

A workshop can become a powerful tool for developing student understanding of concepts. In the preceding example, students learn what text-to-self connections are and how they help with understanding, reflect on samples shared by the teacher, look for connections in pieces of shared reading, and finally, share links they have found on their own. The process of learning the concept is developmental; once students form a solid understanding of making connections, they easily move to make text-to-text and then text-to-world connections.

Theory Into Practice

Comprehension is strengthened when readers make connections to what they read, be it text-to-text, text-to-self, or text-to-world. This is important with content area learning as well. Think about the subject matter learning that you have had difficulty learning or understanding. Was it unfamiliar to you? Were you interested in the topic or content? Were you able to connect the information to other information you already knew? Could you see its relevance in the real world? Keeping these questions in mind when you teach will assist you in making learning for your students more relevant, interesting, and enduring.

The formats for presenting minilessons are as varied as the creativity of the teacher allows. In the beginning of the school year, the teacher generally presents the minilessons. Later in the year, older students who demonstrate a good understanding of the concept may join the teacher in teaching the minilesson or may even do so independently, after rehearsal with the teacher. The teacher may model or demonstrate new concepts, create posters, and so on as part of the minilesson. The concept may be presented directly or the students may be led to "discover" them on their own.

Older students, in particular, may be asked to record information in their reading logs during the minilesson, or they may be given informational sheets to include in their logs as a resource to refer back to as they apply the concepts from their minilesson during independent work time and beyond. Minilesson concepts may also be recorded on posters or charts and displayed in the classroom for future reference. Table 9.2 outlines some additional minilesson ideas for reading and writing workshops.

Table 9.2   Sample Minilesson Ideas for Reading and Writing Workshops

Reading Workshop

Skills & Strategies	Literary Analysis	Management
What good readers do	Responding to reading	Reading logs
Reading for meaning	Author's craft	Where to work
Monitoring comprehension	Genres	Expectations for group work
Making connections	Literary elements	Expectations for individual work
Drawing conclusions	Point of view	Selecting appropriate-level books

Writing Workshop

Skills & Content	Author's Craft	Management
Writing mechanics	Writing process	Conferencing
Editing	Writing for a purpose	Writing expectations
Publishing	Genres	Schedule for workshop
Use of resources	Writing for an audience	Portfolios
Use of technology	Topics for writing	Writing logs
Word analysis strategies	Point of view	Discussing books

Work Session

Following the minilesson, a larger block of time is devoted to reading, writing, discussing, reflecting, or conferencing. Having a minilesson followed by a work session helps teachers ensure they are teaching important concepts that enable students to take what they have learned and apply it directly to their work.

Status of the Class

Before students begin work for the day, teachers may have students articulate their plan for the day using the **status of the class** records to keep track of student work (Atwell, 1998). This can be a single sheet of paper on a clipboard with students' names running down the left side of the sheet and dates across the top. The students quickly report what they will be working on, and the teacher writes it down as anecdotal notes about students' work progress. In reading, the status of the class may be used to record books and page numbers of books students are reading independently. If independent reading is assigned on a daily basis, teachers may record whether students will be reading, responding to reading, or reflecting on reading progress. Dates of conferences might also be recorded on these sheets. Teachers use a shorthand recording system, for example, "r" for reading, "rr" for responding to reading, "rrp" for reflecting on reading progress, and "c" for conference. Once students get accustomed to the status of the class procedure, it takes only a couple of minutes to complete before they move into their work sessions. If little change occurs over several days, the teacher will be certain to check in with that student to determine if there is a problem that needs to be resolved. This might entail setting a deadline with students who are completing little work. By reporting progress on a regular basis, students are able to monitor their own level of work as well.

In writing, as students are engaged in various stages of the writing process, the status of the class will indicate where students are writing a first draft, revising, peer editing, conferencing, or publishing.

Teachers set up the work sessions in a way that enables students to gradually become more independent. In reading, as previously mentioned, the whole class may begin by reading the same book(s). The teacher may then divide the students into guided reading groups and meet with them. Before then, however, the teacher spends time rehearsing with them what they should be working on during that time when they are not meeting with the teacher—including work habits and resources to use when they have questions—so as not to disturb the teacher and others during the guided reading sessions.

Work Session: Writing Workshop

In writing, the status of the class indicates the stage of the writing process in which each student is engaged. Early in the year, the teacher teaches the components of the **writing process** and guides students in applying these stages to the writing workshop. With the introduction of each new step, additional classroom procedures may be added. For example, once students are familiar with **peer editing,** procedures may be reviewed for selecting a peer editor, where peer editing might take place, the role of the peer editor, and how to provide helpful feedback. These may be introduced during minilessons, but the work session is the time when students begin application of the process. Thinking through the most efficient and effective ways to introduce new components will help workshops proceed smoothly.

The role of the teacher during the work session is quite different when compared to that during more traditional classroom learning experiences. The workshop is the place for students to focus exclusively on language arts, including reading, responding, and writing. No worksheets or repetitive skill exercises are included in this model. The teacher, then, serves as a guide to help students examine their use of language arts to deepen their understanding of communication. Reading and writing roles are somewhat different in this aspect, but the common element is that the teacher is aware of the work of each child and discusses new avenues for them to consider.

In writing workshop, many teachers relate that they move from student to student during this time and informally conference with them, saying, "Tell me about your writing." They speak briefly to each student, sometimes asking the student to read a portion of what is written and other times helping him or her puzzle through something of difficulty. It may be that the student is stuck on ending the piece, or the teacher may suggest that the student clarify something that is not clear. Nancie Atwell (1998) moves her chair from desk to desk to maintain a continual presence in the classroom that keeps students focused and allows her to control the length of time she spends with each student. When she does encounter students who are having difficulty, she either asks questions to guide them in coming to their own conclusion or she provides a brief suggestion to try out the new idea.

Writing is also unique in that students may all be at different stages in the writing process. They may be brainstorming what to write next, composing, editing, and so on. It is essential that students know what to do when they finish one stage and are ready to move on to the next. Students who are in the prewriting or drafting stages generally work at their desks or in the writing center. When they finish, they may be instructed to read their work to themselves and self-correct any errors they find, select a partner to peer edit the piece, and submit the piece for editing by the teacher. After that point, students decide whether they wish to **publish** the piece or begin a new writing piece. If they are publishing their writing, they may use a computer and materials in the writing center. Throughout the process, students have access to the materials they need to assist their work as literate persons.

A benefit of the workshop model in writing is that students are able to write at their own pace; upon completion of one piece, they move to another without having to wait for the entire class to finish. Students who work quickly may complete many pieces, though the quality of the work may necessitate having them work more slowly and carefully. Students who work meticulously or who write longer and/or more involved pieces are free to work at their own pace, given that they are accomplishing a sufficient amount of work. Students also work at their own developmental level, with all students actively engaged in writing but each doing so according to his or her stage of development. Taking the pressure off students to complete writing on strict deadlines is refreshing for many students, especially ELLs and students who struggle with writing.

🏠 A View From Home

First grader Charlie is spending the day running errands with his father. After going to the grocery store and dry cleaners, and while walking out of the pet store with his new turtle, Charlie says to his father, "I'm going to write all about my new turtle during writing workshop at school." Encouraging him, his father says, "Don't forget to write about how long it took to pick out just the right one. You picked your turtle because he kept looking at you and didn't put his head into his shell like the others did."

Work Session: Reading Workshop

During the work session of reading workshop, the teacher may meet with guided reading groups for a portion of the time. The other students may be engaged in independent reading in preparation for their guided reading group session, independent reading of other materials, responding to reading, or preparing for conferencing. When the teacher joins the students working independently or in small groups, the role is much the same as in writing workshop. She may ask students to briefly discuss their reading and share their opinions. They may be asked to read a small portion aloud to the teacher to help him or her gauge fluency and comprehension.

Conferencing with students either informally, as suggested above, or in more formal conferences provides both teachers and students a chance to pause and reflect on what is being learned and to set goals for future learning experiences. Some school districts have well-defined statements of standards for each grade/developmental level. In these cases, teachers may use these statements or charts as guides for noting student progress. In other cases, teachers use the list of minilessons they have taught and develop a rubric to gauge how well students have been able to apply the concepts. Students should be informed about what will be reviewed in the conference and how they are expected to prepare for it.

Often teachers conference with small groups of students each day. Those students who wish a conference because they have completed a piece of work and need to review it with the teacher or because they have run into some difficulty that they cannot resolve through other sources are asked to put their names on the board. When teachers move into this phase of the workshop, they know immediately who needs a conference. In addition, teachers may call one or two other students to meet with them as a way to make certain that they are keeping in close contact with each student in the classroom. The boxed text below provides some opportunities for you to reflect on how you might consider establishing various components of the workshop model in your own classroom.

Procedures for Setting Up Work Sessions in Reading and Writing Workshop

The work session is generally the portion of a workshop when students work mostly independently. Think about how you would organize for work sessions in reading and writing workshop. The following questions may be helpful in deciding how to manage this part of the workshop.

- What is the procedure for selecting an editing partner?
- How do students submit their edited pieces to the teacher for review?
- What resources will be made available to students?
- How will you meet with students individually during the work session?
- What should students do if they encounter a problem and you are not available?
- How will you set up conferences?
- How will you prepare students for conferencing with you?
- What will students bring to conferences?
- How will students set goals and then work toward them?

Sharing Sessions

The sharing portion of the workshop is an opportunity for students to review their work, but even more important, it serves as a reflection and assessment vehicle for teachers and students. Students are able to share the work they have done during the work sessions and receive feedback from the teacher and their peers. Obviously, this necessitates guiding students in responding to one another in appropriate ways.

The sharing sessions are a good gauge for the teacher to measure the effectiveness of the minilessons and the guidance given during the work sessions. If students are able to clearly and concisely describe or demonstrate how they applied the concepts from the minilessons, it is a good indication that students understood them and were able to apply them easily. If students appeared confused or unsure of the concepts or have not applied them at all, it is an indication that the teacher will need to find ways to reteach them.

Students learn to give and receive feedback during the sharing session, both of which are helpful to be taught directly. Students learn how to listen to the writing or responses of their peers and note how well the concepts they have learned have been reflected in the work. For example, if the class is working on creating exciting introductions that draw students into the story, their task is to listen for whether their peers have been able to accomplish this. In other words, they have been given specific things to listen for and have had instruction in the particular area. Exciting story introductions begin with a question, a surprising statement, or a puzzling comment or dialogue, and students listen to determine whether the writer has done this. Students also need to know what to do with the feedback they have been given, learning to evaluate the suggestions and then determining whether they will use them as suggested, alter them, or reject them.

As with conferencing, students who complete a piece of work or who want feedback from the class may sign up for the sharing session as well. When teachers note that one or more students have completed work that represents a good application of a concept, they may ask those students to share their work with the class. When students are able to see and hear the work of their peers, it can provide a better sense of application of new concepts.

The sharing session is a good venue for students to reflect on a number of areas, including how well they followed various procedures and what they could do to improve. Reflecting on work habits and making suggestions for improvement is another area that is appropriate to discuss during the sharing session as students self-assess their individual progress and make a mental or written assessment of the quality and quantity of their work during the workshop.

The most significant reflections of the sharing session, though, relate to progress in the development of understandings about the process of reading and writing and how students view themselves as readers and writers (Atwell, 1998; Frey & Fisher, 2006; Routman, 1991). The sharing session of the workshop not only enables students to reflect on how they are using the new skills and strategies they are learning in reading and writing but also encourages them to think about how these skills and strategies impact their own learning.

It is often during the sharing portion of the workshop that students make the connections between the language arts and appreciate how reading, writing, listening, speaking, viewing, and visually representing influence one another. These ideas might be proposed during minilessons, but it is when students are able to articulate the links as they relate to their own use of the language arts that they are able to internalize the integration of the tools of communication.

As might be inferred from the discussion of the workshop model, this learning format often results in the creation of a **community of learners** who support and learn from one another. Teachers and students take on new kinds of roles and responsibilities that assist students in internalizing their development as learners (see Table 9.3). Instruction meets the needs of students and not the dictates of a teacher's guide, though these might serve as meaningful resources for the teacher. Students review their work to improve it, not to have it judged solely by the teacher as an external source. When students carefully and critically examine their work, they often take more ownership because they understand how they are improving and where they need to continue to grow. Minilessons help to continually add depth to their understanding, and sharing sessions allow them to consistently reflect on their progress. With these tools in place, students often develop greater understanding of themselves as learners and of the areas they are studying.

Table 9.3 Teacher Role and Student Responsibility in the Workshop Model

Teacher Role	Student Responsibility
Minilessons	
– Observe and evaluate student work	– Listen to content of minilesson
– Determine student needs	– Think about how to apply concept
– Select appropriate areas for instruction	– Try to apply concept in own work
	– Record information in reading log
Work Session	
– Prepare expectations for workshop	– Engage in own reading/writing
– Assist students with both process and product	– Use a variety of sources for assistance
– Conferencing	– Edit and revise own work
– Provide ongoing feedback to students	– Carefully edit work of peers
– Work with small groups of students	
Sharing Session	
– Prepare students to share work	– Share work
– Teach students how to respond to peers' work	– Respond to work of peers
– Teach students to give helpful feedback	– Give constructive feedback to peers
– Guide students to review progress in subject	– Reflect on progress in subject
– Guide students to review progress as learners	– Reflect on progress as learner

Sharing one's learning and receiving feedback and response is an effective learning mode. Think about the times you have shared your learning (in the form of a written paper or an oral or visual presentation) with your peers and received feedback related to the content and your style. Were these experiences helpful to you in reflecting on your strengths and needs as a learner?

The Reading, Writing, Language Workshop

After some time functioning in a workshop format, students generally become independent in their work. Until then, however, teachers must determine how they will organize the classroom and their materials for instruction and carefully prepare students to carry out the routines. If a school already uses this model, students will already be accustomed to the process and schedule and many of the routines may already be established.

In a classroom that does not include guided reading as part of a reading workshop, the workshop schedule may look something like this at the beginning and later in the school year:

Early in the Year	Later in the Year	
5–10 minutes	5–10 minutes	Minilesson
15–20 minutes	40–45 minutes	Independent working time
10–15 minutes	10–15 minutes	Sharing session

In classrooms where guided reading is part of the workshop, as is occurring in many cases, guided reading may take place during the independent work time. Reading and writing workshops may be scheduled on alternate days and as part of larger literacy blocks, as in Table 9.4, or every day and include both a reading and writing workshop.

Table 9.4 Sample Literacy Block Schedule, Including Reading/Writing Workshop

Time	Monday, Wednesday, Friday	Tuesday, Thursday
9:00–9:15	Word study	Word study
9:15–9:30	Read aloud	Shared writing/writing aloud
9:30–10:30	Reading workshop/guided reading	Writing workshop/guided writing
10:30–10:50	Conferencing	Conferencing
10:50–11:00	Sharing learning	Sharing learning

Organizing for Workshops

Materials

Teachers must think through how they wish to conduct workshops and then determine the teacher and student materials that will need to be prepared. Nancie Atwell (1998) is an excellent resource in this area for upper-grade-level teachers, as are Irene Fountas and Gay Su Pinnell (1996) and Regie Routman (1991) for younger-grade-level teachers.

The teacher may wish to have a folder for each student to keep materials and records related to student work. Often the folder for reading will contain the current book being read and a notebook divided into various sections, for example, reading response, minilesson notes, reading log of books read, and word work. Writing folders generally contain current and past writing samples, including the drafts, editing rubric, and final draft stapled together for each writing piece. The writing notebook may contain a log of pieces written and/or published; minilesson materials, including editing/revising checklists, vocabulary, and grammar notes; and a section for recording ideas for future writing.

Each of the working folders might also contain goal statements, self-assessments of work, and materials currently being used in group work. The folders may be stored in students' desks or in crates divided by groups. Most teachers arrange for different folders for each workshop and store them in separate crates to help students access the materials quickly and easily. The key is that students should be able to access the folders and be responsible, at least in part, for their upkeep.

Establishing **portfolio assessment** is a way to measure progress throughout the year, and a teacher needs to determine how student progress will be highlighted, for example, use of baseline data/progress toward grade-level standards, among other things. Decisions need to be made about which pieces of student work will be included, as well as which assessment, self-assessment, and reflection items (those selected by the teacher and those by the student). Another consideration includes determining if there will be one portfolio for all subject areas per student or separate portfolios. Students will need access to their portfolios to add pieces and to reflect on progress over time, meaning that teachers will need to consider what is most appropriate for portfolio storage.

Teachers may develop a folder of their own for each group or content area for record-keeping purposes. Each folder may contain relevant information about what the group is working on, anecdotal notes about the group or individual student work, assessment information, and materials to be used with a particular group. Teachers also need to determine the reference or work materials needed and make those available. For example, if students are to be writing, will a writing center be created with a variety of writing utensils and paper, dictionaries, and thesauri, and so on?

Teachers must also plan ahead and prepare materials to be used in teaching minilessons, conducting group work, assessments, conferencing, and homework. In reality this is not different from more traditional classroom preparation. The difference emerges in the fact that students will be accessing the materials more independently; they need to know how to easily find and use the materials they need.

Teacher Instruction

In using a workshop approach, teachers do not merely tell students where materials are and how they ought to use them; they recognize that students need time to practice these routines and reflect on how well they are following them. This requires that teachers determine appropriate and manageable ways to introduce the notion of workshops. In reading, teachers often begin with a single book that the entire class reads and then gradually introduce grouping students for guided reading and literature circles. In writing, teachers generally begin with the same writing assignments for the whole class and then move toward individualizing pacing. Asking advice from veteran teachers who hold the same philosophy of teaching and learning may yield valuable suggestions for incorporating workshops in the language arts curriculum.

Minilessons are a critical component of the workshop. Teachers review standards and benchmarks throughout the year to determine what students ought to know and be able to do by year's end. They compare these guidelines to samples and assessment of student work to determine where students are in relation to the standards. This provides good information about the kinds of minilessons various students will need and guides the teacher on a regular basis.

One of the benefits of the workshop model is that the teacher has greater opportunities to get to know and influence the work of individual students. But they must also become expert in reviewing student work that is in process and learning how to nudge students to the next steps, through effective conferencing, while remaining within the instructional level of each student.

Collaborative/Cooperative Learning

A key component of the workshop model is having students work together to complete learning experiences and to extend one another's understanding. The Vygotskian stance reflects the belief that learning is a social endeavor and understanding develops more fully when students are given the opportunity to learn from one another.

There are a number of generic areas teachers need to think about in preparing students to work together, including determining how rules will be established regarding respectful treatment of group members. Will the teacher deliver a set of rules, or will the class develop them together? The first minilessons of the school year during workshops will have more to do with procedures and the day-to-day processes of a workshop rather than content or strategy learning. The sharing sessions at the end of the workshop provide excellent opportunities for students to fine-tune group work procedures and reflect on how effectively they are working together and how working collaboratively makes learning richer.

Reflection Journal 9.1

All students should participate in **collaborative/cooperative learning** situations. Think about and reflect in writing on how you would respond to the following questions:

- What are some ways that you will ensure that each student carries his or her weight in completing group activities?
- What might you do when one or two students dominate the group or exclude a member from participating?
- How can you convince parents of the effectiveness of students working collaboratively?
- How might you guide students in reflecting on how well they work together?

Issues of dominating group members or members who do not complete their part of the work are less likely to occur when students have roles to complete, such as recorder or reporter. The teacher may assign the roles, or if students are already accustomed to this format, they might determine the roles for themselves within the group. When working collaboratively, the group members may divide the work and then put it all together to form a cohesive whole. The challenge in this approach is that students may complete separate parts and not really take advantage of what they could learn from one another. The teacher may wish to structure collaborative work in such a way that opportunities to communicate among members of the group are not lost.

Student reflection on what they are gaining from working together, as well as the progress they are making toward their learning goals, is essential. With practice, they can become good evaluators of their work and their process for completing it.

Independent Work

Another hallmark of the workshop approach is that students will often work independently of the teacher, whether individually, with a partner, or as part of a small group. Guiding students to the point where they are able to work independently can be challenging, as initially some students find it difficult to refrain from interrupting the teacher for assistance when he or she is working with a group or conferencing with a student. Some students may interpret the greater level of freedom as an opportunity to be less engaged. The teacher can establish the rules or design them with the students, as they are good at brainstorming ideas for how best to run the classroom. When students are included in the planning, they are often more willing to cooperate due to feeling invested in the process.

Making the materials that students will need easily accessible and establishing procedures for using them will often eliminate unnecessary interruptions. Misuse of materials may be a topic for students to discuss in a sharing or meeting session.

Designating areas of the room for various activities is another way to help students work independently. For example, a classroom may have a writing center, a **conferencing center,** a shared reading area, and a computer center. If a group of students is working together on a writing project, they could meet in the writing center where they would find writing and editing tools and materials. The teacher would conference with students in the conferencing center. Peer editing or project planning could also be completed in the conferencing center. An easel with big books or multiple copies of books would be found in the shared reading area, and the teacher or a student could share books here with other students in whole or small group settings. Students wishing to publish a piece of writing, or access software or the Internet, would use the computer center. Establishing a schedule for using an area of the room or determining how many students can be in an area at a time is helpful for maintaining a smooth flow of activities.

Content Area Workshops

While most of the discussion in this chapter is centered on the creation of reading and writing workshops, it is possible to extend the workshop model to the content areas of the curriculum. The same three components of a workshop (minilessons, work session, and sharing session) would be followed; however, the difference is that the content would center on the content area concepts. Using a workshop model in content areas of the curriculum would be an effective way to integrate content and the language arts. The following View From the Classroom features a vignette of a fourth-grade math workshop focusing on fractions, which integrates reading and viewing. Figure 9.1 is an example of how

BEAGELS

My favorite dog is the beagel. Beagels sort of look like weiner dogs but they aren't as long as weiner dogs. They also look like lapso apsos. A beagel is about a foot long and about five inches off the ground.

Beagels are a relative of the bassett hounds. There is a close looking resemblance between beagels and bassetts. Beagels and bassetts are the best kind of dogs that a person could want. Beagels have big floppy ears that touch the ground and so do bassetts.

The legs on beagels are short and wrinkly. Beagels are slow but their noses are good for smelling animals out. Beagels can tree raccoons very good and very fast.

I think beagels are cute and I think that they make great pets as well as hunting dogs. I wish that I could get a beagel as a pet some day.

Figure 9.1 Example of a Written Report Created by a Fourth-Grade Student After Researching Beagle Dogs

a fourth-grade student compiled his research about beagles into a written report as the final product in a social studies workshop.

A View From the Classroom: Grade 4 Mathematics Workshop Vignette

Jean recognizes that her fourth-grade students are motivated to work on challenging concepts during reading and writing workshops, and they have improved a great deal in their ability to self-assess their learning process. She has decided to implement the same format in her math class to engage her students in exploring how fractions work and learning to explain their thinking processes more fully.

Jean is planning minilessons in three basic areas, the first dealing with reading mathematics text with greater insights, as many of the students have been struggling to understand content. Jean has noted that they read the text without stopping to think and make little use of additional visual information on the page. She will use overheads to highlight key vocabulary and direction words and encourage students to reread and use reading ahead monitoring comprehension strategies to assist them with some tools to use when meaning breaks down. She will also guide students to use graphics and sample problems to gain additional understanding of the concepts.

Visualizing and predicting will be the focus of the next set of minilessons, as Jean wants students to begin to formulate mental images of fractions and then visualize and predict how fractions

change when something is added to or taken away. Because fractions are difficult for many students to conceptualize, Jean believes that these strategies will aid student understanding in this area. Following this portion of the unit, Jean will incorporate others that focus on adding and subtracting fractions and determining equivalent fractions. They will use manipulatives, visuals, and movement activities to clarify these concepts, and the use of fractions in the real world will also be emphasized.

During the work sessions, students will work in small groups to complete a number of activities, and each group will focus on similar content, yet it will be differentiated by student facility with fractions, though a range of abilities will be represented in each group. The students will interpret a series of newspaper ads and will determine where they will get the best deal on particular items. Other activities will require students to demonstrate equivalent fractions, using visuals and/or graphics, and creating fraction stories that feature adding and subtracting fractions. Jean will meet with one or two of the groups each day in a guided math group, having them talk about how they are using the reading and learning strategies to complete their tasks. Students will

(Continued)

(Continued)

complete written reflections indicating their understanding of fractions and how the strategies affect their understanding.

In the sharing sessions, the students will explain the strategies they use to better understand their math text. They will orally share how visualizing and predicting are impacting their progress in understanding and clarifying the use of fractions. Students will also be invited to share the work they are doing with the ads and the stories and articulate what they have learned about fractions from these experiences. The

sharing session will also include the students bringing in materials to share that demonstrate how fractions are used outside of the classroom for authentic purposes.

Workshops are a beneficial framework to guide the learning of language in elementary and middle school classrooms. With a clear focus and detailed planning, teachers can successfully incorporate this learning method into their language arts curriculum.

End-of-Chapter Reflection

- There are many things to consider and plan for when implementing a workshop framework in language arts classroom. What components do you feel you will have an easy time planning and implementing? Which components may prove to be challenging?

Planning for Teaching

- Develop a weekly schedule for a workshop (reading, writing, or language). Sketch out your ideas for minilessons that you might teach. Think through your role as a teacher during each component of the workshop and that of the students. Share your plan with your peers to get feedback and suggestions.

Connections With the Field

1. Visit a classroom where a teacher is implementing a workshop approach with his or her students. What do you see working well? Where might you change something to make it more meaningful? What ideas do you want to take away to possibly include in your future teaching?

2. Interview a teacher who utilizes a workshop framework in his or her classroom. Prepare a list of questions that reflect the questions you are left with after reading this chapter related to planning for and implementing a workshop.

Student Study Site

The Companion Website for Developing Voice Through the Language Arts

http://www.sagepub.com/dvtlastudy

Visit the Web-based student study site to enhance your understanding of the chapter content and to discover additional resources that will take your learning one step further. You can enhance your understanding of the chapters by using the comprehensive Study Guide, which includes learning objectives, key terms, activities, practice tests, and more. You'll also find special features, such as the Links to Standards from U.S. States and associated activities, Children's Literature Selections, Reflection Exercises, Learning from Journal Articles, and PRAXIS test preparation materials.

References of Professional Resources

Atwell, N. (1998). *In the middle: New understandings about writing, reading and learning*. Portsmouth, NH: Heinemann.

Fountas, I., & Pinnell, G. S. (1996). *Guided reading: Good first teaching for all children*. Portsmouth, NH: Heinemann.

Frey, N., & Fisher, D. (2006). *Language arts workshop: Purposeful reading and writing instruction.* Upper Saddle River, NJ: Pearson Merrill Prentice Hall.

Routman, R. (1991). *Invitations: Changing as teachers and learners K–12.* Portsmouth, NH: Heinemann.

Technology Resources

Guide to writing a basic essay: http://members.tripod.com/%7Elklivingston/essay

Links to resources for learning about writing workshop:
    http://www.indiana.edu/~reading/ieo/bibs/writwork.html

part 3

Language Arts Teaching, Learning, and Assessing From Early Childhood to Early Adolescence

Part III is a detailed look at how teaching and learning language arts can be accomplished in classrooms from early childhood to early adolescence. In this

section, we provide a glimpse at ways to plan for teaching language arts in classrooms of young children through middle school level. It is meant to be a beginning step in thinking about taking what was learned in Parts I and II of this text and applying them specifically to the range of grade levels you may be certified to teach or interested in teaching. Keep in mind, however, that not all aspects of teaching, learning, and assessing language arts are reflected in each chapter, but we have highlighted components in each that we believe are key at that age and grade level, based on children's development.

Chapters 10, 11, and 12 can be accessed in various ways. They can be read before reading Parts I and II to provide an overview of what language arts looks like at various age or grade levels. This method could set the context for the more content-laden chapters in Parts I and II. If you choose to read Part III first, we recommend jotting down notes and questions that can be a guide for you as you read Parts I and II. We also recommend rereading Part III upon completion of Parts I and II, as we presume it will all come together for you and the questions you had upon reading it for the first time will now be answered as you read Part III with new eyes and understanding.

Reading Part III after reading Parts I and II is another option. Using this method could help you understand what language arts could look like in a classroom in relation to the content and concepts you previously read about. One other method we suggest is to use Part III as a guidebook in your future work with children, both in your preservice work and while teaching. If you are doing fieldwork and working with children of a certain age or grade level, it may be beneficial to read the corresponding chapter(s) to familiarize yourself with the key components of language arts at that level.

Each of the following Chapters 10, 11, and 12 is structured using a framework of planning for language arts teaching and learning prior to the first day of school, what is important to implement at the beginning of the year and the middle of the year, and what you need to consider as the school year nears the end. Chapter 10 encompasses curriculum considerations in relation to teaching 3- through 6-year-old children as they begin forming the foundations of literacy at home and in formalized school situations. As you have seen in Chapter 2 while exploring the stages of language development, these are important years in the development of children's literacy and language arts. Chapter 10 provides a model of a first-grade classroom, demonstrating the importance of laying the foundations for future literacy success.

Chapter 11 emphasizes 7- to 9-year-old classrooms and the language arts curriculum and planning that need to be addressed. The model provided is a third- and fourth-grade multiage/multigrade classroom, providing an overview of not only language arts at this level but also how a teacher can successfully meet the needs of a range of age and ability levels in one classroom, as is often the case.

Chapter 12 includes a model eighth-grade language arts classroom example in a middle school setting where language arts curriculum is taught in blocks. We wanted to showcase and suggest ways for encouraging integration of the language arts throughout a middle school student's day.

 **Early Childhood Language Arts**

Kathi Glick's First-Grade Classroom

Context Setting:

After reading this chapter, you will be able to

- Identify aspects of development of 3- to 6-year-olds related to social, cognitive, physical, and emotional growth
- Understand how to plan for and implement language arts at the first-grade level
- Develop an understanding of the development of curriculum in Grade 1 across an academic school year
- Understand how to develop an assessment system for informing instruction and recording student progress in Grade 1 literacy development
- Recognize the importance of guiding students to respond to what they have read and make connections to self, text, and the world

Before We Begin

- Have you ever worked in a classroom or structured child care setting with 3- to 6-year-old children? Reflect on their ability to engage in learning. If you have not, what would you expect 3-year-olds to be like in a classroom setting? Four-year-olds? Five-year-olds? Six-year-olds?

Development of 3- to 6-Year-Old Children

Three- to 6-year-old children are active, energetic, and curious. Learning experiences for children at this age should match the characteristics of their development. Even though they are in the concrete operational stage, they understand a great deal about language and how it is used to communicate. Learning experiences broken into manageable sequences will enable young minds to continue building on their natural inquisitiveness. Table 10.1 outlines the general characteristics of children at the early childhood level and links these characteristics to effective instructional practice in language arts (Wood, 1997). Note, however, that the classroom scenario detailed in this chapter focuses on a first-grade (6- and 7-year-olds) classroom.

Welcome to veteran teacher Kathi Glick's high-energy classroom in Hales Corners, Wisconsin. In this first-grade classroom, students are learning nearly every second of the day. There are 9 boys and 10 girls in this suburban elementary school of 535 students. Two of the children are from India, 1 is Latino, 1 is African American, and 15 are Caucasian. Two of the children are receiving services for speech and language, and two of the children have been diagnosed with special educational needs. The occupations of the parents are varied, with several working in blue-collar jobs and an equal number having professional careers. The classroom is not the quietest one on the first floor, as Kathi recognizes that children learn language by using language. She also firmly believes that children learn a great deal from one another and they learn the most from active, hands-on learning experiences. Although the classroom activities proceed in a very orderly fashion, the children talk and move about while they are engaged in meaningful and authentic learning activities. The district has adopted a balanced literacy approach, which matches well with Kathi's social constructivist philosophy of teaching, learning, and assessment.

During the summer, Kathi takes courses toward completion of her master's degree. She always searches for a professional development course that will give her something to bring back to the classroom in the fall. Recently she has taken a course on research for readiness skills and a course on reader's theater. The resources that she consults most frequently and finds most useful include Lucy Calkins's *The Art of Teaching Writing* (1994), Carol Avery's *And With a Light Touch . . .* (2002), *Word Matters* by Pinnell and Fountas (1998), and Diana Mitchell's *Children's Literature: An Invitation to the World* (2002). She continually thinks about her teaching and ways to improve student learning. Her husband has gotten used to her grabbing the pad of paper she keeps on the nightstand and furiously writing down ideas in the middle of the night.

Kathi admits that she is constantly at her local bookstore, searching for new children's literature to share with her students. She is always on the lookout for quality nursery rhymes and poetry books to use with beginning readers. Each

(Text continues on page 323)

Table 10.1 Developmental Characteristics of 3- to 6-Year-Old Children

3-Year-Old Children	Language Arts Curriculum Connections
• Have a short attention span and move quickly from one activity to another	• Plan for a number of learning activities that match the attention span of young children
• Engage in parallel play, playing next to their friends/peers mostly, not necessarily with them	• Provide introductory opportunities for children to work collaboratively but allow children to work individually on most learning experiences
• Begin to understand the use of language to get what is wanted	• Encourage children to "use words" or "tell me what you want" to redirect their physical reaction to things and to develop language usage
• Enjoy books and language games that include rhyme, repetition, and rhythm	• Reread and use familiar books with rhymes and chants and encourage participation and shared reading
• Produce writing that looks like scribbling, but children typically can detail the message it relays	• Ask children to share what they have written, paying more attention to the message being conveyed than the form of the written communication
• Speak in sentences of five or six words and imitate most adult speech sounds	• Provide multiple opportunities to use extended oral language in the classroom
• Use language to describe things and enjoy telling stories	• Encourage children to describe their experiences
• Are still learning how to use pronouns (*I, me, you, mine*)	• Model proper use of pronouns in everyday speech; point out pronouns and their referents during shared reading
• Begin to copy some capital letters	• Model use of capital letters in shared writing; point out use of capital letters in student writing
• Engage in fantasy play	• Encourage children to use oral and written language as part of play and dress-up centers in the classroom (e.g., post office, travel agency)
4-Year-Old Children	**Language Arts Curriculum Connections**
• Learn through their own play; imitation of adults is common	• Include a variety of dramatic play areas and centers to encourage play and use of language (house/family living center, dress up/dramatic play center); include a variety of real-life objects for students to use as props
• Need a great deal of physical activity, as much of their learning is done through use of large muscles	• At least one quarter of the school day should include active, physical activity such as games played in large spaces to encourage movement
• Have difficulty with paper-and-pencil tasks and visual matching	• Students should not be asked to copy from the chalkboard
• Enjoy large words, explaining and initiating conversations; language is expanding,	• Provide multiple opportunities for children to expand vocabulary through read-alouds, conversations, and exposure to new ideas
• Enjoy being read to	• Plan many opportunities for read-alouds in one-on-one, small group, and whole-group settings
• Enjoy predictable books with few words and repetition	• Use wordless picture books and predictable books to encourage language development and understanding of story elements

(Continued)

Table 10.1 (Continued)

- Begin writing with drawing; scribble writing still apparent; beginning stages of letter formation
- Spelling is at the prephonemic stage; many letters do not correspond to sounds, but represent words and ideas

- Emphasize writing for a variety of purposes

- Encourage children to talk about what they have written as a way to interpret their message; engage in word play activities

5-Year-Old Children

- Follow rules and comply with expectations well

- Experiment with language related to arts and the world around them

- Exhibit strong social development

- Cooperative, like to please adults
- Frequently use thinking aloud to process information, saying things such as "I am . . ." or "I am going to . . ."
- Have an active fantasy element in their lives
- Are very literal in nature

- Spelling is still at the prephonemic and early phonemic stage, but beginning to use initial consonants to represent words (ILKIKM—I like ice cream.)
- Emergent reader stage—typically focus on one word at a time, as visual tracking from left to right has not been fully established
- Begin writing with pictures, which are then labeled with words
- Need large amounts of physical activity; becoming good at participating in group games
- Some letter and number reversals in writing

Language Arts Curriculum Connections

- Develop consistent and clear expectations, routines, and classroom rules
- Use books, games, and activities that include a lot of repetition of language; reread stories, sing songs, and play games many times, including some variations.
- Allow for many opportunities to work and interact with peers (e.g., partner reading, working together at centers, including dramatic play)
- Create and assign classroom jobs and responsibilities
- Encourage thinking aloud to process information, as it is an important good reader strategy students will build on as they become fluent readers
- Use and encourage storytelling and dramatic activities
- State directions succinctly and in a straightforward manner for ease of understanding
- Model "kid writing"

- Model and encourage use of a pointer or finger to track while reading each word

- Writing topics should relate to children's lives, including families, pets, selves, friends
- Include physical games that involve language, and encourage language use and development such as jump rope routines.
- Accept student writing rather than reprimand; model the correct way during group activities such as shared writing

6-Year-Old Children

- Move fast; rush through activities; like to be first; often sloppy work results

- Focus more on process than product
- Have difficulty accepting failure; like to succeed
- Enjoy describing and explaining things

Language Arts Curriculum Connections

- Teach children to read work to themselves and a partner to ensure it makes sense; use an editing checklist for student self-assessment of the quality of their work.
- Engage students in shared writing and editing (process oriented)
- Emphasize that we all make mistakes and model how we "fix up" our mistakes and learn from them
- Utilize show-and-tell in a variety of formats

• Like to play with language	• Play guessing games, engage children with riddles and jokes
• Question things	• Engage students in beginning research projects based on their interests
• Embrace cooperative play	• Discourage competitive interactions through cooperative games and activities
• Have the ability to track as they read, making reading easier at this age	• Encourage children to use their fingers to track print initially
• Explore artistic avenues	• Provide multiple opportunities for children to sing, dance, paint, and act related to stories, poetry, folktales
• Begin to read easy chapter books as well as predictable books	• Select read-aloud chapter books that match the listening and interest level of the children
• Begin to use whole sentences in writing; are at the transitional stage in spelling; have a growing sense of phonics	• Write for multiple purposes and audiences; encourage children to edit and share their writing often
• Write about school, best friends, pets, fantasy	• Talk about ideas for writing as a prewriting activity

summer Kathi teaches drama to older students during the district's summer school session, and the rhyming materials also come in handy when teaching voice projection and expression. The students enjoy practicing these skills with Dr. Seuss material.

Beginning of the Year

Kathi recognizes how important it is to get her first graders off to a positive and successful start right from the beginning of the school year. Even though the curricula of most kindergarten programs now require that children begin learning to read before they leave 5-year-old kindergarten, many come to first grade worried about the expectations for reading and writing. Some will even say to her, "I don't know how to read very well yet." So she works to help them realize that they already have many emerging literacy skills, pointing out that they are readily able to identify fast-food restaurant names and symbols as Kathi holds them up one by one. She arranges the logos on a sentence strip and invites the children to read along with her, "Pizza Hut, Pizza Hut, KFC, Pizza Hut, McDonald's." Next she puts the words to a simple tune, and the children sing along as Kathi points to the names. Finally, she mixes the names up, and the children discuss how to reorder them. They can be heard making comments like "That's not McDonald's. McDonald's starts with an *M*." In this very simple activity, Kathi has accomplished a number of important goals. The students perceive that reading can be fun and that they already know some things about reading. A first lesson in phonemic awareness has taken place as students listen and try to determine the first sound of words in the song. Voice-to-print match is demonstrated as Kathi points to words while putting them to music. Later, the initial and final sounds will be focused on more fully, but for now the children perceive themselves as readers, because even though this is only the first day of school, they have been successful.

Kathi uses the beginning of the school year to set the stage for many things. When the children go out for recess, she mixes up the words for the fast-food song. Upon returning, they exclaim, "Ms. Glick, someone mixed this up." Kathi takes advantage of this opportunity to guide the children in reordering the words, but she also uses it as a first step in getting the children to work together as a team. Even the child who struggles the most can participate successfully in the shared reading activity. As a result, the children go home feeling confident and competent.

The children in Room 118 use a great deal of poetry and nursery rhymes in learning to read. Each child has his or her own binder of class poems to read from each day. In the beginning of the school year, Kathi selects poems that have pictures to accompany the words, which introduces the strategy of using picture clues to obtain meaning from print. Students begin adding their own favorite poems, poems they wrote, and poems written by their peers. Over time, the children become quite sophisticated at recognizing a poet's style. They have been known to identify the poet of new poems even when their names have not appeared on the poetry sheets.

Even a poem written by Kathi in the second grade is included among the poetry selections (see Table 10.2). The students' interest is piqued when they hear about this, and they hurry to their binders to see what their teacher wrote as a young girl. She uses the poem to teach patterns ("He likes to . . .") and rhyming words. The children learn how to use onset and rime to make more /at/ words. These words become the first word wall entries. Kathi believes strongly that learning should be authentic and that skills should be pulled from meaningful reading and writing experiences, not taught in isolation.

To further reinforce this important skill of onset and rime, Kathi brings out magnetic letters and cookie sheets and asks students to form as many /at/ words as they can with a partner. Each pair brings their words to the rug area, and the class compiles a master list of rhyming words that students will use as spelling resources when they are writing. From the very first day of school, Kathi has the children doing as much for themselves as possible. Therefore, they sometimes even do the

Table 10.2   Poem Written by Kathi Glick in Second Grade

Gordo Chan is My Cat

Gordo Chan is my cat.

He is very, very fat.

He likes to play.

He likes to run.

He likes to lay down in the sun.

SOURCE: Kathi Glick, Hales Corners Elementary School, Hales Corners, WI. Used with permission.

writing for lists of rhyming words, writing the onset /c/ in one color and the rime /at/ in another.

After the children have mastered /at/ words, Kathi gives each child a small KitKat candy bar and asks them to analyze the name to see if anything looks familiar. The children quickly figure out the part that says /kat/ and are able to infer that the first part must say /kit/. From here they begin a study of /it/ words. Now that the children know two rimes, Kathi introduces chunking and points out that they can use the chunks or parts of words /at/ and /it/ to figure out new words when they are reading.

Shortly after this strategy is introduced, students begin to bring books to school to show they are finding books at home that have the same patterns they are learning about in school. Kathi shares her favorite poems, and soon the students and even the parents bring in their favorites. Kathi often uses these poems as opportunities for students to make connections and use language. "One child might say, 'My dad's favorite poem is *Take Me Out to the Ballgame,*' and another child might say, 'I saw *Animal Kingdom* last night and they talked about tame animals. Tame rhymes with game.' Language is going on all the time. They are constantly learning from each other," Kathi says.

As the children become familiar with onset and rime, Kathi initiates the Chunking Club. This consists of a large sheet of paper for listing words they have come across in their reading that contain "chunks." For example, the following words might be on a chunking list: c*at*, D*an*, and *Anthony*. They also examine their own names and try to find chunks. The Chunking Club keeps them aware of sounds or words as they become "word detective decoders."

Sometimes Kathi sends her students home with a pencil and a pad of paper. Early in the year she instructs them to go home and make a grocery list of all the foods they really enjoy eating. One parent took her child to the grocery store and reported that they were there for over an hour because the child became so engrossed in reading the labels from favorite foods. From these kinds of activities, students learn that not only can writing be fun, but it is also useful for communicating important information.

Hales Corners Elementary School schedules an Open House for families early in the school year. Kathi takes this opportunity to explain to parents that the district endorses a balanced literacy approach to learning to read and write and explains how listening and speaking are equally important literacy skills to develop. She describes what the children will be learning and emphasizes the importance of continued language or literacy learning even after the children leave school for the day. She encourages parents to help their children read signs they might recognize in the environment and use the word chunks they have studied in school. Turning off the TV and limiting "screen time" or computer use to 45 minutes per day is encouraged.

Parental involvement is invaluable in student achievement, and Kathi spends time informing parents/guardians about how they can best support their sons' or daughters' emotional and academic development. Kathi's warm and enthusiastic personality attracts parents from their first encounter with her as she emphasizes the importance of getting to know the families and creating an open and inviting classroom environment where parents/guardians feel free to visit at any time. She uses many vehicles to involve them in their child's education in simple yet effective ways. Kathi introduces a sheet that she will be sending home with the children after new books have been introduced and children have had an opportunity to learn to read them fairly well (Table 10.3). Parents/guardians are expected to check off the activities as they are completed and describe how well their child was able to complete the activities.

Table 10.3 Parent Letter

Dear Parents,

Periodically I will be sending home a reading book that we used in our group.

Please work with your child TONIGHT on the following:

Name: _____

Title: _____

_____ Review index word cards
_____ Pick 4–5 words and locate them in the book
_____ Read the book
******* Please check off as you do the activity.

Thank you for your continued support,
Mrs. Glick

How did he/she do?

Comments:

_____ Parent Signature

SOURCE: Kathi Glick, Hales Corners Elementary School, Hales Corners, WI. Used with permission.

Daily Language Arts Teaching, Learning, and Assessing

Nursery rhymes are heavily used in designing literacy lessons. The class makes up tunes to go with many of them, and one of the students uses the pointer to follow along as the class recites or sings the nursery rhyme. The children enjoy these sessions, and Kathi takes advantage of every opportunity to continually reinforce phonemic awareness, onset and rime, patterning, and chunking. The children learn these concepts fully in a natural way and rarely through the use of worksheets.

Kathi uses the poem "Chicken Soup With Rice" (Sendak, 1962) throughout the year. Since it has a segment for each month of the year, she introduces a new segment at the beginning of each new month. After they have savored and discussed how Sendak represented the new month in his poem, students find word chunks, patterns, and rhyming words. Some of the words from the poem go on the word wall. It is clear that Kathi systematically introduces students to new strategies and then provides multiple opportunities for them to practice and internalize application of the strategies to support literacy development.

When the students come into the classroom each morning, they study the "Messy Message" board and prepare to help Kathi fix the message that generally refers to what they will accomplish during the day. She tells the children that it is hard for her to spell in the morning before she's had her coffee and invites them to edit the message with her. Words are misspelled, punctuation is missing, and uppercase/lowercase letters are misused. After the students edit the message, they reread it and discuss the content. Kathi prefers the messy message to similar editing formats. The message is meaningful for students, as she selects items that they struggle with in their own writing. Toward the middle of the school year, students may be selected to make up their own messy message for the rest of the class to "fix up." Kathi finds that she frequently refers back to the messy message while guiding students to edit their own work.

Integration across subject areas occurs naturally in this classroom. Students might be working on reading, but they count syllables and the number of letters in words. If they are classifying in science class, they will classify books, or they will classify story settings in their literacy block. The class keeps a log of all the books they've read together. One student will write the next number with the title of the book next to it. In the beginning of the year, Kathi helps the students do this, but they won't need her support later in the year. Together the children determine whether the number for the book entry is even or odd and how many 10s and 1s are represented in the number.

She has designed an integrated social studies curriculum for her first graders in which they study themselves as members of a family, a neighborhood, and a community. They read extensively around the topics, build a model of a community in the classroom, and take several field trips in the neighborhood. Kathi meets with representatives from restaurants, a grocery store, the fire station, and the post office to arrange for the class trips. She outlines the standards she is working toward, and together they design activities for the students' visit. The children read and study before and after each trip, focusing on everything from creating interview questions, to reading about the workers in each establishment, to writing research reports. The children especially enjoy the trip to the post office, where the postal workers place one of the students in a mail cart and demonstrate the route the child would take in getting delivered to his or her final destination. At other sites, the children get to visit behind-the-scenes operations as well. Back at school, they write about what they have experienced and learned.

Kathi estimates that she averages reading three new books per day to the students in addition to the shared reading selections. She uses these books to teach new strategies and practice previously learned strategies. Sometimes she uses a strategy while reading to the students and then asks the children to identify the strategy she used. After lunch the children "buddy-up" for shared reading, and before they begin, they scratch one another's backs and settle in for a good story. Early in the year Kathi reads *Charlotte's Web* by E. B. White (1952) and *Mr. Popper's Penguins* (Atwater & Atwater, 1939/1966). These children's classics prove to be helpful in teaching about character, setting, and the problem in a story. The day ends with a book, as Kathi likes to have the children relax after a busy day of learning. She will announce, "I found another good book," and the children cozy up to hear a story by Kevin Henkes, Eric Carle, or David McPhail, some of Kathi's and the students' favorites.

If a book particularly intrigues the children, they will do additional activities to expand their enjoyment of it. In the beginning of the year, Kathi makes these suggestions, but later on the students take the initiative and come up with unique ways to extend their involvement with the books. Sometimes the students will make a play or do reader's theater from the story. With patterned stories, they might do an innovation on a text where they substitute new concepts into the pattern and write their own version of the story. They are encouraged to look at the author's style and experiment in using that style in their own writing.

When the children have independent reading time, she stresses that everyone can read and that even making up a story while looking at the pictures is reading. Her initial anecdotal records are made on the first day of school. She assembles a large collection of alphabet books for the students to "read" and notes whether they follow the print or illustrations or make up a story.

From that very first day, Kathi wants to immerse her students in text and encourage them to take risks in learning to read. As they read their books, she circulates around the room, stopping at each student's desk to chat with the student. "Tell me what you liked about this book. Was it because it had a lot of bunnies and you have a bunny at home? Draw a picture of something you liked in this book." She wants students to start thinking about books, and it is a busy time of building structures and establishing routines.

Kathi spends a lot of time taking records, but because she considers it an integral part of the teaching and learning process, she doesn't view it as extra work. She reflects on the data she collects to determine how well students are progressing and to design learning experiences that will meet the children's needs. They learn to self-assess their own work early on in this classroom and are given multiple opportunities to describe and take responsibility for their learning.

During the second week of October, Kathi conducts her first formal benchmark assessments, consisting of a running record and comprehension check. This becomes the baseline data against which progress during the year will be measured. By waiting until this point, Kathi has had time to familiarize students with classroom routines and literacy expectations. During the third week of October, students are divided into guided reading groups based on the results of the base-line data and Kathi's observations.

Beginning with the second week of school, students are introduced to five to seven new sight words per week. The words are drawn from books the children will soon be reading. Several kinesthetic and movement activities help reinforce recognition of the sight words. As students read the words, they clap high for "tall" letters (*b, d, f, h, k, 1, t*), clap in the middle for "regular" letters (*a, c, e, i, m, n, o, r, s, u, v, w, x, z*), and clap low for letters that have a tail (*g, j, p, q, y*). Eventually, they will do "baby claps" for short vowels and "big claps" for long vowels. Cheerleading activities get the students moving as they practice the words. Shaving cream, pudding, rice, and sand provide opportunities for tactile stimulation in word identification as the students trace the words in the various media. In pairs, one student traces a new word on his or her partner's back, and the partner works to guess the word. They try to stump their teacher with hard words in this activity. Students write the new words in their word wall booklets to use as a personal reference when writing.

Students generally study five sight words and two challenge words per week. From the second week of the school year, Kathi has them use the sight words in oral sentences and then write the sentence. Early in the year the challenge words might be *like* and *I*, because these are two words they frequently use in their writing. With the word *I*, Kathi introduces uppercase letters and capitals. She will be certain to make errors with this in the messy message to see if the children recognize this new concept. Additional practice with spelling the challenge words will take place, and when Kathi is quite certain they recognize these words in print, they will be added to the word wall.

Photo 10.1 Nag works at revising a piece of writing.

During writing workshop, Kathi guides students to use the word wall as a resource in spelling words correctly. Often she creates chants or pairs the spellings with familiar tunes to help students remember. It is not surprising that she hears them run through the chants when they are trying to recall a particular word. And she smiles to herself when she hears the children out on the playground jumping rope to the chants.

Kathi believes there is a great deal that can be applied from brain research to learning, even at the first-grade level. As she describes it, it is important to "get the dendrites going from right to left in the brain." Early in the year, to provide sound and letter practice, she puts the students' names to the tune of "We've Got the Whole World in Our Hands." They sing "We've Got the Whole World in Our Room," and then Kathi holds up a student name card. They sway back and forth, having their arms cross the midpoint of the body, so important in whole-brain functioning. The song ends with "We have readers and writers in this room." These kinds of activities highlight the importance that Kathi places on building a positive learning environment where all students feel safe and successful.

Reading Workshop

Kathi estimates that it takes from 2 to 3 months to get reading workshop fully operational each year. Table 10.4 provides an example of the reading workshop schedule she uses. She begins with a shorter schedule at the beginning of the year and expands the time by the middle of the year. By the end of the year, Kathi reports that the students could read and write all day.

Several parents are trained by Kathi to work with guided reading groups. They observe her conducting reading workshop and then meet with a group of their own. Each parent receives a laminated sheet of the format and suggestions for the "Workout" and "Response" portions of the workshop. Some parents continue working with groups in Kathi's class long after their own children have completed first grade because they enjoy the experience of working with young readers in this manner.

Table 10.4 Reading Workshop Schedule

Warm Up	10 minutes	Reading previously read books
Work-Out Book	10–20 minutes	Reading instruction with Kathi
		(Guided Reading—per group, depending on need)
Response	15–20 minutes	Respond to reading
Shared Reading	10 minutes	Read new book with partner

At the beginning of each week, Kathi models the strategies the students are to work on. Different strategies are demonstrated for different groups, based on their specific needs. After students do a picture walk of a new book, Kathi asks them to read the book quietly to themselves. As they read, she listens and determines which strategies they are using well and which strategy they need to learn next. It might be "stretching words out," recognizing "*ing* endings," or inferring character traits. Kathi also previews books to determine what students might struggle with, such as /th/ words or the "who, how, what" of a story. Predictable story patterns are invaluable in helping beginning readers expand their sight word vocabularies. Kathi uses basal reading manuals as a resource in determining the focus in literacy instruction. She finds them to be valuable tools and often gets good ideas from them but lets the children's needs guide what she selects to use from them.

A great deal of time is spent introducing students to characters in stories. They pick out their favorite characters and detail why they like them. Kathi wants them to learn to respond to what they read, and this is a concrete way for students to think about the characters and how they act in stories. In addition, it provides students the opportunity to formulate opinions. Reader's theater has proven to be a great venue for students to use in examining characters as they discuss how they will act, and why, as they prepare to portray various characters. Although students have a great deal of fun with plays and reader's theater, they are learning about main and secondary characters, character motivation, and the relationship between character traits and plot. *The Little Red Hen* (Galdone, 1973) and *Stone Soup* (Brown, 1948) are perennial favorites of first graders for reenactment.

Middle of the Year

By the middle of the year, the children select their own "workout" books from among a bucket of books each student has on his or her desk; some are easy books they have read many times before that they can read alone, and others are "just right" books they have read previously and that present a slight challenge to read.

During a study of Dr. Seuss books, Kathi and her students assemble a large collection of these books. She took this opportunity to introduce a number of phonics concepts. In many of the books, there are a number of nonsense and rhyming words. The children preview them and note which patterns they already know, and Kathi introduces new ones as well. Students were given time to review the Dr. Seuss books and select their favorite books as well as their favorite characters. Kathi focuses heavily on metacognition in student learning, so she asks students to reflect on the choices they make. Table 10.5 provides an example of a form students use to reflect on favorite books. They draw a picture from the book and write about what they like about the book.

By March, guided reading sessions last about 30 minutes, depending on student need and ability. Reading workshop can last longer than 1 hour by the end of the year because the students write more in their responses and read longer

Table 10.5   Example of a Form Students Use to Reflect on Favorite Books

Name: _____

Title: _____

Author: _____

Why I liked this book:

_____

_____

SOURCE: Kathi Glick, Hales Corners Elementary School, Hales Corners, WI. Used with permission.

texts. By this point their attention spans have expanded and the longer time frame becomes developmentally appropriate. The membership of the guided reading groups is flexible, and several students have moved from one group to another as their reading needs changed.

Kathi's educational assistant, also a licensed teacher, works with a small group, and parents take smaller groups into the hall to work. Some students have earned "hall privileges" and are allowed to complete their independent work out there. While students are working independently, they listen to a story on tape, read independently, and read with a buddy. Kathi works with groups at a low table off to the side of the room. She positions herself so that she is facing the children working at their desks, even though by this time of the year, the children work well independently and are generally on task. Kathi prepares a sheet of address labels for anecdotal records by writing each child's name and the date on the labels. She jots down notes after meeting with a group or when observing students' independent work and uses the notes later to reflect on students' needs and growth.

One of the activities students participate in during independent reading activities is partner reading. After choosing a reading partner, pairs select a book to read together, complete a book review (Table 10.6), and present the book to the class. The children not only have the opportunity to share good books with classmates, but they discuss the story and new words learned as they prepare to present the book to the class.

In April, a "recording studio" will open in the classroom. Students make recordings of stories with a partner. Even the principal comes in to make a recording, as Kathi likes to provide a variety of audiences for her students to practice for and showcase their reading and speaking. The children determine which parts each person will read and practice reading expressively. When they are prepared, they make the recording and then listen to it to ascertain its quality. The recordings are placed in the listening center, and students enjoy listening to them as part of their independent literacy work. The recordings are especially useful for students with learning challenges and speech and language students in Kathi's classroom, as they can be successful as they listen and read along.

Table 10.6 Partner Reading Task Sheet

_____ 1. Choose a reading partner
_____ 2. Choose a book together
_____ 3. Read the book together
_____ 4. Work on sheet together
_____ 5. Present the book to the class

Names: _____
We read _____
By: _____

We like the book: _____ Yes _____ No

We learned these new words:

_____

_____

Our favorite part was

_____

_____

Here is a picture of our favorite part:

SOURCE: Kathi Glick, Hales Corners Elementary School, Hales Corners, WI. Used with permission.

When Kathi meets with a guided reading group, they talk a lot about connections they have made to what they are reading and prior knowledge they have activated in relation to the text. Sometimes they read favorite parts and occasionally the principal is invited to listen to them read and tell about the connections they have made. On other occasions they discuss and then write about the connections they've made, as in Table 10.7.

On Fridays, Kathi's first-grade students complete language arts activities with their fourth-grade buddies. For example, the buddies guided the first graders in completing *Things I Like About Myself* booklets. By this point in the week, the children are getting weary, and Kathi has them engage in learning experiences that they learn a great deal from but that are a bit less taxing.

Early Spring

In March, Kathi reads *The BFG* (Dahl, 1982) to the students as a read-aloud. Kathi tells them that the giant in the story talks "funny" because he didn't go to

Table 10.7   Making Connections

Name: _____

Date: _____

Title: _____

Author: _____

I have a connection to this story. It is this:

_____

The book was_____ Good _____ So-So _____ Bad

Because_____

_____

SOURCE: Kathi Glick, Hales Corners Elementary School, Hales Corners, WI. Used with permission.

school, and she asks them to concentrate on how he uses language. At certain points, the children pause to reflect on this. They also discuss giants and what the author, Roald Dahl, has done to create humor in the story.

Kathi tries to give her students some world experiences as part of their learning. In this effort, one student per day is selected to be the classroom meteorologist. The student announces the high temperature of the day in Milwaukee and moves the ribbon on the thermometer up or down to reflect this change. They also talk about weather across the country. Students go to weather.com to locate cities or countries on the map that they have studied or are interested in and get the weather information for these locations. By doing this, the children have learned the locations of many states. They link knowledge of the states to books they've read, "*Mr. Popper's Penguins* takes place in Alaska," to popular vacation spots, "Say 'Hi' to Mickey in Florida," and to reading skills, "What letter does *Utah* start with? Can you find it on the map? How many syllables are in the word *Utah*?" Kathi selects children who are less verbal to make the weather reports as a method of providing nonthreatening ways to express themselves in front of the class. By saying "Hi" to the president in the White House every morning, they learn who the president is and where he lives, locating this on the map. The students locate other things on the globe as well. When an alumnus of the school was sent to Iraq, they found Iraq on the map, made a list of questions they wanted to ask him about the country and being in the military, and wrote him a letter. Because he was deployed there during the winter months, the children sent along some drawings depicting winter in Wisconsin. He wrote letters back, and the

Photo 10.2   Shae edits her writing during writing workshop.

children learned a few things about Iraq and his job as a soldier. Another family had relatives from Pakistan, and the students found it on the globe and said "Hi" to the family still there.

The Alignment of Curriculum and Assessment

All of the teaching Kathi does aligns with district standards. Her district has a carefully articulated set of literacy standards that were in place well before the dictates of No Child Left Behind (2001) went into effect. At the beginning of the academic year, teachers receive a sheet for each child that outlines benchmark skills, strategies, and standards for each stage of reading. Teachers mark students' progress toward these goals throughout the school year. Predetermined samples of student work are gathered at regular intervals and placed in a portfolio that moves from grade to grade with the child. Kindergarten materials are placed in a red folder within the portfolio, first-grade samples in a blue folder, and so on. Kathi uses the district benchmarks as a focal point in designing instruction for her students. She considers assessment of these benchmarks to be an integral part of her teaching day, as she uses formative and summative assessments to determine student progress. Kathi considers student self-assessment of their own work to be an invaluable tool in student learning, as she wants them to recognize that they have a role to play in their own learning.

When the students are working on a writing piece in writing workshop, they often have a "Try-ers" Club sheet on their desks to use when they get stuck on a

Table 10.8 "Try-ers" Club

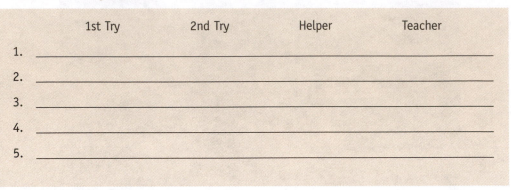

	1st Try	2nd Try	Helper	Teacher
1.	_____			
2.	_____			
3.	_____			
4.	_____			
5.	_____			

SOURCE: Kathi Glick, Hales Corners Elementary School, Hales Corners, WI. Used with permission.

word and the word is not found on the word wall or in environmental print about the room. Similar to the "Have-A-Go" (Routman, 1991; Snowball & Bolton, 1999) model, the students make two efforts to spell the word on their own, consult a "helper," and finally, if needed, ask the teacher for the correct spelling (see Table 10.8). Initiating the "Try-ers" Club is important for two reasons. First, it requires children to become independent in locating resources to assist them in their learning. Second, it provides them with opportunities to closely examine spelling patterns and exceptions.

Kathi devises many such learning tools for her students. When she notes that the children have a particular need that must be addressed or when she perceives that they are ready to move to the next level, she looks for commercially designed materials. If they are not available or do not closely match the needs of her children, she designs her own materials.

The progress the children are making in their writing can easily be traced by comparing pieces of writing from different points in the year. Three samples of Jordyn's writing (Table 10.9) from September, November, and February highlight the growth she is making both in terms of length and development of ideas in her writing.

Working With Students With Special Needs

One of Kathi's students has a learning disability and requires a number of modifications in his learning plan. The district levels trade books according to the Pinnell and Fountas (1998) system of leveling books. According to this system, average readers who are completing first grade should be at about Level J. He has reached Levels D/E in reading, and although this level is well below grade-level expectations, Kathi indicates that he has made a great deal of progress this year. He came to first grade with few emergent literacy skills but now has a good sense of reading processes. Kathi prepares basic reproducible books that this student takes home to practice. He has word wall words, fastened with a metal ring, that he can access for his writing that was developed by Kathi's daughter, a speech and language pathologist.

Kathi also brings in predictable books from the K–5 classroom that the student is now ready to read. When she works with him, they do picture walks and read the predictable book with an emphasis on voice print match. They discuss the story and the strategy, such as making text-to-text and text-to-self-connections as she does with her other groups. They focus on discussing characters in the story as well. Kathi uses components of Reading Recovery (Clay, 1985) to focus on development of comprehension and sight word recognition. She prepares sentence strips from the story, cuts apart the words from each strip, and has the student reassemble and read the sentences. Kathi takes precautions to make sure that he develops a positive sense of himself as a reader by making his experiences as close to those of his classmates as possible. He reads with the fourth-grade buddies when they come to read with the first graders. Kathi trains the buddies to guide their partners to figure things out rather than just give them answers, and she gives his buddy special assistance in how to work with his first-grade friend. The child has his own bucket of books, and he is held to the same guidelines as his classmates. In other words, only books that a student can read with fairly good accuracy may go into the bucket.

For writing, the student is encouraged to use his word ring, which includes words connected to his interests. Currently, he enjoys writing about wrestling. The class celebrated with him when he wrote, "I want," as it represented a milestone in relation to capitalizing the *I*. Great care has been taken in developing a community of compassionate learners in this classroom. They spend time learning how to help one another and to use "kind words." Kathi talks a great deal about how she needs help sometimes and so does everyone else. She stresses that everyone learns differently and that each person can be a helper. A person does not have to observe very long in this classroom to note that the children have learned how to do this.

When students pair up for reading, Kathi partners this student with a stronger reader. Currently the pair is reading Arthur books by Marc Brown (1976, 1979, 1980, 1982, 1990). The student loves these books and is learning a great deal about characters and story structure from these experiences. Kathi knows this because she listens to their discussions as they read together. She makes notes as he says that Arthur is the main character or compares Arthur's experiences from one book to another. He has trouble sequencing and processing information, but these discussions are very helpful for him, especially when he can reference illustrations in the stories to clarify his points.

In the beginning of the school year, Kathi had the student form words with clay as a kinesthetic experience. He would trace over the clay for more tactile experience and then write the words. Kathi would cover up the first letter and check his letter identification ability. From this beginning point he moved to using letter cards and now has moved to recognizing word chunks.

Table 10.9a   Jordyn's Writing Samples From September, November, and February

(I almost know how to ride a two-wheel bike.)

Jordyn 9-14-04
I omos ho
Hiw T rid
a Too Wihel
Bik

Table 10.9b

(I went trick or treating with my sister and my sister's friend Trista and her friend and then we went to Trista's house and we had lots of fun and I ate by her house and we played hide and go seek. It was fun and it was my first time there.)

Table 10.9c1

(One morning I woke up and saw a huge rat. then I woke up my mom to tell her. Then my mom woke my dad then the fat rat woke up my sister and my sister.)

3-9-05
One morning I
worck up and
saw a huge
rat then I
worck up my
mom to tell
her. Then mr
mom work my
dad then the
fat rat wok
up my sister
and my sister

Table 10.9c2

(went uuuuh! Then she ran out the door and the fat rat ran after her. Then she ran down the driveway and then I ran after the rat. then my mom and dad ran after it too. Then)

3-10-05
Went   uuuuh!
The n   She   ran
out The   door
and   The   fat rat
ran   after   her
Then   She   ran down
The   drive wae   and
Then   I   ran after
The   rat   Then
my   mom   and my
dad   ran   after
It   too   Then

Integrated Language Arts Experiences: Reader's Theater

On a sunny March day, Kathi posts a large laminated picture of Mrs. Wishy-Washy, a popular character in children's books by Joy Cowley, on the board and announces that she has returned for a visit. After a picture walk through the big book version of *Mrs. Wishy-Washy's Scrubbing Machine* (2005), Kathi begins reading the story to the children, and they quickly join in the reading as soon as they determine the story pattern. After discussing Mrs. Wishy-Washy's adventures and how they compare to other stories about her, Kathi informs the students that there are several short ŭ words in the story, and as she reads the story again, she asks the children to listen and watch for them. Two older students have come to help out in the room during their recess time. They record the short ŭ words as the students name them.

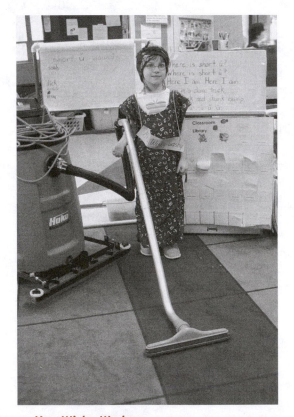

Photo 10.3   Jordyn as Mrs. Wishy-Washy.

Now the students prepare to do a reader's theater with the story. Students are selected for each part, and they dress up in costume props for their roles. Kathi asks the children, "Guess what I have in the back of the room?" The students get excited and begin clapping and cheering when Kathi rolls an industrial rug cleaner borrowed from the school engineers into the middle of the classroom.

The class rereads the story and stops as each character is introduced in the story to determine how each actor should play his or her part. A good bit of discussion takes place as the children decide how the story ought to be performed. During a third reading, the reader's theater is performed, and the children are clearly having fun. Even though this is an enjoyable learning experience, Kathi has specific goals that she wishes to accomplish. In rereading and discussing how each character should act and deliver his or her lines, the children are learning to read with fluency and expression. They are also becoming more familiar with character motivation and story sequence as they plan their dramatic reenactment. Less advanced readers have opportunities to read along and to add words to their sight word vocabulary. Kathi assigns speaking parts to students based on their reading abilities and needs. They receive specialized coaching to make certain they know their parts well before they perform in front of the class.

Photo 10.4 Kathi Glick conducts Reader's Theatre for *Mrs. Wishy-Washy's Scrubbing Machine.*

Guided Reading in First Grade

After the reader's theater activity, Kathi announces that Mrs. Wishy-Washy has some questions for them today. She wants to know what they do to warm up for guided reading, what work they do in guided reading sessions, and what they do when they finish reading their book to one of the parent volunteers. She also wants to know how they are doing as readers and what they could do better. The first questions are reminders of the process they are to follow. Kathi listens carefully to the children's responses to the last two questions, because this gives her a good sense of how accurately they are able to assess their reading progress and set appropriate goals for themselves.

The students "warm up" for guided reading by reading the bucket of books each student has on his or her desk. Many of the children now have more advanced picture books and even some beginning novels in their reading buckets. Kathi has emphasized that reading is an enjoyable activity, and the children really seem to have adopted this attitude. During reading experiences such as this, they are engrossed in their books, as they are at their independent reading levels.

Kathi works with two guided reading groups each day, and the other children meet with the educational assistant, a licensed teacher, or the parent volunteers. In this way, each group gets specialized attention in developing and reinforcing reading skills and strategies. Each group also gets to share reactions and make connections to what they have read. The Guided Reading Session that follows highlights the focus of a session Kathi conducted with two students who are struggling readers.

Guided Reading Session, March 5

Today Kathi meets with two students in a guided reading group. Although their skills and literacy level are well below their classmates, they have made significant progress this year. Kathi has been working with the two girls in identifying the problem in a story and using word length as a decoding skill.

She introduces a new book about a fox and a chick by asking the girls how the fox looks on the cover. After a picture walk through the book, they make predictions about what will happen in the story and stop periodically to check the accuracy of their predictions. The girls have been moving their fingers slowly below each word, and this has slowed down their potential reading rate. Kathi points out that they can move faster below shorter words, as shorter words will take less time to say; the girls focus on this concept while rereading the story.

After the story is read and reread, Kathi poses the following questions and asks the girls to find and share evidence from the story to support their responses:

- What was the problem in this story?
- Why was the fox running away?
- What was the child trying to do?

Kathi reviews a sheet the girls will complete independently (see Table 10.10). They discuss each of the questions thoroughly. When Kathi is confident that they understand the questions and know what to write, she sends them back to their seats to complete the sheets. They are encouraged to help one another if they get stuck.

Table 10.10

Name: _____

Title: _____

Date: _____

What happened in the story?

_____

What was the hardest word in the book?

_____

What strategy did you use to read that word?

_____

SOURCE: Kathi Glick, Hales Corners Elementary School, Hales Corners, WI. Used with permission.

The entire guided reading session with this group took only 20 minutes. Kathi identified key skills and strategies that the girls needed to learn next in their reading. She uses the guided reading session and the text to introduce and practice new skills, strategies, and vocabulary. The true test of how well these concepts have been learned will become evident in how they apply them in independent and shared reading experiences and if they are able to make links between how they read and write.

Kathi continues to work on listening and speaking skills throughout the year. At this time of the year, she focuses on developing descriptive skills as she invites the children to bring "nontoy" items from home that are special to them. In sharing sessions, they describe the item and talk about why it is important to them. The other children listen and ask questions. Kathi encourages parents to support this development at home and sends home suggestions they might find useful. For example, they might look for good describing words while they are reading together, or they might think about words that could be used to describe one of the characters.

Writing workshop is well established by the middle of the year. Although there is a wide range of writing skills in the classroom, all of the children seem to enjoy writing. In large part this is because Kathi continually searches for authentic audiences and purposes for writing. They write letters and poems for a host of situations. By this point in the year, the children are making their own suggestions for shared writing. Therefore, it was no surprise that at the end of their study of

Table 10.11   Wake Up, Mr. Groundhog

Wake Up, Mr. Groundhog
Written by Ms. Glick's First Graders

I have a little groundhog.
I found him in the woods.
He's brown and very fluffy.
And he's very, very good.

Oh groundhog, groundhog, groundhog
I found him in the woods.
Oh groundhog, groundhog, groundhog
He's very, very good.

If he sees his shadow,
He will run away,
If he doesn't see it,
He will come out and play

Oh groundhog, groundhog, groundhog
I found him in the woods.
Oh groundhog, groundhog, groundhog
He's very, very good.

SOURCE: Kathi Glick, Hales Corners Elementary School, Hales Corners, WI. Used with permission.

Groundhog Day, the children spontaneously went to work to write their own groundhog poem (see Table 10.11), which they later put to the music of "Dreidel, Dreidel, Dreidel."

During the Monday workshops, the children write about what they did over the weekend. Kathi guides the students through a series of prewriting activities before they begin writing independently. She reminds them that good writing is like a good meal that starts off with an appetizer, proceeds to the meat and potatoes, and ends with a good dessert. They discuss ideas to write about before they return to their seats. They also play a round-robin story game, where one student starts a sentence by providing the first word and the second person must add a word that makes sense and so on until a sentence has been formed. The last person says "period" or "question mark," and the next person must start a new sentence. After a few of these exercises, the children are energized to get started with their own writing.

Reflection Journal 10.1

What are the elements of Kathi Glick's classroom that appeal to you? Which of the elements do you feel ready to implement, and which elements seem like they would be challenging for you to implement at this point in your preparation to become a teacher?

End of School Year

By the end of the school year, Room 118 has truly become a community of learners who complete language arts activities for a wide variety of audiences and purposes. They move about the classroom with great independence and purpose, barely stopping to notice outside distractions. What is especially striking about this classroom is the level of enthusiasm they have for language arts activities and the great joy they express in being engaged with them.

Every time the children listen to a story in class, they record it on their classroom reading log. Kathi records the first five stories and then lets the children take over. By the end of September, they have logged 42 books read, and by the end of May, they have entered 180 different titles.

Kathi starts the year off reading *Chrysanthemum* by Kevin Henkes (1991) because it deals with an unusual name and accepting differences. Creating a classroom community is an important goal, and this book helps children start thinking about how they treat one another. Some books are selected because (a) they deal with concepts, such as weather, seasons, or fractions; (b) they teach lessons; (c) they focus on word or story patterns; or (d) they have great characters or plots or are just plain fun to read.

During the course of the year, the students have listened to and discussed several novels, including *The BFG* (Dahl, 1982), *Charlotte's Web* (White, 1952), *Trumpet of the Swan* (White, 1970), *Because of Winn Dixie* (Dicamillo, 2000), and *Junie B., First Grader (At Last!)* (Park, 2002). Kathi firmly believes in the importance of having children respond to what they have listened to or read. She relies heavily on reader response theory (Rosenblatt, 1978, 1995) in making a great deal of room in her agenda for students to discuss and form opinions about what they have read. She also stresses the importance of making connections between themselves and what they know of the world and what they have read.

Many of the children are now reading beginning novels for both guided and independent reading sessions. A favorite among the children is the Henry and Mudge series by Cynthia Rylant (1987, 1990, 1991, 1992, 1994). Students are encouraged to alert one another to good books they have come across. They do this both in class discussions and through book reviews, such as the one in Table 10.12.

Table 10.12   Book Reviews

The name of my book is _____

The characters are _____

The story takes place _____

The story is about _____

_____

I think that you would like to read it because

_____

My favorite part is

_____

Draw a picture of your favorite part.

SOURCE: Kathi Glick, Hales Corners Elementary School, Hales Corners, WI. Used with permission.

From April on, the students spend a great deal of time publishing books in the publishing center that opens each spring in the school. Kathi models writing stories with them. First she shares a very bland story without detail and then a very interesting story. The students discuss which one they like better and determine what made one better than the other. She has been teaching them how to use graphic organizers to plan their writing, and they are now ready to use them independently. Figure 10.1 illustrates a graphic organizer that students use in developing a beginning, middle, and end to their stories. Student growth from the beginning of the year to the present is quite remarkable.

End-of-Year Assessment

Kathi has a very well-organized assessment system to measure student progress and to determine student needs. She maintains a folder for each of her guided reading groups. The names of the children are on the front of the folder, and records for each student are clipped together inside the folder. Table 10.13 outlines the contents of each group's folder.

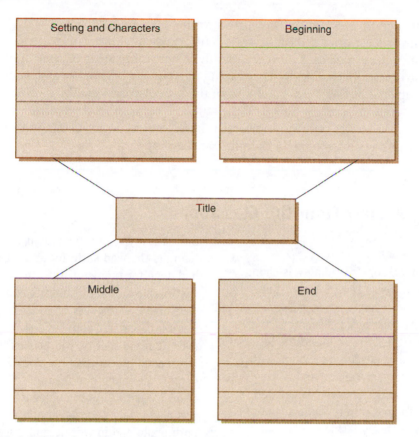

Figure 10.1   Story Organizer: Beginning, Middle, End

SOURCE: Kathi Glick, Hales Corners Elementary School, Hales Corners, WI. Used with permission.

Table 10.13   Guided Reading Group Folders

Contents of Reading Group Folders

List of books read by the group

Anecdotal records on the work of the group

Individual student records (clipped together by student)

- Reading level grid
- Log of books read
- Formal running records from January and June
- Monthly informal running records
- Parent sheets
- Group working materials (Ex: Venn diagram, word cards)

Kathi completes either formal or informal Running Records for each of her students at least once a month. If students are struggling or moving slowly, she completes the evaluations more frequently, determining areas of need and designing instruction that will move them along most quickly. More formal assessments are completed at the middle and end of the school year. Retellings provide Kathi with a sound measure of how well the students comprehend what they are reading. She also makes notes to indicate strategies students are using and to articulate learning goals for next steps in literacy development.

A View From the Classroom

Student 1:

In October, John's reading was choppy, even with basic Level C books. Kathi had to provide several cues to get him to retell even the most basic elements of these simple stories. He confused the letters /b/ and /d/ and needed instruction with basic, emergent reading and writing skills. Behavior issues also challenged John's ability to concentrate and complete his work in a timely fashion.

Kathi worked all year long to improve both John's literacy skills and his confidence as a reader and writer. Early in the year, he refused to even try, because he was certain he could not learn. But Kathi was persistent, and slowly he started to make an effort and then began to surprise himself with what he could do.

As John gained momentum, his language arts skills began to soar. This didn't mean that Kathi's work became easier. John continued to need reinforcement to use the strategies he'd been learning. Even his final report indicated that he needs to remember to "get his mouth ready to say unknown words" rather than looking to a classmate or an adult to provide the word for him.

On the last day of school, John's parents tearfully thanked Kathi for all that she had done for their son. They recognize that because of Kathi's efforts and John's developing willingness to cooperate, he is leaving first grade with solid skills that make it likely that he will be successful in the second grade. His final Book Interview Conference found him reading solidly at Level I/J with 99% comprehension. He was able to analyze the story accurately both orally and in writing and came to the main idea immediately.

John has gotten excited about the Henry and Mudge series (Rylant, 1987, 1990, 1991, 1992, 1994). During the summer, his parents plan to keep him supplied with these books and others so that they can continue to support the joy in books that he discovered this school year.

Student 2:

Juan's progress was quite remarkable this year also. He started out with Level E books and plateaued at this level for the entire first semester. Though he remained at this level for a long time, he was not standing still. In the beginning of the year, he could read some books, but he largely memorized the text, paid little attention to story structure, and took little pleasure in language arts activities. Retellings were difficult for Juan, and he often looked to Kathi for help.

Through all of the reading experiences in the classroom, Juan began to get a sense of how reading worked. His comprehension improved a great deal, and he began to look for humorous books to read during independent reading time. In Kathi's anecdotal records, she noted that Juan laughed at funny parts in stories and later brought them to share with the class during whole group sharing time. This indicated to her that he was connecting to what he was reading.

Early in January, Juan jumped two levels and was solidly reading at Level G, but just one month later he moved to Level H. By the end of the school year he was reading at Level I. The time that it took him to develop and consolidate his reading skills and strategy use were paying off. Juan now often chooses to read during free time, and his mother reports that she rarely has to prompt him to read each evening any longer.

Kathi keeps a pack of index cards handy when she meets with her guided reading groups. She also maintains an ongoing list of books read by the group and staples these cards to the inside pocket of each folder. Notes about concepts the entire group or individual students struggle with and need to focus on are also included in the folder. For example, if students are confused by the word *bump*, Kathi shows them how it is related to the word *jump*, which they already know, or they might do work with short ŭ onset and rime patterns. Her folder for each group, therefore, is a working document that she uses to evaluate student performance and guide instructional decisions.

The top sheet of each child's papers is titled *Record of Book Reading Progress K–3*. (See Figure 10.2 for examples of John and Juan's first-grade reading progress sheets.) The recording sheet contains a dated record of books that have been read and for which running records have been compiled. The district has identified several books at each level that are used as assessment books and are not included in instructional or independent reading materials. At a glance, Kathi is able to note the progress of each child. She keeps track of progress with phonemic awareness, letter recognition, and phonics in much the same way. Many of her incoming first graders already know their letters and many of their sounds and have a good handle on phonemic awareness. Kathi determines which skills the students need work in for these areas and reinforces these skills in language arts, including guided, shared, and independent reading and writing activities, throughout the day.

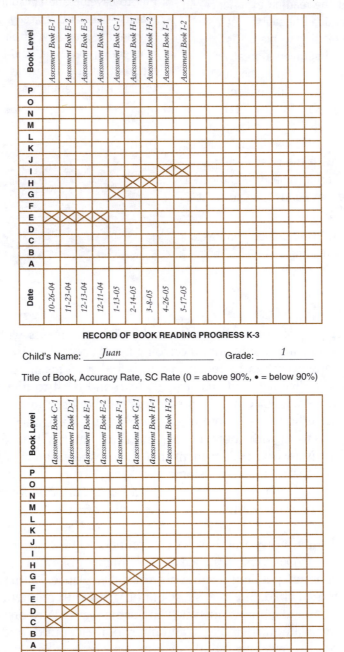

Figure 10.2 Examples of John and Juan's First-Grade Reading Progress Sheets

SOURCE: Kathi Glick, Hales Corners Elementary School, Hales Corners, WI. Used with permission.

The folders serve as excellent resources for parent-teacher conferences. The assessment pieces have been collected on an ongoing basis, and the record of language arts and reading advancement allows parents/guardians to know how well their children are progressing.

End-of-Year Celebration

An easel outside of Room 118 today announces, "Welcome to Authors' Tea." Half of the families have been invited to attend the morning tea, and the other half will come to the afternoon session. The room has been rearranged into rows of chairs for guests, and a table with two chairs has been placed in the front of the room. All the desks have been pushed to the back of the room. Family members begin to arrive and take their seats for the big event. The children are excited and a bit nervous. They take a few minutes to review a few final details, and they are ready to begin.

Today is the culmination of a writing project that began in February. Kathi slowly and carefully led the students through the process of writing their own books. They selected topics, developed and edited their stories, and then moved to the final step of having their books typed and bound by volunteers in the school's publishing center. The students are now prepared to share their hard work with their families.

The tea is completely hosted by the students, though Kathi sits nearby in case she is needed. A student welcomes guests and explains the event. Students come to the table in pairs, proudly carrying their books along with them. The students introduce one another by reading the About the Author notation on the final page of their books. One student holds the microphone while the other reads his or her book and shows the illustrations.

The children have rehearsed everything several times, and their readings go very smoothly. They enjoy having an audience for their work, and many smile and swing their legs as they share their stories. In a question-and-answer session following the readings, the students talk about the process they went through in writing and publishing their work. They share cookies and punch with their families, and the Authors' Tea comes to a satisfying close.

The book dedications are charming and provide an indication of how seriously the students take their writing. For example, Chastity wrote a book called *My Hair* (Price, 2005), and her dedication reads, "Dedicated to Brittany Spears because she has nice hair." Alexa wrote *Little Butterflies* (Jifas, 2005) and included the dedication, "Dedicated to my mom because she helps me and gives me butterfly cookies." Mitchell dedicated his book, *The Black Dragon* (Schold, 2005), "To Mrs. Glick because she taught me how to write," a sentiment echoed in many of the books. Perhaps the most creative dedication was made by Austin when he wrote, "Dedicated to myself because I like dragons" from his book, *The Big Red Dragon* (Brault, 2005).

Photo 10.5   Michael and Lauren Share Their Stories at Authors' Tea

Before the children leave for summer vacation, Kathi playfully has her students take an end-of-year oath in which they promise to come back to visit and to continue using the literacy strategies they learned during the year (see Table 10.14). Early in the second grade, Kathi visits her former students and reminds them of the strategies they already know and encourages them to use them in their reading and writing in their new classrooms.

This summer Kathi is taking the final two courses for her master's degree in reading, where she will focus on district-level management and assessment of language arts programs. When asked to articulate her goals for next year, Kathi readily describes her plans to develop more parent involvement in their children's literacy development. She outlines her belief that most parents are truly interested in supporting their children's education, but they are not always certain of the best

Table 10.14   End of Year Oath

I promise to come back to
First grade to visit Ms. Glick.
I promise to use all of my
Strategies when I read and write.

Photo 10.6   Koby and Mitchell at Authors' Tea

ways to help them. She would like to provide parents with ongoing education about how best to help their children and would like to invite parents whose children struggle in school to special sessions. Other sessions might focus on selecting quality learning materials for children. Parents would be given guidelines to assist them in selecting resources and enable them to recognize which computer games, books, and puzzles are useful educational tools for them to purchase or check out of the library. Other suggestions would be simple for parents/guardians to engage in with their children but would have a huge impact on their literacy development, including reading and writing with children and getting them excited about literate activities, regular trips to the library or bookstore, and reciting nursery rhymes together.

Kathi would also like to take a course in adaptive education to better understand options available to her in working with children with special needs. Like a true teaching professional, Kathi is always anxious to learn more about effective teaching, learning, and assessment in early childhood education.

At the close of the school year, Kathi sends home the children's writing notebooks and other things they have worked on during the year. She attaches the poem found in Table 10.15 to the front of the materials in hopes that parents will sit down with their children and savor their accomplishments this year.

Table 10.15   Letter Attached to Student Work

In these folders you will see
Lots of first-grade memories.

Take the time and share the fun,
Reading, writing, and math well done.

It's very hard to say good-bye
When you see how hard they try.

So off to second grade they go,
Watch them closely as they grow.

Thank you for all of your support.
Have a wonderful summer.

End-of-Chapter Reflection

- What areas of planning language arts instruction and assessment do you feel you want to learn more about for students at the 3- to 6-year-old levels?
- What are some of your ideas for teaching, learning, and assessing young children?

Planning for Teaching

1. Think about the areas of planning instruction and assessment for 3- to 6-year-old students in language arts that you feel you want to learn more about. There are numerous resources through print, the Internet, and people resources available for teachers related to teaching and assessing language arts. Search out supplemental resources that could help you further develop your understanding of these components and begin a resource list.

2. After reading about how Kathi Glick plans and implements language arts in her first-grade classroom, sketch out a rough plan or list of things you want to make sure to include in your future primary-level classroom. Share your ideas with peers.

Connections With the Field

- Visit a 3- or 4-year-old classroom and a first-grade classroom (6-year-olds) and observe how language arts plays a role in the curriculum and throughout the typical daily schedule. Compare it to Kathi Glick's classroom. What are the similarities and differences that you noted between the two classrooms?

Student Study Site

The Companion Website for Developing Voice Through the Language Arts

http://www.sagepub.com/dvtlastudy

Visit the Web-based student study site to enhance your understanding of the chapter content and to discover additional resources that will take your learning one step further. You can enhance your understanding of the chapters by using the comprehensive Study Guide, which includes learning objectives, key terms, activities, practice tests, and more. You'll also find special features, such as the Links to Standards from U.S. States and associated activities, Children's Literature Selections, Reflection Exercises, Learning from Journal Articles, and PRAXIS test preparation materials.

References of Children's/Young Adult Literature

Atwater, R., & Atwater, F. (1966). *Mr. Popper's penguins.* New York: Scholastic. (Original work published 1939)
Brault, A. (2005). *The big red dragon.* Hales Corners, WI: Gold Medal.
Brown, B. (1948). *Stone soup.* New York: Scribner.

Brown, M. (1976). *Arthur's nose*. Boston: Little, Brown.

Brown, M. (1979). *Arthur's eyes*. Boston: Little, Brown.

Brown, M. (1980). *Arthur's valentine*. Boston: Little, Brown.

Brown, M. (1982). *Arthur's Halloween*. Boston: Little, Brown.

Brown, M. (1990). *Arthur's pet business*. New York: Little, Brown.

Cowley, J. (2005). *Mrs. Wishy-Washy's scrubbing machine* (E. Fuller, Illus.). New York: Philomel.

Dahl, R. (1982). *The BFG*. New York: Knopf.

Danzinger, P. (2003). *Get ready for second grade Amber Brown* (T. Ross, Illus.). New York: Putnam.

Dicamillo, K. (2000). *Because of Winn Dixie*. Cambridge, MA: Candlewick.

Galdone, P. (1973). *The little red hen*. New York: Seabury Press.

Henkes, K. (1991). *Chrysanthemum*. New York: Greenwillow.

Jifas, A. (2005). *Little butterflies*. Hales Corners, WI: Gold Medal.

Park, B. (2001). *Junie B., first grader (at last!)* (D. Brunkes, Illus.). New York: Random House.

Price, C. (2005). *My hair*. Hales Corners, WI: Gold Medal.

Rylant, C. (1987). *Henry and Mudge: The first book of their adventures* (S. Stevenson, Illus.). New York: Simon & Schuster.

Rylant, C. (1990). *Henry and Mudge and the happy cat*. New York: Bradbury.

Schold, M. (2005). *The black dragon*. Hales Corners, WI: Gold Medal.

Sendak, M. (1962). *Chicken soup with rice*. New York: Harper.

White, E. B. (1952). *Charlotte's web*. New York: Harper & Row.

White, E. B. (1970). *Trumpet of the swan*. New York: Harper & Row.

References of Professional Resources

Avery, C. (2002). *And with a light touch . . . : Learning about reading, writing and teaching with first graders* (2nd ed.). Portsmouth, NH: Heinemann.

Caukins, L. (1994). *The art of teaching writing*. Portsmouth, NH: Heinemann.

Clay, M. (1985). *The early detection of reading difficulties* (3rd ed.). Auckland, New Zealand: Heinemann.

Mitchell, D. (2002). *Children's literature: An invitation to the world*. Boston: Allyn & Bacon.

No Child Left Behind Act. (2001). Conference Report to Accompany H.R. 1, Report No. 107-334, House of Representatives, 107th Congress, 1st Session.

Pinnell, G., & Fountas, I. (1998). *Word matters: Teaching phonics and spelling in the reading/writing classroom*. Portsmouth, NH: Heinemann.

Rosenblatt, L. (1978). *The reader, the text, the poem: The transactional theory of the literary work*. Carbondale: Southern Illinois University Press.

Rosenblatt, L. (1995). *Literature exploration* (5th ed.). New York: Modern Language Association of America.

Routman, R. (1991). *Invitations*. Portsmouth, NH: Heinemann.

Snowball, D., & Bolton, F. (1999). *Spelling K–8*. York, ME: Stenhouse.

Wood, C. (1997). *Yardsticks: Children in the classroom ages 4–14: A resource for parents and teachers*. Greenfield, MA: Northeast Foundation for Children.

Other Children's/Young Adult Literature Resources

Henkes, K. (1988). *Chester's way*. New York: Greenwillow.

Henkes, K. (1991). *Julius, the baby of the world*. New York: Greenwillow.

Henkes, K. (1991). *Lilly's purple plastic purse*. New York: Greenwillow.

Henkes, K. (1991). *Owen*. New York: Greenwillow.

Henkes, K. (1991). *Sheila Rae, the brave*. New York: Greenwillow.

Henkes, K. (1991). *A weekend with Wendell*. New York: Greenwillow.

McPhail, D. (1984). *Fix-it*. New York: Dutton.

McPhail, D. (1993). *Pigs aplenty, pigs galore*. New York: Dutton.

Rylant, C. (1991). *Henry and Mudge and the bedtime thump*. New York: Bradbury.

Rylant, C. (1992). *Henry and Mudge and the long weekend*. New York: Bradbury.

Rylant, C. (1994). *Henry and Mudge and the careful cousin*. New York: Bradbury.

Seuss, Dr. (1937). *And to think I saw it on Mulberry Street*. New York: Vanguard.

Seuss, Dr. (1957). *The cat in the hat*. New York: Random House.

Seuss, Dr. (1960). *Green eggs and ham*. New York: Random House.

Seuss, Dr. (1960). *One fish, two fish, red fish, blue fish*. New York: Random House.

Seuss, Dr. (1963). *Hop on pop*. New York: Random House.

Seuss, Dr. (1965). *Fox in socks*. New York: Random House.

Seuss, Dr. (1979). *Oh, say can you say*. New York: Random House.

Technology Resources

A book-related site that includes read-alouds of picture books, poetry, learning games, and sing-along songs (a small yearly subscription fee is required):
http://www.mightybook.com

Discovery School lesson plans for Grades K–5, includes language arts and other content areas for integration purposes: http://school.discovery.com/lessonplans/k-5.html

Rhyme-a-week cards and lesson ideas:
http://curry.edschool.virginia.edu/go/wil/rimes_and_rhymes.htm#Week1

Early Literacy Advisor: http://www.mcrel.org/programs/literacy/ela/index.asp

Assessment tools for K–3 learners:
http://teams.lacoe.edu/reading/assessments/assessments.html#top

 **Middle Childhood Language Arts**

Sandy Cabernathy's Third- and Fourth-Grade Classroom

Context Setting:

After reading this chapter, you will be able to

- Identify aspects of development of 6- to 9-year-olds related to social, cognitive, physical, and emotional growth and how this knowledge informs language arts teaching and learning
- Understand a variety of factors to consider when planning for, implementing, and assessing language arts in a classroom for 7- to 9-year-old children
- Gain an understanding of the various stages of the school year and how literacy planning, instruction, and assessment change to meet students' development

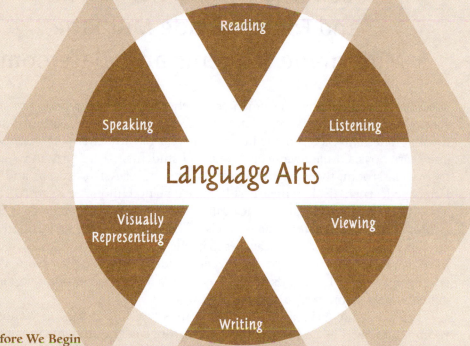

Before We Begin

- When you think about second-grade (7-year-old) children, what do you expect physically, emotionally, and cognitively? What about third-grade (or 8-year-old) children? Fourth (9-year-old)? What are some ways to capitalize on this knowledge when planning for language arts instruction?

Development of 7- to 9-Year-Old Children

Seven- to 9-year-old children are inquisitive and independent in nature and enjoy taking control of their learning. Table 11.1 describes some of the characteristics of children at these ages and how a teacher can capitalize on them in a language arts curriculum (Wood, 1997). Note, however, the classroom scenario detailed in this chapter focuses only on a third- and fourth-grade (7- and 8-year-old) classroom only.

Introduction to Sandy Cabernathy and Her Third- and Fourth-Grade Multiage, Multigrade Students and Classroom

Meet Sandy Cabernathy, an elementary teacher for 12 years, working in an urban school, teaching twenty-seven 8- and 9-year-old children in a combined third and fourth grade. The class is made up of ten 8-year-old students, 4 of whom are girls and 6 are boys. Of the seventeen 9-year-old students, 10 are girls and 7 are boys. In her classroom, there are five students who are of Asian descent and English language learners (ELLs), their first language being Hmong or Korean. There are also three students who are of Mexican descent, whose first language is Spanish, two of whom are at intermediate levels of English language acquisition. Twelve students are of African American descent, and seven are Caucasian. Two children have diagnosed learning needs and receive additional instruction from a specialist in the school who spends an hour each day in their classroom working individually with them on regular classroom work.

The academic makeup of the classroom is typical and similar to most classrooms of today. The developmental reading range of the students includes those who are "on grade level," meaning they test academically at their average age and grade level. There are also students who are "below grade level," including seven of the ELLs, and those who are "above grade level." Therefore, Sandy must plan her instruction for a wide range of student abilities.

Sandy believes strongly in a balanced or comprehensive literacy curriculum, highlighting the fact that language arts is fully taught and learned at this level for large blocks of time but is also integrated within the content area learning during

Table 11.1   Developmental Characteristics of 7- to 9-Year-Old Children

7-Year-Old Children	Language Arts Curriculum Connections
• Enjoy working and playing alone	• Include ample opportunities for working alone, e.g., independent reading and writing experiences, individual projects
• Hardworking, tend to be perfectionists, take a long time in completing tasks	• Have a predictable language arts curriculum/schedule, e.g., reading workshop daily from 9:00 to 10:30, writing workshop daily from 11:00 to 12:00
• Love routine and structure	• Allow students to play with language and words in activities such as "What makes these words similar?"
• Have a natural curiosity and like to make discoveries on their own	• Integrate language arts activities such as reading, writing, and readers' theater into content area curriculum such as social studies and science
• Begin to take an interest in the outside world	• Incorporate daily read-alouds, shared reading, and writing
• Need to have time to complete work and have closure	• Use one-on-one conferencing in reading and writing workshops
• Well-developed listening skills	
• Enjoy one-on-one conversation	• Do not penalize students for not reading perfectly silently
	• Encourage alternating between starting with a picture and text first to move students into getting ideas into words
• Silent reading time is not yet "silent," but still includes some whisper reading	• Encourage writing topics related to students' lives
• Writing comes before drawing	
• Themes in their writing: family, friends, trips, pets, serious issues such as death and war	

8-Year-Old Children	Language Arts Curriculum Connections
• Energetic, developed imaginations	• Read aloud a variety of genres, including fantasy, science fiction
• Tend to overestimate their abilities and are not aware of the limits of the risks they take	• Help children break tasks/projects into smaller portions so they can be completed successfully and well
• Enjoy humor, jokes, and riddles	• Stock classroom library with joke books, encourage verbally sharing and writing jokes, do book talks using humorous texts
• Tend to want to work and play with their own gender	• Encourage productive collaboration and communication
• Talkative, enjoy group work	• Vary grouping, allow for independent, small group, and large group work to allow for movement and activity
• Tend to work quickly, not always thoroughly	• Develop student self-assessment to judge quality of work
• Need frequent physical activity but tire easily	

(Continued)

Table 11.1 (Continued)

- Themes in their writing: varied topics, including adventure and breakfast to bed stories, variety of genres explored, lengthy pieces; beginning to experiment with drafts and revision

- Teach the process of narrowing a topic in writing

9-Year-Old Children

Language Arts Curriculum Connections

- Often worriers and anxious in nature, self-critical
- Focus often on "fairness" issues
- Tend to use negative language: "I can't," "This is boring"
- Enjoy playing with language and learning vocabulary
- Concerned with their final products and give much attention to detail

- Focus on reading to learn rather than learning to read

- Themes in their writing: dark topics such as death and wars

- Encourage risk taking and experimentation in reading and writing activities

- Incorporate word work into daily shared reading activities
- Help students see the value in rough drafts of their writing as a way to develop ideas and experiment with writing technique
- Stock classroom library with a variety of genres of literature, including informational books, magazines, resource books, online encyclopedias and Web sites, software

science and math. One of the ways she highlights language arts throughout her curriculum is using authentic children's literature for many purposes. For example, she uses quality literature while reading aloud to her students each day, as primary texts for guided reading and literature circles, as texts for shared reading experiences, as models for writing, and as supplementary material for topics in social studies such as the use of the Mexican folktale *Borreguita and the Coyote* (Aardema, 1991) when studying folk literature from around the world. To effectively incorporate literature to this extent, Sandy has to keep current on new children's literature, so she spends some of her free time visiting libraries and bookstores and reading for pleasure.

Another key aspect of being an effective teacher, in Sandy's opinion, is knowing her students' abilities and academic capabilities. In order to know her students in this manner, she uses a variety of assessment tools and collaborates with colleagues in determining ways she can help them grow. Let us now peek into her classroom and see how language arts is taught and learned in this 7- and 8-year-old classroom.

Planning for the School Year and Language Arts Curriculum

For Sandy Cabernathy, planning for the upcoming school year begins during the summer after she has had time to relax and reflect on the previous school year. After getting her garden planted and taking a vacation, she is energized to begin some preliminary planning for the fall. Part of this includes reading as many children's books as she can. She has befriended the children's librarian at her local library, who often shares new books she thinks Sandy's 8- and 9-year-old students would enjoy reading. Sandy reads them herself first, determining if they would be valuable as part of her curriculum and how she might use them with her students. She creates a list of these books, deciding those that would be appropriate for read-alouds, shared readings, literature circles, content area learning, and guided reading. She found some interesting books whose topics tie in well with a unit in her social studies curriculum. Her students study farming and production as part of learning about agriculture in their home state, so she plans to incorporate these new texts into the unit later into the school year. Sandy decides to use *Farmer's Market: Families Working Together* (2005), by Marcie R. Rendon and photo illustrated by Cheryl W. Bellville, as a read-aloud to provide an overview of the topic. She also plans to incorporate other books about markets around the world to use as a text set while studying this subject in social studies and language arts. The local librarian helps her find other appropriate texts. Table 11.2 details the text set she plans to use with her students focused on markets.

Especially important to Sandy this upcoming school year is developing her writing program so that her students can become more effective writers. As she reflected on her previous year of teaching, she felt that teaching writing was an area she needed to develop. Therefore, she dedicated time right after school ended to attend a 2-day workshop focused on writing workshop, as well as read a professional book, *Writing Essentials: Raising Expectations and Results While Simplifying Teaching* (2004) by Regie Routman, on the topic. She is excited to implement what she has learned in her classroom.

She spends time thinking about her assessment system within her language arts curriculum and is happy with the methods she used previously and wants to continue to use both the formative and summative assessments she used last year. Although she receives the academic records for her new students from their previous teacher, in addition she plans to sit down with each child in the first 3 weeks and conduct an interest inventory and running record to confirm each student's current reading interests, strategy use, and reading level. She finds that doing this helps her get to know her students as literate persons more quickly and she can get them started with guided reading after the first month of school and literature circles shortly thereafter.

Table 11.2 Markets Text Set

Use in Language Arts/Social Studies Curriculum	Book	Publishing Information
Read Aloud/Social Studies Comparison of market places around the world, including Uganda, Morocco, New York City, Ecuador, Ireland. Identify all locations on a large wall map.	*Market!* by Ted Lewin	HarperCollins, 1996
Read Aloud/Social Studies Irish village marketplace, good text to contrast with Mexican marketplace and culture using a graphic organizer.	*Market Day* by Eve Bunting, illustrated by Holly Berry	HarperCollins, 1996
Read Aloud/Guided Reading Read aloud to provide background on topic and also use with small groups of students focusing on various aspects of the text and text design. Highlights two families, one of Hmong descent, one of Polish-German descent, working together to run their farms and sell their American and ethnic produce at a local farmer's market.	*Farmer's Market: Families Working Together* by Marcie R. Rendon and photo illustrated by Cheryl W. Bellville	Carolrhoda Books, 2001
Social Studies Depicts a Saturday market in Oaxaca, Mexico. Text will correlate well with study of Mexican culture. Some Spanish words interspersed representing Mexican objects, traditions, clothing, and patterns.	*Saturday Market* by Patricia Grossman, illustrated by Enrique O. Sanchez	HarperCollins, 1994
Independent Reading Beginning reader informational text that depicts a variety of things available in markets around the world.	*Markets* (Social Studies Emergent Readers) by Pamela Chanko, illustrated by Samantha Berger	Sagebrush, 1998
Independent Reading Good follow-up after the read-aloud of *Saturday Market* by Grossman.	*Taste of the Mexican Market/Gusto Del Mercado Mexicano* by Nancy Tabor (Spanish/English text)	Sagebrush, 1999
Shared Reading/Writing Repetitive text, play on nursery rhyme. Students could add new lines to story following pattern.	*To Market, To Market* by Anne Miranda, illustrated by Janet Stevens	Harcourt, 1997

Two weeks before school begins, Sandy crafts a letter to her students that she sends to their homes to prepare them for the first days of school. District translators prepare the letters in Korean and Spanish for Sandy. Hmong translators relay the contents of the letters to parents/guardians by phone, as few are literate in their first language. She likes to get to know her students' interests and what they like to read as soon as possible so she can begin connecting them with appropriate books that will get them excited about reading. In her letter, she asks them to bring a life box (Taberski, 2000) on the first day of school and be prepared to talk about its contents. She encourages them to include items that tell about themselves and things of importance to them. She suggests such things as photographs of loved ones, a favorite toy or stuffed animal, memorabilia from experiences they have had, and a favorite book. On the first day of school, she will have students share these with the class as a way to get to know one another and as a means for engaging the students in meaningful listening and talking. She has found this to be a successful and enjoyable activity that engages students in literate activity. As an informal assessment, she will jot down anecdotal notes related to what she learns about each child. Of course, she will model the sharing process for her students first, and she has her life box already packed with her favorite books (one children's book, *Ramona Quimby, Age 8,* by Beverly Cleary, 1982, and one adult book), photos of her husband and dog, a seed package from the flowers she planted this spring, her journal, a bag of popcorn seeds (her favorite food), a travel brochure to signal her love of traveling to exotic places, and a note card with a picture of children from around the world to depict her dedication to her profession as a teacher and her love of children.

Beginning of the School Year

Sandy is careful to prepare a classroom for her students that is inviting in nature but not too "finished," as she wants them to assist with this task so that they feel the classroom belongs to them. She posts the alphabet in print and manuscript format for students' reference and large blank pieces of poster board that will serve as the word wall. The only words she includes on the wall are the names of her students and herself, as she plans to use them for language and word study activities beginning on the first day of school. She knows that the word wall will fill up quickly as her students learn new words through their language and content area studies. She purposely leaves most of the bulletin boards bare, covered only in colored or decorative paper so that students feel invited to add to them with their writing and artwork. A few of Sandy's favorite wall hangings and art pieces representing the cultures of her students are placed about the room, and families will be invited to loan other items to the classroom.

The furniture is arranged to create centers and areas around the classroom. Sandy has included a writing center stocked with writing utensils, art supplies, various types of paper, a range of writing reference books such as dictionaries and thesauri appropriate for a variety of reading levels, envelopes, staplers, paper clips, and a date stamp. She wants to make this area inviting and allow students access to needed writing materials as well as encourage them to engage in all kinds of writing, from story to letter writing to illustrating their pieces.

The small group area includes a lima-bean-shaped table where students will gather for guided reading and writing, as well as for working on independent group projects. In this area Sandy stores supplies she will use when working with small groups, such as Post-it notes, pens, markers, chart paper, and a clipboard on which she will record assessment data.

The classroom contains a large carpeted area where students will gather for group activities such as shared reading and writing, read-alouds, and language arts minilessons. Sandy places a rocking chair in the area and designates it as the "author's chair," where students will sit as they share their writing with the class. It will also serve as Sandy's chair as she reads aloud to the students and as a quiet place for an individual student to read during independent reading. In this area, she sets up a white board, markers, and bookstand where instruction can take place.

Part of the carpeted area includes bookshelves where Sandy has created a well-stocked classroom library with the books she has been collecting over the years. Books are organized in baskets in a number of ways, including genre, readability level, author, and topic. Throughout the year, she asks students to rearrange the books using categories of importance to them. Included in the class library is a check-out chart that includes a pocket with a card with each child's name that the child will fill out when borrowing a book.

Sandy knows the importance of making sure her language arts curriculum is tied to her school district, state, and the national standards. Therefore, she finds it helpful to note the standards in her lesson plan book, along with the objectives for each language arts activity. For example, when doing her initial planning for her integrated social studies and language arts unit related to farming, production, and markets, and she aligns the students' learning not only with the social studies standards but also with the correlating language arts standards. In choosing and using the wide range of literature in the markets text set, the National Council of Teachers of English standard that states, "Students read a wide range of literature from many periods in many genres to build an understanding of the many dimensions (e.g., philosophical, ethical, aesthetic) of human experience" (National Council of Teachers of English, 1996), is what guided her choice, as she made sure to include both fiction and informational genres representing a variety of cultures.

Sandy plans for the first day of school, wanting to make sure her students understand that literacy and language arts is the framework of their day (see Table 11.3). She chooses a few books for read-alouds, *First Day Jitters* (Danneberg, 2000) and *Sumi's First Day of School Ever* (Pak, 2003), and a poem and book for shared reading. Wanting her students to acclimate to the daily schedule, she tries to keep the plan for the first day of school as close to what their daily schedule will be all year long. Sandy knows that she must be flexible and has planned this schedule loosely, aware of the fact that she will take cues from the students and will make changes as warranted.

Table 11.3   First Day Plan

	Activity/Lesson	Objective/Standard/Assessment
9:00	Student arrival and individual greeting Instruct students to find book in class library and sit in carpeted area and read Teacher takes care of attendance/lunch preferences	• Determine which students are motivated to read and are independent • Determine which students like to read with peers
9:15	Large group (meet in large group carpeted area) Read aloud: *First Day Jitters* by J. Danneberg Introductions of selves using life boxes (1/2 of the class) • Shared reading experience: poem • Minilesson: How independent reading time works, and how to use classroom library to check out books	• Opportunity to connect personally with students and get to know them individually • Begin to develop a classroom community of literate persons • Provide teacher opportunity to informally assess students' speaking skills (IRA/NCTE Standard 4: Students adjust their use of spoken language to communicate effectively with a variety of audiences and for different purposes) • Begin to set expectations for students' literacy development
10:00	Independent reading time (includes choosing books from classroom library)	• Observe student interaction with text
10:30	Writing workshop: What is writing workshop? • Minilesson: How to get ideas for writing • Group sharetime: Sharing of ideas, expectations, and routines of writing workshop	• Determine students' enthusiasm and interest in writing • Learn beginning stage of process writing
11:30	Large group sharetime (1/2 of class share life boxes)	• Provides teacher opportunity to informally assess students' speaking skills (IRA/NCTE Standard 4: Students adjust their use of spoken language to communicate effectively with a variety of audiences and for different purposes)
12:00	Lunch	
1:00	Math	• Introduce math journals
1:45	Integrated curriculum (including social studies, science, health, language arts, etc.) First unit of study: Who are we? Read aloud: *Sumi's First Day of School Ever* by S. Pak Social studies lesson related to communities	• Begin to develop a classroom community of literate persons • Help students get to know themselves, others, and their community
2:30	Specials (physical education, music, art): Specials begin the second week of school	
3:20	Dismissal	

First Day of School: Laying the Groundwork for a Literate Classroom Environment

On the first day of school, Sandy is excited and nervous, just as her students are, and as a read-aloud she has chosen *First Day Jitters* by Julie Danneberg (2000). It's a picture book about the character Sarah, who is very anxious to go to school on the first day. The twist at the end of the book reveals that Sarah is the teacher and that teachers too can be nervous about the first day of school. Sandy enjoys sharing this book, as she feels it helps her students understand her nervousness of beginning a new school year. She also likes to begin teaching students that making text-to-self connections can assist in comprehending and appreciating text.

She is looking forward to getting to know her students and working with them as they continue to develop as literate persons. ELLs are invited to have a friend who speaks both languages come along for support, as needed.

This shared literacy time begins with the students sitting on the carpeted group meeting area. Sandy sits in the rocking chair, providing the students a good view of her and the texts she shares with them. After the read-aloud, she models the process for sharing their life boxes as she begins talking about her own. The students enjoy learning more about their teacher and have many questions related to the objects in her box. Time is then spent having half of the class share their life boxes and take turns sitting in the rocking chair to be in the spotlight.

Shared Reading and Writing

Shared reading and writing begins with Sandy sharing a format for a poem the class will write together. On the easel where chart paper is attached, she has written

We have a classmate named _____.

_____ enjoys _____, _____, _____

Welcome to our class, _____.

She chose this poem format as a way to emphasize what the students have learned about one another through their life box sharing. Keeping in mind third- and fourth-graders' need for movement and shorter spans of inactivity, Sandy wanted to include some movement and actions that would encourage pantomiming. Each child who shared his or her life box is called on to fill in the information for his or her three-line stanza. At the end of each stanza, Sandy asks for a movement or motion that the students could do before moving on to the next stanza. The students suggest clapping, snapping their fingers, swaying back and forth, stomping their feet, and calling out "yee ha!" Later, after all the students have shared their life boxes and added their stanzas, she will have them each create their page for a class book, including a collage of items that represent the things they enjoy. She will then bind the book and place it in the class library for all the students to read throughout the year.

After working with the poem, Sandy also wanted to emphasize the theme of working together to become a community and getting to know one another beyond just outside appearances, and thus she chose *The Island of the Skog,* written and illustrated by Steven Kellogg (1973), to read aloud to the students.

Independent Reading

After shared reading, Sandy conducts a minilesson to help her students understand the concept of independent reading and how to choose books from the classroom library. She begins by touring the students around the class library, pointing out how books are arranged by topic, author, and level and how to keep it orderly. She demonstrates the process for borrowing books, modeling how to take the cards out of their assigned pocket on the chart and write down the date and title of the book. She plans to teach them how to choose appropriate books in the next few days. Today she only wants to expose them to the library, allow them to browse and see what is available, and make a first choice on their own. She informs them that during independent reading time they will be visiting the class library in small groups to choose a book and try out the checkout system.

She then discusses with the students the expectations for independent reading time. Although Sandy knows they have been exposed to independent reading before this year, she wants to make sure they understand the purpose and develop the rules for this daily event. After explaining that they will read each day for about 30 minutes, she asks them what they need to read productively. Students respond based on their prior knowledge and develop a list of Responsibilities for Independent Reading. See Table 11.4 for a list of the responsibilities that evolved over time, not the initial responsibilities. Sandy allows the students to develop the list of responsibilities as she guides their ideas, knowing they will be adjusted as new components to independent reading are added, as when reading response is incorporated. Sandy likes students to sit at their tables during this time, as she

Table 11.4   Responsibilities for Independent Reading

1. I will read silently so I do not disturb others.
2. I will choose books I like to read and that are "just right" for me.
3. I will read continuously.
4. I will keep up with my reading records and reading responses.
5. I will conference with my teacher about my reading.

feels she can better monitor their reading and can more easily conference with them on an individual basis. She feels they have created a good beginning list, so she moves them on to beginning independent reading for the first time. She informs them that while they wait for their turn to browse the class library, she will place baskets of books on their tables, and they are to read those until called. She tells them that to help them gauge the length of independent reading time, she will set a timer for 15 minutes. They will be working up to 30 minutes of reading time in the coming month. The students return to their seats and independent reading time begins, with small groups of students rotating in and out of the class library, choosing their first books for independent reading time.

Writing Workshop

Writing workshop begins Day 1 as a means for getting students to see the importance of writing throughout the curriculum and as a focused time to develop writing skills. Again, Sandy gathers the students on the carpet in the large group meeting area. She believes students can stay focused longer when gathered in an intimate setting such as this, and she feels that it is helpful to have students in close proximity to one another so they can "pair and share," a strategy she uses often to encourage all students to share their ideas and have an audience. Sandy begins her first writing workshop minilesson using the ideas she learned during her summer workshop. She asks the students about their previous experiences with writing workshop, knowing that they have had a variety of different experiences, not all of them positive. She wants to help them see the value of writing on a daily basis so they will look forward to writing workshop, knowing that before now they may have dreaded writing.

She decided that she wanted to get the students actually writing first before discussing the format and expectations for writing workshop, so she talks about the fact that they will be writing every day for the entire school year.

"'What will I write about if I have to write every day?' you might be asking yourself," she tells the students. "Today I am going to help you think about this and help you get started making a list of all the things you might write about." She has the overhead projector readied with a blank transparency and pen. She stands near it and begins to engage in using the think-aloud strategy to model the process of generating ideas. She places her name and the date on the top of the paper and explains why she has done this. "I want to make sure I keep a record of all the writing I do this year, so I will make sure I always have the date and my name on each piece of writing I do. I have heard famous writers say that they get their ideas for writing from their own lives and experiences, that their ideas come right from what they do every day. Now, what do I know about that I could write about? What do I do every day that I could maybe write a piece about? I could write about brushing my teeth, since I do it every day. That might be kind of boring, unless I maybe was writing a poem about it, or even a list of instructions for brushing your teeth that an alien to our planet could understand." She continues to think aloud as she writes her list, detailing each item and talking to herself about why it is something she knows about and possibly something about which she could write a piece. Table 11.5 is a list of the topics she brainstormed and shared with her students.

Sandy then instructs her students to think to themselves for a few minutes about some of the things they could write about. She then asks them to turn to a neighbor sitting next to them and each talk about their ideas and why they might be good to write about during writing workshop. Some of the bilingual students speak excitedly to one another in their native languages. Sandy is happy to see this, as they are discussing writing topics that are important to them. A few students are called upon to share their ideas with the class. Sandy feels that hearing a variety of ideas will assist students as they engage in silent writing time for a short while to generate their list. Some ELLs, who are not yet writing much in English, draw pictures to represent their ideas, and Sandy provides them with one-word or short-phrase labels to write under each picture.

Students then are gathered for a group sharetime. Sandy shows them what she has added to her idea list and asks a few students to share some ideas they have generated. She passes out writing folders and tells students to place their lists into their folders and tomorrow they will narrow down their ideas and choose one to begin writing about. To provide further details about writing workshop, she tells them that each day from 11:00 to 12:00 they will engage in writing workshop and will be writing about topics of their choice. She encourages them to always be thinking about writing topics they could use. She shows the students the file boxes labeled with their table numbers and instructs one person from each table to return the folders of the students in their groups. She explains that this is where the folders will be when they are not using them so that they can always be easily found and accessible when writing workshop begins. Further management minilessons and details about how writing workshop works will be shared as students progress through their first pieces of writing in the first few weeks.

Table 11.5

Ms. Cabernathy
September 2

My Writing Ideas

1. Brushing my teeth (poem?)
2. Flowers
3. My favorite books
4. My dog Lewis (told from his point of view)
5. The park by my house and what I like to do there
6. Vacation to the Grand Canyon
7. Sharing a bedroom with my sister when I was young

Integrated Curriculum

Integrated curriculum is the time of the school day where content area study, including social studies, science and health, and other subjects, is integrated with language arts. The first unit of study Sandy has established for her students is "Who are we?" In this unit, the students will explore themselves as individuals, both as a way for Sandy to get to know her students but also to allow them to get to know one another and develop a classroom community. Sharing life boxes was the way this unit of study was initiated on the first day of school. Sandy feels it is important to model fluent reading even within the teaching of content area subject matter and likes to include more than one read-aloud each day if time warrants. Today she chooses to read *Sumi's First Day of School Ever* by Soyung Pak (2003) about a young Korean girl who comes to school for the first time and the only English she knows is "Hi, my name is Sumi." Understandably, she feels lonely and scared and finds school to be a cruel place until her teacher does a number of things to make her feel included. Sandy likes to use this book as part of the Who-We-Are unit to encourage working together and getting to know and accept one another, and as a means for including books that reflect the cultures of the students in her class.

Some of the learning the students will be involved in within this 2-month-long unit includes learning about their own families and investigating the school and the surrounding neighborhood as a community. Students will engage in interviews with their families, school personnel, and neighborhood businesses and organizations. Before the interviews, however, students are taught and practice the many skills of this learning method, including writing and asking open-ended questions, telephone skills to call interviewees for interview appointments, taking abbreviated notes, proper use of a tape recorder to gather information, courtesy skills needed when meeting face to face with interviewees, writing a thank-you note, synthesizing information, and writing a report. As you can see, many of these skills encompass language arts processes as put forth in the IRA/NCTE Standards for the English Language Arts, including reading, spoken, and written language; media and technology use; gathering and synthesizing information, inquiry and research; use of conventions in language; and communicating knowledge. Although this is largely a social studies unit, Sandy's students can only be successful if they ardently use their skill and competence in language arts processes.

On this first day of school, Sandy has her students create semantic maps about themselves, detailing their likes, dislikes, and interests. She models the process using the overhead projector and information about her. As with writing workshop, the students are interested in learning about their teacher, and she capitalizes on this fact by telling them about herself while at the same time teaching the useful organizational technique of semantic mapping or webbing. Figure 11.1 depicts a semantic web that one of her third-grade students created about himself.

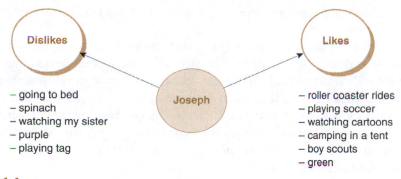

Figure 11.1

At the end of the day, Sandy tells her third- and fourth-grade students that they have homework tonight and every night: read at home! She expects her students to read at least 15 minutes a day and provides a calendar for students to fill out documenting their daily reading that also includes a place for the signature of a parent or guardian to verify. At the end of the month, the students will return their calendars and will engage in tallying the data and using mathematical and graphing skills to reflect on their at-home reading habits and set goals for future reading.

Reflection Journal 11.1

What has Sandy Cabernathy done on the first day of school to ensure that her students understand that language arts and literacy are key components of their learning in her classroom? How does this contribute to the development of a classroom community?

Reflecting on the First Day of School

After the students have left, Sandy sits down to reflect on what she has learned about her students and plan for the following days. She reviews the notes she took while students were sharing their life boxes and thinks about how students interacted with one another and her during group times such as shared reading and read-alouds. She decides that students are learning the ways in which the classroom works and the school day progresses. She is pleased that the students seem willing and eager to engage in language arts learning. She likes that they were enthusiastic as they learned about one another during the sharing of life boxes, and she is able to ascertain which students she might need to provide more guidance with oral presentation skills. Sandy had noticed that the presentations to the whole class had been stressful for the two Hmong students, so she plans more small group sharing sessions, where the students would feel more comfortable speaking English.

She looks over the students' writing they created during writing workshop and makes anecdotal notes related to the strengths she sees in each student's writing. She also documents skills and areas related to writing development that she would like to work on with the students based on initial needs she identifies.

She is happy with the books she chose to use on this first day of school, noting that the students seemed to enjoy the twist in *First Day Jitters.* She plans to find other books that have surprise endings to help students continue to develop their prediction and inference skills.

Assessing Students' Literacy

Sandy helps her students learn and practice self-assessment of their reading through minilessons she conducts during the first week of school as she teaches them to choose books that are at the appropriate level for them to read during independent reading. As the students come into the classroom on the second day of school, she instructs them that one of their morning tasks is to find three books in the classroom library that they will share with the class. She asks them to find a book that is easy for them to read, one that is just right in their opinion, and a book they feel is challenging for them to read. Later, during reading workshop, she conducts a minilesson where the students place their books in the appropriate piles: easy, just right, and challenging. She has them page through them, getting a feel for what their classmates feel is appropriate for their age and grade. She then leads them through a brainstorming session to create a chart listing the general criteria for each level. Sandy makes sure to use the language that the students use in describing the books, as this chart is to be reflective of the strategies they use. Table 11.6 is the chart that her class created.

Another monitoring and self-assessment minilesson Sandy conducts the first week of school to assist her students in choosing appropriate books is the five-finger strategy. She gives them each a bookmark with a picture of a hand on it with the directions, "Read a page in a book and put up a finger for each word that you don't know. Read each finger below to determine if the book is right for you." Each finger on the hand is labeled:

Finger 1 - Easy

Finger 2 - Just Right!

Finger 3 - Challenging

Finger 4 - Very Challenging

Finger 5 - Too Hard

Table 11.6   How We Choose and Level Books

Easy	Just Right	Challenging
• Words are small, short, and common	• Can pronounce words easily	• Longer words
• Book short in length	• Can understand what is happening	• Difficult to understand most of the time
• Many illustrations	• Can read all the words	• Don't know meaning of many of the words
• Big print	• Longer words than in easy books	• High reading level
• Can understand what is happening	• Challenging at times, easy at times	• Smaller print than easy or just right books
• Fairy tales are easy	• Chapter books	• Hard to sound out words
		• Long in length
		• Complicated story
		• Can have dialect or different language

She models the process using adult books, making sure she has chosen books that will reflect each of the fingers' levels, and connects to the previous day's mini-lesson related to easy, just right, and challenging. She requests that each child try this method in the next few days as they are choosing books to read during independent reading. At the end of the week in reading workshop sharetime, the students share their process and discuss how the strategy is useful to them as readers. Sandy encourages students to use this self-assessment technique as one option when choosing books to read. She then adds the five-finger strategy to a chart in the classroom where they have been adding reading strategies they use and learn.

After a couple of days of kidwatching (Goodman & Owacki, 2002) and informally assessing her students engaged in language arts, Sandy feels the students are ready to be formally assessed to ascertain their reading levels. She begins by planning time to meet with each student individually in the next 2 weeks, scheduling 15 minutes per child. Sandy uses an informal reading inventory assessment to determine both the reading levels and reading strategies that each of her students use while reading. Knowing this information allows her to plan instruction for her students to meet their individual needs as well as helps her to group them in short-term groups to target their reading needs.

In assessing students' spelling, Sandy assigns a written response to the prompt "My favorite book/game/food is . . . because . . ." She asks that the students write at least a three-sentence paragraph and provide at least two reasons for their

Table 11.7   Reading and Writing Conference Conduct

- Be prepared to talk about what I am currently reading and writing.
- Bring updated reading and writing records with me.
- Be open to setting goals for myself as a reader and a writer.
- Use strategies for being both a good listener and speaker.

choice. She uses a spelling assessment tool to determine each student's spelling ability through determining the percentage of correctly spelled words. She will conduct similar spelling assessments every 5 weeks or so to provide her with ongoing information about each child's spelling growth and to help inform her spelling curriculum and instruction. Sandy has the prompt translated into both Korean and Spanish for her ELL students who learned to read in their home language. With the help of the translators, she gains a sense of how well the students write in their first language and how they view themselves as writers.

Sandy teaches the students how to conduct themselves in teacher/student reading and writing conferences through modeling both appropriate and inappropriate behaviors. She then leads the students in a brainstorming session to develop a list to hang in the classroom for monitoring themselves during writing workshop (see Table 11.7). Sandy begins having a weekly conference with each student and keeps anecdotal notes about each conference in a three-ring binder that has a page allocated for each student. At the end of each week, she skims over these pages, looking for commonalities in language arts needs to assist her in planning minilessons and small group guided reading and writing lessons.

Typical Language
Arts Learning Schedule

After the first few weeks, Sandy's classroom has a predictable schedule, and the curriculum is running smoothly. See Table 11.8 detailing a typical day in the classroom and how the language arts curriculum plays an integral part in the scope of the day.

Reflection Journal 11.2

What are the elements of Sandy's classroom that appeal to you? Which seem to be the most difficult to employ? Why?

Table 11.8   Typical Day in Ms. Cabernathy's 8- to 9-Year-Old Classroom

9:00–9:15	Settling in, independent reading
9:15–9:45	Word study
9:45–10:15	**Reading Workshop** Community meeting, read-aloud, shared reading
10:15–11:00	Independent reading (guided reading, literature study—not started yet)
11:00–12:00	**Writing Workshop**
Lunch and Recess	
1:00	Math
1:45–3:20	Integrated curriculum and content area learning (science, social studies, health, gym, music, art, etc.)

After getting used to the schedule and routines, Sandy decides it is time to begin implementing guided reading during the reading workshop block because she now has a solid understanding of the students' reading levels and needs. She uses the information she has collected in the first few weeks related to the students' reading levels and interests to begin grouping students. Knowing that guided reading groups are fluid and changing and that students will be a part of many different groups throughout the year, she determines that students can be placed into four groups for their first guided reading experience of the year. Table 11.9 depicts the four groups, the reading need and skill or strategy she has diagnosed, and the text she has chosen to use. Sandy plans to meet with each group four times a week, beginning with Groups 1 and 2 the first week and Groups 3 and 4 the next week, so that each group has sustained teaching and practice with the new strategy they will learn. Although all students begin in guided reading groups, they will also be participating in literature study groups on and off later in the year.

Middle of the School Year

By the middle of the school year, students are engaged meaningfully in reading and writing workshop and have become independent in their ability to make decisions related to reading choices during independent reading and creating writing pieces in writing workshop. Sandy has been using individual conferencing to keep up with students' reading and writing during both daily workshops. Early on she introduced the practice of keeping track of reading and writing development through records students keep and update in their reading and writing record

Table 11.9

	Reading Need	Text to Be Used
Group 1	Understanding how stories flow: understanding the major story elements of problem, events, and resolution	*Encyclopedia Brown Solves Them All* by Donald Sobol • Each chapter has a case to solve, thus helping students to understand a mystery (problem), clues (or events = things that happen), and a resolution (solution to the mystery)
Group 2	Comprehending what is read using the context (surrounding words in a sentence and sentences in a paragraph) and own schema	*Amelia Bedelia Goes Camping* by Peggy Parish • Students will learn that words can have multiple meanings as they use the context clues and background knowledge to decode and understand such things as "pitching a tent" and "hitting the road"
Group 3	Using schema to bring information and understanding to what you are reading	*Hungry, Hungry Sharks* by Joanna Cole • Students, several of them ELLs, will brainstorm what they already know about sharks and create a web containing this information. Many visuals will be added to the chart to support learning. They will be guided to take what they know and apply it to new information, building their schema and comprehending what they read.
Group 4	Monitoring one's own comprehension by asking questions through think-alouds	*Locked in the Library!* by Marc Brown • Sandy demonstrates self-questioning for comprehension through thinking aloud using the text. Students read with partners practicing the strategy.

folder. Students use and bring up to date their records each day and learn that this is an important part of their development as readers and writers. The quality and quantity of most students' work continues to improve throughout the year, as they are given the opportunity to monitor their own progress.

The students' reading records include a list for recording the books that they read during independent reading so that they and Sandy can monitor the number and type of books they are reading. Table 11.10 is a sample of one student's use of this form. Through a series of management minilessons, Sandy models how to record the date they began reading the text, the date they completed reading the text, the title, author, challenge level of the text (easy, just right, or challenging), genre, and personal comments and reflection related to the text. This record serves as a tool both for the students and Sandy to monitor if they are reading at an appropriate pace, level, and variety of genres and as a means to help set personal reading goals.

Another form that students keep in their reading and writing record folders is "What I Need to Work On in My Reading" (Table 11.11). This form is used by the

Table 11.10

Books I've Read - Name: <u>Maggie O.</u>						
Title	**Author**	**Date Began**	**Date Finished**	**Level E/JR/CH**	**Genre**	**Comments**
• *Little Red Riding Hood*	T. Hyman	8/31/04	8/31/04	E	FT	I like this story.
• *The Paper Bag Princess*	R. Munsch	9/1/04	9/1/04	E	FT	Different fairy tale story.
• *The Korean Cinderella*	S. Climo	9/1/04	9/2/04	JR	FT	Same & different story.
• *The Turkey Girl: A Zuni Cinderella*	P. Pollack	9/6/04	9/7/04	JR	FT	Kind of weird.
• *Anansi and the Moss-Covered Rock*	E. Kimmel	9/7/04	9/8/04	E	FT	Funny
• *Mufaro's Beautiful Daughters*	J. Steptoe	9/8/04	9/8/04	JR	FT	Cinderella but different.
• *Amber Brown Wants Extra Credit*	P. Danzinger	9/9/04	9/26/04	JR	Fic	I like Amber books.

Table 11.11   What I Need to Work On in My Reading

Name: <u>Maggie O.</u>

Date	Comments
9/2/04	I need to remember to fill out my reading records every day.
9/9/04	Try to read different books other than fairy tales.
10/1/04	Use the skip-and-return strategy when reading hard words.
10/21/04	I need to write more descriptive comments about the books I read.

students to record their reading goals based on feedback received during one-on-one conferences and things students notice about themselves as readers. As Sandy perceives areas that need emphasis in students reading, or strategies that would benefit them while reading, she will briefly reteach and model its use during the conference, typically using the text students are currently reading. The students will then add this goal to their list as a reminder to use it while reading.

Another part of the students' reading records is the monthly At-Home Reading Record, a graph that includes the months of the school year (extending through July to encourage students to keep up with the reading habit) and records the total number of minutes of completed at-home reading. This serves as a reference and tool for setting goals for future reading as homework. As the students tally their minutes each month and chart them, they are often excited and motivated to read even more. Figure 11.2 is an example of one student's reading for the school year. Although reading much more than the required 15 minutes each day at home, Sandy conferenced with Maggie and talked about the kinds of things that she does besides reading that cause her reading minute totals to fluctuate each month. Upon calculation at the end of the year, Maggie found that she averaged 997 minutes per month, equaling about 33 minutes of reading each day, including weekends. Sandy congratulated her on her reading habit and encouraged her to continue to read each day for personal pleasure.

The writing records that students are taught to use include a running list of pieces they have written during writing workshop, a form to record what they need to work on in their writing similar to their reading record of the same type, and a list of written pieces they have taken to publication. Examples of each of these can be found in Tables 11.12, 11.13, and 11.14.

In order to meet with students for conferencing related to their reading and writing, Sandy developed a schedule where she works with five or six students

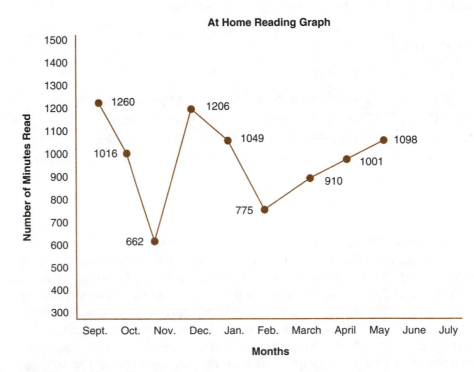

Figure 11.2 At-Home Reading Record

Table 11.12   Pieces I've Written

Name: Maggie O.

Title of Piece	Date	Comments
That's Pretty Much My Vacation	8/30/04	It's about my vacation
The Little Mermaid	9/10/04	Like the movie
Delaware	10/1/04	Trip
The Frog Prince	10/3/04	
My Life as an Ant	10/11/04	Continued again
Hurricane's Coming	10/25/04	Rewriting Dad story
Baticula	11/7/04	
Peace Piece	11/9/04	School contest piece
The Candy Alphabet	11/20/04	Alphabet study

Table 11.13   What I Need to Work on in My Writing

Name: Maggie O.

Date	Comments
9/6/04	I need to work on my capitalization.
10/12/04	I need to remember to reread my pieces to proofread and edit them.
11/1/04	I want to use more sound in my writing to make my pieces more descriptive.

Table 11.14   Pieces I've Published Record

Name: Maggie O.

Title of Piece	Date Published
That's Pretty Much My Vacation	9/20/04
Delaware Trip	10/30/04
Make Peace Work	11/18/04

each day. The schedule is predictable, as she will meet with the same five or six students on the same day each week. This schedule allows both her and her students to be prepared, with the students coming to their conference ready to share what they have been reading or writing and ready to ask for specific assistance if needed. Sandy prepares for them the night before, using the students' records to assist her in planning for what to emphasize in the conferences.

Writing Portfolios

By midyear, students have produced and accumulated numerous writing pieces and have engaged in a lot of reading as evidenced on their Books I've Read record (Table 11.10). Sandy believes it is important for students to reflect on their literacy development and make choices in selecting evidence that reflects their growth. Every other month, students spend time in writing workshop perusing their writing folders, rereading all of their writing (drafts and published pieces), and culling through them to make decisions about which pieces they want to continue working on, which are completed, and which demonstrate strengths and areas needing growth. The pieces they feel are finished are filed in a Completed Writing folder. Sandy wants students to keep all their writing at school so that they can reread and possibly go back to work on prior writing throughout the year. Sandy has students reflect on how they feel their writing has progressed as a way to help them set goals for their writing and provide direction with where they want to go with their writing topics and skills.

Author Study

A part of the language arts curriculum that Sandy and her students thoroughly enjoy is the author study. Working from her ever-growing knowledge of appropriate and enticing authors for her third- and fourth-grade students, she chooses the first author for the class to study. This year she has chosen to begin the year with Eve Bunting and her books, since she has such a wide range of work that spans many topics, interests, and reading levels. The books she has chosen to bring into the classroom are mostly Bunting's picture books, so that all of the students feel comfortable with the format of the texts and the perceived ease of reading these books (see Table 11.15). This author's work is especially helpful for her ELLs, as the illustrations are vivid and provide additional prompts to aid in predicting and comprehending text. Sandy has dedicated a corner of the classroom library to display the books and a trifold poster she created that details highlights of Bunting's life, accomplishments, and writing information. She has included photographs of Eve Bunting to provide students with a visual of the author; graphics that highlight themes in her books, including the Statue of Liberty, as many of her books' themes include various types of freedom; an outline map of Ireland where Bunting was born; pictures of various family configurations signaling the element of family and community; and pictures of animals and nature, representing the ecological and naturalistic themes in many of her books. Sandy feels that her students are sure to find a topic of interest in Bunting's books. As well, the books are illustrated by different illustrators, and therefore she can help them learn more about art and design elements and various artistic styles as she uses the books for interactive read-alouds.

Table 11.15   A Sampling of Some of Bunting's Books Used in the Author Study

Butterfly House Illustrated by Greg Shed	*Smoky Night* Illustrations by David Diaz
Cheyenne Again Illustrated by Irving Toddy	*Ducky* Illustrations by David Wisniewski
Can You Do This, Old Badger? Illustrated by LeUyen Pham	*I Have an Olive Tree* Illustrations by Karen Barbour
The Days of Summer Illustrated by William Low	*Jin Woo* Illustrations by Chris Soentpiet
A Day's Work Illustrated by Ronald Himler	*A Picnic in October* Illustrations by Nancy Carpenter
The Day the Whale Came Illustrations by Scott Menchin	*Sunshine Home* Illustrations by Diane De Groat
December Illustrations by David Diaz	*The Summer of Riley* (novel)

Students are introduced to an author's work through the read-alouds that Sandy leads at least three times a week focused solely on Eve Bunting. As they read the books as a class, they will create a chart that compares various elements of Bunting's work, especially focusing on their themes.

She also conducts book talks that highlight Bunting's books, inviting students to choose these books to read independently. One requirement during the study is to read at least three of Bunting's books and write a response in their reading response journals before the author study is complete.

Sandy finds that as the students learn about how an author writes, they often use components of an author's style in their own writing. Students often get topic ideas for their writing as well, as in the example of Kris after reading *Sunshine Home* (Bunting, 1994c), a story of a boy and his family who visit their aging grandmother in a retirement home. Having similar experiences, Kris writes a piece about the fun times he had with his grandfather before he moved into a home where he was limited in his capabilities. *Sunshine Home* helped Kris make text-to-self connections while sharing family memories in a written form.

The last part of the Bunting author study is a celebration of her work, as the students vote on which books they liked the best and the least. They evaluate what makes the books their favorites and complete this first study by reading the class favorite and brainstorming a list of other possible authors they would like to study next.

End of the School Year

Students have learned so much this year. Sandy is pleased with her language arts curriculum and especially the changes in writing workshop she implemented. By this time, things flow smoothly in the language arts curriculum, and the students have shown tremendous growth in their literate ability.

Student Self-Assessment and Goal Setting

Throughout the school year, students used their reading and writing records to reflect on their literacy learning. By now, they have accumulated many pages of records that they organize by date. Sandy provides them with some prompts to assist them in looking for patterns over time and to help them reflect on what they have learned and how they have grown as readers, writers, and language users over the year. The written reflections they complete are a valuable tool for both students' self-assessment and overall assessment for Sandy.

Reading and Writing Workshop Celebrations

Sandy wanted a way to celebrate all of the hard work her students had been doing throughout the year related to language arts and literacy development. They had read many books and had written and published many pieces during writing workshop, as well as during content area learning. She had read about authors' day conferences (Langman, 1990), where students reflect on and celebrate the writing they have done and the skills they have learned through writing workshop. She thought this would be a reflective and celebratory way to self-assess their learning as well as share their growth with others. With preplanning and organizing, Sandy and her students dedicated a morning in late May in which the students celebrated with their families and other school personnel, including the reading specialist, counselor, principal, and school secretaries. Prior to their Literacy Celebration Day, as they deemed it, Sandy's students reviewed all of their reading and writing records from the entire year and culled through all of their written pieces, especially focusing on their published pieces. They then wrote a reflection related to the following questions that they devised together as a class:

1. The types of writing I have done this year are . . .

2. My favorite piece(s) of writing is/are . . . because . . .

3. I read ___ books this year

   ___ Easy books

   ___ Just right books

   ___ Challenging books

4. I read the following genres: . . .

5. My favorite book(s) is/are . . . because . . .

6. My favorite author(s) is/are . . . because . . .

7. One important thing I learned about writing this year that I won't ever forget is . . .

8. One important thing I learned about reading this year that I won't ever forget is . . .

9. About the author/reader (personal information that people will be interested in knowing about me as a famous reader/writer): . . .

These reflections were published and posted on the Literate People bulletin board that all were encouraged to peruse during the celebration. The class voted on three classmates that they wanted to have read a published piece aloud during the celebration.

Time was allocated for favorite books to be read aloud, chart stories and poems, picture books, or portions of novels the class had enjoyed. Prior to the celebration, the class brainstormed lists of their favorites and voted to determine the "best of the best." Of course, no celebration is complete without food, and Sandy and her class planned simple snacks that parents helped to contribute.

The final piece of the celebration had students set goals for themselves as literate people. Throughout the year, Sandy taught a series of minilessons related to goal setting. Drawing on these previously learned strategies, students used the information from the reflections they created before the Literacy Celebration Day and created a written set of goals. Sandy photocopied her students' goals and kept one copy to give to their next year's teacher and sent the original home with the students as a reminder for them. The students were proud of themselves, and the Literacy Celebration Day was an appropriate and exciting way to highlight all of their hard work.

Teacher Reflection and Future Planning

Sandy is pleased with how writing workshop progressed in her classroom this year. She feels that she and her students came a long way further than her former classes, and she credits the time she took over the summer and throughout the year to try out the new components. Although successful, there are a few things she wants to tighten up and modify for next year. One component is the writing workshop minilessons. Although she feels that she did teach a range of skills and strategies to help her students become better writers, she found that many of them needed help throughout the year in getting ideas for writing, since they were writing every day and sometimes the well would run dry. A colleague told her about writer's notebooks and suggested she learn about them, implementing them within the language arts curriculum as a means to alleviate students' problems coming up with writing topics. Currently Sandy has three books—*Lasting Impressions: Weaving Literature Into the Writing Workshop* (Harwayne, 1992), *Notebook Know How: Strategies for the Writer's Notebook* (Buckner, 2005), and a book that her students can read about writer's notebooks, *A Writer's Notebook: Unlocking the Writer Within You* (Fletcher, 1996)—on the top of her "to read" pile over the summer. She is anxious to get started in planning to include this component in her curriculum.

Sandy felt that the end of the year literacy celebration was a tremendous success, and she wants to implement this more than just at the end of the year. She plans to have a literacy celebration at least three times a year, which would be ideal to help students see their growth over time.

A major goal Sandy sets for next year is to include a stronger tie of language arts to the content area curriculum. She does methodically integrate reading and writing into social studies and math but wants to emphasize word work components as her students learn new vocabulary in content area studies. Sandy is pleased with her teaching and her students' learning this year but anxiously looks forward to getting her garden planted, vacationing, and starting to think about next year's students and the language arts learning in which they will engage in her classroom.

End-of-Chapter Reflection

- Sandy is an experienced teacher and is comfortable juggling all of the language arts instruction and components in her classroom. Which areas seem the most challenging to implement and/or plan?

- How does knowing about the developmental stages of your students help in planning language arts instruction?

- What areas of planning language arts instruction and assessment do you feel you want to learn more about for students at the 7- to 9-year-old level?

Planning for Teaching

1. Think about the areas of planning instruction and assessment for 7- through 9-year-old students in language arts that you feel you want to learn more about. There are numerous resources related to teaching and assessing language arts through print, the Internet, and people available for teachers. Search out supplemental resources that could help you further develop your understanding of these components.

2. After reading about how Sandy Cabernathy plans and implements language arts in her third- and fourth-grade classroom, sketch out a rough plan or list of things you want to make sure to include in your future intermediate-level classroom. Share your ideas with peers.

Connections With the Field

- Visit a 7-, 8-, or 9-year-old classroom and observe how language arts plays a role in the curriculum and throughout the typical daily schedule. Compare it to Sandy Cabernathy's classroom. What are the strengths and weaknesses of each classroom?

Student Study Site

The Companion Website for Developing Voice Through the Language Arts

http://www.sagepub.com/dvtlastudy

Visit the Web-based student study site to enhance your understanding of the chapter content and to discover additional resources that will take your learning one step further. You can enhance your understanding of the chapters by using the comprehensive Study Guide, which includes learning objectives, key terms, activities, practice tests, and more. You'll also find special features, such as the Links to Standards from U.S. States and associated activities, Children's Literature Selections, Reflection Exercises, Learning from Journal Articles, and PRAXIS test preparation materials.

References of Children's/Young Adult Literature

Aardema, V. (1991). *Borreguita and the coyote* (P. Mathers, Illus.). New York: Knopf.

Brown, M. (1998). *Locked in the library!* (M. Brown, Illus.). New York: Little, Brown.

Bunting, E. (1994a). *A day's work* (R. Himler, Illus.). New York: Clarion.

Bunting, E. (1994b). *Smoky night* (D. Diaz, Illus.). New York: Harcourt Brace.

Bunting, E. (1994c). *Sunshine home* (D. De Groat, Illus.). New York: Clarion.

Bunting, E. (1995). *Cheyenne again* (I. Toddy, Illus.). New York: Clarion.

Bunting, E. (1996). *Going home* (D. Diaz, Illus.). New York: HarperCollins.

Bunting, E. (1996). *Market day* (H. Berry, Illus.). New York: HarperCollins.

Bunting, E. (1997). *December* (D. Diaz, Illus.). New York: Harcourt Brace.

Bunting, E. (1997). *Ducky* (D. Wisniewski, Illus.). New York: Clarion.

Bunting, E. (1998). *The day the whale came* (S. Menchin, Illus.). New York: Harcourt Brace.

Bunting, E. (1999). *A picnic in October* (N. Carpenter, Illus.). New York: Harcourt Brace.

Bunting, E. (1999). *Butterfly house* (G. Shed, Illus.). New York: Scholastic.

Bunting, E. (1999). *Can you do this, old badger?* (L. Pham, Illus.). New York: Harcourt.

Bunting, E. (1999). *I have an olive tree* (K. Barbour, Illus.). New York: HarperCollins.

Bunting, E. (2001). *The days of summer* (W. Low, Illus.). New York: Harcourt.

Bunting, E. (2001). *Jin Woo* (C. Soentpiet, Illus.). New York: Clarion.

Bunting, E. (2001). *The summer of Riley*. New York: HarperCollins.

Chanko, P. (1998). *Markets* (S. Berger, Illus.). Minneapolis, MN: Sagebrush Press.

Cleary, B. (1982). *Ramona Quimby, age 8* (A. Tiegreen, Illus.). New York: HarperCollins.

Climo, S. (1993). *The Korean Cinderella* (R. Heller, Illus.). New York: HarperCollins.

Cole, J. (1986). *Hungry, hungry sharks* (P. Wynne, Illus.). New York: Random House.

Danneberg, J. (2000). *First day jitters* (J. D. Love, Illus.). Watertown, MA: Charlesbridge Press.

Danzinger, P. (1997). *Amber Brown wants extra credit* (T. Ross, Illus.). New York: Scholastic.

Grossman, P. (1994). *Saturday market* (E. O. Sanchez, Illus.). New York: HarperCollins.

Hyman, T. S. (1983). *Little Red Riding Hood* (T. S. Hyman, Illus.). New York: Holiday House.

Kellogg, S. (1973). *The island of the Skog* (S. Kellogg, Illus.). New York: Puffin.

Kimmel, E. (1988). *Anansi and the moss-covered rock* (J. Stevens, Illus.). New York: Holiday House.

Lewin, T. (1996). *Market!* New York: HarperCollins.

Miranda, A. (1997). *To market, to market* (J. Stevens, Illus.). New York: Harcourt.

Munsch, R. (1988). *The paper bag princess* (M. Martchenko, Illus.). Toronto, Ontario, Canada: Annick.

Pak, S. (2003). *Sumi's first day of school ever* (J. Kim, Illus.). New York: Viking.

Parish, P. (2003). *Amelia Bedelia goes camping* (L. Sweat, Illus.). New York: Harper Trophy.

Pollock, P. (1996). *The turkey girl: A Zuni Cinderella* (E. Young, Illus.). New York: Little, Brown.

Rendon, M. R. (2001). *Farmer's market: Families working together* (C. W. Bellville, Illus.). Minneapolis, MN: Carolrhoda.

Sobol, D. (1992). *Encyclopedia Brown solves them all.* New York: Yearling.

Steptoe, J. (1987). *Mufaro's beautiful daughters* (J. Steptoe, Illus.). New York: Lothrop, Lee & Shepard.

Tabor, N. (1999). *Taste of the Mexican market/Gusto del mercado Mexicano.* Minneapolis, MN: Sagebrush Press.

References of Professional Resources

Buckner, A. (2005). *Notebook know how: Strategies for the writer's notebook.* Portland, ME: Stenhouse.

Fletcher, R. (1996). *A writer's notebook: Unlocking the writer within you.* New York: HarperTrophy.

Goodman, Y., & Owacki, G. (2002). *Kidwatching: Documenting children's literacy development.* Portsmouth, NH: Heinemann.

Harwayne, S. (1992). *Lasting impressions: Weaving literature into the writing workshop.* Portsmouth, NH: Heinemann.

Langman, G. (1990, November). Celebrate with an author's day. *Writing Teacher,* pp. 30–31.

National Council of Teachers of English and the International Reading Association. (1996). *Standards for the English language arts.* Urbana, IL: Author.

Routman, R. (2004). *Writing essentials: Raising expectations and results while simplifying teaching.* Portsmouth, NH: Heinemann.

Taberski, S. (2000). *On solid ground: Strategies for teaching reading K–3.* Portsmouth, NH: Heinemann.

Wood, C. (1997). *Yardsticks: Children in the classroom ages 4–14: A resource for parents and teachers.* Greenfield, MA: Northeast Foundation for Children.

Technology Resources

An interactive Web site that includes resources for all aspects of teaching and learning language arts at the elementary level. Although a subscription is needed to access all the materials and games, there is much to be found for use in a language arts curriculum: http://www.enchantedlearning.com/Home.html

Early Adolescence Language Arts

Joelle Quimby's Eighth-Grade Language Arts Classroom

Context Setting: After reading this chapter, you will be able to

- Identify social, emotional, cognitive, and physical aspects of development of 10- to 13-year-old students related to teaching, learning, and assessing language arts
- Describe the various language arts curriculum components that are appropriate to teach at the 10- to 13-year-old level
- Broadly conceptualize the year-long curriculum and planning necessary for language arts in an eighth-grade classroom

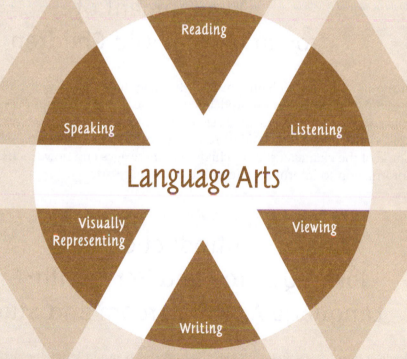

Before We Begin

- Middle school is a time of both physical and emotional change, with students moving toward independence and individuality. How do you feel about working with students at this age level? What do you consider are the challenges a teacher faces? What might be the benefits of working with 10- through 13-year-old students?

Teaching language arts to 10- to 13-year-old children is a rewarding venture. Students of this age are motivated and energetic, and involving them in language arts activities can be a remarkable experience for teachers at this level. As is typical across the country, the curriculum in the middle school that is highlighted in this chapter is largely departmentalized, where the students switch classes for each content area and teachers have special training in their content area. In this chapter we highlight the planning, implementing, and assessing of language arts by Joelle Quimby (who has a minor in English language arts) and one of her eighth-grade language arts classes, beginning with her before-school-year planning through her reflecting on her students' learning and her teaching for the next year. To provide a broader view of teaching 10- to 13-year-old children, interspersed within the chapter are brief vignettes that are a compilation of a number of sixth-grade language arts classrooms used to demonstrate other appropriate methods for teaching and assessing in the language arts curriculum.

Development of 10- to 13-Year-Old Children

Although this chapter highlights eighth-grade students (13-year-olds) and provides a glimpse into sixth-grade students' language arts curriculum (11-year-olds), it is important to understand the basic developmental level of students who are typically housed together in middle schools (Wood, 1997). Therefore, Table 12.1 details some of the characteristics of children at these ages and how teachers can use this information to inform their teaching of language arts.

Introduction to Joelle Quimby and Her Eighth-Grade Language Arts Classroom and Students

Joelle Quimby teaches two eighth- and ninth-grade language arts classes in an urban middle school. She has been teaching for 2 years and finds this age group both invigorating and challenging at times.

Once a week she meets with a team of teachers who share the same students: a social studies teacher, math teacher, science teacher, and herself. Although the program is departmentalized, the team works together to integrate the curriculum and design learning experiences and assessments for the students as much

Table 12.1

10-Year-Old Children	Language Arts Curriculum Connections
• Receptive learners and listeners, enjoy factual information	• Engage in read-alouds daily; include informational book genre
• Enjoy group work and group games	• Include language and word play games
• Need outdoor activity	• Plan for outdoor reading and writing experiences and activities
• Like joining clubs	• Involve in newspaper club, foreign language clubs, book clubs
• Conscientious, hardworking, follow directions easily, organized	• Design integrated language arts/content areas projects
• Memorization is easy at this time	• Involve students in plays, choral reading, recitation activities
• Enjoy independent reading time, read lengthy books	• Allow for 30 minutes of independent reading time daily
• Writing topics: friends, adventures	• Explore adventure genre and authors, minilessons on using graphic organizers to plan elements of an adventure story

11-Year-Old Children	Language Arts Curriculum Connections
• Girls hit adolescence and a growth spurt, begin forming cliques, awkwardness of adolescence begins	• At times, allow students to choose their partners to encourage comfort with learning, both same-sex and mixed-gender groupings
• Easily embarrassed, frustrated, moody, sensitive	• Limit student reading aloud in front of others, break large projects into smaller pieces so success is seen in smaller steps
• Need and enjoy authentic learning experiences in the curriculum	• Research, field trips that tie in with content area studies
• Motivated to learn new areas of knowledge (foreign language, music)	• Capitalize on the visual and symbolic nature of music and language
• Love to argue and debate, begin to see world from multiple perspectives	• Engage in variety of debate and perspective-sharing experiences on topics related to current events, social issues
• Enjoy humor, puzzles, word games	• Include jokes, riddles, word play books in classroom library, use for read-aloud and breaks in instruction
• Can establish and modify rules	• Teach grammar rules, encourage finding "exceptions" to the rules
• Longer reading assignments are appropriate	• Allow for sustained reading periods, 30 minutes or longer
• Increase use of informational books and biography	• Stock classroom library with variety of informational books and biography and use as models during read-aloud and writing workshop
• Writing topics: fantasy, science fiction	• Expose students to these genres in books as models for own writing

12-Year-Old Children	Language Arts Curriculum Connections
• At times can be both responsible and irresponsible	• Make good tutors/buddies for young children
• Growth spurts occur for both boys and girls	• Incorporate word puzzles and trivia games
• Enjoy challenges, physically and academically	• Have students develop rubrics and criteria for assignments and projects

(Continued)

Table 12.1 (Continued)

- Capable and interested in making rules, setting criteria for assignments
- Enjoy group sports and clubs
- Peers become more important than adults
- Word and language play, focusing on the double meaning of words of interest
- Conversation with peers and adults is important
- Interested in current events, social justice issues
- Can sustain activity for longer time periods

- Both serious and playful

- Work better when content is integrated rather than isolated

- Enjoy a variety of reading materials, including trade books, magazines, newspapers
- More willing to revise writing
- Writing topics: teen issues

- Engage students in creating and writing a class or school newspaper
- Peer editing and revision can be taught and encouraged

- Conferencing during reading and writing workshop is a good time for conversation with an adult in a meaningful context
- Include activity with and reading of newspaper and current events

- Set aside blocks of time for sustained activity such as independent reading and computer use time; longer projects and assignments done over time
- Engage in group activity such as drama and reader's theater, debate; encourage performance for others
- Work with content area teachers (social studies, science, math, health) to incorporate meaningful reading, writing, listening, and speaking activities
- Build up classroom library to include a variety. Use a variety of genres in literature study and book clubs
- Encourage revision after sharing writing pieces with others

13-Year-Old Children

- Can be sensitive, withdrawn, confused, apprehensive, judgmental
- Great difference between boys and girls both emotionally and physically
- Need social interaction to stimulate them intellectually and cognitively
- Music becomes important
- Peer pressure is highly evident
- Use a lot of slang and sarcasm
- Feel journaling reveals too much of themselves, shy away from this
- Write more proficiently than they speak
- Enjoy exploring multiple perspectives of issues
- Enjoy read-alouds, especially related to social issues and issues of conformity
- Capable of revising their writing

- Writing topics: social justice and injustice, being included and excluded

Language Arts Curriculum Connections

- Capitalize on their self-critical nature by utilizing self-assessment related to abilities in language arts (writing, speaking)
- Encourage both same-sex and mixed-gender groupings

- Build in literature discussion, book clubs, opportunities for debate

- Work in song lyrics; listening to music, writing lyrics and poetry
- Group work can result in high levels of interaction
- Teach and encourage writing of essays, letters to the editor
- If using journals, develop ways to ensure privacy

- Create many opportunities for oral communication
- Include discussions and debates within language arts
- Include read-alouds and activity with reading the newspaper and current events
- Teach revision methods, provide appropriate resources to revise writing
- Focus on critique of writing and not personal criticism

as possible. There is adequate communication between the members of the team that assists them with their teaching and the students with learning.

We follow Joelle and one of her classes of eighth-grade students each day for a 55-minute block of time throughout the year. Her class is made up of 25 students: 12 males and 13 females. A majority of the students are of Latino and African American origin, seven are Hmong, and two are Caucasian. Half of the students in Joelle's class are English language learners (ELLs), and five of the students have diagnosed learning differences. There is an ELL teacher who works with the students, primarily on language-arts-related instruction in their native language. Some are pulled out for a part of the class period, which Joelle finds challenging. To ensure that these students get enough quality language arts instruction in English, she will often pull them together as a group to work with while the rest of the class is engaged in independent activities such as writing workshop. She believes that a student's home language should be accepted and valued, understanding that this can assist them in acquiring English as a second language (Cummins, 1984). One way she practices this is by incorporating their ideas in additional comments, using standard English form, often followed by a question related to the meaning of the student's comment (Strickland, Ganske, & Monroe, 2002).

Planning for the School Year and Language Arts Curriculum

Many of Joelle's students are struggling readers and writers, and due to this fact, they try to avoid reading and writing as much as possible. She knows that they need to be motivated to practice and use their literacy skills, since avoidance causes students to read and write less, when what they really need is to be practicing more. This is a goal she has set for herself this year, as she wants to ensure that she is meeting the needs of all her students as fully as possible. To assist in motivating her students, she provides a large collection of reading materials that are interesting and engaging to 13-year-old students and written at a range of reading levels so that all students can easily access the texts. She includes magazines, newspapers, brochures and pamphlets, short story collections, poetry, and picture books in the classroom library collection. She knows that for students to be motivated, they need to feel in control and proficient as readers and writers. Her goal is to develop a risk-free and engaging classroom environment that includes collaborative activities and appropriately challenging tasks (Strickland et al., 2002).

Another way Joelle carefully works at developing a positive and motivating classroom culture is by allowing many opportunities for student choice within the language arts curriculum. She plans to begin the year providing numerous mini-lessons that will assist her students in choosing books to read independently that are appropriate for them as readers. During writing workshop, she wants to encourage students to choose their own topics and genres about which to write in addition to having some assigned topics and pieces.

She plans to incorporate many opportunities for students to know more books and authors and be exposed to books in various settings and situations. One way she will address this is by inviting the school librarian and others to participate in frequent book talks and author talks to entice students to read good books through sharing short commercials about them and the authors that students enjoy at this level. Eventually, she wants to encourage students to lead book talks related to good books that they have read. Students will also be encouraged to share books through a student book exchange program she plans to implement, where once a month they can bring in books they own that they would like to exchange with their classmates as a way to rotate their personal book collections. She knows that some students do not own books of their own, and she will provide them with a book or two that she receives free with bonus points from book clubs that she and her students order throughout the year, to allow everyone to be a part of the exchange.

Joelle knows that it is important to model an appreciation and use of literacy in her own daily life and that of others in the community. She plans to do this by reading aloud quality, engaging literature to her students daily, inviting other readers from the community such as the students' parents, the school principal, the corner storekeeper, and local personalities such as the sports reporter from the local newspaper, and modeling writing about her own experiences and elements of her life when teaching minilessons in writing workshop. Along with modeling literate behavior, she knows that it is imperative that her students engage in large amounts of literacy-related social interaction to get and keep them motivated as language learners. One way she intends to incorporate this is through frequent use of the "Think, pair, share" (Kagen, 1994) strategy discussed later in this chapter.

Sixth-Grade Vignette: Struggling Readers at the Middle School Level

Leticia Smith's sixth-grade language arts classroom includes a number of struggling and reluctant learners. She is careful to gear her instruction to meet the needs of these students. She makes sure that her classroom library collection contains literature that is of high interest for her students and includes low vocabulary and predictable text where possible. By providing texts that are geared for her students' literacy levels and interests, she feels they are more apt to read and continue developing their skills as readers. Following is a sampling of texts she includes in her collection:

Picture Books:

- *Pink and Say* by Patricia Polacco
- *Weslandia* by Paul Fleishman

Chapter Books/Novels

- *I Hadn't Meant to Tell You This* by Jacqueline Woodson
- *Soccer Duel* by Matt Christopher (and others by Christopher that include a sports focus)
- *Holes* by Louis Sachar
- *Stone Fox* by J. R. Gardner
- *The Friendship and the Gold Cadillac* by Mildred Taylor (and others by Taylor that include the same characters and setting)
- *Darkness Before Dawn* by S. Draper

Fairy Tale Variants

- *The Time Warp Trio* by John Sciezska
- *The Wolf at the Door and Other Retold Fairy Tales* by E. Datlow and T. Windling
- Cinderella Stories

  - *Cinderella: An Art Deco Love Story* by L. and D. Roberts
  - *Sootface: An Ojibwa Cinderella* Story by R. San Souci
  - *Little Gold Star/Estrellita de oro: A Cinderella Cuento Retold in Spanish and English* by J. Hayes
  - *Jouanah: A Hmong Cinderella* by J. R. Coburn
  - *Lily and the Wooden Bowl* by A. Schroeder
  - *Sumorella* by S. Takayama

Nonfiction/Informational Books

- *Things I Have to Tell You: Poems and Writings by Teenage Girls* by B. Franco
- *Born Beautiful: The African American Teenager's Complete Beauty Guide* by A. Books
- *The Guy Book: An Owner's Manual* by M. Jukes
- *Caught by the Sea: My Life on Boats* by G. Paulsen

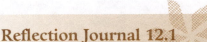

Reflection Journal 12.1

What are some ways that you might motivate 11- through 13-year-old students who are not necessarily interested in language arts? What would have motivated you as a 13-year-old student?

Overall Curriculum Planning

Joelle likes to plan her school year by focusing on the language arts content and skills she wants to teach and the students learn for each quarter. At the end of last year, the eighth-grade teachers discussed the overall goals they had for their students using both state and district standards. Each teacher then added goals related to their content area. This integrated planning assists Joelle in setting the curriculum for English language arts. She looks at each 8-week quarter and plans a 3-week unit focused on reading, 3 weeks focused on writing, a week to correlate with school-theme-based curriculum, and 1 week of test-taking strategy teaching and learning. Table 12.2 shows an outline of her basic planning.

Although reading and writing are integrated into the daily curriculum, Joelle organizes each quarter in the described manner to ensure an in-depth emphasis on reading and writing units. She feels 3 weeks is an appropriate amount of time to fully study literature at this level and learn about and practice writing in predetermined genres. By organizing around a writing and reading focus for each quarter, students are exposed to more reading and writing than done typically on a daily basis. Table 12.3 shows what each 55-minute class period looks like in general, with the bulk of the class devoted to language workshop, where a variety of activities take place that integrate all the language arts.

Reading Program and Foci

Joelle's reading program is part of the language workshop she runs in her classroom, where students are involved in a variety of reading-related activities and within a variety of groupings: individual, paired, small group, and whole class. Her goals for her students as readers are influenced by the state and national language arts standards related to reading and include the following:

- Reading by choice and often, having confidence in oneself as a reader
- Learning and applying an understanding of literary analysis when reading fiction
- Reading and appreciating poetry and other genres
- Competently using effective reader strategies while reading all texts in all content areas
- Connecting personally to what is read and sharing one's responses with others while effectively listening to others' responses

Table 12.2

	Quarter 1	Quarter 2	Quarter 3	Quarter 4
Reading Focus (3 Weeks)	Reading in our daily lives How language workshop runs during reading study	Engaging in book clubs and literature discussion—reading response	Biography and autobiography (literary elements: setting, character, theme)	Poetry and drama (reader's theater)
Writing Focus (3 Weeks)	Writing in our daily lives How language workshop runs during writing study	Responding to reading through writing	Memoir writing Using technology to share one's writing (iMovie book reviews and/or autobiographies)	Poetry writing
School- or Grade-Level Theme Focus (1 Week)	Who are we? Celebrating our diversity	Our school (how to improve it, celebrating its uniqueness)	Social activism in our neighborhood (the power of language)	Social activism in our neighborhood and beyond
Test-Taking Strategies (1 Week)	Understanding reading in the classroom versus reading required by tests	Reading multiple-choice questions Understanding rubrics (writing)	Responding to writing prompts, writing tests	Short answer and extended response question strategies

Table 12.3   Daily/Weekly Schedule—55-Minute Block

5–8 Minutes	Warm Up	
10 Minutes	Read-Aloud	
10 Minutes	Minilesson	Monday: Spelling/Word Study Tuesday: Reading Wednesday: Grammar Thursday: Writing Friday: Varied, based on student need/current project

22 Minutes	Language Workshop	Reading Focus (First 3 weeks of quarter)
		Writing Focus (Second 3 weeks of quarter)
		Theme Focus (Third week of quarter)
		Test-Taking Focus (Fourth week of quarter)
		Teacher Roles:
		    Joelle works with individuals, small groups (reading, writing)
		Student Roles:
		    Independent work: reading, writing, spelling, grammar activities
		    Partner/Group work: literature discussions, partner reading and writing

5 minutes	Sharing/Wrap Up	

Much of the reading component of the language art curriculum consists of using authentic literature in the form of shared texts and text sets. She has accumulated multiple copies of texts for literature groups/book clubs, as well as small sets of texts that students can follow along in while she reads aloud. She knows that many of her students need more modeling and practice with strategies for comprehending texts that they read, and therefore she builds in time for them to see her using the strategies during minilessons related to strategies, read-alouds, and shared reading experiences.

During the 3 weeks of reading emphasis in the language workshop, the students will be engaged in independent reading, literature discussion groups, and focused guided language groups as needed. Joelle must stay organized to keep all students' needs met, and she uses a variety of anecdotal records to assist her with this. Table 12.4 shows her planning for instruction for her students during

Table 12.4   Planning for Language Block: Reading Focus

Week 1	Week 2	Week 3
Independent Work: (When not in group activities)		
• Grammar/Vocabulary/Spelling Activities		
• Independent Reading		
• Reading Response Activities		
• Partner Reading		
Literature Discussion Group • David • Pa • Amanda • Eric • Rita • Houa Text: *The Watsons Go to Birmingham* (C. P. Curtis, 1997) Literature Discussion Group • Tara • Pao • Princess • Sarah • Jesus • Sher Text: *From the Notebooks of Melanin Sun* (J. Woodson, 1997)	Literature Discussion Group • Rattanasavanh • Tony • Donna • Justin • Rick • Kerala • Drew Text: *Monster* (W. D. Myers, 2001)	Literature Discussion Group • Odemaris • Shoua • Keisha • Dan • Steve • Maria Text: *Esperanza Rising* (P. M. Ryan, 2000)
Guided Language Groups *Group 1* (Students: Keisha, Steve, Maria, Justin) **Focus:** How characters change *Group 2* (Students: Rick, Tony) **Focus:** Reading through a portion of text, then asking if it made sense	**Guided Language Groups** *Group 1* (Students: Shoua, Sarah, Odemaris) **Focus:** Visualizing *Group 2* (Students: Shoua, Amanda, David, Sher, Princess) **Focus:** Figurative language	**Guided Language Groups** *Group 1* (Students: Eric, Drew, Tony, Kerala, Tara) **Focus:** Inferring main ideas *Group 2* (Students: Rattanasavanh, Jesus, Pa, Rita) **Focus:** Text to self-connections

the 3-week reading focus during the language workshop portion of class during Quarter 2 of the school year.

Joelle likes to have each student take part in a literature discussion group for 1 week during this 3-week time span. These groups are usually formed by interest and by allowing students to choose the text they will be reading. By midyear, the students become very self-reliant and work well within their literature discussion groups without assistance, thus freeing up Joelle. During each week she plans to work with two to three groups of students she has determined need extra guidance in a variety of skills and strategies, such as practicing comprehension strategies, understanding components of nonfiction text, and others. She will often use texts for these guided language groups that the students are familiar with (for example, those previously used for read-alouds) so that she can maximize the teaching and learning time within these groups. When students are not in literature discussion groups or guided language groups, they are working independently, mostly reading independently, writing responses to what they have read, or completing assigned grammar, vocabulary, and spelling activities.

Sixth-Grade Vignette: Individualized Spelling Program

Leticia Smith's sixth graders partake in an individualized spelling program that is modeled after the buddy system spelling program (Fountas & Pinnell, 2001). Students learn spelling principles and ways of applying spelling knowledge to their writing through a 5-day cycle of activities. On Monday, Leticia begins the cycle with a spelling minilesson. The focus of the current week is on understanding the Greek roots of *bi* (two) and *morph* (form) and their meaning in words. She wants the students to look for these roots to assist in understanding word meaning.

Students choose words for their lists, including a few that have the characteristics from the minilesson (words that contain *bi* and *morph*) and others from their personal word lists generated from their own writing during writing workshop and other words suggested by Leticia. Each word is written on an index card, and students practice spelling them using rubber or foam stamps and magnetic letters and by writing them out and spelling them aloud.

On the second day, students work on a "have a go at it" sheet that contains four columns, where the first two columns are for students to write the word two times, spelling it from memory and trying out different

(Continued)

(Continued)

letter/sound configurations. This practice encourages students to look deeply at words and determine spelling using word knowledge they already possess. In the third column, the students look at the correct spelling and write it down. The fourth column provides the students another opportunity to write the word correctly, copying it from the previous column.

On Day 3, the students pair up with their spelling buddies and take a pretest, self-correcting when complete, as a way to continue to work with the words. During the fourth day of the cycle, the students are to make connections to their words, finding other words with similar sounds in them, rhyming words, and other words with similar meanings. These activities help them connect their words to others and see patterns and similarities, as well as expanding their vocabulary. On the last day, spelling buddies give each other a final spelling test, which is corrected by Leticia. She finds that this spelling program does more for her students than a traditional program where the teacher (or textbook) assigns the spelling words and nothing truly meaningful is done with them. By capitalizing on the students' need for individuality, social interaction, and choosing words that are meaningful to them, students do well on the tests and retain their new spelling knowledge longer than if they just learned them as a means to complete the final test.

Writing Program and Foci

The writing program is also situated within the language workshop portion of the class and, like reading, includes a wide variety of writing-related activities. During the 3 weeks that the curriculum centers on writing, the workshop begins with a minilesson or activity specifically related to the daily writing focus. In each period there is a specific writing project that students work on independently or in pairs or sometimes small groups. During the first quarter, Joelle's writing focus is writing in daily life, and her minilessons will focus on helping the students understand the writing they do on a daily basis and its importance. They are taught how to do writing that is essential for daily living, such as making lists; writing out directions in a clear, concise manner; filling out applications (for jobs, health forms); the proper way to write out checks; and other important writing tasks. The project for the first week is for students to pay attention to the writing that guides their daily life and that of others and write up an informative essay detailing these things. Tying in to career education, the students research an occupation they are interested in and determine what types of writing are needed. They are taught how to write an article describing the occupation and the forms of writing that are essential to complete this role.

In addition, during the first quarter of school, the students need to understand how the language workshop will run while they are engaged in the 3-week writing study. They learn (a) the practical components of the activities they will be doing; (b) the process they will engage in during writing; (c) where to find and access writing materials and tools such as thesauri, dictionaries, and telephone books; and (d) expectations for working independently and with others.

The rest of the year will include 3 weeks of a writing focus each quarter. The second quarter's emphasis will be on the various ways to respond in writing to what is read, and the third quarter will engage students in writing their own memoirs or autobiographies and creating an iMovie video production (Apple Computer, 2005) to share their writing with others. Finally, the fourth quarter will engage students in writing poetry after they have learned about and read poetry during the prior 3 weeks.

School- or Grade-Level Theme Foci

Joelle's school's philosophy states that students should have opportunities to learn from one another across grade and age levels. Therefore, the school has instituted a schoolwide theme for one week each quarter that runs across all content areas. The teachers have collaboratively determined the major themes, making sure that they cut across all content areas and would be interesting for 11- to 14-year-old students to explore. They are largely based on who the students are, diversity, and becoming socially active within their neighborhood and larger community. At the end of each semester, schoolwide celebrations of the theme take place so that the students can share what they have learned and accomplished with one another.

During the second quarter, Joelle's plans are to engage her students in a variety of language-arts-related learning situations around the theme Our School—Celebrating Its Uniqueness and How to Improve It. Some of the activities the students will partake in include interviewing a range of students related to their opinions and ideas about the school community and writing and producing a play to share their findings. This play will be performed during the end-of-semester schoolwide celebration.

Test-Taking Strategies Foci

During the last week of each quarter, Joelle dedicates time to an in-depth study of test-taking strategies. Understanding that her students have been and will be required to take standardized tests throughout their educational careers, she believes it is important to directly teach students the keys to taking tests to help them be confident with this skill. During the first quarter, she wants students to learn about the different types of reading they must do when taking tests versus the reading they do in their daily lives and in school. She will

Sixth-Grade Vignette: Pairing With Little Buddies

The sixth graders in Kim Xiong's class spend time each week with their first-grade little buddies, a connection Kim made with their teacher, Karen Klaus. Both groups of students enjoy this time together and look forward to Friday mornings when they get together. Kim believes that having her sixth graders work one on one with beginning readers and writers will benefit not only the first-grade students but help her students strengthen their own language arts skills at the same time. Every week they begin with a 10-minute read-along, where the big buddy sixth graders model reading a variety of books that are at or just above the first-grade students' reading level. The sixth graders were taught how to encourage the first graders to join in and read along, as well as how to ask questions they have about their own books to help enhance comprehension. Kim's sixth graders read through the books before visiting their buddies and plan for general questions and discussion.

The rest of the 30-minute block is spent in a variety of activities that include language arts such as writing a story together, role-playing characters from a book, illustrating a story that was written by the big buddy, whole-group-shared readings of poetry or rhymes that are then practiced and illustrated in buddy pairs, and engaging in various art projects related to books or well-loved characters.

This buddy time assists sixth graders in being role models of literate behavior and allows the first graders to engage in language arts activities in a motivating and engaging manner.

have the students compare samples of tests and pieces of writing they encounter in books, advertisements, and other media. She will teach them ways to pay attention to the details and key words to look for when reading tests so that they can feel more confident with their answers and better decipher the instructions and purpose of the standardized tests they will be required to complete. The following three quarters of the year will include learning about how multiple-choice questions are constructed, how to create and use a rubric for assessment purposes, how to respond effectively to writing assessment prompts, and how to read and answer short-answer and extended-response questions on tests.

This last week of each quarter is an important piece of Joelle's language arts curriculum, as all standardized tests require students to be effective readers and often writers. She will integrate understanding and practice with content area tests as well as show students that reading and writing are integral to being successful with test taking in general.

Grammar Integration

Grammar is an important component of the eighth-grade language arts curriculum, and Joelle feels it is best taught in an authentic manner, that is, applying grammar concepts to actual reading and writing versus completing a series of isolated worksheets or grammar lessons, so that students will see the importance of correct grammar usage. One way she does this is through minilessons done on a weekly basis, but she will also integrate lessons and the application of grammar into all reading and writing activities as they arise within her class. One way students practice their growing grammar skills is through the writing activities they engage in and often during the warm-up at the beginning of each class. Some of the concepts that are integrated throughout the year include (a) capitalization and punctuation rules such as appositives and phrases/clauses in a series, (b) parenthetical expressions, (c) parts of speech review, (d) pronoun antecedent agreement, (e) commonly confused words, and (f) adjective and adverb usage.

Newspaper Club

Many varied clubs within the school hold meetings on a weekly basis outside of class time. Joelle is the faculty adviser of the newspaper club, and she opens it up to any student who is interested in writing and producing a school newspaper. She finds that many of her eighth-grade students join, and she uses this time as a way to extend their language arts learning through a clublike environment. The kinds of items typically included in the newspaper are major articles related to topics of interest and relevance to the school in general, articles about students and teachers with various talents and experiences, interviews with students and community people, poetry written by club members and others who submit jokes and puzzles, and activity highlights from the scope of clubs, to name a few.

Joelle helps the students research, write, and edit the newspaper, which is published once a month. She works at encouraging the students to be as responsible for all stages as possible, with her role being final editor and technical support person. Digital cameras help add visuals to the newspaper, and the paper is designed using Microsoft Publisher software (Microsoft Corporation, 2005). The newspaper is photocopied and made available to each student and staff member in the school. Joelle believes this club is an authentic way for students to use their language arts skills meaningfully, and she encourages all students to take part in this monthly venture.

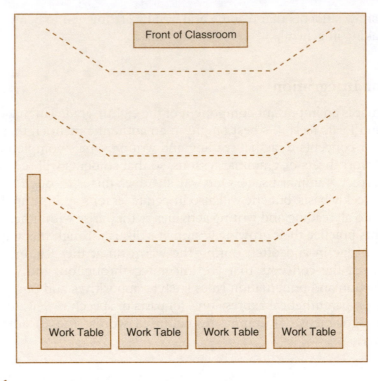

Figure 12.1

Classroom Setup and Materials for Language Arts Curriculum

Joelle sets up her classroom so that students can interact with one another easily yet have a personal space for independent work. Using a semicircle shape, she arranges students' desks so that two are placed together and eight are arranged per row (Figure 12.1). Since she knows that interaction and having choices are important to 13-year-old students, she allows students to pick their seats, provided they are conducive to positive work habits.

Four worktables sit at the back of the room for small group meeting space and instructional time either for Joelle to work with students or for students to work with one another. Along the left side wall, she places a supply table that includes writing materials that students have free access to such as paper, writing instruments, dictionaries, and thesauri. Built-in bookcases line the right side wall, housing the amply stocked classroom library. After learning the classroom checkout system, students have open access to these materials as well. Over the past 2 years, Joelle has built up her collection, especially emphasizing multicultural literature and books emphasizing social issues, as she has found that eighth-grade students are particularly interested in this. She uses this and other literature to hook the students' interests from Day 1 and makes sure she has a wide range of genres, formats, and reading levels reflected in this collection. A small sampling of her collection of picture books appropriate for older readers are found in Table 12.5. Table 12.6 provides a short list of some of the well-loved novels, poetry, fiction,

Table 12.5   Literature for Older Readers: Picture Book Format

Text Title	Author/Illustrator	Comments
Rose Blanche	Gallaz, C. Innocenti, R. (Illus.)	Holocaust
Faithful Elephants: A True Story About Animals, People and War	Tsuchiya, Y.	Impact of war on animals
We Are All in the Dumps With Jack and Guy: Two Nursery Rhymes With Pictures	Sendak, M.	Social issues
Gawain and the Green Knight	Shannon, M. Shannon, D. (Illus.)	Retelling of the meeting of a knight in King Arthur's court
Reach for the Moon	Abeel, S. Murphy, C. R. (Illus.)	Poetry by seventh-grade girl with learning disabilities
Wilma Unlimited: How Wilma Rudolph Became the World's Fastest Woman	Krull, K. Diaz, D. (Illus.)	Biography
Too Far Away to Touch	Newman, L. Stock, C. (Illus.)	Relationship between a girl and her uncle with AIDS
Alia's Mission: Saving the Books of Iraq	Stamaty, M. A.	Hiding of 30,000 books to escape destruction during bombing of Iraq
Animalia	Base, G.	Complex alphabet book
Starry Messenger	Sis, P.	Galileo's biography
Dia's Story Cloth: The Hmong People's Journey to Freedom	Cha, D. Thao Cha, C. (Illus.)	One woman's travel to freedom. Illustrations stitched in story cloth
The Story of Ruby Bridges	Coles, R. Ford, G. (Illus.)	Ruby's story of going to a segregated school
The Great Migration	Lawrence, J.	Migration of southern U.S. African American migrating north

and nonfiction in her class library as well. Please note that many of the authors listed have other books that are excellent for middle school students, and helping students move to another book by a favored author is an effective way to keep them reading.

Joelle has two large bulletin boards in her classroom, one that she uses to post student writing and other language arts work. The second bulletin board she uses to post language-related news items, posters related to language arts skills and strategies (e.g., the steps to the writing process, the 100 most commonly misspelled words, hints for using the 6+1 Traits of Writing rubric), and photographs and biographical information of popular authors. She encourages students to add to this bulletin board whenever they have language-related news or information that they would like to share.

Table 12.6   Sampling of Literature for Older Readers: Fiction, Nonfiction, Poetry

Nothing but the Truth	Avi	Fiction
Weetzie Bat	Block, F. L.	Fiction
The Chocolate War	Cormier, R.	Fiction
The Redwall Series (Redwall)	Jacques, B.	Fantasy
A Wrinkle in Time	L'Engle, M.	Science Fiction/Fantasy
Somewhere in the Darkness	Myers, W. D.	Fiction
His Dark Materials, Book I (Series)	Pullman, P.	Fantasy
Nightjohn	Paulsen, G.	Historical Fiction
Dicey's Song	Voigt, C.	Fiction
The Lord of the Rings	Tolkien, J. R. R.	Fantasy
The Pigman	Zindel, P.	Fiction
The Complete Collected Poems of Maya Angelou	Angelou, M.	Poetry
Joyful Noise: Poems for Two Voices	Fleischman, P.	Poetry
This Same Sky	Nye, N. S.	Poetry
Prince of the Fairway: The Tiger Woods Story	Teague, A.	Nonfiction/Biography
Fannie Lou Hammer: A Voice for Freedom		
Heart to Heart: New Poems Inspired by Twentieth-Century Art	Fiorelli, J. E. Abrams, H. N.	Nonfiction/Biography Poetry/Art
19 Varieties of Gazelle: Poems of the Middle East	Nye, N. S.	Poetry
Love That Dog		
Stop Pretending: What Happened When My Big Sister Went Crazy	Creech, S. Sones, S.	Novel in verse Novel in verse
Kira-Kira		
An American Plague: The True and Terrifying Story of the Yellow Fever Epidemic of 1793	Kadohata, C. Murphy, J.	Novel Nonfiction

Sixth Grade Vignette: Using the "Say Something" Strategy

Jay Costello's class of sixth-grade students effectively engages in oral response using the "Say Something" strategy (Short, Harste, & Burke, 1996). This strategy provides an interactive format for students to initiate conversation about texts and to encourage oral communication. Jay taught the students how to use it early in the school year through modeling, and the students use it frequently during paired reading or small group literature discussions. Today the students are learning the strategy of identifying important ideas and words while reading nonfiction texts. Cal and Aiden are reading *Sugaring Time* (1983) by Kathryn Lasky while practicing and using the Say Something strategy.

Aiden [quietly reading aloud]	The sugar sap is made in the tree primarily for its own use, not for people's use. It helps the tree to live and grow. Sunlight and warmth start the sugar-making activity beneath the surface of the tree. Say something.
Cal	I think that it's important to know that trees make the sap for themselves, not just for people to get maple syrup. It makes me think about the tree and what it needs and not just what we people want. My turn to read.
	[Reading aloud] Some people, especially a long time ago, gashed maple trees with an ax or chopped big notches into their trunks. Like gaping wounds, these cuts would pour forth the sap, but they would never heal and within a few years, the sugar maples would die. Say something, Aiden.
Aiden	The word *gashed* seems important. That's kind of sad that people do that. I think an important idea from this paragraph is that trees can't just be hacked up because people want maple syrup; they're being greedy. It needs to be done right to keep the trees alive.

Cal and Aiden continue reading the assigned section using this strategy, helping one another understand the main ideas and key words. It is easy to see the personal connections that students can make using this strategy, thus making the comprehension task easier.

Beginning the School Year: Basic Framework of Joelle Quimby's Eighth-Grade Language Arts Curriculum

First Day of School

Beginning with Day 1, students know what their 55 minutes in language arts will entail, as Joelle has clearly written the daily schedule on a whiteboard posted at the front of the room. She believes that by sharing the schedule and daily expectations, students are more comfortable knowing what to anticipate and will rise to her expectations for them. On this first day she tells them that they need to read the board and begin working on the introductory language arts activity she has planned for them. Since this is the first day of class, she orally describes the 5-minute activity. Today they are to interview another classmate, finding out his or her name and likes and dislikes, and to be prepared to introduce their partner to the class. Joelle finds this is a good way to get students interacting and learning about one another, and it provides her with a sample of each student's oral speaking skills through a low-stress situation.

Joelle does not believe in writing and posting the classroom rules without input from the students, and she finds that an effective way to get them to feel like valued members of the classroom community is to ask them, "What do you need in this classroom to be effective learners?" From this question, the students are able to develop a list of classroom rules based on their needs and input. She has never had to impose her own rules, as each class comes up with appropriate rules for themselves that are often more stringent than she would even suggest.

Because getting students enjoying language is a key objective in Joelle's plan, she shares a read-aloud with her students, *Family Pictures/Cuadros de Famila*, written and illustrated by Carmen Lomas Garza (1990). She chose this book because it's a picture book, and she can read the complete book in one sitting. She also wants her students to know that it is perfectly fine to read picture books and that many of them truly are not written for young children but for older readers and even adults. She tells the students that every day she will read aloud to them from a variety of genres, topics, and types of books, including novels, poetry, picture books, newspaper articles, and so on. To encourage discussion and response during and after the daily read-aloud, Joelle stops frequently and models thinking aloud about what she has read or poses questions to the students to encourage them to make text-to-self, text-to-text, and text-to-world connections. *Family Pictures* portrays the author/illustrator's childhood in a rural Mexican American community in southern Texas and depicts memories of vacations, food, parties, spirituality, and daily events. Joelle shares some of her own personal childhood stories and invites her students to make text-to-self connections as a way for them to comprehend the text and to begin developing a classroom community.

Joelle likes to present her students with a general overview of what they will be studying throughout the year in her language arts class to help them set goals for themselves and think about future learning. She has them create a written reflection about where they are now as readers, writers, listeners, and speakers as well as any preliminary goals they have for themselves. Joelle models this through a brief minilesson using an overhead projector so students can watch as she does a think-aloud sharing reflection on herself as a literate person. She keeps this short and focused, knowing that this is just the first time students will be reflecting on themselves in her language arts class. This written reflection will be a good baseline sample of their writing and their beliefs about themselves, providing Joelle with a starting point for the individual conferences she will have with her students on a monthly basis.

Near the end of class, Joelle informs the students that they will have homework every evening. One of the assignments will be to read at least 10 pages of something every day. Those 10 pages could be from the Bible, from the newspaper, a sports magazine, or from a book they are reading aloud to their younger siblings. The key is active reading of something for an extended period, and 10 pages is a good number to keep them reading for an appropriate amount of time each day. Joelle will informally talk to students about what they read at home and what they are learning and enjoying from it as a way to keep track of their reading homework. There will often be other homework as well that will be closely tied to the language arts curriculum, including spelling, word study work, writing assignments, and preparing for speaking roles such as reader's theater.

Sixth Grade Vignette: Read-Aloud

Rob Cannon, a sixth-grade teacher, believes that daily interactive read-aloud times should be special. Currently he is reading *Esperanza Rising* by Pam Muñoz Ryan (2000). He feels that placing the read-aloud first thing at the beginning of the hour-long block is a good time to set the mood and emphasis on language for his language arts classes. After the students are seated, he turns off the lights and lights a candle, then seats himself on the high stool at the front of the room. The atmosphere set, he looks out at the students and begins reading.

A Typical Day/Week in Joelle Quimby's Eighth-Grade Language Arts Classroom

This is a typical day in Quarter 2, Week 3, of the school year. The current focus is on reading, and the students have been engaged in book clubs and literature discussion groups as well as using writing to respond to what they are reading. The students have internalized the routine well and move through the 55-minute class period smoothly and efficiently. As students file into class on this Tuesday, they know they are to begin work on the warm-up of the day (see Table 12.7) that Joelle has posted on the whiteboard. One activity Joelle has students engage in regularly is "think, pair, share" (Kagen, 1994). She will post something to reflect on that is

Table 12.7   Sampling of Literature for Older Readers: Fiction, Nonfiction, Poetry

Activity	Purpose	Suggested Topics/Ideas
Think, Pair, Share (Kagen, 1994)	To encourage discussion and conversation, practice oral and listening skills and, at times, written reflection.	– Current event topics – Discussion of words with two meanings – Quotations – Questions – Language concepts
Write Letter to Teacher	Teacher learns more about her students as well as encourages written communication with a specified audience.	Letter Prompts: – Tell me about the last movie you saw. – Write about a suggestion you have to improve our school.
Sentence/ Vocabulary Examination	Sentence written on chalkboard with an unfamiliar vocabulary word. Students must use context clues and reading strategies to decipher and determine meaning.	– The *herpetologist* closely studied the specimens, carefully comparing one amphibian to another.
Poetry Exploration	To expose students to poetry and provide ample opportunity to read and listen to it read.	– Find a poem from classroom library that reflects "you" today. – Read a poem out loud to yourself, then a partner (teacher-chosen/photocopied). – Write a biopoem about yourself, a sibling, a parent/guardian, your best friend (format for biopoem previously learned).

related to language or current events and ask students to do a quick write about the topic. After a few minutes, students pair up with a classmate near them and share their ideas and reflection. Joelle modeled this process at the beginning of the school year, demonstrating sharing ideas and engaging in discussion and questioning one another related to the topic. The main goal is to get students to use written and spoken language to think in depth about meaningful topics.

The text that Joelle is reading aloud to her students currently is a novel, *Al Capone Does My Shirts*, by Gennifer Choldenko (2004), a coming-of-age story about Moose Flanigan, who lives with his family on Alcatraz Island where his father works as a guard in 1935. As she reads, she allows students to share their brief responses, helping them comprehend and make connections to the text.

Today's minilesson focuses on reading, and Joelle wants her students to learn another way to respond to the texts they read: double-entry responses. They have already been writing letters to her that she responded to and have also kept reading response journals. On the overhead projector, she has placed a copy of the

Table 12.8   Double-Entry Reading Response Form Book Title: *Rose Blanche* **(Gallaz & Innocenti, 1985)**

Quotes/Text From Book	Response
"They drive tanks that make sparks on the cobblestones. They are so noisy and smell like diesel oil. They hurt my ears and I have to hold my nose when they pass by."	I can't imagine living with tanks of war, driving right down the streets. Living every day like this would be very scary, in my opinion.
"Lots of times I walk by the river, just looking at it. Branches float along and sometimes old, broken toys. I like the color of the river. It looks like the sky."	Even in times of hardship and darkness and ugliness, Rose still is able to find some beauty. I like how the author contrasts the broken toys that symbolize broken lives with the blue, beautiful river. Almost like he is saying there is hope amid despair.

double-entry response form that she duplicated (see Table 12.8). Using a text they are already familiar with, she uses the think-aloud strategy describing how to use the form while at the same time writing her responses.

Joelle instructs the students that by the end of the week, they are to complete a reading response with the book they are currently reading independently or with their literature response group using the double-entry format.

The language workshop then begins as students engage in various language activities. There is currently one literature discussion group meeting and two guided language groups. Joelle stops for a few minutes to check in with the literature discussion group, who are reading *Esperanza Rising* by Pam Muñoz Ryan (2000). She listens in to their discussion about a few of the events in the story thus far, using a literature discussion group assessment form (Table 12.9). Students have been introduced to this form and know that they are to come to discussions prepared, adhere to established guidelines for discussions, and demonstrate their understanding of literary elements to exhibit comprehension and appreciation of the text. Joelle makes notes related to the points she observes and hears from two of the six students in the group and will continue to make a stop at this group each day for the rest of the week to obtain data about each student. She leaves after asking the students about their plans for finishing the text by the end of the week.

She then moves on to work with the guided language groups, taking 8 minutes with each group, modeling the focus strategy and leading them in practice. While working with the groups, the rest of the students are reading independently or with a partner, responding to reading through writing, or involved in grammar, vocabulary, or spelling activities.

Table 12.9   Literature Discussion Group Assessment Form

Text: _____ Date: _____			
Student	**Preparedness**	**Participation**	**Response**
	– Reading complete – On task	– Responds/listens appropriately – Actively engaged	– Exhibits comprehension – Discusses literary elements – Appreciation evident
Odemaris			
Keisha			
Steve			
Shoua			
Dan			
Maria			
Comments			

Five minutes before the period ends, Joelle calls the students together for a brief group share time. She asks if anyone has completed a double-entry reading response during workshop and encourages Odemaris to share her book and a sample response. Justin shares a book talk, highlighting the plot of the book he is reading, *Olive's Ocean* by Kevin Henkes (2003). Students then take a minute to complete a productivity rubric (see Table 12.10) that helps self-assess their learning and their impact on their classroom community. Joelle has students complete this rubric at least once a week.

End-of-Quarter Self-Assessment Portfolios

Joelle and her students accumulate all the work they do for the quarter in a language arts collection portfolio, which will contain writing samples of a variety of genres and formats, reading responses, grammar work, spelling tests, and literature circle projects and responses. At the end of the quarter, the students spend time going through their portfolios, reflecting on the work they have done and the growth they have demonstrated over an 8-week period. Joelle will provide guidelines for choosing items from this collection portfolio to be included in a showcase portfolio, and the students will help develop some criteria as well. Some of

Table 12.10   Productivity Rubric

Name: _____

Always/Almost Always	Most of the Time	Some of the Time	Never/Almost Never	Productivity Rubric
3	2	1	0	I stay on task.
3	2	1	0	I ask thoughtful questions of the teacher(s) and my classmates.
3	2	1	0	I listen attentively and reflectively.
3	2	1	0	I contribute positively to the work of my group/class.
3	2	1	0	I do high-quality work.
3	2	1	0	I take responsibility for my own learning.
3	2	1	0	Other: (optional)

the items she requires are a writing sample, a reading response, evidence of grammar learning and usage, and a spelling test. She encourages students to find items that they are proud of and that show them as effective users of all modes of communication—reading, writing, listening, speaking, viewing, and visually representing. After the students have chosen their items, they write a cover letter detailing how their portfolio reflects their learning in language arts over the quarter. They include comments on their favorite book read during the quarter, favorite unit, what stands out in relation to their development, and goals for improving in subsequent quarters.

Students share their portfolios one on one with Joelle during a conference and twice a year share with their parents during parent-teacher conferences. Joelle's students are proud of their work, and using portfolios to assess their growth over an 8-week period is motivating and insightful for both her and her students.

Sixth-Grade Vignette: Research Projects and Project Fairs

Part of the integrated curriculum at Longfellow School is for students to learn the many steps and processes of doing research. Throughout the year, they are expected to engage in at least one in-depth independent research project. Much of the learning of research skills occurs in language arts and social studies classes, as much of their foci is on the many modes of communication.

(Continued)

(Continued)

In Jenny Rand's language arts classroom, she teaches the steps and skills of effective interviewing as a way for students to prepare for an interview they must do of school personnel to create a collaborative newsletter highlighting the faculty and staff at the school. Interviewing is a skill that is valuable for doing research, especially when obtaining information from human resources.

Students learn oral communication skills when focusing on (a) the etiquette of setting up interviews, (b) greeting and using manners, (c) courtesy while interviewing, and (d) how to graciously end an interview and follow it up with a thank-you note. Some of the skills they learn prior to engaging in the interview include how to (a) listen effectively, (b) take abbreviated notes, (c) write good open-ended questions that elicit quality information, (d) ask follow-up questions, and (e) efficiently use a tape recorder. After the interview, students learn how to reread their interview notes and organize the information into a written report format (article, story, question/answer interview format). Other research-related skills Jenny teaches in her language arts class include a variety of note-taking methods while reading or while viewing media such as documentaries. There are other research-related skills taught within the social studies classes that complement the learning of the students in language arts.

Sixth-grade students are expected to engage in an individual research project at least once during the school year that is supported by all of their teachers, with one being their main guide. The topics for research are varied, and students are encouraged to study topics of interest in any content area. Four times throughout the year, students who have completed their research take part in a project fair that is set up for all students in the school. The students stand by their projects, which include written and visual components; sharing information; answering questions from the other students, teachers, and parents who attend; and receiving accolades for their hard work on their research. The project fair is motivating for students, and knowing the dates that they will be held helps the students practice goal setting and meeting deadlines.

End of the School Year

At the end of the year, students review the portfolio they created each quarter and engage in a similar process as a culminating assessment tool. They write a final letter detailing their growth over the span of the school year and reflect in depth on future goals in language arts as they move into high school. Joelle has a final conference with each student where she orally provides her assessment of his or her growth over the year. She also uses this time to personally share a comment or compliment about each student related to literacy, learning in general, or what she has learned about the student as a person.

Joelle also likes to get feedback about her teaching from her students and provides class time for them to write her a final letter, addressing some prompts related to her teaching style and methods, or students can choose to free write their responses. She finds this is valuable information, which allows her to understand 13-year-old students better as well as get advice for improving her teaching.

Each summer Joelle learns a bit more about best practices for ELLs. This summer she wishes to focus on scaffolding learning experiences and assessments so that her ELLs can participate as fully as possible in class activities. Learning about the stages of English language acquisition last summer really helped her to monitor the progress her students were making in both acquiring English and literacy development. Since she understands that ELLs go through a silent period before beginning to try out their new skills in English, she was not as worried when some of them were not speaking much in English. She thinks that took some of the pressure off the students, and they felt more comfortable in the classroom.

One of her other goals is to learn more about content area literacy and how to help her students become more proficient in using language arts skills in all their content area classes. She plans to work with the math teacher on her team to help her institute the use of math journals as a way to integrate writing and mathematics.

End-of-Chapter Reflection

- Reflect on your feelings about working with middle-school-age students in language arts after reading this chapter. Have your ideas changed about this age level? Do you feel that you could competently work with 10- to 13-year-old students? Why or why not?

- There are many challenges to working in a school that has isolated content area classes and short periods for teaching and learning. What are some ways you might overcome this challenge if you were teaching language arts in a middle school with only 55 minutes to an hour each class?

Planning for Teaching

1. Think about the areas of planning instruction and assessment for 10- to 13-year-old students in language arts that you feel you want to learn more about. There are numerous resources through print, the Internet, and people resources available for teachers related to teaching and assessing language arts. Search out supplemental resources that could help you further develop your understanding of these components.

2. After reading about how Joelle Quimby plans and implements language arts in her eighth-grade classroom, sketch out a rough plan or list of things you want to make sure to include in your future middle school classroom. Share your ideas with peers.

Connections With the Field

- Visit a middle school classroom and observe how language arts plays a role in the curriculum and throughout the typical daily schedule. Compare it to Joelle Quimby's classroom. What are the strengths and weaknesses of each classroom?

Student Study Site

The Companion Website for Developing Voice Through the Language Arts

http://www.sagepub.com/dvtlastudy

Visit the Web-based student study site to enhance your understanding of the chapter content and to discover additional resources that will take your learning one step further. You can enhance your understanding of the chapters by using the comprehensive Study Guide, which includes learning objectives, key terms, activities, practice tests, and more. You'll also find special features, such as the Links to Standards from U.S. States and associated activities, Children's Literature Selections, Reflection Exercises, Learning from Journal Articles, and PRAXIS test preparation materials.

References of Children's/Young Adult Literature

Abeel, S. (1994). *Reach for the moon* (C. R. Murphy, Illus.). New York: Pfeifer-Hamilton.

Base, G. (1986). *Animalia*. Ringwood, Victoria, Australia: Viking Kestrel.

Choldenko, G. (2004). *Al Capone does my shirts*. New York: Putnam.

Curtis, C. P. (1997). *The Watsons go to Birmingham—1963*. New York: Yearling.

Gallaz, C., & Innocenti, R. (1985). *Rose Blanche*. Mankato, MN: Creative Education.

Garza, C. L. (1990). *Family pictures/Cuadros de familia*. San Francisco: Children's Book Press.

Henkes, K. (2003). *Olive's ocean*. New York: Harper Trophy.

Krull, K. (1996). *Wilma unlimited: How Wilma Rudolph became the world's fastest woman* (D. Diaz, Illus.). New York: Harcourt Brace.

Lasky, K. (1983). *Sugaring time*. New York: Macmillan.

Myers, W. D. (2001). *Monster*. New York: Amistad.

Newman, L. (1995). *Too far away to touch* (C. Stock, Illus.). New York: Clarion.

Ryan, P. M. (2000). *Esperanza rising*. New York: Scholastic.

Shannon, M. (1994). *Gawain and the green knight* (D. Shannon, Illus.). New York: Putnam's.

Woodson, J. (1997). *From the notebooks of Melanin Sun*. New York: Scholastic.

References of Professional Resources

Apple Computer. (2005). iMovie HD [Computer software]. Cupertino, CA: Author.

Cummins, J. (1984). *Bilingualism and special education: Issues in assessment and pedagogy*. San Diego, CA: College-Hill.

Fountas, I., & Pinnell, G. S. (2001). *Guiding readers and writers grades 3–6: Teaching comprehension, genre and content literacy*. Portsmouth, NH: Heinemann.

Kagen, S. (1994). *Cooperative learning*. San Juan Capistrano, CA: Kagen Cooperative Learning.

Microsoft Corporation. (2005). Microsoft Publisher [Computer software]. Redmond, WA: Author.

Short, K. G., Harste, J. C., & Burke, C. (1996). *Creating classrooms for authors and inquirers* (2nd ed.). Portsmouth, NH: Heinemann.

Strickland, D., Ganske, K., & Monroe, J. K. (2002). *Supporting struggling readers and writers: Strategies for classroom intervention 3–6*. Portland, ME: Stenhouse.

Wood, C. (1997). *Yardsticks: Children in the classroom ages 4–14: A resource for parents and teachers*. Greenfield, MA: Northeast Foundation for Children.

Other Resources

Benedict, S., & Carlisle, L. (1992). *Picture books for older readers and writers*. Portsmouth, NH: Heinemann.

Technology Resources

First established in 1996, this site is a resource for teachers, schools, and districts to assist with raising the achievement of middle-school-level students. Includes a strong emphasis on language arts topics, curriculum, and resources. Especially interesting is the reading/writing project: http://www.middleweb.com

An excellent Web site that contains information about fairy tales and their variants. Includes a comprehensive listing of books, including similar tales across cultures and literary analysis done on fairy tales. Appropriate to use with middle school through adult-level students: http://www.surlalune fairytales.com/goldilocks/books.html

Kay Vandergrift's Web site with an in-depth study of *Snow White* and variants. Appropriate for engaging middle school students in a study of folk literature: http://www.scils.rutgers.edu/~kvander/snowwhite.html

Epilogue

Reflecting on Your Future
Teaching of the Language Arts

Having had the opportunity to study the teaching, learning, and assessment of language arts that span kindergarten through Grade 8, it is a good time to complete one last reflection on the major ideas and evaluate your knowledge base and level of confidence in preparing to teach in the language arts. For each area, rate yourself from 1 to 5, with 5 being very confident/ready to do this tomorrow. Your ratings may provide you with ideas for the goals you wish to set for yourself in preparing to teach. You can jot those down where appropriate.

1. I can articulate my philosophy of teaching, learning, and assessment in literacy development.

1	2	3	4	5
Not at All	Somewhat	Fairly Well	Very Well	Very Confident

Goals:

2. I feel confident in linking standards, instruction, and assessment related to the language arts.

1	2	3	4	5
Not at All	Somewhat	Fairly Well	Very Well	Very Confident

Goals:

3. I have a good sense of how to set student expectations.

1	2	3	4	5
Not at All	Somewhat	Fairly Well	Very Well	Very Confident

Goals:

4. I have a good understanding of how to teach children to self-assess their work.

1	2	3	4	5
Not at All	Somewhat	Fairly Well	Very Well	Very Confident

Goals:

5. How well do I understand the components of the language arts: reading, writing, listening, speaking, viewing, and visually representing? (Reflect on the major considerations of each area. How well do you think you would be able to integrate teaching, learning, and assessment in the language arts?)

Reading:
1	2	3	4	5
Not at All	Somewhat	Fairly Well	Very Well	Very Confident

Writing:
1	2	3	4	5
Not at All	Somewhat	Fairly Well	Very Well	Very Confident

Listening:
1	2	3	4	5
Not at All	Somewhat	Fairly Well	Very Well	Very Confident

Speaking:	1	2	3	4	5
	Not at All	Somewhat	Fairly Well	Very Well	Very Confident

Viewing:	1	2	3	4	5
	Not at All	Somewhat	Fairly Well	Very Well	Very Confident

Visually Representing:	1	2	3	4	5
	Not at All	Somewhat	Fairly Well	Very Well	Very Confident

Goals:

6. I feel confident about implementing a balanced literacy approach to literacy development.

1	2	3	4	5
Not at All	Somewhat	Fairly Well	Very Well	Very Confident

Goals:

7. I feel confident that I can excite students through language arts activities.

1	2	3	4	5
Not at All	Somewhat	Fairly Well	Very Well	Very Confident

Goals:

8. I am familiar with a wide range of children's/young adult literature, magazines, Web sites, and software.

1	2	3	4	5
Not at All	Somewhat	Fairly Well	Very Well	Very Confident

Goals:

9. I feel confident about selecting quality literature to use in my classroom.

1	2	3	4	5
Not at All	Somewhat	Fairly Well	Very Well	Very Confident

Goals:

10. I have a good understanding of how to integrate the language arts across the curriculum.

1	2	3	4	5
Not at All	Somewhat	Fairly Well	Very Well	Very Confident

Goals:

11. I have good ideas about how to keep track of student progress in the language arts.

1	2	3	4	5
Not at All	Somewhat	Fairly Well	Very Well	Very Confident

Goals:

12. I know how to develop a schedule for literacy instruction.

1	2	3	4	5
Not at All	Somewhat	Fairly Well	Very Well	Very Confident

Goals:

13. I have a good idea of how to physically arrange my classroom for literacy instruction.

1	2	3	4	5
Not at All	Somewhat	Fairly Well	Very Well	Very Confident

Goals:

14. I am confident about meaningful planning, implementation, and assessment of language arts instruction.

Planning:

1	2	3	4	5
Not at All	Somewhat	Fairly Well	Very Well	Very Confident

Implementing:

1	2	3	4	5
Not at All	Somewhat	Fairly Well	Very Well	Very Confident

Assessing:

1	2	3	4	5
Not at Al	Somewhat	Fairly Well	Very Well	Very Confident

Goals:

15. I feel confident about designing instruction to meet the needs of English language learners in language arts.

1	2	3	4	5
Not at All	Somewhat	Fairly Well	Very Well	Very Confident

Goals:

16. I can articulate my philosophy of classroom management.

1	2	3	4	5
Not at All	Somewhat	Fairly Well	Very Well	Very Confident

Goals:

17. I feel confident that I know how to design and implement an effective classroom management/climate plan.

1   2   3   4   5
Not   Somewhat   Fairly   Very   Very
at All   Well   Well   Confident

Goals:

18. I have a plan for involving parents in the literacy development of their children.

1   2   3   4   5
Not   Somewhat   Fairly   Very   Very
at All   Well   Well   Confident

Goals:

19. I feel confident in knowing how to deal with a classroom of diverse learners.

1   2   3   4   5
Not   Somewhat   Fairly   Very   Very
at All   Well   Well   Confident

Goals:

20. I have a good understanding of how to be a reflective practitioner related to language arts.

1   2   3   4   5
Not   Somewhat   Fairly   Very   Very
at All   Well   Well   Confident

Goals:

The teachers in Chapters 10 through 12 are exemplary teachers who are reflective practitioners. On a daily basis they evaluate their teaching and their students' learning. They ask themselves if their students are making progress in developing voice in their ability to communicate effectively through the language arts. They regularly review their records to verify these impressions. Teaching and learning standards serve as a guide and a framework for establishing short- and long-term goals for the class, as well as for individual students.

In addition to cognitive factors, reflective practitioners also examine affective factors that impact learning, and they recognize that learning does not happen in a vacuum. Students learn best when they feel motivated and appropriately challenged by learning experiences that are authentic and worthwhile. Positive self-esteem and confidence in themselves as learners are two important elements that they strive to help their students develop. These teachers recognize the importance of getting to know the whole child and his or her family and use this knowledge to make learning relevant and the classroom experience positive for all students. Differences in language and culture are seen as enrichments rather than distractions.

It is also clear that the teachers in Chapters 10 through 12 are lifelong learners. They spend countless hours in bookstores, on the Internet, or scouring other resources to find materials that will support learning for all students in their classrooms. They take courses, read books and articles, and seek out teachers, parents, and community members who can help them expand their understanding of all aspects of teaching and learning. Lifelong learners immerse themselves in the latest theoretical learning experiences and technology related to teaching. They evaluate and adapt each to make certain they are appropriate for the children they teach.

An innovation on *The Important Book* by Margaret Wise Brown (1949/1990) in the poem that follows may help capture these sentiments.

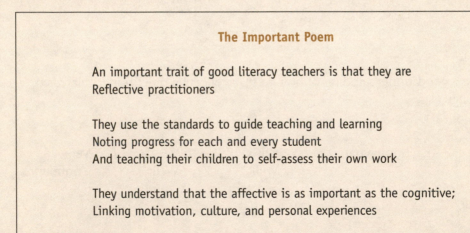

The Important Poem

An important trait of good literacy teachers is that they are
Reflective practitioners

They use the standards to guide teaching and learning
Noting progress for each and every student
And teaching their children to self-assess their own work

They understand that the affective is as important as the cognitive;
Linking motivation, culture, and personal experiences

They think about how effective their teaching has been
And continually make improvements

An important trait of good literacy teachers is that they are
Reflective practitioners

Another important trait of good literacy teachers
Is that they are lifelong learners
They are always informing themselves about kids and learning
And teaching too

You'll find them in bookstores and meetings
And at conferences too

Avid reading and writing by the teacher influences
Students to read and write, they know

New ideas for learning experiences never
Fail to excite them

Another important trait of good literacy teachers
Is that they are lifelong learners

End-of-Chapter Reflection

- Write your own important poem to capture what you feel are the most important critical traits of an effective language arts teacher or to reflect on where you are in your preparation to teach in the language arts.

Planning for Teaching

1. Share your survey with a group of your peers. Discuss the areas you feel you need to continue to learn about. Celebrate those areas that you feel comfortable teaching and assessing.

2. Based on your responses on the survey, set goals for yourself to become more adept in the areas in which you feel deficient. Locate professional resources that you feel will be helpful to reach your goals. Continue to stay abreast of current language arts research and children's literature so you can continue to grow as a professional.

Reference

Wise Brown, M. (1990). *The important book* (L. Weisgard, Illus). New York: Harper & Row. (Original work published 1949)

Glossary

Active learning   opportunities for students to explore concepts through a problem-solving process, often using prompts, manipulatives, and/or movement activities.

Aesthetic stance   reading for pleasure.

Anecdotal records   notes about student progress recorded by teachers in a variety of formats.

Anecdotal Records Assessment (ARA)   a process of linking teacher notes about student learning and teaching standards.

Anticipation guide   a series of true/false statements that students respond to before reading a passage, designed to activate prior knowledge prior to reading.

Appreciative listening   the listener listens for enjoyment or pleasure.

Assumptions   what we believe to be true. In relation to language arts teaching, that could include a teacher's beliefs, either true or false, about students' motivations and ability to become competent users of language.

Auditory acuity   physical reception of sound waves involved in hearing.

Author studies   teachers guiding students in reading and analyzing several books by the same author. Students determine the author's style and use of literary elements in writing.

Author's craft   the style of writing used by an author.

Autobiography   a biography or narrative of one's life.

Backdrop setting   a setting that does not have an impact on the actions of the characters or the direction of the plot.

Balanced or comprehensive approach   an approach to reading instruction that combines a variety of teaching methods from a skill-based and meaning-based approach as a way to meet the needs of all learners.

Basal reading textbook   typically textbooks developed for each grade level that include a collection of written pieces that are organized by reading level or difficulty and skills that students progress through as they continue to develop reading ability.

Benchmarks   goals set for students to attain.

Bilingual   being proficient in communicating in two languages.

Bloom's taxonomy   a hierarchy of thinking skills developed by Benjamin Bloom.

Book talks   brief descriptions of books that entice others to read them.

Center   typically an area in a classroom set up with its own direction, materials, and activities designed for students to work at their own pace and often to make their own choices. Also called a learning center or literacy learning center when related to language arts curriculum.

Characterization   characters created by the author in a story.

Collaborative/cooperative learning   students work together to complete learning tasks. Often students learn skills to assist them in working collaboratively/cooperatively.

Common Underlying Proficiency (CUP)   the theory that a "bilingual" language learners' understanding in one language is understood in a second language.

Community of learners   a classroom where students work collaboratively and respectfully in their learning activities.

Comprehend   accurately understanding what is written or spoken.

Comprehension   the meaning-making process of reading.

Comprehension strategies   various strategies a reader uses before, during, and after reading a text to understand it clearly and meaningfully.

Comprehensive or balanced approach   an approach to reading instruction that combines a variety of teaching methods from a skill-based and meaning-based approach as a way to meet the needs of all learners.

Concept   an idea, thought, or general notion to be learned by students.

Concept books   informational picture books for young children. The most basic concept books deal with alphabet, numbers, colors, and shapes.

Concepts of print   understandings that emergent readers develop about how text is organized, such as the left to right and top to bottom direction of print (in English), the front/back of a book, and so on.

Conceptual knowledge   understandings that students possess about specific concepts.

Conceptual load   the proportion of different ideas accessible in a text in relation to the length of the text.

Conferences   meetings between teachers and students to review work, receive feedback, and set goals for further learning.

Conferencing center   an area of the classroom reserved for student-teacher conferences.

Conflict   the struggle experienced by main characters in a story. Conflict may involve person-against-person, person-against-society, person-against-nature.

Content area instruction instruction in subject areas such as mathematics, science, and social studies.

Content area workshops a workshop approach to learning in specific or integrated subject areas such as mathematics, science, and social studies.

Context clues information from the text surrounding a word or word cluster that helps to provide meaning for new or difficult words.

Creative listening the listener uses input from the message to develop a unique response.

Critical listening the listener analyzes and evaluates input and formulates an opinion or response.

Critical thinking skills skills acquired by students that enable them to analyze, evaluate, synthesize, and apply what they have learned.

Cueing systems the sources of information that assist readers in identifying words and making meaning of them.

Data-driven instruction analysis of test scores and other data to make decisions to continually improve student learning.

Decode analyzing written or spoken symbols of a language; to decipher meaning using spelling-sound relationships.

Dialogue journals notebooks used by students to write about their reactions to what they have read, and teachers or other students respond with their own reactions and questions.

Didactic children's books that are designed to teach children a lesson or advocate for a certain type of behavior.

Digital storytelling students create digital stories on computer from their own writing by adding visuals and narrating the text.

Directed reading-thinking activity (DRTA) a predicting, reading, confirming, predicting cycle in which students learn to think closely about what they have read.

Discriminative listening the listener differentiates the sounds that make up the message and begins to attend to what is being said.

Dynamic characters characters that change as a result of experiences they undergo in the course of the text.

Early stage of reading the stage of reading development that occurs approximately from 6 to 9 years of age as a reader focuses heavily on print and the use of a variety of reading strategies to make meaning from a text.

Effective teacher of literacy a teacher who is able to excite children about literacy and guide them in the development of high-level literacy skills.

Efferent stance   reading for information.

Electronic books   book text that can be viewed online or downloaded from the Internet.

Emergent stage of reading   the beginning stage of reading from approximately age 3 to 7 where the reader begins to explore print in general, beginning to notice and appreciate rhyme, sounds, the fact that illustrations hold meaning as well as text.

English language learners (ELLs)   students who speak a language other than English as their primary language and are in the process of learning English.

Episodic novel   a novel that is composed of a series of episodes, each complete in itself and not reliant upon the other chapters of the novel.

Expository text   text that primarily relates information.

Expressive language functions   the speaker or artist makes a verbal or graphic response to stimuli. Speaking and visually representing are expressive language functions.

Figurative language   use of similes, metaphors, or personification to create images of characters or events.

Fluency   reading smoothly with accuracy and appropriate flow and expression.

Fluent stage of reading   the stage of reading from approximately age 9 and beyond where readers use strategies effectively and automatically to gain meaning from a wide range of text.

Folk literature   the body of oral literature that has been preserved across multiple generations and whose authors are unknown. Folktales, myths, fables, legends, and fairy tales are all considered folklore or traditional literature.

Foreshadowing   clues in a story that lead the reader to speculate on what will happen in the story.

Frustration level   a level of reading material that is too difficult for a reader to process and comprehend successfully.

Genre   a category used to categorize literary works usually by form, content, or writing style.

Genre studies   teachers guiding students in reading and analyzing several books in the same genre to better understand the characteristics of the particular genre.

Gradual release of responsibility model   students are guided to continually take on more responsibility for their own learning.

Graphic organizers   charts, graphs, or visuals used to organize information.

Graphophonics   the recognition of the letters of the alphabet and the understanding of sound-spelling relationships.

Graphophonemic cueing system one of the four cueing systems a literate person needs to use to read effectively, which involves the relationship between single letters or sets of letters and the speech sounds they represent.

Guided reading a reading approach done with small groups of flexible, homogeneously grouped students who have the same reading needs. Strategies are taught to support and guide readers to become independent and fluent readers.

Hearing receiving sound waves through the ear.

High-frequency words one hundred of the most frequently used words in the English language, including such words as *our, I,* and *the.*

Historical character maps a web of a character's attributes and/or accomplishments in historical fiction/nonfiction literature.

Historical fiction a genre of literature that includes realistic characters, settings, and plots from a historical time period.

Holdaway's model of student learning a model for learning devised by Don Holdaway in which the teacher's role gradually diminishes as students are able to accept more responsibility for their own learning.

Independent reading one of the components of a balanced literacy program where students read independently for pleasure and to solidify reading strategies.

Informal reading inventory (IRI) an assessment tool that uses graded text passages to determine readers' strategy use, strengths, and areas of need in relation to decoding and reading comprehension.

Informational literature a genre of literature designed to inform readers about a particular topic.

Integral setting a setting that influences the actions of the characters or the direction of the plot.

Integrated units units of study that integrate one or more content areas.

Interactive read-aloud a fluent model orally shares a text with listeners and invites interaction through personal response, response to questions, and other modes of responding to text.

Interactive writing creating a piece of writing in collaboration, where both the teacher and students taking turns with the writing utensil to document the groups' ideas.

International Reading Association (IRA) an organization of elementary classroom teachers and reading specialists dedicated to improving the understanding of literacy development and instruction. The IRA and the National Council of Teachers of English (NCTE) formulate nationally recognized literacy standards.

Jigsaw activity a learning activity where individual students or groups of students hold separate pieces of information. The students must share all of the pieces of information to complete an activity.

Key concepts   the most important ideas being learned or researched.

Key information   important information needed in learning about a new topic or in completing a research project.

Key vocabulary   the most important new terms in a learning activity. Often key vocabulary is bolded or highlighted in content area texts for children.

Kidspiration   software that guides students in outlining and organizing ideas for writing.

Kidwatching   an assessment method and concept described by Yetta Goodman that includes observing students as a way to gather information about them while they are engaged in learning and activities in the classroom.

Language experience approach   an approach to teaching language arts whereby students' oral speech is transcribed and used as curriculum materials for teaching and learning language arts.

Learning logs   notebooks in which students record important information around a particular topic and analyze what they have learned.

Learning strategies   plans to help students reach specific learning goals.

Letter recognition   recognizing the letters of the alphabet.

Listening   the ability to focus on gaining meaning from sound.

Literacy   the ability of a person to use the language arts skills required for effective functioning in school and community settings.

Literacy development   the complex process of becoming literate.

Literacy learning environment   an environment designed to encourage students to participate in meaningful literacy-related activity and development.

Literal language   use of words and phrases that do not have an underlying or alternative meaning.

Literary elements   elements of a narrative story, including plot, characterization, setting, theme, style, and point of view.

Literate activities   lessons and engagement that encourage students to develop and use their literacy skills.

Living Books   software programs developed from children's literature. Living Books software contains colorful graphics, clickable hotspots, and text, allowing students to interact with the book.

Making connections   readers relate what they read to themselves (text-to-self), other texts they have read (text-to-text), and to the world around them (text-to-world).

Making Words©   an activity developed by Marie Clay where students explore patterns in words.

Metacognition thinking about one's own thinking processes.

Minilesson a brief lesson of about 5–10 minutes in which a single concept is taught or reinforced as part of reading or writing workshop.

Modern fantasy a genre of literature that features imaginary characters, settings, or plots. Magic, personification, and supernatural characters or phenomena are often components of modern fantasy.

Monitoring comprehension a strategy that students use to ensure that they are taking meaning from print.

Monolingual the ability to understand or speak reasonably well one's first language and the ability to speak only that language.

Narrative literature text that primarily relates a story.

Narrative text a story or set of experiences and events that is written or expressed orally.

National Council of Teachers of English (NCTE) an organization of literacy professionals. NCTE joined the International Reading Association (IRA) to formulate nationally recognized literacy standards.

National Reading Panel a panel of reading experts that outlined effective, research-based literacy instruction for children and young adults.

No Child Left Behind Act (NCLB) an act put forth by the George W. Bush administration in 2001 related to quality in education that states there must be "stronger accountability for results, expanded flexibility and local control, expanded options for parents and an emphasis on teaching methods that have been proven to work."

One-to-one correspondence this skill indicates that children are reading the word they are pointing to as they read text.

Onset the part of a syllable that precedes the vowel, such as *sh* in the word *ship*.

Open-ended learning experiences students are given choices in how they meet specific criteria.

Paralinguistic cues cues that provide clues to a speaker's message, such as use of visuals, tone of voice, facial expressions, and gestures.

Passive listening students listen but are not expected to respond orally to what they hear.

Peer editing students are trained to edit one another's writing, using a rubric or specific set of criteria.

Phonemic awareness the ability to distinguish the difference between the 44 sounds (or phonemes) within spoken language.

Phonemes see *phonemic awareness*

Phonics   see *phonological system*.

Phonological awareness   the understanding that speech can be divided into words and sentences, including syllables, onsets, and rimes.

Phonological system   the sound system of language. Although there are 26 letters in the English language, there are 44 sounds or phonemes, adding up to a large combination of letters and sounds to form many words with various pronunciations; also referred to as *phonics*.

Picture books   a genre of literature that includes illustrated books written for young children.

Picture clues   analyzing illustrations or photographs in a story to support understanding and enjoyment of text.

Plot   plan of action of a story or novel.

Point of view   the perspective from which a story is told or perceived. A story may be told from a first-person or third-person perspective.

Portfolio assessment   a collection of student work that is evaluated against a rubric or specific set of criteria.

Power   used in relation to the viewer's angle in illustrations to depict the level of influence or "power" the viewer has over those represented in the illustration or photo.

Pragmatic cueing system   one of the four cueing systems that a literate person needs to utilize to read effectively. This system is based on tapping into one's prior knowledge, background experiences, and culture to help make sense of the written word.

Pragmatics   the language system that deals with the social and cultural aspects of language use.

Presentation skills   effective abilities to formally share information and insights on a given topic.

Prior knowledge   knowing based on previous experiences and knowledge learned. A learner can comprehend better when prior knowledge is activated.

Problem-solving process   a series of logical steps to resolve a problem, often associated with solving problems in mathematics.

Publish   prepare a final edited copy of writing to be shared with an audience.

Purposeful listening   the listener attends to the message to complete a task.

Reader's theater   a read-aloud performance of literature using a variety of genres. The focus is on the language and oral expression, not the acting out of the text. Students read scripted versions of stories, portraying the characters' emotions.

Reading   the act of making sense of text, understanding, and comprehending text (where text can be anything that can be "read," including visuals, music, performances, etc.).

Reading First Initiatives   funding made available by the No Child Left Behind Act to support reading development.

Reading management programs   computerized software, such as Accelerated Reader, that is used to monitor the independent reading and comprehension of students.

Realistic fiction   a genre of literature that includes realistic characters, settings, and plots.

Receptive language functions   the listener and viewer receive information from the environment. Listening and viewing are receptive language functions.

Receptive vocabularies   words that listeners understand but do not use in their own vocabulary.

Reciprocal teaching   students refine understanding of a particular skill, strategy, or concept by teaching it to other students who have not yet mastered the material.

Reflection   the process of thinking about one's experience or performance.

Reflective teacher   a teacher who thinks about his or her teaching, students' learning, and evaluating the impact of each on the other.

Registers   the variety of speaking situations we may find ourselves in. We adjust our speech according to who we are communicating with and the purpose of the communication.

Resolution   the way in which a conflict is resolved. The resolution may be either satisfactory or unsatisfactory.

Return sweep   the act of diagonal eye movement from one line of print to the next line.

Rime   a vowel and the following consonants of a syllable in a word.

Round-robin storytelling   the reading method of students taking turns reading aloud one after another.

Running records   an assessment method that includes a teacher marking the miscues that readers makes while reading aloud as a way to determine the strategies they use and with which they need further instruction.

Scaffolding   providing support for student learning through a variety of means.

Scanning   quickly looking through print to find key words or phrases.

Schema   understandings we have about particular concepts based on prior experiences.

Scientific method   a process of solving problems and completing experiments in science.

Self-assessment   the act of assessing one's own abilities and performances through a variety of methods, including such things as written reflection, oral assessment, and visually representing.

Semantic cueing system   using meaning cues to make sense of print.

Semantic feature matrix   a graphic organizer grid that highlights similarities and differences among items in a specific category or topic.

Semantics   clues that reveal the meaning of a word, phrase, sentence, or passage.

Sequential bilinguals   a learner who learns one language first, then another language (for example, a child learning one language at home before beginning school and learning a second language in school).

Shared reading   a teaching method where a fluent reading model reads aloud but invites listeners to share in the reading process as they view the text, gradually working up to fluent reading of the text themselves in the process.

Sharing session   the last stage of a workshop, such as reading or writing workshop, where the class gathers together to share what was accomplished, learned, and practiced within the work time of the workshop.

Sight words   words that can be identified quickly and easily and do not require any word analysis.

Signal words   words such as *therefore, however, then,* and *later* that help students interpret information.

Simulations   classroom enactments of aspects of the outside world (for example, simulating a post office in a classroom or school to teach about the postal service).

Simultaneous bilinguals   a learner who learns two languages simultaneously.

Skills   an acquired aptitude to perform well.

Skimming   briefly perusing materials to determine what information might be included.

Speech registers   a wide range of speaking situations in which speakers adjust what they say and how they speak depending on the listener and the setting.

Standardized testing   normed measures of academic student performance and progress.

Standards   guidelines for student performance at various levels.

Status of the class   a quick method for assessing where students are in a process such as during writing workshop. Students quickly report to the teacher

4

what stage of writing they are in with their current writing project and their plans for the current day's workshop.

Strategic readers   readers who use strategies such as predicting, using picture clues, and activating prior knowledge to understand what they read more fully.

Strategies   a systematic plan intentionally modified and monitored to develop one's ability in learning.

Student centered   when individual and collective needs of the learners are analyzed and instruction is designed to meet those needs, a classroom is student centered.

Style   the way in which a book is written. The elements of style include use of words, images, metaphors, sounds, and voice.

Summative assessment   a summary or final evaluation pulling together all parts and assessments of what was learned.

Syntactic cueing system   the system readers use when they understand how sentences are formed and the grammatical rules that preside over them.

Syntax   the order of words in a sentence (e.g., in English we generally have an adjective followed by the noun it is describing: "the blue car." In Spanish we find the opposite: "el carro azul"—"the car blue").

Talking   to communicate by speaking.

Telecommunicating   electronic means of communication via Internet and e-mail.

Text directionality   the ability to perceive left to right orientation of text for reading purposes.

Text features   components of subject-area texts such as maps, bolded vocabulary, headings, pictures, and captions.

Text-to-self connections   connections students make between themselves and/or their life experiences and the literature they read.

Text-to-text connections   connections students make between what they are currently reading and what they have previously read.

Text-to-world connections   connections students make between what they read and what they know of the world around them.

Theme   what a reader is "left with" after reading a text. A message or idea that leaves an impression on a reader.

Think-alouds   a strategy in which a model (teacher) or learner verbalizes the thought processes that are used during learning a new concept or skill.

Trade books   a book published for sale to the general public.

Traditional basal approach   a program consisting of student textbooks and workbooks, teachers' manuals, and supplementary materials for developmental reading and language arts development.

Transitional stage of reading   the stage of reading development where readers become more fluent and integrate a variety of self-monitoring and fix-up strategies while reading a variety of genres and forms of text.

Trilingual   being proficient in communicating in three languages.

Viewing   the communication process involved when students watch or examine print or graphic stimuli. Information gathered by seeing or sight.

Visual demands   character shots in visual media in which the character seems to be looking directly at the viewer.

Visual literacy   refers to the process of learning by viewing print or graphic stimuli. Use of illustrations and graphics to gain greater meaning from text.

Visual media   print, electronic, or visual performance modes of communication.

Visual offers   portray characters in visual media that do not appear to gaze at the viewer and do not suggest a relationship.

Visually representing   messages that are conveyed through graphics, video, computer, or dramatic media.

Vocabulary maps   webs of new words that highlight meanings and/or uses of new words.

WebQuest   a preselected set of Web sites that a teacher may direct students to use in researching a particular topic.

Whole language approach   a philosophy for teaching language that is based on the notion that students learn language best beginning with whole texts and moving to understanding parts.

Word analysis strategies   strategies whose purpose is to assist a reader in the decoding and identification of words.

Word sort   a method for finding common elements and patterns between and among words through the process of manipulating word cards. Two types of sorts include the open sort, where students find a pattern among words on their own, and closed sort, where word cards are sorted into predetermined categories or patterns.

Work session   the stage within a workshop where students typically work independently or in pairs to apply what they have learned during the minilesson.

Workshop model   a model that encourages a variety of groupings and instructional models, including minilessons where (a) the teacher models and teaches strategies, skills, conventions, and procedures; (b) a work session where students apply their new learning independently; and (c) a sharing session where students give and receive feedback to peers related to the content and processes shared.

Writing   the process of recording language graphically.

Writing process   the stages, decisions, and actions a writer goes through when producing a piece of writing.

Zone of proximal development   the distance between what the child is capable of doing alone and the problem-solving level accomplished with guidance.

Index